The New Class Society

The New Class Society

Robert Perrucci
and Earl Wysong

ROWMAN & LITTLEFIELD PUBLISHERS, INC.
Lanham • Boulder • New York • Oxford

ROWMAN & LITTLEFIELD PUBLISHERS, INC.

Published in the United States of America
by Rowman & Littlefield Publishers, Inc.
4720 Boston Way, Lanham, Maryland 20706

12 Hid's Copse Road
Cumnor Hill, Oxford OX2 9JJ, England

British Library Cataloguing in Publication Information Available

Library of Congress Cataloging-in-Publication Data

Perrucci, Robert.
    The new class society / Robert Perrucci and Earl Wysong.
       p. cm.
    Includes bibliographical references and index.
    ISBN 0-8476-9172-1 (alk. paper).—ISBN 0-8476-9173-X (pbk. :
alk. paper)
    1. Social classes—United States. 2. United States—Social
conditions—1980–   I. Wysong, Earl, 1944–   . II. Title.
HN90.S6P47   1999
305.5'0973—dc21   99-11242
                                        CIP

Printed in the United States of America

∞™ The paper used in this publication meets the minimum requirements of
American National Standard for Information Sciences—Permanence of Paper
for Printed Library Materials, ANSI Z39.48–1992.

Contents

Tables and Figures

TABLES

FIGURES

Preface

The dawning of industrial capitalism in England in the eighteenth century was accompanied by severe and often violent dislocations in the lives of agricultural workers. Land that had for generations been held in common and used for grazing animals was enclosed for use in sheep raising, an industry that was essential to the capitalists who owned the burgeoning textile industry. Peasant villages were destroyed, and agricultural workers were forced off the land. Deprived of their jobs and the means of making a living through agriculture, dislocated peasants were also faced with a hostile government eager to serve the needs of a powerful new capitalist class. The enactment of vagabondage laws and poor laws forced displaced peasants—men, women, and children—into the factories where they found long hours, extremely harsh working conditions, and low wages. A modern-day economist looking at this transition from a feudal agricultural society to an industrial capitalist society might describe it as an example of "creative destruction"—the painful but necessary "shock therapy" that often accompanies technological and economic change.

The experiences of eighteenth-century peasants bear a striking resemblance to those of manufacturing workers in the United States in the 1970s and 1980s. Forced out of their high-wage manufacturing jobs, their unions under attack by both government and corporations, workers were forced into the burgeoning service industries where they found low wages, no benefits, and exploitative working conditions. The "end of welfare" legislation of 1997 has the ring of eighteenth-century vagabondage and poor laws, forcing displaced and threatened workers to accept increasingly onerous working conditions and wages.

The experiences of the eighteenth-century peasant and the late-twentieth-century blue-collar worker were both a part of a larger transformation in the structure of class inequality taking place in the respective historical periods. The post-World War II period in the United States provided economic growth for society and consumer prosperity for millions of Americans. The idea of America as a middle-class society gained prominence as the sons and daughters of working-class Americans went, in increasing numbers, to college, into high-wage skilled jobs, and into the professions. Then something happened: Beginning in the 1970s and continuing into the 1980s, the once powerful high-wage auto, steel, textile, rubber, and consumer electronics industries went into a tailspin. Competition from the Far East and Europe led to a wave of plant closings in the United States and the transfer of manufacturing jobs to lower-wage areas abroad. Millions of high-wage, blue-collar jobs disappeared, and the existence of middle-class, blue-collar "aristocrats" became a fiction. The rapid introduction in the 1980s of advanced computer technology and information systems helped facilitate the dramatic "downsizing" of millions of white-collar middle-management employees by major U.S. firms. This trend continues to be encouraged by ongoing waves of corporate mergers and acquisitions.

This book is about the transformation of the mid-century "middle-class" American society into a bifurcated and polarized two-class society. This "new class society" consists of a privileged class made of 20 percent of the population and a new working class composed of the other 80 percent. A person's position in the new class society is determined by access to four types of scarce resources, which together we call *generative capital*: consumption capital, investment capital, credentialed-skill capital, and social capital. The privileged class is composed of those who have access to these resources over time, which means that they are stable and predictable. The new working class, in contrast, has limited access to generative capital, and their resources have become more unstable and unpredictable. Moreover, the privileged class uses its resources to maintain and legitimate the new class society. This is achieved through its control of large-scale organizations and institutional networks in the areas of the economy, politics, and culture.

The first two chapters set the stage for the book by providing the lens of class analysis for viewing American society. Chapter 1 introduces our "new class" theoretical model, compares our approach with previous class analysis traditions, and describes the main features of what we view as the emerging new class society. In chapter 2 the ideals of the American Dream are contrasted with the major features of the new class society. It documents recent notable class trends and introduces two "hidden" class realities explored in detail in later chapters: conflicting class interests and the organizations that maintain and legitimate the class system.

The middle section of the book (chapters 3 through 7) examines how the privileged class maintains and extends its advantages by holding positions of dominance in the major institutional sectors of U.S. society. The global economy, government policy, education, and the information industry are examined as settings in which class inequalities are created and reinforced. These chapters use material reported daily in the media to demonstrate how class interests and privileged-class power are used to make decisions about jobs and wages, health care and social security, taxes and television, and the education of the next generation of Americans.

In the final chapter we consider the prospects for both continuity and change of the new class society. It reviews current class-based imbalances in institutional power; it revisits the populist movements of the past as a potential guide to understanding future challenges to class inequalities; and it explores the emerging struggle between privileged-class policies that would reinforce class inequalities and challenges from working-class organizations to such policies.

Acknowledgments

There are a great many steps between the completion of a manuscript and a published book. First you have to find someone who believes in what you are trying to do. We are indebted to Dean Birkenkamp for his strong support of this project and for sharing in our effort to present a fresh view of class in the United States. Several people at Rowman & Littlefield helped to bring the project to completion: Rebecca Hoogs, Scott Horst, and Katherine Kimball. Candy Lawson worked on numerous drafts of chapters and helped to prepare the final manuscript. Tony Faiola was our graphics specialist who helped to convert our primitive tables into attractive and informative images. Joyce Webb was helpful in printing multiple versions of several chapters.

1

Class in America

My momma always said that life is like a box of chocolates. You never know what you're gonna get.

—Forrest Gump, 1994

The lead character of the popular film, *Forrest Gump*, illustrates that despite limitations of intellect, his pure heart, guileless character, sincerity, hard work, and positive mental attitude enable him to prevail over life's hardships. Gump's disarming qualities defrost the cynicism of a heartless world and open the path to material success, social respect, and personal fulfillment. His achievements appear to affirm his momma's homily, reinforce belief in the American Dream, and give testimony to the pervasive ideological belief that all men are created equal.

However, movie ideals often clash with social realities. Is life really like a box of chocolates—unpredictable and capricious in detail but essentially rewarding to the pure of heart? Consider the contrast between the fictional experiences of Forrest Gump and the real-life experiences of Jim Farley.

> Jim Farley's fellow workers at Federal Mogul Corporation's roller bearing plant on the east side of Detroit called him Big Jim—not so much because of the size of his body, they said, as because of the size of his heart.
>
> They liked the soft-spoken yet tough manner in which he represented them as a union committeeman. And they liked his willingness to sit down over a shot and a beer at the nearby Office Lounge and listen to the problems they had with their jobs, their wives, or their bowling scores.
>
> Jim Farley had come North from eastern Kentucky, because mechanization of the mines and slumping demand for coal made finding work there impossible. The idea of leaving behind the mountains where he had grown up for the punch-in, punch-out factory life in a big city like Detroit didn't appeal to him much—but neither did the thought of living on relief, like so many unemployed miners in his hollow and most others in Pike County. . . .
>
> Federal Mogul announced that it would be phasing out its Detroit operations by early 1974 and moving bearing production to a new plant in Alabama. Farley, say those who knew him, became a different man almost overnight—tense, moody, withdrawn. A month after the announcement he suffered a heart attack. Physically, he recovered rapidly. Mentally, things got worse. His family and friends called it "nerves." . . .

With close to 20 years at Federal Mogul, the thought of starting all over again—in an unfamiliar job, with no seniority and little hope for a decent pension—was not pleasant. But Farley had little choice. Three times he found work, and three times he failed the physical because of his heart problem. The work itself posed no difficulty, but none of the companies wanted to risk high workers' compensation and health insurance premiums when there were plenty of young, strong workers looking for jobs.

As Farley's layoff date approached, he grew more and more apprehensive. He was 41 years old: what would happen if he couldn't find another job? His wife had gone to work at the Hall Lamp Company, so the family would have some income. But Farley's friends were being laid off, too, and most of them hadn't been able to find work yet either—a fact that worsened his outlook.

Farley was awake when Nancy left for work at 6:15 A.M. on January 29, but he decided to stay home. His nerves were so bad, he said, that he feared an accident at work. His sister-in-law Shirley stopped by late that morning and found him despondent. Shortly before noon he walked from the kitchen into his bedroom and closed the door. Shirley Farley recalls hearing a single click, the sound of a small-bore pistol. She rushed to the bedroom and pounded on the door. There was no response.

Almost 20 years to the day after Jim Farley left the hills of eastern Kentucky, his dream of a secure life for his family was dead. And so was he."[1]

Most people would see Jim Farley's death as an unnecessary personal tragedy. Here was a man with severe psychological problems who simply could not cope with the stress of job loss. "Millions of people lose a job in this lifetime, but they don't commit suicide" might be the typical response. There is a strong tendency to see unemployment as individual failure and the inability to "bounce back" as further evidence of that failure.

But there is another way to look at Jim Farley's death, one that recognizes a long chain of life experiences that produce patterns of predictable hardship and limited opportunities. Farley's chances in life are powerfully shaped by his social-class location, which constrains opportunities. His life is like that of millions of others who barely finish high school and move through half a dozen different jobs hoping to find one that will provide a decent wage and long-term security. Yet, just as the class structure constrains the lives of people like Jim Farley, it confers numerous advantages and opportunities on others. The same class structure that shapes laws denying workers a right to a job gives companies like Federal Mogul the right to do what they wish with their property. They can close a plant with little or no consideration of their workers or the community. In fact, tax laws may provide incentives for closing plants and building new ones in countries with lower-wage workers. The conditions leading to Jim Farley's death some twenty-five years ago have now spread across the land. Millions of workers in stable, high-wage jobs in America's basic industries have been told they are no longer needed. Thousands of plants are closed and sit empty in steel towns along the rivers of the Monongahela Valley in Pennsylvania. They were among the first to go in the dramatic reshaping of America's class structure, which eliminated the middle-class worker, and they were soon followed by similar dislocations in the auto, textile, glass, and electronics industries.

After the flight of manufacturing to foreign shores, corporate America's appetite for profits began to turn to their white-collar labor force. Suddenly, the giant corporations like IBM, AT&T, and GM discovered "downsizing" or "right-sizing" or "restructuring," in which the use of new technology and new work organization resulted in a 10–20 percent reduction in employees. The 1990s brought the global economy, and it became the corporate "bogey-man," disciplining workers with the constant threat of further shutdowns and layoffs to allow American firms to compete with other firms and other workers across the globe.

What are we to make of America's love affair with Forrest Gump? Why the attraction to the Gump myth in the face of the harsh realities? Maybe believing that life is like a box of chocolates leads to an expectation of sweet (but mixed) outcomes and makes predictable class-based disappointments and hardships easier to bear. After all, during the Great Depression of the 1930s, Hollywood produced some of its most upbeat and fanciful films.

To make sense of Jim Farley's death (and maybe even the popularity of Forrest Gump) we need to recognize that the American class structure in the past twenty years has been dramatically altered. What we are seeing is not a temporary aberration that will be soon put right but a fundamental shift in the distribution of economic and political power that constitutes the class structure. To understand the declining fortunes of millions of Jim Farleys and the corporate decisions of thousands of Federal Moguls, it is necessary to examine the workings of class structure and how it shapes the lives of workers, the decisions of politicians, and the actions of corporations.

INEQUALITY

The real news is that the median wage—the take-home pay of the worker smack in the middle of the earnings ladder—is still less than it was before the last recession. At the same time the upper reaches of America have never had it so good.

—Robert B. Reich, *Nation*, February 16, 1998

Most Americans have a keen sense of the presence of inequality. We learn about it in many ways on a daily basis, from our observations of people, homes, cars, neighborhoods, and news accounts of the "rich and famous." There is good evidence that we start to learn about inequality at a very early age and accumulate additional knowledge throughout our lives.[2]

If we were to talk with a group of "average" Americans about their awareness of social differences among people in our society, we might hear something like the following:

It's those ballplayers and movie stars that make all the money. Millions of dollars a year for playing a game or acting like a jerk in front of a camera. Then there's the rock stars getting rich off the videos they sell to kids.

The middle class is getting a screwing. The honest, hard-working slob pays taxes, tries to raise a family, and has a helluva time making ends meet. It used to be that hard work would pay off with a steady job, a house of your own, and a decent car. But you can forget about that happening today.

There are lots of people in this country who are called poor, because their income is below some official poverty line. Some of these people are probably in bad shape through no fault of their own. But there's a lot who just don't want to work, who would rather get a government check and food stamps. I would rather take a minimum-wage job than lose my self-respect by taking handouts.

Most Americans are aware of different forms of inequality. They know about income inequality and the patterns of discrimination against women and racial and ethnic groups. This awareness can be traced to stories in the mass media or what they may have learned in courses in high school or college. Knowledge of inequality is often conveyed in stories about the gender gap in salary, or the homeless, or the number of children or older Americans living below the poverty line. But what about the social arrangements that produce inequality and are responsible for its persistence? A pervasive form of inequality cuts across age, race, ethnicity, and gender to confer privilege on a minority of Americans while relegating the rest to varying degrees of insecurity, need, or despair. This is class inequality, a structured system of unequal rewards that provides enormous advantages to a small percentage of people in the United States at the expense of the overwhelming majority. Inequality is contained within a class system that resembles a game of monopoly that is "rigged" so that only certain players have a chance to own Park Place, and a great many others go directly to jail.

The discussion of class in America is a taboo subject because of the national reluctance to examine how the class system of the United States operates on a day-to-day basis. We do not learn from our schools or media how a privileged but organized minority of Americans is able to amass a disproportionate share of our national wealth and to transmit that privilege across generations to create a permanent economic, political, and social elite class. This structured class inequality is both the cause and the consequence of the ability to control important resources such as money, education, votes, or information. And for this system to work, the majority of disadvantaged Americans must be persuaded to believe that the way things work out for people is fair. This is done by distracting attention from class inequality and focusing the national spotlight on conflict between blacks and whites, women and men, gays and straights, pro-choice and antiabortion partisans.

American society is complex. It contains a diverse population of people of different races, ethnic origins, and religions. The people are divided across a complicated and shifting political spectrum spanning liberalism, the radical right, the religious right, conservativism, libertarianism, and democratic socialism. Politics are played out across a dizzying array of interest groups concerned about the environment, abortion, flag burning, animal rights, prayer in schools, gun ownership, sexual harassment, and sexual lifestyles and hundreds of other groups that are for or against something. Some of these interest groups confront each other over their different ideas on rights, justice, and freedom—or what we might call the "pursuit of happiness." However, most of the interest groups try to use the powers of government to aid them by changing tax law, funding health care, or reducing air pollution. This means that to be successful interest groups have to lobby members of Congress. And government, with its millions of employees and thousands of agencies and departments, oversees the use of a $1.6 trillion budget, a task that entails taking money from most people and giving some of it to other people.

The day-to-day operation of this society is made possible by the 130 million Americans who are in the labor force. The work they do is described in the sixty-five thousand occupational categories. The economy, often described as if it were separate from the rest of society, is made up of thousands of establishments where people make a living, from the multinational General Motors with 745,000 employees worldwide to the family-owned Korean grocery in Brooklyn.

Many of those Americans who are still socially alert and concerned about how our society works read newspapers and magazines, watch news programs on television, or belong to an interest group. But the socially aware are probably also overwhelmed by this entity we call society (a nineteenth-century French sociologist called it "the Great Being"). The complexity, the contradictions, the madness of modern life lead the average American to alternate between anger, involvement, and frustration and often finally to withdraw into some safe haven or escapist activity.

Everyday life has become so complicated that we have created a host of new occupations for people whose job it is to keep us informed about the workings of "The Great Being." These jobs are found in what is humorously referred to as the "hot-air sector" of our economy, where "experts," "pundits," and "advocates" give us an hour-by-hour, blow-by-blow account of the number of jobs created or lost, the strength or weakness of long-term bonds, the creeping or waning of inflation, and the international crisis of the week involving famines, floods, and "ethnic conflicts" (although the Russian bear has been caged, the world is still portrayed as a dangerous place). We get some relief from the hot-air sector by tuning in on the "drop your pants in public" talk shows like the Jerry Springer Show. The daily accounts of murder and mayhem (especially gang violence and drive-by shootings) are presented as if they are happening in our own city or on our own block. This image of complexity is intimidating and keeps millions of Americans from taking an active interest in civic life.

Amid all this complexity and contradiction and conflict, is it any wonder that most Americans have lost confidence in their elected officials, corporations, schools, or unions? Is it any wonder that fewer than four in ten citizens vote in presidential elections? Americans seem to be constantly off balance, unsure about what to believe, suspicious of every leader who promises a "better way," and ultimately cynical about the possibilities for change. Escape may be the only way out, or so it seems. If we have the money, or credit cards, we can escape into consumerism. If not, there is television, booze, or drugs.

But there is another way to look at American society; it is a view that is rarely presented in newspapers, discussed on television, or taught to our school children. This view says that it is possible to understand how society works and how the pursuit of happiness becomes available to some but not to others; that amid all the complexity, one can find stable and enduring patterns in our collective lives. The stable and enduring pattern that is the focus of this book is the new class system.

MAPPING THE CLASS STRUCTURE: PAST TRADITIONS AND NEW REALITIES

Mapping the U.S. social class structure and defining what *class* means in America have always been difficult and slippery tasks. Academic sociologists, journalists, and pundits have applied a variety of contrasting images and approaches to these topics. The use of such varied approaches has contributed to confusion and inconsistencies in academic and public arenas concerning the nature of the American class structure and how *class* can best be defined. Even so, poll data indicate that most Americans recognize the existence of a clearly identifiable, patterned U.S. class structure as well as the reality and importance of class inequalities. Survey findings suggest that Americans tend to view class structure in terms of a cake-like image, with groups of people organized into layers and stacked in a ranking system that ranges from low to high across gradual and shaded degrees of class differences. Such a view implies that the people grouped together within each layer are part of a specific social class and that class location is based on the possession of similar shares of important resources. This image appears to include the notion that class is partly a function of economic factors as well as cultural and lifestyle differences among people.

Sociological models of class structure and definitions of social class have sought to achieve greater precision and clarity than public views and images. But whereas some academic maps and definitions are similar to public perceptions, others are strikingly different. Although past sociological efforts to map the class structure and define class have not been uniform, they have tended to be organized around one of two distinct traditions or approaches: the production model and the functionalist model.

The production model is a kind of single-factor approach in which people's positions in the production process (and their possession of economic wealth) occupy center stage. It views class structure as organized on the basis of the relationship people have with the means of production: people tend to be either owners of productive wealth, like factories, offices, malls, airlines, rental properties, small businesses, or nonowners—workers.

This approach is grounded in the work of Karl Marx. But some contemporary sociologists (neo-Marxists) have refined and extended the original two-class model to reflect the reality that the production and corresponding occupational structures are much more complex today than they were in the 1880s.[3] Recent sociological variations of this approach also produce a kind of cakelike image of class structure with a relatively short list of layers—or classes. However, unlike the public image of classes shading into one another because of gradually shifting economic and lifestyle differences, production models view the class structure as more sharply divided by wealth inequalities that reflect people's positions in the production process. In these models, classes are typically labeled as owners, managers, small employers, workers, and the poor (or underclass). In each instance, class position is based on a person's location in the production process—which also closely corresponds to the possession of wealth and to the occupational roles people perform. Owners (big and small) set policy and control the production process; managers assist owners and act as "order givers" who oversee the production process and often accumulate portions of productive wealth themselves; workers are "order takers" and typically do not share in the ownership of productive wealth (or at most own only very small portions); the poor are excluded from both ownership and most forms of desirable work. (But according to this model some segments of the poor may be used by owners and managers from time to time, as a force to pressure workers into accepting lower wages or less desirable working conditions.)

The functionalist model was partly inspired by Max Weber's view that social stratification is a complex, multidimensional phenomenon and can not be understood on the basis of a single factor. Unlike the production model, in which ownership (or the lack of it) is critical to producing the class structure (and defining class), the functionalist approach views the layers (classes) as organized according to variations in the levels of prestige. Prestige levels are viewed as reflecting a combination of several qualities individuals possess. These include the level of importance attached by cultural values to different occupational categories individuals occupy, educational levels they attain, and variations in their incomes. Although money does matter somewhat in some functionalist models, prestige, especially occupational prestige, not wealth per se, is the critical factor shaping the class structure and locating people within it. According to functionalist models, occupations requiring advanced formal education such as teaching and social work confer high levels of prestige on people who work at them, even though their income levels may be lower than some factory or business occupations requiring less education.

Like production models, functionalist models also encourage a layer-cake view of the class structure. However, in contrast to production-model views of sharp class divisions based on production positions and economic wealth, functionalist models envision a multilayer class structure with shaded degrees of prestige and income dividing the social classes. Thus, functionalist models are somewhat similar to the public image of class structure. But functionalist models often completely omit references to class and substitute the term *socioeconomic strata* as a way of describing the layered rankings of people possessing similar levels of prestige and economic resources. The strata that make up the class structure are typically arranged by functionalist models into descriptive class categories that are further subdivided. For example, the highest class is often divided into upper-upper-class and lower-upper-class groupings, with the same *upper-* and *lower-* prefix designations applied to the middle and lower classes as well. Approached in this way, class structure takes on a kind of shaded, layer-cake image, with classes more akin to statistical categories than to groupings of real people.[4]

BEYOND TRADITION:
NEW CLASS REALITIES AND THE DISTRIBUTIONAL MODEL

> If calling America a middle-class nation means anything, it means that we are a society in which most people live more or less the same kind of life. In 1970 we were that kind of society. Today we are not, and we become less like one each passing year.
>
> —Paul Krugman, *Mother Jones*, November–December 1996

The production and functionalist models differ in many respects, but both produce layer-cake images of class structure. Both models also emphasize the importance of occupation as a key factor in determining class location—although for different reasons. As we have seen, the production model emphasizes the links between occupation, production position, and class, whereas the functionalist model emphasizes the links between occupation, prestige, and class. Although both models have made useful contributions in analyzing class inequalities in the past, their focus on the occupationally linked factors of production and prestige is inadequate to the tasks of both describing and understanding the emerging realities and complex dimensions of the new American class system.

To more fully understand the origins, nature, and dynamics of the new class system, in this book we develop and apply a new model of class analysis. Our model builds, in part, on some features of, but is also distinct from, the production and functionalist models of the past. We refer to our approach as the distributional model of class analysis, and it includes at least four major features that distinguish it from previous models of class analysis.

The first distinctive feature of our model is our view that the emerging new class system is organizationally based. This means that the class structure is viewed as increasingly organized around and through large organizational structures and processes that control the distribution of several forms of valuable economic and social resources. We maintain that large organizations—through various levels and groups of "gatekeepers" within them—direct, channel, and legitimate the distribution of these resources to individuals and groups. Occupations are still important in our approach, not simply because of their role in production but because of the organizations in which their work is conducted. Lawyers are not important as lawyers; they are important because of the firms in which and for which they do their lawyering. This view is directly linked to the second important feature of our approach: class location reflects the extent to which people possess combinations of four forms of generative economic and social resources—investment, consumption, skill, and social capital (to be discussed below). People possess variations in these forms of capital in large measure owing to the nature and extent of the links they have to upper-level authority positions within corporate, government, and cultural structures. Thus, we view the class structure as being largely shaped by the distribution of organizationally controlled forms of capital, which, held in greater or lesser amounts, determine the class locations of individuals and groups.

A third major feature of our approach concerns the idea that large organizations are centrally involved in legitimating the distributional processes as well as the class inequalities that arise from them. As we will see in later chapters, this means that large organizations are key sources for generating various forms and kinds of idea systems and explanations that justify the distribution of the four forms of capital to various individuals and groups as fair and legitimate. The fourth and final major feature of our approach rests on our assertion that the U.S. class structure is increasingly polarized by class inequalities into two broad class divisions. This leads us to argue that the new class system more closely approximates a double-diamond image of class structure than the cakelike, stacked-layer images evoked by earlier models of class analysis.

Our distributional model takes into account the reality that large organizations dominate the economic, political, and cultural landscapes today and through complex distributional structures and processes shape the nature and details of the new American class system. In this system, social classes are defined as collections of real people (not statistical categories) who hold similar levels of, and have similar access to, the four forms of generative capital. These forms of capital are distributed to class members through organizationally based structures and processes that, as we will see, are dominated by privileged groups who themselves possess high levels of all four forms of capital.

Control of mass media - advertising education -

GENERATIVE CAPITAL AND CLASS STRUCTURE

Our image of a double-diamond class structure is based on the way that vital life-sustaining resources are distributed and the availability of these resources over time. In some societies the most important resource is land, because it allows one to grow food to eat and to exchange the surplus food for housing, health care, and seeds to grow more food. Peasant farmers in Central America are permanently impoverished because most land is held in large estates. These estates produce coffee or cotton for export, that is, they produce for foreign exchange or money. Peasants, without land, face the choice of starvation, working for the owner of a large landholding, or moving to the city in search of work.

In American society today, capital is the main resource used in exchange for what we need and want, and it is found in four forms: consumption capital, investment capital, skill capital, and social capital.

Consumption Capital

Consumption capital is usually thought of as income—what we get in our wages and salary, unemployment check, social security, or welfare check. The lucky people have enough of it to buy food and clothing, pay the rent or mortgage, and make payments on the furniture or car. The really lucky people have a little money left over. But for most people, there is plenty of month left over when the money runs out.

When thinking about how much consumption capital families have and how they spend it, we immediately recognize that food can mean lobster or macaroni and cheese; clothing can mean second-hand from the thrift shop or name brands and fashionable labels. People vary in their weekly or monthly consumption capital, and two families with the same monthly income may choose to spend it in very different ways.

Figure 1.1 describes the distribution of income in 1995 for about 100 million households in the United States. Twenty-one percent of the households have annual incomes of less than $15,000. At the other extreme, 32 percent have annual incomes in excess of $50,000. In 1970, 16 percent of household incomes were below $15,000 (in constant 1992 dollars), and 23 percent were about $50,000. Thus, the inequality in income has increased over the past two decades, with one-quarter of households hovering at or below the poverty level.

Investment Capital

Investment capital is what people use to create more capital. If you have a surplus of consumption capital (the money left over when the month runs out) you can save it and earn interest each month. You can buy a house, or you can invest in stocks or bonds and earn dividends and capital gains. You can buy an old house, a "fixer-upper," renovate it, divide it into apartments, and collect rent. If your annual rent receipts exceed the combined cost of mortgage payments, property taxes, insurance, and maintenance costs, you will earn a profit.

If you have a great deal of investment capital, you can live off returns on investments in stocks or investments in a business. If you own a business, it probably means that you will employ others and will have to decide how much to pay workers and whether or not to provide them with health insurance or retirement plans. The less you need to pay them, the more you will have for yourself.

The varied ways in which investment capital is used produce wealth, which provides power and independence and is a major source of well-being for families. Wealth is determined by the total current value of financial assets (bank accounts, stocks, bonds, life insurance, pensions) plus durable assets such as houses

Figure 1.1   Money Income of Households, 1995

Source: U.S. Department of Commerce, 1997.

Note: 1995 median income is $34,076.

or cars, minus all liabilities such as mortgages and consumer debt. Thus, we can describe a family's wealth in terms of *total net worth* (financial assets, plus durable assets, minus liabilities) or *total financial wealth* (only financial assets). The distinction is important, because financial assets can generate income (interest, dividends) but durable assets are "lived in" or for "driving around."

The level of wealth inequality in the United States is much greater than the level of income inequality. Much less is known about wealth than about income distribution in the United States, but wealth is probably a more significant indicator of inequality because of its role in transmitting privilege across generations. Some sociologists have described wealth inequality as "the buried fault line of the American social system."[5] Figure 1.2 presents the shares of total net worth and total financial wealth in 1983, 1989, and 1992 for the top 1 percent, the middle 19 percent, and the bottom 80 percent of households. It is clear that there is enormous disparity in wealth controlled by the top 20 percent of the population compared with that of the bottom 80 percent. The privileged classes in 1992 controlled 83.8 percent of total net wealth and 92.3 percent of financial wealth—both figures representing increases over 1983. Wealth provides security, well-being, independence, and power to a privileged minority in American society, who can use that wealth to advance their privileged-class interests. The members of this privileged class are likely to be the corporate elite, top managers, doctors and corporate lawyers, members of Congress, White House staff, cabinet officials, professors at elite universities, media elite, "talking heads" on television, and assorted cultural elites. They are Democrats and Republicans, conservatives and liberals, Christians and Jews, pro-choice and antiabortion, radical feminists and Promise Keepers. They have a common commitment to keeping 80 percent of the population "bamboozled" while pretending to represent their interests. They have a common bond, which is high income, job security, and wealth, and they will rig the rules of the game in order to preserve and extend their privilege.

Skill Capital

Skill capital is the specialized knowledge that people accumulate through their work experience, training, or education. Skilled plumbers learn their craft through apprenticeship programs and years of on-the-job experience. Skilled doctors learn their craft primarily in medical schools, but their skills are developed further through work experience.

Skill capital is exchanged in a labor market, just as investment capital is used in connection with a financial market. Both plumbers and doctors try to get the highest return for their skill in the form of wages or fees, and they do this through collective associations like labor unions (United Auto Workers) or medical societies (American Medical Association). When skill capital is organized in the form of collective associations, there is greater likelihood of job security or high wages. Workers with unorganized skills (i.e., nonunion) or with low levels of skill are more vulnerable when dealing with employees or clients.

Figure 1.2   Percentage Shares of Total Net Worth and Total Financial Wealth, by Percentile Groups, 1983, 1989, and 1992

	Financial Wealth 1992	Financial Wealth 1989	Financial Wealth 1983	Net Worth 1992	Net Worth 1989	Net Worth 1983
Top 1%	45.6	48.2	42.9	37.2	38.9	33.7
Next 19%	46.7	45.7	48.4	46.6	45.6	47.5
Bottom 80%	7.8	6.1	8.7	16.3	15.4	18.6

Source: Wolff, 1996, 67.

The most important source of skill capital in today's society is located in the elite universities that provide the credentials for the privileged class. For example, the path into corporate law with six-figure salaries and million-dollar partnerships is provided by about two dozen elite law schools where the children of the privileged class enroll. Similar patterns exist for medical school graduates, research scientists, and those holding professional degrees in management and business. After the credentialed skill is provided by elite universities, the market value of that skill (and its income- and wealth-producing capability) is protected by powerful corporations and professional associations. People in high income- and wealth-producing professions will seek to protect their market value not only for themselves but also for their children, who will enter similar fields.

Social Capital

Social capital is the network of social ties that people have to family, friends, and acquaintances. These ties can provide emotional support, financial assistance, and information about jobs. Social capital is used by immigrants in deciding which communities they will settle in when they come to the United States. These same immigrants use social capital to get settled and to find jobs. Social ties are also used by doctors, lawyers, and other professionals to start practices.

The basis of social ties can be found in school ties and in kinship, religious, and political affiliations. For example, graduates of elite universities often become the new recruits at national law firms, major corporations, foundations, and government agencies. A study by the Office of Management and Budget reports that 40 percent of foreign service professionals in the State Department come from eight Ivy League colleges. Another example is found in a story in the *New York Times* (November 10, 1995) about some of the appointments made of new lawyers to join the staff of New York State's new attorney general. One new employee is the daughter of the best friend of the state's U.S. senator; she is paid $75,000 a year. Another employee just admitted to the bar is the daughter of another lawyer who served on the attorney general's election committee; she is paid $60,000 a year.[6]

But social capital is used for more than just getting high-paid secure jobs. It is also used to solidify class interests by making sure that people marry within their corporate or professional class. For example, consider the type of "personal ad" that appears in many upscale magazines for the young urban professional: "Join the Ivy League of Dating. Graduates and faculty of the Ivies, Seven Sisters, Johns Hopkins, M.I.T., Stanford, U. of Chicago, CAL Tech, Duke, U.C. Berkeley, Northwestern, meet alumni and academics. The Right Stuff! Call XXX-XXX-XXXX."

One has to wonder what the "right stuff" is. These ads may appeal to people who are simply trying to meet someone on their intellectual level; but they could instead join MENSA, an association of people with high IQs. More likely it is an effort to match same-class individuals with credentialed skills. This is the way to get dual-earner-household doctors, attorneys, and corporate elites or the "mixed marriages" of doctors and fashion designers or artists who become the "darlings" of *People* magazine fare.

Although everyone has at least a minimal level of social capital, it should be clear that access to different forms of social capital (like consumption, investment, and skill capital) is distributed very unequally. Having a family member loan you $100 or a friend who works in a retail store tell you about a job opening is not the same as being a member of a fraternity or sorority at an elite university. Social capital refers to current memberships people hold in social networks that are linked to varying levels of organizational power, prestige, and opportunities. Individuals can be connected by strong ties (e.g., family members) or weak ties (e.g., acquaintances) to formal and informal social networks that are associated with varying levels of organizational resources and power. A person's position in these social networks provides access to information and opportunities that can be converted into important financial and social benefits. For example, the extent of investment capital owned or controlled can be the result of holding high positions in large organizations; paid and unpaid leadership positions in economic, political, or cultural organizations can be used to advance personal careers or provide opportunities for relatives and friends. Thus, social capital must be viewed as a class-linked resource that both protects and advances privilege and provides a barrier for those "upstarts" seeking to expand their generative capital.

GENERATIVE CAPITAL AND POWER

> The residents of one zip code—10021—on New York City's Upper West Side contributed more money to Congress during the 1994 elections than did all the residents of 24 states.
>
> —Ellen Miller and Randy Kehler, *Dollars and Sense*, July–August 1996

The distribution of these scarce and valued resources—consumption capital, investment capital, skill capital, and social capital—is the basis for class inequality among individuals and families in America. This inequality is revealed when resources are converted into economic power, political power, and social power. Economic power is based on the resource of money (consumption capital and investment capital), and it usually is used to provide food, shelter, and clothing. People who have more economic power can buy more things and better things and thereby make their lives more comfortable and enjoyable. Money can be converted into other valued things like health care, which enables those with more money to live longer and healthier lives. Money can protect people when unfortunate or unforeseen events occur, like an earthquake, tornado, or flood. Recovering from these natural disasters and from human disasters like unemployment or illness is possible when you have economic power. Money also has the special quality of being transferable to others and can also be used to transmit advantage.

Consumption capital can be used to procure social capital. For example, families with money can use it to help secure the futures of their children by purchasing special experiences through travel, tennis lessons, scuba diving, dance, and creative arts in the hope that such experiences will foster or strengthen social relationships with others having similar experiences. It is also done by buying entry into prestigious educational institutions that provide their students with lifelong advantages. Families who buy elite educational degrees for their children are using their investment capital to develop both social capital and skill capital. Graduates of elite universities have a special advantage in converting their credentialed skill capital into better jobs. They establish the social contacts that can be used later in life to solidify or enhance their social position. Many families, recognizing the payoff that comes with a degree from an elite college, prepare their children with SAT prep courses in the eighth grade and private school education. In 1995, Harvard University received eighteen thousand applications for sixteen hundred places in the entering class. Those lucky enough to be selected can expect to pay about $150,000 for the four-year degree. Clearly, these families are using their consumption capital to invest in the education of their children.

Three out of four families in the United States have little economic power. Even so-called middle-class families on the "brink of comfort" (as they were described in a *New York Times* article by Charisse Jones, February 18, 1995) find themselves in a constant struggle to make ends meet. Consider Bill and Brenda Jones, both of whom have full-time jobs that pay about $8.00 an hour. Their combined gross pay is $33,000 per year, with take-home pay being $27,000, or about $2,200 a month. Their income is below the national median income of $34,076 (see figure 1.1). They have a son in high school and a daughter who lives at home while studying at a local college. This "middle-class" family has a monthly budget of $2,123 that meets basic expenses:

Rent	$676
Groceries	400
Telephone	50
Electricity	60
Tuition	300
Car insurance	50
Cable	37
Health insurance deductible	50
Clothing, auto, misc.	200
Car payments	300

The Jones family is much better off than many, but they have no savings, no pension plan, and no job security. The two children in the family work at part-time jobs to cover their own entertainment and school-related expenses. If either parent should lose his or her job, the Jones family would be in serious trouble.

If the Jones family is on the "brink of comfort," what must things be like in a female-headed household with one or two children, where the mother brings home about $1,000 a month from a $7.00 an hour job as a retail clerk? This family is sitting on the official poverty line, or maybe one paycheck above or below it. Clearly, a household budget for three or four persons of $1,000 a month generates no economic power.

The problem facing three of every four families in the United States is not simply that they are just making ends meet—whether on $30,000 a year or $12,000 a year—but that their consumption capital is limited, unstable, and unpredictable. They cannot count on these resources over time in any predictable way, and if they should experience any period of joblessness they will face a serious crisis. Possession of stable and secure resources over time is the key to economic power. The predictability of resources allows people to plan and save in order to provide for the future. They can think about buying a home, sending a child to college, saving for retirement, or starting a business. Most American workers have very unstable incomes, even if they are sometimes earning what seems like a "high" salary. For example, take the case of the United Auto Worker employed in a General Motors assembly plant. During periods of peak production and heavy overtime, a worker might earn $4,000 per month. This is a $50,000-a-year job, assuming that the monthly salary continues all year. But that's the rub. When overtime disappears and production schedules are cut back because of overproduction, that $50,000 salary is cut in half, at best; at worst, the plant may be shut down and production moved to a lower-wage area in the United States or some other country—which is exactly what happened to hundreds of thousands of high-wage blue-collar workers in the 1970s and 1980s.

Political power is the result of collective actions to shape or determine decisions that limit or enhance peoples' opportunities. The tenants of a housing project can combine their time to collect signatures on a petition calling on the housing director to provide better services. Corporations in a particular sector of the economy can combine their money (economic power) to hire lobbyists who will seek to influence members of Congress to support or oppose legislation that will affect those corporations. Individuals and organizations with more economic power have a different set of opportunities for exercising political power than groups without economic power.

The clearest examples of how collective economic power can be converted into political power is in the area of corporate welfare—the practice of congressional action that provides billions of dollars in federal loans and subsidies to specific industries. More than $100 million a year goes to corporations like McDonald's, Pillsbury, and Sunkist to help them advertise their products in foreign countries. The Pentagon provides another $100 million a year to a group of semiconductor firms to help them compete internationally. This money goes not to small, struggling firms but to giants like Intel and National Semiconductor Corporation. The total annual corporate welfare bill has been estimated at between $85 billion and $100 billion.[7]

Groups with little economic power usually try to exercise political power through mass mobilization of persons with grievances. Bringing together hundreds or thousands of persons for a march on city hall conveys a visible sense of a perceived problem and an implied threat of disruption. The capacity to disrupt may be the only organized weapon available to those without economic resources. Such actions usually get the attention of political leaders, although it does not always produce the results desired by aggrieved groups.

Social power involves access to public services and the interpersonal networks that can be used to solve many of the day-to-day problems that confront most families. Public services like police, fire protection, and public transportation can provide people with the security to use public space for living, leisure, and getting to and from work, stores, and day-care facilities. Interpersonal networks consist of the informal groups and formal associations that are available in a community for persons with certain interests and concerns. The availability of community groups concerned about the presence of toxic waste dumps, the spread of crime, and the quality of the schools in their community provides opportunities for people to learn about many things in addition to toxic waste, police protection, and education. Such groups often provide links to information about jobs, or how to approach a local banker for a loan, or how to obtain information about financial aid for college students.

Opportunities to develop social power vary widely across groups. People who have jobs that provide little flexibility in their work schedules or are physically demanding may have little time or inclination for participation in community groups at the end of a hard day. Similarly, some jobs offer more opportunities than others to develop the interpersonal networks that can be drawn upon to help a family member find a job or to help in finding good and affordable legal assistance.

There is considerable evidence from social research that Americans with greater economic resources, and those holding upper managerial positions in organizations, are more likely to actively participate in a variety of community affairs.[8] These active participants accumulate information about community affairs and social contacts that can be used to advance or solidify the interests of one's social group. Some of the key players in this process of accumulating social power have been identified as women from professional families who are out of the labor force and have the discretionary time for civic affairs.[9]

An interesting example of how social power operates among the privileged classes is provided by the case of the Morrison Knudsen Corporation.[10] It happened that the chairman's spouse started a private charity organization to provide young women with alternatives to abortion. The spouse served as unpaid executive director of the charity and was apparently successful in obtaining donors to support its activities. The success of the charity could perhaps be traced to the fact that five of the charity's directors are the spouses of directors of Morrison Knudsen, and three of the directors of the charity are senior executives of the corporation. Thus, the spouse of the board chairman of Morrison Knudsen was able to use her social power to put together a charity organization capable of drawing upon the political and economic power of directors from the privileged elite. Such opportunities would certainly not be available to a community organization trying to oppose the location of toxic waste sites in their area or one trying to get the local police to be more responsive to the concerns of local citizens.

CLASS STRUCTURE AND CLASS SEGMENTS

The combination of capital and power can be used to describe the class structure of American society. One popular way of describing the class structure of a society is with a physical or geometric shape or image. The shape or image conveys the relative proportions of people in a society who have some valued thing, like money or education. The pyramid (figure 1.3), for example, illustrates a class structure in which a small percentage of a society (10 percent) has a great deal of the commodity, another 30 percent has a little less, and the majority (60 percent) has the least amount of the valued commodity.

Another frequently used image is the diamond (figure 1.4), which provides a different picture of the way valued things are distributed. The diamond image says that a small percentage (10 percent) of a society has a lot of something, another small percentage (10 percent) has very little of something, and most of the people (80 percent) are in the middle, with moderate amounts of the valued commodity.

Figure 1.3　Pyramid Diagram of Class Structure and Class Segments

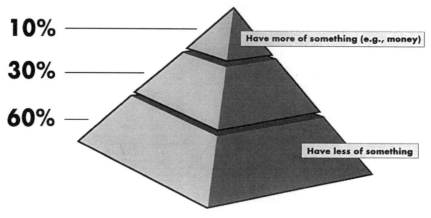

Figure 1.4　Diamond Diagram of Class Structure and Class Segments

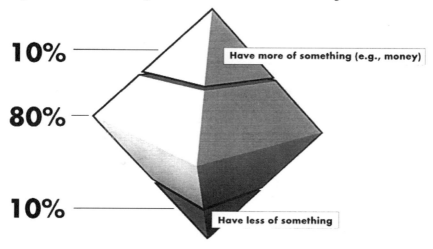

In each of these class structures, the class positions of people can be simply designated as upper class, middle class, or lower class. Thus, the pyramid image represents a society in which most persons are lower class, and the diamond image represents a middle-class society. If asked to choose between the two societies depicted here, most people would probably choose the society represented by the diamond image, because the majority of the people are in the middle class. If you chose to live in the pyramid society, you would have a 60 percent chance of being in the lower class.

However, before choosing one of these societies in which to live, you might want a little more information. You might want to know about the particular attribute or characteristic that puts people in each class. Is it something they are born with, like skin color or physical size, or is it some characteristic they learn or acquire, like being a good hunter or a skilled craft worker? You might also want to know something about how people in each class live, in terms of basic necessities, material comforts, physical security, and freedom. Finally, it might be important to know if it is possible for people to change their class position within a lifetime or across generations, or if there are opportunities for their children to rise above the class into which they were born.

Thus, the image of a society as pyramidal or diamond-shaped provides an overall view of how people in that society are distributed on some valued characteristic or attribute. But it does not tell about the society's "rules" for determining or changing their class position.

Let us try to make all this a little more concrete by examining American society. Most efforts to portray the American class structure have focused on occupations as the main determinant of the class structure and of people's positions in that structure. Occupations have been classified according to the public's opinion of the social standing or prestige associated with being a public school teacher, or a dentist, or a mechanic, or a machine operator. When large numbers of Americans are asked to rate occupations on a scale ranging from "excellent" to "poor" in social standing, they consistently place U.S. Supreme Court justice, physician, and corporate manager at the top of the list; at the bottom are garbage collector, filling station attendant, and janitor. The prestige hierarchy of occupations has remained pretty stable in studies done over several decades and in different countries.[11] This has led some analysts to see occupational prestige as the basis of class structure in American society. They also assert that the term *class* is not meaningful because prestige is determined according to a continuous system of rankings of occupations, without any sharp boundaries or divisions between occupations.

However, if you look behind these prestige rankings to ask what it is that people are actually ranking, you will find that what is being evaluated is not simply the prestige of an occupation but also its income and power. In our society, the occupational structure as embedded in organizations is the key to understanding the class structure, and a person's occupation is one aspect of class position. But how do the hundreds of different occupations combine to create a structure of distinct classes with different amounts of economic, political, and social power? What aspects of occupations determine their position in the class structure?

People often speak of their occupation or their job as what they do for a living. An occupation or job describes how a person is related to the economy in a society or what one does in the process of the production of goods and services. An occupation or job provides people with the means to sustain life ("to make a living"); and the sum total of the work done by people in their occupations or jobs is the wealth generated by the economic system. In one sense there is a parallel or symmetric relation between the availability of jobs and the amount of wealth that is generated. The more people in a society are working at making a living, the better the economic health of the total society. But there is also a sense in which there is an asymmetric relationship between the well-being of working people ("how much of a living they make") and the total wealth that is generated. Some people contribute more to the total wealth than they receive for their work, as in the case of some workers whose wages are a fraction of the value of their products when they are sold. And some people may receive ten or twenty times more in income for their work than that received by others. So although there may be 130 million Americans involved in occupations and jobs for which they are compensated, their amount of compensation varies widely according to how they are related to the production process. There are a variety of ways in which people are related to the production process in today's economy.

The Privileged Class

The activity of some people in the system of production is focused on their role as owners of investment capital. Such a person may be referred to colloquially as the "boss" or, in more respectful circles, as a "captain of industry," an "entrepreneur," or a "creator of wealth," but in the language of class analysis they are all owner-employers. The owner may actually be the sole proprietor of the XYZ Corporation and be involved in the day-to-day decisions of running that corporation. But ownership may also consist in the possession of a large number of shares of stock in one or several corporations in which many other persons may also own stock. However, the ownership of stock is only socially and economically meaningful when (1) the value of shares owned is sufficient to constitute "making a living," or (2) the percentage of shares of stock owned relative to all shares is large enough to permit the owner of said shares to have some say in how the company is run. Members of this group (along with the managers and professionals) control most of the wealth in America. The point of this discussion is to distinguish owners of investment capital from the millions of Americans who own shares of stock in companies, who own mutual funds, or whose pension funds are invested in the stock market. The typical American stock owner does not make a living from that ownership and has nothing to say about the activities of the companies he or she "owns."

On the lower rungs of the owner-employer group are the proprietors of small but growing high-tech firms that bring together venture capital and specialized knowledge in areas involving biomedical products or services and computer software forms. These are "small" businesses only in Department of Commerce classifications (less than $500,000 in sales), for they bear no resemblance to the Korean grocer, the Mexican restaurant owner, or the African American hair salon found in many American cities. They are more typically spin-off firms created by technical specialists who have accumulated some capital from years of employment in an industrial lab or a university and have obtained other investment capital from friends, family, or private investors.

A second activity in the system of production is that of manager, the person who makes the day-to-day decisions involved in running a corporation, a firm, a division of a corporation, or a section within a company. Increasingly, managers have educational credentials and degrees in business, management, economics, or finance. Managers make decisions about how to use the millions of dollars of investment capital made available to them by the owners of investment capital.

The upper levels of the managerial group include the top management of the largest manufacturing, financial, and commercial firms in the United States. These managers receive substantial salaries and bonuses, along with additional opportunities to accumulate wealth. Table 1.1 presents a typical pattern of "modest" compensation for the officers of a large firm. We refer to this compensation as "modest" because it is far below the multimillion-dollar packages of compensation for CEOs at IBM, AT&T, Disney, and Coca-Cola (which range from $20 million to $50 million). But such distinctions are probably pointless, because we are describing executives whose wealth is enormous in comparison with others not in their class. For example, the top CEO in the listing above also owns 102,772 shares of stock in the corporation he heads. The value of these shares is $8,220,000. The executive vice president owns 166,488 shares, and the other VPs own "only" 25,000 to 75,000 shares.

The lower levels of the managerial group carry out the important function of supervising the work done by millions of workers who produce goods and services in the economy. The success of these managers, and their level of rewards, is determined by their ability to get workers to be more productive, which means to produce more at a lower cost.

Professionals carry out a third activity in the economic system. This group's power is based on the possession of credentialed knowledge or skill, such as an engineering degree, a teaching degree, or a degree in public relations. Some may work as "free professionals," providing service for a fee, such as doctors, dentists, or lawyers. But most professionals work for corporations, providing their specialized knowledge to enhance the profit-making potential of their firm or of firms that buy their services. The professional group is made up of university graduates

Table 1.1   Compensation for Corporate Executives

Position	Annual Compensation	Bonus	Stock Options
President and chief executive officer	$608,846	$325,000	$2,159,916
Executive vice pres. and financial officer	376,769	142,000	732,493
Senior vice president	267,861	146,000	390,663
Vice president	292,577	86,000	488,324
Vice president	262,500	67,000	488,329

Source: Based on data from the Annual Report and Proxy Statements, Great Lakes Chemical Corporation, 1997, West Lafayette, IN.

with degrees in the professional schools of medicine, law, business, and engineering and in a variety of newly emerging fields (e.g., computer sciences) that serve the corporate sector. The possession of credentialed knowledge unifies an otherwise diverse group, which includes doctors who may earn $500,000 a year and computer specialists who earn $50,000 a year.

The potential to accumulate wealth is very great among certain segments of professionals. Median net salary in 1995 for all doctors was $160,000, ranging from a high median salary of $240,000 in radiology to $125,000 in family practice. Unfortunately, these averages hide the salaries of graduates from elite medical schools and those affiliated with the most prestigious hospitals. Also absent is information about doctor's entrepreneurial activities such as ownership of nursing homes or pharmaceutical firms.

Similar opportunities for high income exist among lawyers, where partners at the nation's elite law firms average $335,000 and associates average $80,000 (1988). Even law professors at prestigious law schools have a chance to amass a small fortune while teaching and practicing law or consulting. A recent *New York Times* story reported that a professor at Harvard Law School gave the school a bequest of $5 million.[12] The *Times* reported that the professor is "not one of the school's prominent moonlighters" and is "unlike Prof. Alan M. Dershowitz, the courtroom deity who has defended Leona Helmsley and Mike Tyson and is on the O. J. Simpson defense team." So how did the professor do it? By "writing and consulting."

Professors at elite universities who are in selected fields like law, medicine, business, biomedical engineering, or electrical engineering have opportunities to start high-tech firms and to consult for industry in ways that can significantly enhance income. Even "modest" activities, like becoming an outside director for a bank or industrial firm, can be very rewarding. A colleague in a business school at a Big Ten university who is a professor of management has been on the board of directors of a chemical corporation for twenty years. His annual retainer is $26,000. He gets an additional $1,000 a day for attending meetings of the board or committee meetings and $500 a day for participating in telephone conference meetings (the board meets six times a year, and committees from one to six times a year). Each nonemployee director gets a $50,000 term life insurance policy and a $200,000 accidental death and dismemberment insurance policy. After serving on the board for a minimum of five years, directors are eligible for retirement benefits equal to the amount of the annual retainer at the time of retirement. Retirement benefits begin at the time of the director's retirement from the board and continue for life.

Why does the president of this university, or its Board of Trustees, allow a professor to engage in such lucrative "outside activities"? Maybe it's because the president, whose annual salary is $200,000, holds four director positions that give him more than $100,000 a year in additional income.

Professionals in elite settings not only make six-figure salaries, but they have enough "discretionary time" to pursue a second line of activity that may double or triple their basic salaries. Not a bad deal for the professional class.

Not everyone with a credentialed skill is in the privileged professional class. We exclude from this group workers like teachers, social workers, nurses, and most university professors at nonelite schools. They are excluded because of where they obtained their degrees, where they are employed, and the market for their skills. Each of these factors limits job security and provides very modest levels of income (i.e., consumption capital) and little investment capital. Thus, we distinguish between elite and marginal professional groups, with only the former being in the privileged class.

The New Working Class

Finally, there is the large majority of Americans: employees who sell their capacity to work to an employer in return for wages. This group typically carries out its daily work activities under the supervision of the managerial group. They have limited skills and limited job security. Such workers can see their jobs terminated with virtually no notice. The exception to this rule is the approximately 14 percent of workers who are unionized; but even union members are vulnerable to having their jobs eliminated by new technology, restructuring and downsizing, or the movement of production to overseas firms.

This working group also consists of the many thousands of very small businesses that include self-employed persons and family stores based on little more than "sweat equity." Many of these people have been "driven" to try self-employment as a protection against limited opportunities in the general labor market. But many are attracted to the idea of owning their own business, an idea that has a special place in the American value system: it means freedom from the insecurity and subservience of being an employee. For the wage worker, the opportunities for starting a business are severely limited by the absence of capital. Aspirations may be directed at a family business in a neighborhood where one has lived, such as a dry-cleaning store, a beauty shop, a gas station, or a convenience store. Prospects for such businesses may depend upon an ethnic "niche" where the service, the customer, and the entrepreneur are tied together in a common cultural system relating to food or some personal service. The failure rate of these small businesses is very high, making self-employment a vulnerable, high-risk activity.

Another sizable segment of wage earners, perhaps 10–15 percent, has very weak links to the labor market. For these workers, working for wages takes place between long stretches of unemployment, when there may be shifts to welfare benefits or unemployment compensation. This latter group typically falls well below official poverty levels and should not be considered as part of the "working poor." The working poor consists of persons who are working full-time at low wages, with earnings of about $12,000 a year—what you get for working full-time at $6.00 an hour.

Table 1.2 provides a summary of these major segments of Americans with different standing in the current economy. The groups are distinguished as

Table 1.2   Class Structure in America

Class Position	Class Characteristics	Percentage of Population
Privileged Class		
Superclass	Owners and employers. Make a living from investments or business ownership; incomes at six- to seven-figure level, yielding sizable consumption and investment capital.	1–2%
Credentialed Class		
Managers	Mid- and upper-level managers and CEOs of corporations and public organizations. Incomes for upper-level CEOs in seven-figure range, others, six-figures.	13–15%
Professionals	Possess credentialed skill in form of college and professional degrees. Use of social capital and organizational ties to advance interests. Wide range of incomes, from $75K to upper-six figures.	4–5%
New Working Class		
Comfort Class	Nurses, teachers, civil servants, very-small-business owners, and skilled and union carpenters, machinists, or electricians. Incomes in the $35–50K range but little investment capital.	10%
Contingent Class		
Wage earners	Work for wages in clerical and sales jobs, personal services, and transportation and as skilled craft workers, machine operators, and assemblers. Members of this group are often college graduates. Incomes at $30K and lower.	50%
Self-employed	Usually self-employed with no employees, or family workers. Very modest incomes, with high potential for failure.	3–4%
Excluded class	In and out of the labor force in a variety of unskilled, temporary jobs.	10–15%

(1) those who own capital and business, (2) those who control corporations and the workers in those corporations, (3) those who possess credentialed knowledge, which provides a protected place in the labor market, (4) the self-employed, small-business owners who operate as solo entrepreneurs with limited capital, and (5) those with varying skills who have little to offer in the labor market but their capacity to work.

These segments of the class structure are defined by their access to essential life-sustaining resources and the stability of those resources over time. As discussed earlier, these resources include consumption capital, investment capital, skill capital, and social capital. The class segments differ in their access to stable resources over time, and they represent what is, for all practical purposes, a two-class structure, represented by a double diamond (see figure 1.5). The top diamond represents the privileged class, composed of those who have stable and secure resources that they can expect will be available to them over time. This privileged class can

Figure 1.5   Double-Diamond Diagram of Class Structure and Class Segments

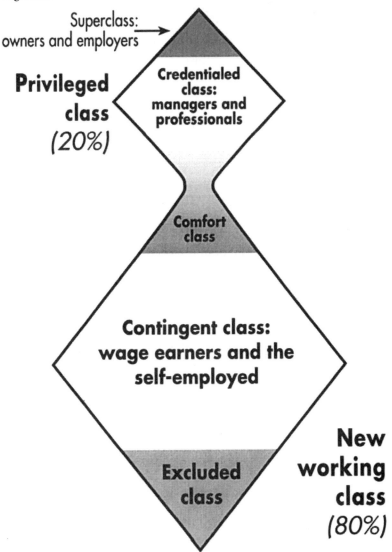

Superclass: owners and employers →

Privileged class (20%)

Credentialed class: managers and professionals

Comfort class

Contingent class: wage earners and the self-employed

Excluded class

New working class (80%)

be subdivided into the superclass of owners, employers, and CEOs, who directly or indirectly control enormous economic resources, and the credentialed class of managers and professionals with the knowledge and expertise that is essential to major industrial, financial, commercial, and media corporations and key agencies of government. The bottom diamond is the new working class, composed of those who have unstable and insecure resources over time. One segment of this class has a level of consumption capital that provides income sufficient for home ownership and for consumption patterns that suggest they are "comfortable." Thus, we label this segment the comfort class, represented by school teachers, civil servants, social workers, nurses, some small-business owners, and skilled unionized carpenters, machinists, or electricians. Despite their relatively "high" incomes ($35,000–$50,000), the comfort class is vulnerable to major economic downturns or unforeseen crises (e.g., health problems) and has limited investment capital to buffer such crises.

The largest segment of the new working class is composed of the wage earners with modest skills and unpredictable job security. This group includes the machine operators in a manufacturing plant, bank clerks, and the supervisors who could be displaced by new production technology, computerized information systems, or other "smart" machines. Their job insecurity is similar to that of the growing segment of temporary and part-time workers, thereby making them the contingent class.

At the bottom of the new working class are those without marketable skills who move in and out of the labor force in temporary jobs or in seasonal employment. They are the excluded class, who either are treated as "waste," because they are no longer needed as either cheap labor or as consumers, or fill the most undesirable jobs in restaurant kitchens or as nighttime cleaners of downtown buildings.

It is important to keep in mind that a person's location in the double-diamond class structure is related to his or her occupation but not determined by that occupation (as is the case in the production and functionalist models of class, discussed earlier in this chapter). Some lawyers are in the top diamond, and some in the bottom. Some engineers, scientists, and professors are in the privileged class, and some in the new working class. It is not occupation that determines class position but access to generative capital—stable, secure resources over time.

THE NEW AMERICAN CLASS STRUCTURE DEFINED

Figure 1.5 provides a picture of the new American class structure as a "double diamond," divided between the privileged and those lacking the privileges that come with money, elite credentials, and social connections. This two-class structure is composed of approximately 20 percent privileged Americans and 80 percent nonprivileged Americans. Members of the employer, managerial, and professional classes have a stable income flow, employment stability, savings, pensions, and insurance. Their positions in the economy enable them to use their resources to accumulate more resources and to insure their stability over time. The new working class has little in the way of secure resources. Their jobs are unstable, as they can be eliminated by labor-replacing technology or corporate moves to off-shore production. Only marginal professionals and craft workers possess some skills that provide short-term security, but even their skills are being eroded by new technology, the reorganization of work, and the decline of union power.[13]

This image of class structure in American society is based on three important principles that define the new American class structure and how it works in practice.

Class Structure Is Intergenerationally Permanent

One of the most significant aspects of class structures is their persistence over time. The inequality that a person experiences today provides the conditions that determine the future. This aspect of class structure is rarely discussed by the media or even by scholars devoted to the layer-cake image of inequality. In fact, most discussion of class structure views that structure, and one's place in it, as temporary and ever changing. The belief in equality of opportunity states that regardless of where a person starts out in life it is possible to move up through hard work, motivation, and education. Similarly, the overall structure is viewed as changing, as revealed in statistics on the median income, the expanding middle class, or the declining percentage of the population living below the poverty line. In short, the popular image of class differences is that they are temporary and constantly changing. But in fact, nothing could be further from the truth when it comes to the new class system in the United States.

The "rules of the game" that shape the class structure are designed to reproduce that structure. Let's consider a few of those "rules" and how they work.

First, our legal system gives corporations the right to close down a plant and move the operation overseas, but it does not give workers a right to their jobs. Owners and employers have property rights that permit wide latitude in making decisions that impact on workers and communities. But workers' jobs are not viewed as a property right in the law. The protected right to a secure job would provide workers with a stable resource over time and modify their vulnerable situation in the class system.

Second, people in privileged classes have unrestricted opportunities to accumulate wealth (i.e., extensive consumption capital and investment capital). The accumulation process is based on tax laws that favor the rich, a variety of loopholes to avoid taxes, and an investment climate that enables the rich to get richer. The share of net worth and financial wealth going to the top 20 percent of the population is staggering (see figure 1.2). One out of five Americans owns almost everything, while the other four are on the outside looking in.[14]

This extraordinary disparity in wealth not only provides a clear picture of the polarized two-class structure, it also provides the basis for persistence of that structure. Because inheritance and estate laws make it possible to do so, wealth is transmitted across generations, and privilege is thereby transmitted to each succeeding generation.

Another feature of the American class structure that contributes to its permanence is the sheer size of the privileged class. It consists of approximately twenty million households, or between forty million and fifty million people. A class of this numerical size, with its associated wealth, is able to fill all the top positions across the institutional spectrum. Moreover, it is able to fill vacant positions or newly created positions from among its own members. Thus, recruitment of talented women and men from the nonprivileged class will become increasingly rare.

Third, the so-called equality of opportunity in America is supposed to be provided by its system of public education. Yet anyone who has looked at the quality of education at the primary and secondary levels knows that it is linked to the class position of parents. Spending-per-pupil in public schools is tied to property taxes, and therefore the incomes of people in school districts. Schools in poor districts have the poorest physical facilities, libraries, laboratories, academic programs, and teachers.[15] Some of the children who survive this class-based public education are able to think about some sort of post-secondary education. But even here the game is stacked against them.

Going to college is based on the ability to pay the costs of tuition and, unless the student lives at home, room and board. Even at low-cost city colleges and state universities the expenses exceed what many working-class families can afford. On the other hand, even if college attendance were not tied to the ability to pay, it is not likely that many youngsters from low-income families would think of college as a realistic goal, given the low quality of their educational experience in primary and secondary grades.

Thus, the "rules of the game" that are the foundation for the class structure are designed primarily to transmit advantage and disadvantage across generations. This persistence of structure exists even when there are instances of upward social mobility—the sons and daughters of working-class families who move into the professional classes. This upward mobility occurs in a very selective way and without changing the rules of the game. For example, when the birthrates among the privileged class fail to produce enough children to fill all the jobs for doctors, lawyers, engineers, computer specialists, and managers, it is necessary to recruit the most talented young men and women from the working class. The most talented are identified through special testing programs and curriculum tracking and are encouraged to consider advanced education. "Elite" colleges and universities develop special financial and academic programs for talented working-class students, and a variety of fellowship programs support those with financial need. Upward mobility is made possible not by changing the rules of the game but by "creaming" the most talented members of the working class. The "creaming" process has the dual effect of siphoning off potential leaders from the working class and supporting the belief in equality of opportunity and upward mobility.

There Is No Middle Class

Most views of class structure, as noted earlier, present a "layer-cake" image of class differences. There are six or eight classes made up of groups of occupations that differ in prestige, education level, or income. These differences between classes are not sharp and discontinuous but gradual shadings of difference between one class and another. The layer-cake image encourages a belief in a "center" or a "middle class" that is large and stands between the upper and lower classes. The different groups in the middle may think of themselves as being "better off" than those below them and may see opportunities to move up the "ladder" by improving education, job skills, or income.

This image of class structure is stabilizing, in that it encourages the acceptance of enormous material inequality in American society because of the belief that anyone can improve his or her situation and become one of the "rich and famous." It also encourages greater attention to the small differences between groups and tends to ignore the large differences. For example, many Americans are hard-working men and women who often work two jobs to make ends meet but are limited by these low-wage and no-benefit jobs. These people are often most hostile to the welfare benefits provided for people who are just below them in income. A working poor person gets $12,000 a year for full-time work, whereas a welfare family may get the same amount in total benefits without working. However, these same working poor rarely have their hostility shaped and directed toward the rich, who may be more responsible for the low wages, limited benefits, and inadequate pensions of the working poor.

The belief in a middle class also allows politicians to proclaim their support for tax breaks for what they call the middle class while debating whether the middle class includes those with incomes up to $150,000 a year or only those earning up to $100,000.

In our conception of class structure, there can be no middle class. Either you have stable, secure resources over time, or you do not. Either you have a stable job and income, or you do not. Either you have secure health insurance and pensions that provide adequate income, or you do not.

Classes Have Conflicting Interests

In the layer-cake theory of class structure, each class is viewed as having more or less of some valued quality or commodity such as education, occupational skill, or income. Members of each class may aspire to become members of classes above them, and they may harbor negative opinions and prejudices of those in classes below them. But classes, in this theory, are not fundamentally opposed to one another. Of course, there is often discussion of why members of certain classes might support or oppose particular political candidates because of their social or economic policies. But these alliances or oppositional views are seen as linked to shifting issues and are not tied to class interests.

In our view, the two large classes of privileged and working-class Americans have fundamentally different and opposed objective interests, so that when one class improves its situation the other class loses. The advantages of the privileged class, expressed in its consumption capital, investment capital, skill capital, and social capital, are enjoyed at the expense of the working class. Any action to make the resources of the working class more stable, by improving job security or increasing wages and pensions, for example, would result in some loss of capital or advantage for the privileged.

Consider the most extreme test of the existence of oppositional interests between the privileged and exploited classes. One might expect that the highest unifying symbol of the country—the presidency—might be above the taint of class interests. However, a recent unauthorized disclosure of a transcript of President Bill Clinton's meeting with President Boris Yeltsin of Russia sounds like two "petty professionals" trying to make the best deal for their services. "Collusion was recently exposed in a classified transcript of the Presidents' private meeting at the anti-terrorism summit in February [1996]. According to the leaked memorandum, Clinton promised Yeltsin support for his reelection bid with 'positive' U.S. policies toward Russia. In exchange, Clinton asked Yeltsin to lift trade barriers on imports of U.S. chicken parts (40 percent of which come from Arkansas—specifically, a large portion from Tyson Foods, a heavy contributor to Clinton's campaign)."[16] "Pimping" for chicken parts! If this is what goes on at the level of presidential discourse, what might be discussed at meetings of corporate executives, doctors, lawyers, and other credentialed elites? How do the sons, daughters, nephews, nieces, and probably even cousins of the elites get their jobs in the media, foundations, and other plush appointments in the nation's institutions? Slim chance that some bright graduate of a regional college (one with a direction in its name) who submits a resumé believing that the potential employer wants "the best person for the job" will ever be considered.

Given the existence of oppositional interests, it is expected that members of the privileged class will work to advance their interests. As employers they will seek to minimize worker wages and benefits and to fight efforts by workers to organize. As media owners, filmmakers, and writers they will produce cultural products and information that undermine efforts by the working class to organize and advance their interests. Think, for example, about how the media and opinion makers are quick to cry "class warfare" whenever someone points to the wealth of the privileged. Think also about how the opinion makers reacted to the role of Nation of Islam leader Louis Farrakhan in the Million-Man March on the Capitol mall in October of 1995. Every effort was made to discredit Farrakhan and to separate him from the march. The integrationist ideology of the slain civil rights leader Martin Luther King Jr. was resurrected over and over again, as if to say that the privileged class supports the legitimate aspirations of African Americans but not their efforts to develop their own social and economic communities and to ignore white society while doing so.

These three principles—Class structure has intergenerational permanence, There is no middle class, and Classes have conflicting interests—provide a basis for understanding the central defining features of the American class structure. We have, in effect, tried to answer the question, What is class inequality? In the next chapter we address the question, How does class inequality work?

NOTES

1. Don Stillman, "The Devastating Impact of Plant Relocations," *Working Papers* (July–August 1978): 42–53.

2. Cecelia Burns Stendler, *Children of Brasstown: Their Awareness of the Symbols of Social Class* (Urbana: University of Illinois Press, 1949); Robert G. Simmons and Morris Rosenberg, "Functions of Children's Perceptions of the Stratification System," *American Sociological Review* 36 (1971): 235–49; Scott Cummings and Del Taebel, "The Economic Socialization of Children: A Neo-Marxist Analysis," *Social Problems* 26 (December 1978): 198–210; Anthony M. Orum and Roberta S. Cohen, "The Development of Political Orientations among Black and White Children," *American Sociological Review* 38 (1973): 62–74; Jeannette F. Tudor, "The Development of Class Awareness in Children," *Social Forces* 49 (1971): 470–76.

3. For an orthodox Marxian view, see Charles H. Anderson, *The Political Economy of Social Class* (Englewood Cliffs, N.J.: Prentice Hall, 1974). For a sophisticated neo-Marxian analysis, see Erik O. Wright, *Classes* (London: Verso, 1985), and *Interrogating Inequality* (London: Verso, 1994. Wright's early analysis emphasizes ownership and control of the means of production and control of labor as the defining conditions for determining class location; his more recent work adds control of organizational assets and ownership of skill assets.

4. For a good example of the functionalist multidimensional model of class, see Dennis Gilbert and Joseph A. Kahl, *The American Class Structure* (Chicago: Dorsey Press, 1987). For an approach that emphasizes the status or prestige of occupations, see Peter M. Blau and Otis D. Duncan, *The American Occupational Structure* (New York: Wiley, 1967).

5. Melvin Oliver, Thomas M. Shapiro, and Julie E. Press, "'Them That's Got Shall Get': Inheritance and Achievement in Wealth Accumulation," in *Research in Politics and Society*, vol. 15, ed. Richard E. Ratliffe, Melvin Oliver, and Thomas M. Shapiro (Greenwich, Conn.: JAI Press, 1995).

6. Clifford J. Levy, "New York Attorney General Remakes Staff by Patronage," *New York Times*, November 10, 1995.

7. This estimate was provided by the Cato Institute and reported in Stephen Moore, "How to Slash Corporate Welfare," *New York Times*, April 5, 1995.

8. See Robert Perrucci and Marc Pilisuk, "Leaders and Ruling Elites: The Interorganizational Bases of Community Power," *American Sociological Review* 35 (1970): 1040–57; Robert Perrucci and Bonnie L. Lewis, "Interorganizational Relations and Community Influence Structure," *Sociological Quarterly* 30 (1989): 205–23; David Knoke, *Organized for Action: Commitment in Voluntary Associations* (New Brunswick: Rutgers University Press, 1981).

9. Arlene Kaplan Daniels, *Invisible Careers: Women Civic Leaders from the Volunteer World* (Chicago: University of Chicago Press, 1988).

10. Diana B. Henriques, "Ties That Bind: His Directors, Her Charity," *New York Times*, March 21, 1995.

11. Robert W. Hodge, Paul M. Siegel, and Peter H. Rossi, "Occupational Prestige in the U.S.: 1925–1962," in *Class, Status, and Power*, ed. Reinhard Bendix and Seymour M. Lipset (New York: Free Press, 1966); Robert W. Hodge, Donald J. Treiman, and Peter H. Rossi, "A Comparative Study of Occupational Prestige," in Bendix and Lipset, *Class, Status, and Power*.

12. David Herzenhorn, "The Story behind a Generous Gift to Harvard Law School," *New York Times*, April 7, 1995.

13. Harley Shaiken, *Work Transformed: Automation and Labor in the Computer Age* (New York: Holt, Rinehart and Winston, 1985); David F. Noble, *Forces of Production: A Social History of Industrial Automation* (New York: Knopf, 1984).

14. Edward N. Wolff, *Top Heavy* (New York: Twentieth Century Fund, 1996).

15. Jonathan Kozol, *Savage Inequalities: Children in America's Schools* (New York: Harper, 1991).

16. "Chicken on Chechnya?" *Nation*, April 29, 1996, 3.

2

Separate Realities:
The Dream and the Iceberg

Why should the strong—The beautiful strong—Why should they not have the flowers?

—Stephen Crane, *The Red Badge of Courage and Other Writings*, 1960

The first lesson of sociology . . . [is] the importance of class consciousness.

—Charles H. Anderson, *Toward a New Sociology*, 1974

"The fruit doesn't fall far from the tree." Prior to the first three decades of the post-World War II period, this aphorism linking children, parents, and social class stood at the intersection of commonsense observations and social science research.[1] From wealthy elites to white trash, personal experiences, popular culture, and sociological data supported the widely shared consensus that social class tends to "run in families." But following World War II, real wages (adjusted for inflation) for working-class Americans began trending in an upward direction. At the same time, the postwar period witnessed improving opportunities for advancement from the working class into more prestigious occupations.[2] For members of the newly forming blue- and white-collar middle-income groups of the 1950s and 1960s, these patterns provided a reassuring vision of a comfortable and secure future for themselves and their children. Improving living standards combined with traditional beliefs in the open-ended economic and social opportunities in America contributed to an enthusiastic, shared embrace of the American Dream as a cultural ideal among members of virtually all social classes.[3]

The American Dream is predicated on the belief that humble class origins are not destiny. It is grounded in the faith that American society offers unlimited opportunities for upward mobility for anyone firmly embracing the work ethic, regardless of class origin. Although the details of the dream vary, Americans typically envision it as including economic comfort and security (an above-average and secure income), higher educational levels (for themselves and their children), a rewarding job, home ownership, and personal freedom.[4]

35

Somewhat paradoxically, the dream runs both parallel with and counter to the general trend whereby children tend to replicate the class ranking of their parents. For privileged-class families, the dream offers a reassuring sense of continuity: the advantaged positions of parents can and will be passed on to, and extended by, their children. For working-class families, the dream represents a possible future of reward, fulfillment, and affluence—especially for their children. To some extent, the early post-World War II period seemed to provide middle-income families with evidence that the dream was within reach. Thus, among members of the nonprivileged classes, the dream has resonated powerfully as a mythic cultural ideal and—at least for a time—as an attainable reality. Today, however, there is growing evidence that opportunities for realizing the American Dream, especially for those in the new working class, are being shredded by powerful economic, political, and cultural forces that are part of the emerging, iceberg-like American new class society.

The purpose of this chapter is threefold. First, we clarify our iceberg metaphor and consider the taboo nature of class analysis. Second, we identify three important "above the waterline" trends associated with the new class system that are at odds with the ideals of the American Dream. Third, we consider two dynamic dimensions of the new class system (discussed in detail in later chapters) that we view as submerged "beneath the waterline" of conventional social analysis: conflicting class interests and the structures and processes that maintain and legitimate the class system.

This chapter stands at the brink of truth concerning the dynamics of the new class society. Like a breaking TV-news report with "film at eleven," it previews themes of betrayal, heartbreak, power, greed, deception, resistance, and hope that are central to the story of social class in America. It is a twisted tale previewing a long, strange trip intended for travelers, not tourists.

THE THREE-THOUSAND-MILE ICEBERG

Strange and Ugly things are about to happen.

—Hunter S. Thompson, *Generation of Swine*, 1988

Like a huge iceberg stretching coast to coast across the American social horizon, the new class society combines a dramatic profile of sharply defined and disturbing visible features with a submerged and hidden mass of potentially society-wrecking forces and consequences. Compared with the social structure of the recent past, the new structure is sharply leaner in the middle, larger and much meaner at the bottom, and increasingly "secessionistic" among the privileged few at the top. In the terms of figure 1.5, it is a structure that combines privilege, security, and affluence for those in the upper diamond with increasing peril, insecurity, and eroding incomes for those in the lower diamond.

Recent political events and public opinion trends suggest that many Americans are interested in social-class issues and increasingly aware of some of the most visible features of the class iceberg. The evidence includes widespread public interest in the class-based politics of Patrick Buchanan and Ralph Nader during the 1996 presidential campaign, grassroots interest in progressive Senator Paul Wellstone's (D-Minn.) 1998 exploratory presidential bid (ended by his 1999 decision to withdraw), and polls indicating growing public disenchantment with the rich and large corporations.[5] At the same time, other evidence indicates that many Americans are confused about or distracted from class issues. This tendency is illustrated by public interest in militias, religious fundamentalism, and escapist popular culture trends such as lotteries, casinos, celebrity-lifestyle reports, and diversionary films—from the sentimental *Forrest Gump* to the "romantic" *Titanic* to Bruce Willis-style action flicks. These conflicting trends suggest that Americans lack a consistent focus on, or clear understanding of, the submerged dimensions of the class iceberg—including conflicting class interests, the structures and processes that legitimate the class system, and the possibilities for changing it.[6] We think these paradoxical trends of interest and confusion stem, at least in part, from the taboo nature of social class in America.

SOCIAL CLASS: THE LAST TABOO

Mainstream American social institutions today openly address a wide range of issues that until recently have been considered taboo as topics for public discussion. Despite the expanding inventory of previously censored cultural and lifestyle issues (e.g., abortion, drug use, rape, family violence, race and gender inequalities, homosexuality), social class analysis remains the last taboo. In fact, as far as class analysis is concerned, a virtual blackout exists among mainstream social institutions, and few public forums exist for wide-ranging discussions of the nature and consequences of social-class structures and inequalities. It is one topic that has been consistently marginalized and ignored by the schools, the mass media, and by most political leaders.

Class analysis is not a curricular theme or topic at the primary or secondary level and is seldom included in university-level courses.[7] In the print media, newspaper editors have little interest in, or sympathy for, working-class interests or issues. Majorities ranging from 54 percent to 60 percent of editors report that they side with business in labor disputes and also on business-worker conflicts involving issues such as minimum-wage increases and plant-closing legislation.[8] Every major U.S. daily newspaper includes a separate business section, but none includes a separate "class" or even "labor" section, and none of the 1,533 daily U.S. newspapers includes a regular commentary column written by a socialist or social democrat.[9] A similar situation exists in the electronic media, as illustrated by a study of the three network television evening news programs, which found the networks devote only 2 percent of total airtime to workers' issues.[10]

Politicians typically avoid class-based rhetoric—especially the use of language and policy labels that might openly emphasize or reveal the conflicting economic and political interests of working-class versus privileged-class members. Sometimes this avoidance is openly acknowledged, as illustrated by a *Newsweek* report, "Why Clinton Won't Play Class War," which points out that "aides push him to bash the rich, but he seeks a middle way."[11]

President Clinton's approach is consistent with the unwritten rule that politicians should avoid raising class inequalities as public issues. Only two exceptions exist to the political taboo on class issues. First, it is acceptable to discuss the "middle class." Because large numbers of Americans identify themselves as middle class, references to this group actually serve to disguise and mute class differences because the term is so inclusive: it embraces nearly everyone. When the mainstream media profile "middle-class" problems, as in the *New York Times* 1996 "Downsizing of America" series, it creates public interest and a large market. (The series was reprinted as a best-selling book.) However, such accounts do not address conflicting class interests. For example, the central message of the *Times* series was one not of class interests but of individual effort: "The lesson, heard again and again, [is] that while government and business can do some things, in the end workers have little to fall back on but themselves."[12]

The second exception to avoidance of the class issue includes mass media glimpses into the lives of the privileged class as well as tours of the excluded class. Television programs often take viewers to both destinations. The glamour of life at the top is routinely showcased on tabloid-style TV "newsmagazine" (e.g., *Hard Copy, Inside Edition, Extra!*) profiles of wealthy show business, sports, and occasional charismatic corporate elites. The grim realities of life-at-the-bottom experiences turn up on occasional PBS and HBO documentaries concerning homelessness, welfare, and related issues. However, these inside looks at the extremes do not involve class analysis. Instead, they serve as models or morality tales, the first to aspire to and the other to avoid. The two models are never presented as causally related: one is not rich because the other is poor.[13]

When a mainstream politician does openly address class issues, especially in terms sympathetic to workers, the responses of other politicians, pundits, and the mass media tend to be swift, dismissive, and derogatory. Pat Buchanan's 1996 Republican presidential primary campaign illustrates the pressures to keep class analysis out of politics. His message of economic populism resonated strongly with working-class concerns over the growing economic insecurity and marginalization of workers in the emerging new class system. But this message violated the taboo against class analysis in politics, and his candidacy was greeted by an almost universal fear and loathing by the privileged class—as evidenced by numerous negative print and television reports and disparaging commentary from mainstream politicians of both parties. A 1996 *Newsweek* cover story depicted Buchanan as a demagogue "preaching fear" and included several related stories, the details and tone of which were clearly aimed at discrediting his message, his supporters, and his candidacy.[14]

Buchanan's conversion to populism struck many as disingenuous and opportunistic—especially given his personal history of promoting privileged-class interests in several capacities ranging from his work as a speechwriter for Richard Nixon and Spiro Agnew to his job as a conservative commentator on the CNN *Crossfire* program. Nonetheless, his candidacy registered strongly with many voters and mobilized many mainstream, privileged-class political, economic, and media leaders into actions aimed at marginalizing Buchanan's appeal and at keeping class-based messages and analysis out of politics.

The taboo nature of class is a product of institutional biases that discourage and deflect media and public discussions of class issues—especially conflicting class interests. These biases are grounded in privileged-class interests in encouraging public silence on, or even confusion about, class issues. Members of the superclass have an especially strong interest in not having public attention called to their class-based advantages or to broader class inequalities, because a close examination of the origins of and basis for these inequalities—including the wealth, power, and privileges of this class—might call the entire class system into question.[15]

Superclass preferences for avoiding public discussions of class inequalities are paralleled by the interests of credentialed-class members in maintaining their own positions of comfort and security. Allied with and following the lead of their superclass sponsors, many credentialed class members are rewarded for helping to keep class analysis out of the arena of public discourse. In their roles as government officials, organizational managers, media producers, and community leaders, members of the credentialed class often pursue organizational policies and practices that have the effect of deflecting public attention away from class inequalities and class-based analysis of social problems.[16]

Individuals and groups proposing higher taxes on the wealthy are attacked by many credentialed-class political leaders and media editors as advocating destructive and divisive "class warfare."[17] Whether the topic is taxes, income, educational opportunities, or other class-based inequities, privileged-class advantages and working-class disadvantages are topics to be avoided, not discussed.[18] Social inequalities (when they are considered) are most often framed by credentialed-class leaders as problems of race, gender, or other cultural-ethnic divisions—or perhaps the result of personal or genetic flaws (e.g., a "predisposition" to problems limiting "achievement," such as alcoholism, drug use, mental illness, etc.).[19] Class analysis is out of the picture.

Although privileged-class interests are a major factor underlying the class taboo, we do not see a "class conspiracy" driving the neglect of class issues in public discourse. Rather, we see the superclass and its credentialed-class allies as bound by shared cultural assumptions, values, experiences, worldviews, and organizational memberships.[20] These shared qualities lead to strong, common commitments to maintaining the economic, political, and cultural status quo.[21] Such views lead members of these two classes (and most Americans) to explain material and social success (or failure) on the basis of factors other than class-based resources.[22]

The shared values and worldviews common to the privileged class help explain why most members of this class prefer public policies, corporate practices, and media content that ignore or deflect attention away from the importance of class resources in understanding life experiences and life chances in the United States. Members of the privileged class tend to favor a class-doesn't-count orientation that leads, from their perspective, to eminently reasonable, sound, and sensible public policies and corporate practices that contribute to the common good—as they define it. This approach, combined with the enormous resources controlled primarily by the superclass, helps ensure that privileged-class-based ideas, policies, and lifestyles exert a kind of hegemonic grip on the economic, political, and cultural structures of the society and upon the imaginations and aspirations of most members of this class as well as upon many members of the new working class.[23]

Despite the taboo driving public neglect of class analysis, it has become virtually impossible for workers and their families, politicians, reporters, and even privileged-class members to ignore several class-related trends that are transforming the nature of social geography and social experiences in the United States today. Although these trends are increasingly obvious and growing in significance as subjects of public commentary and even political discourse, they are only the most visible and obvious features of the social-class iceberg today.

ABOVE THE WATERLINE: NEW CLASS-SOCIETY TRENDS

> The Four Horsemen of the workplace—global competition, technology, downsizing and the growth of the contingent work force—will cause wages to continue to fall, creating a nation increasingly divided into haves and have-nots.
>
> —G. Pascal Zachary and Bob Ortega, *Wall Street Journal*, March 10, 1993

Although American society has always been divided by substantial class inequalities, recent developments in the economic, political, and cultural arenas have produced substantial changes in the U.S. class system. Three important class-related trends fall above the waterline of the class iceberg in the sense of being increasingly visible and obvious sources of growing public concern and commentary: (1) class polarization, (2) downward mobility, and (3) class secession.

Class Polarization

> We are now the "two nations" predicted by the Kerner Commission thirty years ago. Only the dividing line . . . is class.
>
> —Patrick Buchanan, *The Great Betrayal*, 1998

Class polarization refers to the growing division of the United States into two main classes: the privileged class and the new working class. This trend is the result of four convergent developments that have become increasingly evident since the early 1970s. First, a pattern of growing income inequality has placed increasing numbers of persons and families in the upper- and lower-income ranges, with declining numbers in the middle. Second, a corresponding pattern of falling real wages for most working Americans has eroded living standards for all but those in the highest-income groups. Third, a pattern of shrinking fringe benefits for more and more workers has emerged, particularly in the areas of health care and pensions, resulting in ever higher levels of economic insecurity among middle- and low-income groups. Finally, the increasing use of contingent, contract, temporary, and part-time workers by a wide range of employers has contributed to a growing "contingency workforce" characterized not only by low pay and prestige but also by vanishing-point levels of job security.

Once upon a time—and not too long ago—the material realities of life for middle-income Americans were such that references to this group by social scientists and journalists as the "middle class" were understandable, if overstated. Of course, as is often the case with class issues, the precise meaning of this concept was (and is) somewhat elusive and subject to debate. Even so, since the end of World War II, for most mainstream academic researchers as well as for the American public, middle-class status has typically been associated with an identifiable core of economic and social resources. These include "respectable" jobs (mid-level prestige or higher), stable, mid-level (or higher) incomes, security benefits (health care, pensions), and participation in conventional social institutions such as churches, schools, community groups, and other voluntary organizations.[24]

For the first three decades of the post-World War II period, most academic definitions and popular perceptions of an American middle class were grounded in an economic reality whereby a majority of middle-income individuals and families possessed stable jobs and experienced gradually rising real incomes.[25] The reinforcement of these core features among middle-income groups by additional material resources anchored middle-class status (e.g., expanding levels of employer-provided benefits including health care, life and disability insurance, vacation time, and pensions).[26] This stable resource base made it possible for many middle-income families, over time, to increase their stock of investment capital (by homeownership and investment savings), skill capital (by additional education and by sending children to college), and social capital (using more free time to participate in various social groups and organizations). The material and social resources of middle-income Americans, combined with widespread egalitarian cultural beliefs of America as a middle-class nation, were reflected in subjective class-identification studies that from the 1940s through the 1980s consistently found majorities of Americans identifying themselves as members of the middle class or upper-middle class.[27]

In short, the middle income-middle class linkage was predicated on workers' access to organizational resources that went beyond income alone. In post-World War II America, job stability and rising real wages combined with other forms of

economic and social resources typically available to middle-income groups produced a large group that could readily realize a modest version of the American
Dream. The resource base of middle-income Americans at this time could even
provide a platform for upward mobility, especially for their children. However,
"sometime around 1973, the American dream stopped working. That's the year
that the real (inflation-adjusted) hourly wage for nonsupervisory workers—almost three-quarters of the workforce—peaked. Since then, its [*sic*] fallen."[28] As
real wages fell, other major structural changes in this period transformed the national economy in ways that produced a "crisis of the American Dream."[29]

Although not causes in and of themselves, as the most visible features of the
class polarization process, the four convergent developments cited earlier in this
section offer a starting point for understanding the extent to which the material
realities of the U.S. middle-income group have been transformed. An examination of these developments, in conjunction with the evidence concerning the distribution of consumption capital (income) and related material resources in the
last thirty years, supports our view that a polarized new class system has
emerged—minus a middle class. (A portion of what has been called the middle
class is best understood as part of the comfort class segment in our model.) To
many who considered themselves part of the middle class, the period since the
early 1970s brought the "end of the world"—as they knew it.

Many may not agree with our view that America has no middle class; but national polls reflect a growing public awareness of major changes in the class system. In a significant shift from previous studies of class membership perceptions,
by the mid-1990s a majority (55 percent) of Americans identified themselves not
as members of the middle class but as members of the working class.[30] As the century ended, most sociologists also agreed that at the very least, the middle class
was under siege or declining. By the late 1990s, most major introductory sociology college texts included discussions of the declining or disappearing middle
class as a separate topic, typically in chapters dealing with stratification or class
inequalities.[31]

Declining Middle Incomes and Wages

Although all U.S. national income studies include middle ranges, middle-income
levels do not necessarily translate into middle-class status. Moreover, even the
numbers of what are often called middle-income households have declined since
the 1970s. The realities of shrinking numbers of middle-income households and
of declining real wages for average wage earners over the past three decades are reflected in a variety of income studies reported in the 1990s. One comparison of
1979 and 1993 worker and household incomes found (reporting all amounts in
1993 dollars) that the proportion of workers with mid-level earnings ($7.00 to
$27.99 per hour) from households with mid-level annual incomes ($14,000–
$55,999) decreased from 39.1 percent of all workers in 1979 to 34.3 percent in

1993. By contrast, the proportion of low-earning workers (those earning less than $7.00 per hour) from households with annual incomes of less than $42,000 increased from 19.5 percent in 1979 to 22.7 percent in 1993. While some workers' incomes did go up, the increase in the proportion of higher-earning workers ($14.00 to more than $28.00 per hour) in households with upper-level incomes (more than $56,000) from 16 percent in 1979 to 19.5 percent in 1993 was not sufficient to offset the loss of middle-income workers.[32]

Another study of the distribution of persons, households, and families by income levels over the 1979–95 period defined middle income for individuals as spanning a range from 50 percent to 200 percent of median family (size-adjusted) income. (In 1995, the U.S. median family income was $40,611 for all families—unadjusted for size.) Middle-income households and families were defined as those earning between $15,000 and $50,000 (in annual incomes, 1995 dollars). From 1979 to 1995, this study found decreases in the percentages of middle-income persons (from 68 to 60 percent), households (from 49.7 to 47.0 percent), and families (from 51 to 47 percent). Some of the decline in the percentages of middle-level family and household incomes occurred as a result of shifts into the top level (incomes in excess of $50,000); but the decline also reflected an increase in the percentages of families and persons in the bottom income level during this period.[33] Underscoring the drift toward greater income inequality during this same period, the Gini Index (a measure of income inequality whereby zero equals total equality and one equals total inequality) increased from .365 in 1979 to .426 in 1995.[34]

The decline in the percentage of middle-income families is especially interesting in that it occurred during a period when the annual number of paid working hours logged by husbands and wives increased sharply—and 77 percent of all family households consist of married-couple families.[35] Husbands' hours increased from an annual average of 2,096 in 1979 to 2,159 in 1994, and wives' hours increased from an annual average of 851 in 1979 to 1,168 in 1994.[36] Despite the fact that husbands, wives, and unmarried individuals spent more hours in the paid labor force as the 1990s unfolded, not only did the number of middle-level income families and individuals fall, but real (inflation-adjusted) median family income remained virtually stagnant, inching up only $272 in sixteen years—from $40,339 in 1979 to $40,611 in 1995 (in 1995 dollars).[37]

Although the period from the 1970s through the 1990s witnessed declining numbers of mid-level incomes and stagnating real family incomes, it also saw substantial declines in real wages for many American workers. During the 1989–95 period, average per-hour real wages (in 1995 dollars) declined both for production or nonsupervisory workers, from $11.87 to $11.46, and for white-collar workers, from $18.31 to $18.05.[38] More recently, in January 1998 the average weekly earnings of nonsupervisory workers (about 80 percent of the workforce—excluding agriculture) were $436.[39] If a worker earned this amount for fifty-two weeks, his or her annual income would be $22,672. That may not sound too bad, but if we compare workers' average wages in January 1998 with those in January

1973, we find average real wages (adjusted for inflation) were 22.6 percent lower in 1998 than they were in 1973.[40] More generally, median household income (which includes families of all types as well as single-person households) fell from $35,526 in 1989 to $34,076 in 1995 (in 1995 dollars).[41]

One result of the declining numbers of mid-level income groups and falling real wages and the growing numbers of low-income workers has been a sharp redistribution of income upward to those in the top-income-earning groups. The U.S. Census Bureau provides a useful way of illustrating income redistribution trends. The bureau reports the shares of aggregate (total) national income received by U.S. families divided into five quintile groups, arrayed by income levels from the lowest 20 percent to the highest 20 percent.

Using Census Bureau data, figure 2.1 summarizes several aspects of family income levels and redistribution trends in recent years. First, it illustrates, using side-by-side comparisons, the shares of national income received by families in each quintile group for 1980 and 1995. Second, the first line at the bottom of the figure reports the percentage changes in family income shares from 1980 to 1995 for each quintile group. Finally, the last line at the bottom of the figure provides a "snapshot" of 1995 family income ranges for each quintile (in 1995 dollars).[42]

During the 1980–95 period, each quintile group experienced changes in the percentage of aggregate income received ranging from highly positive to highly negative. The top 20 percent experienced a 13 percent increase in its share of national income (from 41.1 percent in 1980 to 46.5 percent in 1995), whereas the other four quintiles all experienced decreases in their shares of national income. These ranged from a modest loss of 5 percent for the fourth quintile (dropping from 24.4 percent to 23.2 percent) to a whopping 17 percent loss for the bottom quintile (dropping from 5.3 percent to 4.4 percent). The changes in income shares for these five groups reflect the reality that income was redistributed over the 1980–95 period—in an upward direction.

The income ranges reported as the last line of figure 2.1 provide a context for considering the impact of upward income redistribution. The income range for the bottom quintile in 1995 included all families with incomes up to $19,070 (in 1995 dollars). This means not only that families in this group have the lowest incomes but also that they will be most affected by income losses because they have the fewest resources to begin with. Yet this group suffered the greatest loss in income share during the 1980–95 period (17 percent). The income ranges for the second quintile ($19,070 to $32,985), the middle quintile ($32,985 to $48,985), and the fourth quintile ($48,985 to $72,260) provided these groups with greater cushions (compared with the bottom quintile) to absorb income losses. Of course, the top quintile, with an income range of $72,260 and up, needed no "cushion" because it increased its income share by 13 percent.

The growing gap between top and bottom wage earners is even more starkly evident when we compare changes in the income shares received by the top 5 per-

45

Figure 2.1 Family Income Share and Changes, by Quintile Group, 1980–1995

Quintile	Bottom 20%	Second 20%	Third 20%	Fourth 20%	Top 20%
Percentage change in family income shares: 1980 – 1995	-17%	-13%	-10%	-5%	+13%
Dollar amount limits for each quintile (1995 Dollars)	Up to $19,070	$19,070 to $32,985	$32,985 to $49,985	$49,985 to $72,260	$72,260 & Up

Source: U.S. Department of Commerce, 1997, 470.

cent with those of the bottom 40 percent of American families over time. In 1980, families in the top 5 percent income group received 14.6 percent of all income, while the bottom 40 percent received only 16.9 percent. But by 1995 the income share of the top 5 percent (earning $123,656 or more annually) had grown to 20 percent, while the bottom 40 percent share had shrunk to 14.5 percent.[43] A separate analysis of Congressional Budget Office data for families in the top 1 percent income group ($330,000 and up per year, in 1994 dollars) further underscores the pattern of upward income redistribution. During 1979–93, this elite group experienced an 83 percent increase in real income.[44]

Top earning groups have far outdistanced average wage earners over the past two decades, but the very highest-paid groups have done even better. In the 1980–95 period, the compensation of corporate chief executive officers (CEOs) increased by 500 percent while factory wages increased by only 70 percent.[45] In 1996, CEO pay and bonuses (including stock options) for 365 major U.S. corporations increased 54 percent (over 1995) to an average of $5.8 million. In 1997 this same group received another 35 percent increase (over 1996), which brought average CEO compensation to $7.8 million.[46] If factory and minimum-wage workers had received pay raises comparable to those of CEOs since 1980, their wages would have been $90,000 and $39,000, respectively, in 1995.[47]

In 1973, total annual CEO compensation was 44.8 times what average workers earned. But like the Energizer Bunny, the CEO group kept going and going: by 1989, the CEO:average worker pay ratio grew to 122:1. It jumped to 212:1 in 1996 and then skyrocketed to 326:1 in 1997.[48] According to *Forbes*, in 1997 four CEOs received hundred-million-dollar-plus incomes: Sanford Weill (Travelers Group, $227.6 million), Stephen Hilbert (Conseco, $124.5 million), Richard Srushy (HealthSouth, $106.7 million), and Ray Irani (Occidental Petroleum, $104.5 million).[49] The stock option portion of CEO compensation can grow dramatically in value over time, as illustrated by Disney's Michael Eisner, who collected more than $400 million in 1997 by exercising just some of his earlier-awarded stock options.[50]

The upward CEO pay trend covered all industries—including health care. Income inequality in this field was evident by the incredible range between executive and shop-floor pay levels. In the 1990s, health company CEOs pulled in stratospheric incomes: Thomas F. Frist, of Health Corporation of America, received a total of $127 million in 1992, and in 1997, Richard Srushy was paid a total of $106.7 million.[51] Compared with the terms of the 1995 Minneapolis Nurses Association contract with twelve Minneapolis-St. Paul hospitals, which established a $33,288 annual starting wage for nurses,[52] these CEOs received incomes more than thirty-four-hundred times the pay of a nurse. It is clear that in health care, as in other fields, privileged-class incomes have soared over the past two decades. At the same time, the real wages of average workers have stagnated or declined as middle-income households sent more members to work at longer hours and still saw their numbers—and real incomes—decline.

Losses in Benefits and Growing Contingent Labor

In addition to income losses, reductions in job benefits and increasing job insecurity for many middle-income groups have intensified class polarization. When fringe benefits for average-wage, private-sector workers are defined as employer-paid pension plans, insurance (health and life), and payroll taxes (the employer portion of Social Security and unemployment taxes), these factors account for about 18 to 20 percent of workers' total compensation.[53] In the 1979–94 period (adjusted for inflation), "the average value of benefits including employer-provided health insurance, pension plans, and payroll taxes grew [by] just $.04 per year." In the more recent 1987–95 period, employee benefits (in 1995 dollars) fell from an average of $3.38 to $3.26 per hour.[54]

Looking only at pension benefits, we find that the proportion of workers in medium-size and large firms with employer-paid pension plans decreased from 84 percent in 1980 to 59 percent in 1991 (a 30 percent decline).[55] Also, the proportion of full-time employees in large and medium-size firms directly funding their own pensions through deferred savings such as 401(k) plans increased from 26 percent in 1985 to 44 percent in 1991.[56] A disturbing corollary of this latter trend has been the increase in reports of employer abuse and fraud involving misappropriation of employee contributions to 401(k) plans, which highlights growing retirement insecurities for workers.[57]

Regarding health care, the share of workers covered by employer-provided health care plans, where employers pay amounts ranging from partial to full premiums, declined from 71 percent of private-sector workers in 1979 to 64 percent in 1993.[58] More-comprehensive employer-paid health plans went from covering a majority of workers to covering only a minority. From 1980 to 1991, the proportion of workers under the age of sixty-five who had 100 percent employer-paid family health care dropped from 54 percent to 31 percent.[59] Also, the percentage of health care costs paid for by employers declined from 80 percent in 1980 to 69 percent in 1991, while the average expenditure on health care per family doubled between 1980 and 1991.[60] These trends are understandable, as employers have increasingly shifted health care costs to employees. For example, "the average monthly contribution for family coverage for workers in small firms (fewer than 200 workers) [increased] from $34 to $175 between 1988 and 1996."[61]

Workers' wages and benefits fell in part because of the growing use by employers of more workers who were defined as other than conventional, full-time employees. The alternatives to full-time employment include a number of labels, with "contingent" being the most common. "The term 'contingent work' was first coined by Audrey Freedman at a 1985 conference on employment security to describe a management technique of employing workers only when there was an immediate and direct demand for their services. Within a few years of its initial usage . . . the term came to be applied to a wide variety of employment practices . . . [other than] full-time [jobs]."[62]

Definitions of contingent work vary, but there is no doubt that employers are employing more workers outside of conventional, full-time work arrangements. Surveys of 521 major U.S. companies reveal that in 1989, 97 percent used workers from temporary agencies and 78 percent used independent contractors (up from 77 and 63 percent in 1986).[63] The temporary-help industry increased the numbers employed as temps from 417,000 in 1982 to 1,411,000 in 1995.[64] By 1995, 18.5 percent of the U.S. workforce consisted of non-full-time workers. This figure included involuntary part-time workers (3.7 percent), contingent workers (those who do not expect their jobs to last more than one year—4.9 percent), and workers in all other forms of "alternative arrangements" (contract, on-call, temps—9.9 percent).[65] Other estimates placed the mid-1990s share of "contingent workers" (broadly defined) at 25 to 35 percent of the total U.S. workforce.[66]

The trend of increasing contingent labor is paralleled by declining levels of job security as measured by workers' attachment to employers over time. The recent past has witnessed a decline in the percentage of workers with "strong employer attachment" (defined as no more than one job change in ten years) and an increase in the percentage of workers with "weak employer attachment" (indicated by four or more employers in ten years). The proportion of workers in the first category decreased from 67 percent in the 1970s to 52 percent in the 1980s, and the proportion of workers in the second category increased from 12 percent in the 1970s to 24 percent in the 1980s.[67] These data indicate that as contingent work has expanded, job security has been diminished. When we combine the trends of declining real wages, fringe benefits, and job security for more and more members of the new working class with the sharp increases in income and wealth for members of the privileged class, the result is a growing division of the United States into a society of haves and have-nots: class polarization.

Downward Mobility

> For fifteen years, ordinary Americans have been working harder and getting less. . . . The rich are getting ahead; the rest are getting nowhere.
>
> —Robert Reich, *UAW Solidarity*, December 1995

Downward mobility is one type of vertical movement possible in class-stratified societies. Vertical social mobility refers to movements by individuals or groups up or down across class boundaries and often involves generational comparisons. Intergenerational vertical mobility occurs when an individual rises above or falls below the class ranking of his or her parents (e.g., an individual with working-class parents rises as an adult to membership in the superclass). Intragenerational vertical mobility occurs when an individual rises above or falls below the class ranking he or she held at an earlier point in adult life without reference to his or her parents' class ranking (e.g., a physician who—for whatever reasons—falls to a position as a laborer). Social mobility can also be horizontal—as might occur when an adult worker moves from one occupation of average prestige and pay to another with similar prestige and pay levels.[68]

When sociologists track vertical social mobility, those using functionalist models typically utilize a combination of income, job prestige, and educational attainment as indicators of class. Production-model advocates are more likely to focus on an individual's role in the production process (laborer, manager, owner) as a guide to class rank. Functionalist model studies of vertical social mobility in the United States in the 1960s and 1970s using occupational prestige rankings as indicators of class position found substantial occupational mobility occurring mainly in an upward direction.[69] By contrast, production model studies focusing on capitalist property ownership as an indicator of class found little evidence of intergenerational mobility into the "capitalist property ownership class" in the 1980s and 1990s.[70] More recent research using functionalist model approaches suggests that upward vertical intergenerational social mobility in the 1990s was becoming more difficult in the United States—especially for the poor.[71]

Downward mobility emerged as a high-profile, savage social trend in the 1980s and continued throughout the 1990s as a major source of anxiety, grief, dislocation, and frustration for millions of American workers and their families. In general, *downward mobility* refers to the "falling from grace" experience of formerly middle-income workers who individually and collectively have suffered substantial losses of income, usually combined with parallel declines in health, pension, and job security benefits. For many affected workers, the results include sharp, permanently impaired standards of living, diminished long-term economic security, anger, self-doubt, guilt, and dislocated personal relationships. Personal effects of downward mobility have been the primary topics of mass media reports on this issue as illustrated by the 1996 *New York Times'* "Downsizing of America" series and book.[72]

Stories of downward mobility made (and still make) for compelling, first-person media reports, and as a social trend downward mobility is hard not to notice. Public opinion polls suggest many Americans recognize—as least indirectly—the consequences of downward mobility. Following a decade of job losses, a 1995 Gallup poll found that 60 percent of Americans believed the future would be worse than the present, and only 23 percent believed it would be better.[73]

Research from the 1990s using functionalist- or production-model approaches tends to agree that downward mobility became an increasingly common experience for large numbers of American workers and their families in the 1980s and 1990s.[74] Although our distributional model does not include a middle class, we also agree that downward mobility was an obvious and important economic trend in the 1990s. From the perspective of the distributional model, downward mobility occurs when members of class segments in the new working class experience substantial resource losses related especially to the consumption capital and economic power dimensions of our model. When such losses shift working-class members and their children into the depths of the contingent or excluded-class segments, then downward mobility has occurred.[75]

As a social trend and experience, we generally agree with the conventional meaning most often applied to *downward mobility*: the term typically refers to workers' economic and social losses resulting from job displacement (jobs lost due to plant closings, automation, or layoffs). *Downward mobility* was initially used by researchers to describe the experiences of blue-collar workers who lost unionized, middle-income jobs with company-paid fringe benefits (typically health and life insurance, vacations, and pensions) and who were forced to take jobs paying much less and offering few or none of the benefits they had previously enjoyed. More recently, the term has also been applied to diverse groups of workers, including managerial and professional white-collar employees who have lost their jobs due to corporate "restructuring" or "downsizing" (permanent staff reductions).[76]

Although job displacement represents one factor driving downward mobility, this trend is reinforced by three other developments that to some extent are driven by job losses but which also increase the extent to which downward mobility is experienced by workers and their families: declining numbers of middle-income families or households, declining real wages of workers, and downward intergenerational drift among young adults raised in middle-income (or upper-middle-income) families who cannot find jobs that will allow them to replicate their parents' income level or living standards.

Down by Work: Lost Jobs

Regarding the first measure, one study from the late 1980s estimated that as many as one-fifth to one-third of all workers experienced downward mobility in the 1970s and 1980s because of job displacement, resulting in substantial income losses or loss of full-time work.[77] Data on job loss for the 1979–91 period show that 14.3 million blue-collar and 9.5 million white-collar employees became "displaced workers." This means they experienced permanent job loss as a result of a facility closing, job elimination, or slack work.[78] More recently, in the 1993–97 period more than 2.4 million jobs were lost because of downsizing.[79] This trend continued in 1998, with layoffs in the first five months "running 26 percent above the same period last year."[80]

The income consequences of job displacement are typically disastrous for what were formerly middle-income wage earners. Workers displaced from the auto, steel, meatpacking, and aerospace industries in the the mid-1980s report income losses of about 44 percent of their pervious earnings in the first two years after being laid off.[81] More recently, of the 2.2 million full-time workers laid off in 1993 and 1994, only two-thirds had found full-time work by 1996. More than one-half of this group were earning less than what their previous jobs paid, and more than one-third experienced pay cuts of 20 percent or more. The average weekly median earnings for this group declined about 14 percent, but older full-time workers in this group (those in their late fifties and early sixties) who found new jobs experienced pay decreases averaging 37 percent.[82]

Down by Money: Lost Income

As we documented in the earlier discussion of class polarization, the past few decades have witnessed a real and demonstrable downward drift in the number of middle-income Americans. The 1979–95 study cited earlier found declines in the proportions of middle-income persons, households, and families.[83] Falling real wages for average workers also added to the downward-mobility drift brought on by job displacement and declining numbers of middle-income positions. This trend is evident in the 1989–95 declines in average per-hour real wages for production and nonsupervisory workers from $11.87 to $11.46 and for white-collar workers from $18.31 to $18.05 (in 1995 dollars).[84] And it is evident again in more recent data showing that average real wages (adjusted for inflation) were 22.6 percent lower in 1998 than they had been in 1973.[85]

Down by Age: Lost Living Standards

The extent of recent downward intergenerational mobility is difficult to determine, in part because of definitional issues concerning the meanings of *class, generations,* and *downward mobility.* Despite these problems, recent income-based research findings and poll data indicate that by objective measures and subjective impressions, young workers today are finding it difficult to match the living standards achieved by older workers in the previous generation.

One 1998 study compared the earnings of young adult workers (twenty-five to thirty-four years old) from the baby-boom generation (born from 1946 to 1964) with those from the baby-bust generation (born from 1965 to 1976). In 1979 the median weekly earnings (in all occupational categories) for young adults (mostly baby boomers) averaged $545 (in 1996 dollars). By contrast, in 1996 the median weekly earnings for young adults (mostly baby busters) averaged $463 (in 1996 dollars). This means that the 1996 real earnings of young adult baby busters were 15 percent lower than the 1979 real earnings of young adult baby boomers. Moreover, the relative earnings ratio of young adults (the earnings of young adults compared with those of the total adult workforce—twenty-five to sixty-four years old) declined from 95 percent in 1979 (for the baby boomers) to 89 percent in 1996 (for the baby busters).[86]

A second 1998 generational study assessed how the incomes of unmarried eighteen-to-twenty-nine-year-old workers in the 1990s compared with the incomes of their single counterparts in the early 1970s and mid-1980s. With all income reported in 1994–95 dollars, the study found the average real income of young single workers in the 1972–73 period to be $22,413 (before taxes). By 1984–85 this figure had declined to $21,928, and it then fell even further to $19,891 in 1994–95. This means that in 1994–95, young adult workers' real earnings were 11.3 percent lower than those of young adult workers in 1972–73, with more than 80 percent of the total decline occurring between the 1984–85 and 1994–95 periods.[87]

The findings from these studies (and others) clearly illustrate that young workers today are disadvantaged in terms of earnings compared with young workers twenty or more years ago. Moreover, the studies also suggest that the low base earnings of young workers today (combined with falling real wages) make it unlikely that future wage increases will allow them—in later years—to match the current earnings of their parents or other workers twenty or more years senior to them. This is the case because older workers today started at a higher real-earnings base, and their current earnings reflect twenty years (or more) of pay increases built on a higher wage base (except for older workers downsized out of their jobs). Thus, based on a variety of evidence, it appears that downward intergenerational mobility is a relatively common experience among young adults today. The authors of an intergenerational income study covering the 1954–94 period conclude that "it is very possible that the recent (and some future) cohorts will have lifetime earnings inferior to those of their parents' generation."[88] This empirically based conclusion is also supported by national surveys of young adults' subjective perceptions, such as a 1995 Gallup poll in which 52 percent of Americans said they were worse off than their parents and only 35 percent said they were better off.[89]

The Social Consequences of Downward Mobility

The consequences of the downward mobility experience (from all causes) for millions of new working-class members and their families over the past two decades include a growing sense of insecurity and pessimism among middle-income Americans. These trends are reflected in public attitudes, lifestyle choices, and even the popular music of today's youth. In a mid-1990s National Opinion Research Center poll, 67 percent of Americans agreed that "the lot of the average man is getting worse," and 38 percent felt it is "not fair to bring a child into the world."[90] In a 1996 *Time*/CNN poll, 63 percent agreed with the statement that "the American Dream has become impossible for most people to achieve."[91]

Consistent with American workers' pessimistic views concerning economic opportunities, marriage rates and traditional family lifestyles have declined. Twenty years ago married couples with a child (or children) made up 40 percent of all households and constituted the most common type of household. In 1994 such households were the third most common (26 percent) after nonfamily households (30 percent—including singles and unmarried couples living together) and married couples without children (29 percent).[92] As income inequalities have become more pronounced, shrinking incomes and benefit levels have increasingly placed traditional lifestyles and the economic security associated with the American Dream out of reach for middle-income Americans.

"The world is a vampire—Set to drain [you]" sings Smashing Pumpkins, a popular Generation X alternative rock band. This grim take on the life chances of the young is not an isolated image. It is a theme frequently repeated in the lyrics of today's popular music. Sometimes cynicism and pessimism are seamlessly woven together. In a later verse of the same song, the band sings, "Despite all my rage I am still just a rat in a cage." In short, the band, and their youthful audience, know that they're being used, and they don't like it. But they do not offer any emancipatory vision or see any alternatives to a life of rage in the cage. There is no message of hope, just "Birth, school, work, death," as the Godfathers band sings. The music conjures up a bleak iron-cage imagery of their world; they feel trapped in a predictable, downsized, dead-end society. The children of post-World War II middle-income Americans have created a subcultural zeitgeist that appears to reflect their feelings of increasing anxiety and frustration about a class system they were born into but which they feel they neither understand nor control.

Class Secession

> More than ever, the American upper classes live in a world of their own, divorced from any interest in anyone else's fate.
>
> —Doug Henwood, *Utne Reader*, January–February 1992

As income erosion, economic insecurity, and downward mobility increase among the new working class and are manifested in a tight spiral of community tensions and social problems, the privileged class is increasingly distancing itself from public institutions in ways that suggest not simply more suburbanization but rather class secession. Of course, the very wealthy have always separated themselves from the nonwealthy through exclusive neighborhoods, clubs, and schools. However, what Robert Reich terms the "secession of the successful" combines traditional forms of physical and social separation and increasing numbers of privately provided services with an ideology that encourages and legitimates hostility to public institutions serving members of nonprivileged classes.[93] In short, this trend involves a separatist social identity and a secessionistic mentality.

One measure of the increasing physical separation of the privileged class from the working class is the growing number of home-owner associations, which typically govern details of home and property maintenance in neighborhoods and communities that are physically separate and sometimes walled off from surrounding areas. The Community Association Institute estimates that 190,000 community associations existed in 1996 and that they are growing at the rate of about 10,000 per year.[94] These organizations are typically initiated by developers to supervise upscale housing developments. Membership is usually mandatory for home owners. An association board of directors (appointed first by the developer and later elected by home owners) enforces developer-designed codes, covenants, and restrictions regarding property use, maintenance, and services, and each home buyer must sign a contract in which he or she agrees to abide by the association's rules. Association-provided services are financed by membership fees and may range from basics like trash collection to maintenance of parks, recreation sites, private security guards, and even lobbying activities. The latter service logically follows the reality that associations are private concerns representing groups with narrow, private interests. Thus, associations lobby state and local governments on various issues such as zoning decisions and tax relief for services they already provide—like garbage collection.[95]

Of all community associations, those that govern physically walled and gated upscale residential developments are among the fastest growing. In 1987 there were an estimated twelve thousand U.S. gated communities, but by 1997 the number had grown to twenty thousand, encompassing more than 3 million housing units, which were home to about 8.4 million Americans. Developers estimate that eight of ten new urban projects today are gated. In the suburbs, the numbers are more difficult to determine, but regional data suggest that gated suburban communities are also growing in numbers. In the late 1980s one-third of Orange County, California, suburban developments were gated. A 1990 survey of southern Californians looking for a house found that 54 percent wanted a home in a walled, gated community. But this trend is not limited to the western United States: "On Long Island, gated communities were rare in the mid-1980s, but by the mid-1990s they had become common. . . . Chicago, suburban Atlanta, and nearly all other large U.S. cities report similar trends."[96]

Although a few gated communities now cater to middle-income families, researchers estimate that about one-third of new gated communities are luxury developments for the upper-middle and upper classes and another one-third are retirement oriented but typically for upper-income retirees. This means that about two-thirds of new gated communities cater to Americans in the top 20 percent income group. By contrast, earlier gated communities were almost exclusively restricted to "retirement villages and compounds for the super rich." If we combine older (pre-1980s) and new gated (post-1980s) communities, we find they are largely populated by privileged-class families or individuals. As a recent book on this subject put it, "In the [1880s] private gated streets were built . . . for the mansions of the rich. . . . Now the merely affluent, the top fifth of Americans . . . can have barriers between themselves and everyone else as a sign of their joining the ranks of a new separate—but never equal—American elite."[97]

The combination of high income, physical isolation, and privately provided services in gated communities encourages what political scientist Evan McKenzie refers to as an "ideology of privatism—an ideology that overlays and reinforces sentiments favoring exclusiveness, exclusion, and isolation." In his study of homeowners' associations, McKenzie maintains that this ideology, when combined with the physical isolation that "privatization for the few" produces, can lead to "an attenuated sense of loyalty and commitment to public communities." As a result, he believes there could be "a gradual secession from the city . . . [with the city becoming] financially untenable for the many and socially unnecessary for the few. Certainly this steady secession would make the lives of those who remained in the city increasingly difficult."[98]

The expansion of private, class-segregated communities, the erosion of privileged-class support for mixed-class, public institutions (residential neighborhoods, municipal services, public schools), and the crystallization of a secessionist ideology supporting these trends are apparent to commentators from different points on the political spectrum today. Conservative Charles Murray sees current income trends "producing something very like a caste society" in which the wealthiest 10 or 20 percent of the population will simply "bypass the social institutions it doesn't like."[99] He explains that when public services fall apart, the privileged class will retreat to private enclaves complete with private services like schools and police—as in the gated community model.

Writing from a liberal perspective, Robert Reich sees members of the privileged class as increasingly identifying with private rather than public interests in terms of where their allegiances lie—producing both secessionistic ideas and consequences. Top executives of American firms declare that "their job is to maximize shareholder returns, not to advance public goals."[100] As a senior Colgate-Palmolive executive put it in 1989, "The United States does not have an automatic call on our resources. There is no mind-set that puts this country first."[101] The triumph of private-over-public-interest sentiment at the highest levels of the corporate community is also evident in an event, reported by Ralph Nader, that occurred at a 1996 General Motors stockholders meeting:

> At one point a lone stockholder gained recognition to speak, and noting that GM had eliminated some seventy-three thousand U.S. jobs in the past decade, asked politely if [General Motors CEO John] Smith and the members of the board would rise and join him in pledging allegiance to the American flag on display on the side of the platform. After some embarrassed tittering among the board members and scurrying of legal counsels back and forth behind the podium, Smith announced that the bottom line was no, they would not.[102]

"Middle of the road" writers and publications also openly acknowledge the realities of growing class segregation. A mid-1990s *Newsweek* cover story offered the following view of class secession from the political center: "Increasingly the [privileged class] is choosing to live in ways that minimize its mixing with . . . [other classes]. . . . Sometimes it just moves farther out into the suburbs, or higher up the high rise. But increasingly often it chooses to live in a walled and gated community guarded by private security forces."[103]

The Twenty Percent Solution

The combination of class polarization, downward mobility, and class secession has produced two American nations—somewhat akin to the feudal systems of European societies in the Middle Ages and in Third World nations today. In our modern society, the fortunes of the richest superclass Americans are protected, along with affluence and security for their credentialed-class allies. Together, these two groups make up the privileged class—the most affluent 20 percent of the population, who possess the most stable shares of consumption, skill, social, and investment capital resources. In 1996, family incomes for the top 20 percent averaged $120,400 (in 1996 dollars—before federal taxes) and $632,330 for the top 1 percent.[104]

As noted in chapter 1, below the privileged class is the new working class. Comprising 80 percent of the population, it is divided into three broad class segments. At the top of the lower-class diamond—attached like a barnacle to the most affluent 20 percent—is an assorted collection of income groups that make up what we term the comfort class. It includes some workers and families that can and do achieve income levels above—sometimes well above—the national average. Many in this class work at positions that attend to the needs of the privileged class for various services or for material production. Others oversee the labor power of, or monitor and manage members of, the contingent and excluded classes. The comfort class also includes an ever-shrinking group of blue-collar, unionized workers who, because of their collective social capital, retain a tenuous hold on above-average incomes.

Members of the comfort class are compensated at wage and benefit levels that range from relative affluence to modest but comfortable incomes. Total household incomes for individuals and families in this group can sometimes approximate the mean household incomes of the top 20 percent. More typically, comfort-class incomes fall well below those levels but are often above the 1995 U.S. family median income of $40,611.[105] However, retaining above-average incomes over time is problematic for members of this class, because they and their children face increasingly uncertain economic futures.

Rank-and-file community professionals from working-class backgrounds, unionized skilled workers, experienced teachers, travel agents, social workers, and police officers are some examples of workers whose combination of skill, social, and consumption capital allow them to cluster near the top of the lower class diamond (the comfort class). However, these positions are not part of a middle class—to the extent that this term implies income security and realistic opportunities for advancement to the upper reaches of the class system. Rather, these positions are increasingly uncertain and contingent upon structural, personnel, and income policy decisions made by the superclass and executed by credentialed-class members in the top class diamond. The uncertainty experienced by members of this group is linked to their possession of only modest levels of the four generative forms of capital, their lack of power to influence policies that could eliminate (or downgrade) their positions, and their permanent exclusion from the upper class diamond. Most comfort-class members work in dead-end positions in the sense that they are almost totally disconnected from career ladders leading to positions in the privileged class.

Beneath the comfort class are the contingent and excluded classes. These groups shade downward from the insecure working poor to the homeless and destitute at the bottom. Members of these classes are virtually locked out of opportunities for movement into positions in the comfort class and live out their lives as part of a permanent, serf-like American underclass.

BENEATH THE WATERLINE: CONFLICTING CLASS INTERESTS

Although the class iceberg thrusts some obvious features of the system into view, with the right kind of conceptual sonar gear we can also peer beneath the waterline. There we can glimpse some hidden features of the new class society. To begin, we view the preceding three trends as closely related to, and reflective of, conflicting class interests. Contrary to the "win-win" language and imagery so prevalent in media accounts of business and labor relationships, we see superclass corporate owners and their credentialed-class allies as having interests that are fundamentally opposed to those of working-class Americans. It is our view that privileged-class interests trend in the direction of preserving and extending class-based economic, political, and cultural inequalities. Such interests translate into a privileged-class agenda centered on maintaining and enhancing the wealth, power, privilege, and security of the superclass and of its credentialed-class allies. This agenda is pursued through privileged-class dominance of the major economic, political, and cultural organizations of society.[106]

Protecting Privilege

Large corporations and corporate-generated wealth are at the heart of conflicting class interests and privileged-class power. The economic resources controlled by major U.S. corporations are staggering. Although the total U.S. "corporate population" consists of 3.9 million firms with total annual receipts of $11.8 trillion (1993), a few huge companies dominate all major sectors of American business.[107] In 1992 the top one hundred industrial firms controlled 74.6 percent ($1.2 trillion) of all industrial assets. The fifty largest banks controlled 62 percent ($3.5 trillion) of all banking assets, and two insurance companies (Prudential and Metropolitan) controlled nearly 30 percent of all insurance assets.[108] Many of the largest companies are multinational firms with corporate headquarters in the United States and subsidiaries scattered around the globe.

These giant corporations are, in turn, largely owned and controlled by a small number of superclass elites who are assisted in various ways by their credentialed-class allies. In general, the superclass includes the top wealth-owning and income-receiving groups in the United States—including the 149 U.S. billionaires in 1997.[109] It comprises the wealthiest 1 percent of the U.S. population, which, in 1992, owned 49.6 percent of all corporate stock, and the next wealthiest 9 percent which, in the same year, owned 36.7 percent. (The bottom 90 percent owned only 13.6 percent.)[110] As wealth and income shade downward, this class gradually merges into the credentialed class. In terms of income, superclass members are typically found among the 87,000 taxpayers (individuals and families) filing returns with incomes of more than $1 million (in 1995). Members of the credentialed class are found in the second-from-the-top income tier—including most of the 1.1 million taxpayers filing returns with annual incomes of $200,000 or more (in 1994)[111] as well as among taxpayers with incomes of $120,400 or more (which was the average income for the top 20 percent of U.S. families in 1996).[112]

Members of the superclass who are actively involved in organizational governance occupy top positions of power and authority in the largest and most powerful economic, political, and cultural organizations in the society. Such superclass executives—along with their credentialed-class subordinates—are considered, by social science researchers, to form the heart of an American "power elite." Members of this group play active, corporate officer and board member roles and occupy public-policy-influencing positions in public and private organizations—and have been the focus of research documenting this group's membership, power, and self-conscious and cohesive nature.[113]

A recent study of the dimensions of elite power and influence illustrates that major corporations—and other powerful organizations—are dominated by a very small, privileged-class group. This study identified 7,314 top positions of power and authority in the dominant economic, political, and cultural organizations that together represent the institutional foundation of American society. Most of these positions (5,303) were located in the largest corporations, including media companies and law firms.[114] Although this study identified more than 7,000 elite positions, they were occupied by just 5,778 individuals, with 30 percent (1,733) coming from upper-class—what we call superclass—family backgrounds. The remaining 4,045 positions were occupied by individuals from primarily upper-middle class—what we call credentialed-class—family origins.[115] Although this study could be faulted for being too limited in terms of identifying powerful institutional elites, it does illustrate that even in a nation as large as the United States, the superclass portion of the "power elite" corresponds in size to a neighborhood in a small town.

The size of the institutional power elite and the precise ratio of superclass to credentialed-class members that make up this group may be subject to debate (as are the boundaries that divide these two classes); but there is no doubt that superclass members owe their stratospheric incomes and huge concentrations of wealth to corporations. These organizations serve as the conduits through which most superclass income is channeled—primarily in the form of stock dividends, corporate bond payments, capital gains, and other forms of corporate-based compensation.[116] Corporate-based, nonwage compensation is also important to credentialed-class incomes, but far less so than to superclass incomes.

Various forms of data concerning income levels and sources illustrate that the higher the income, the lower the percentage derived from salaries and wages and the greater the percentage derived from dividends, interest, and other forms of corporate-based compensation. In 1989, 80 percent of income for families in the top 20 percent income group came from wages or salaries, while 13.8 percent came from investment capital income of various types. But for the top 1 percent income group, only 57.6 percent of income was derived from wages and salaries, and 41 percent came from investment capital income.[117] More recently, in 1994 the 5 percent of Americans with incomes of $100,000 or more filed federal tax returns reporting that only 58 percent of their income came from salaries and wages, with the remainder coming from nonwage sources.[118] Moreover, as 1998 reports on top executive pay illustrate, for CEOs awarded massive long-term stock options, salaries plus bonuses represent only 3 percent (or less) of their total annual compensation.[119] Even under more typical circumstances, as illustrated by

General Motors CEO Jack F. Smith Jr.'s 1995 salary of $1,500,000 and total compensation package of $13,887,931, CEOs' salaries at major firms often represent only 10 to 20 percent of their total compensation.[120]

The incomes of credentialed-class managers and white-collar professionals who assist superclass elites in sustaining the corporate project are nowhere near those of the superclass, but they are still substantial. In 1992 the incomes of these two groups averaged $159,575 and $57,675, respectively (compared with a $27,606 average for manufacturing operatives).[121] For these groups, at these income levels, nonwage compensation is still less important than wage and salary income. Even so, the incomes of these groups are directly derived from corporate resources; and as credentialed-class executives advance up the corporate hierarchy, their nonwage income shares also grow.

From newly rich corporate officers to the oldest American family fortunes, skybox-level incomes and wealth are clearly linked to the ongoing production of corporate profits. Privileged-class corporate officers understand this connection. Therefore, superclass members actively involved in corporate governance, along with a select group of upwardly mobile credentialed-class members groomed by superclass sponsors, work diligently to ensure the continued financial health, power, and survival of the corporate enterprise. At the highest levels of wealth, the corporate basis of immense personal wealth is clearly illustrated by CEO fortunes linked to specific firms. Examples include Bill Gates's $51 billion Microsoft-based fortune, Warren E. Buffett's $33 billion Berkshire-based empire, and Philip H. Knight's $4.7 billion Nike-based holdings.[122] In short, large corporations are the engines that generate the income and wealth of the superclass and also of its credentialed-class allies.

As a result of privileged-class ownership and control of large firms, the class interests of this group are served in three ways. First, much of the value of the goods and services produced by workers is transferred (at an increasing rate) to superclass corporate owners and to their credentialed-class allies. The heart of this process is simple and increasingly transparent today. It involves paying workers far less (in wages and benefits) than the market value of what they produce, retaining the difference as rising profits, and then distributing these huge sums to CEOs and managers as salaries, bonuses, and stock options, and to stockholders, as dividends. When the U.S. fast-food industry pays most of its workers at or near minimum wage rates of $5.15 per hour (1999) and provides virtually no paid fringe benefits, it is not surprising that in 1997 McDonald's could easily afford an $8,151,000 total compensation package for CEO Michael R. Quinlan.[123] Similarly, when Nike pays its Indonesian workers $2.50 per day to make shoes that sell for $125 per pair in U.S. markets, it's no surprise that Nike CEO Phil Knight is a billionaire.[124]

Second, the corporate-derived income and wealth of the privileged class are used as class-based resources for penetrating and controlling government to develop and reinforce a body of law and public policies that legitimate privileged-class dominance and institutionalize class inequalities. Such arrangements make class-based social inequities and biases in the economic and political order favoring the privileged class appear to be "normal" or even "natural." Also, control of government allows the privileged class to actively pursue public policies that serve its immediate interests—such as tax cuts (primarily benefiting higher-income groups), reducing the size of government (fewer business regulations mean more profits), and welfare cuts (creating a larger pool of low-wage workers, using the poor as scapegoats). Third, privileged-class control of public-opinion-shaping institutions such as the state, the mass media, and the educational system is used to ignore, conceal, marginalize, contest, disguise, or misrepresent issues and information that would expose class-based inequalities and legitimate class-based grievances of workers.

We believe the interests of the working classes, in contrast with privileged-class interests, trend in the direction of reducing existing class-based economic, political, and cultural inequalities. This means, first, that workers have economic interests in receiving a larger share of the value of the goods and services they produce in the form of higher wages as well as more extensive and secure fringe benefits. Such outcomes would occur at the expense of superclass owners of productive property and their credentialed-class allies by reducing profit margins. Second, workers also have political interests in contesting privileged-class control of government in order to use law and public policies on behalf of the working class as instruments for reducing economic and political class inequalities. For example, workers' opportunities and economic security would be enhanced by an expansion of social spending for education, a national health care system, and additional protections for the environment. Third, at the cultural level, workers also have interests in using the mass media and schools to expose class-based inequalities and to legitimate the class-based grievances of workers.

Our view of the existence of conflicting class interests does not mean that we see the privileged and working classes as equally aware of or equally well organized to work toward the active realization of their interests. To the contrary, as the later chapters illustrate, we see privileged-class members as much more conscious of their collective class interests, more cohesive in pursuing them, and in possession of much greater (and more unified) organizational resources than the working class. The net result is that compared with the working class, the privileged class is much more aware of, and able to effectively pursue and realize, its common class interests.

Class War in America

> There is a class war underway in the U.S. of A., and a growing majority of Americans knows it.
>
> —Jim Hightower, *Dollars and Sense*, July–August 1996

Nowhere is the reality of conflicting class interests, privileged-class consciousness, and the overwhelming power of superclass-dominated organizational resources more apparent than in the story behind the transformation of the American class system in the period from the 1970s to the 1990s. The trends of class polarization, downward mobility, and class secession are the direct result of policy decisions made and sponsored by superclass-controlled organizations over the past thirty years that collectively represent nothing less than total class war. Although varying explanations exist for the current configuration of the American class system, none approaches the explanatory power of a class-war analysis. Although the details of the story are complex, the main actors, events, and policies underlying it are stunningly simple. They are fundamentally grounded in conflicting class interests and linked to the dynamics of an almost totally one-sided class war sponsored and directed by the superclass and driven by corporate resources.

The story behind today's new class society begins in the late 1960s and early 1970s. Several working-class political movements initiated during this period led to an expansion of New Deal-based national policies that effectively increased opportunities for, as well as the economic, occupational, and physical well-being of, working-class Americans. Such policies included numerous Great Society programs such as Medicare and Medicaid, as well as several new federal regulatory acts in six major areas, including consumer products, discrimination in employment, traffic safety, consumer finance, job safety, and the environment.[125] Among these acts were groundbreaking measures such as the 1966 Coal Mine Safety Act, the 1969 National Environmental Policy Act, and the 1970 Occupational Health and Safety Act. For workers, the net effect of the progressive legislation enacted in the 1960s and early 1970s was a welcome expansion of the welfare state.

Members of the superclass viewed pro-worker policy developments with fear and loathing: "The expansion of the welfare state in the 1960s and 1970s created panic among the U.S. capitalist class."[126] This reaction was undoubtedly magnified by the parallel trend of declining corporate profits during this period.[127] The superclass response was a concerted, large-scale mobilization for total class war. At the heart of this effort was the conscious creation of a two-pronged political and economic strategy for the purpose of waging class war on a scale unprecedented in American history. The following sections introduce two key dimensions of this class war, both of which are explored in more detail in later chapters.

The Political Dimension of the Class War

At the political and public-policy level, the superclass dramatically expanded the organizational and resource base undergirding its political lobbying and policy-influencing capacity. The list of heavyweight superclass-promoted lobbying developments that emerged during this period begins with the Business Roundtable. Organized in 1973 by John Harper, head of Alcoa Aluminum, and Fred Borch, the CEO of General Electric, it included two hundred CEOs from the largest banks and corporations, and it remains one of the most formidable corporate lobbying organizations today.[128] In that same year, to further beef up superclass political pressure on Congress, the National Association of Manufacturers moved to Washington, D.C. Also, the number of corporations represented by registered lobbyists grew dramatically, from 175 in 1971 to 650 in 1979, and membership in the Chamber of Commerce more than doubled, from 36,000 in 1967 to 80,000 in 1974.[129] The 1970s and 1980s also witnessed the development and growth of an extensive corporate-funded network of conservative "think tanks" aimed at influencing public policy with conservative ideas and policies such as "supply-side" economics and "welfare reform."[130]

To help fund the political campaigns of candidates favorable to privileged-class business interests, the number of corporate political action committees (PACs) grew from 89 in 1974 to 1,206 in 1980.[131] Business mobilization of PACs continued throughout the 1980s and 1990s, with corporate and related trade association PACs totaling 2,489 by 1995 and accounting for 54 percent of the $388 million disbursed by all PACs in 1993–94.[132] In addition to the expansion of corporate PACs, the amounts of money from business-based political contributions of all types also increased dramatically, as election expenditures for all congressional candidates spiraled up from $354.7 million in 1981–82 to $765.3 million in 1995–96.[133]

The increasing cost of political campaigns has led to an ever greater dependence—especially at the national level—by both Republicans and Democrats on high-dollar contributions from both corporate PACs and wealthy individuals. Funds from these sources include both "hard" and "soft" money, with the former subject to federally regulated limits on amounts donated, whereas the latter is largely free from donation limits and loosely regulated in terms of how the monies may be spent.[134] In the 1995–96 national elections, business contributions of all types (hard and soft money from corporate PACs and wealthy individuals) totaled $654.4 million, split 60 percent for Republicans and 40 percent for Democrats.[135] The tilting effect of privileged-class dominance of national election funding in favor of candidates supporting the interests of this class was evident in 1996, when business contributions of all types (hard and soft dollars) to all federal candidates totaled eleven times more than the amount spent by organized labor.[136]

The political mobilization of superclass-funded organizations hit the jackpot with the election of the Ronald Reagan and George Bush administrations. Their record of strong support for superclass-based corporate interests and hostility to welfare-state programs is well known. As David Stockman, the architect of Reagan's economic policies, put it, "The Reagan Revolution required a frontal assault on the American welfare state."[137] Superclass interests received further boosts in the 1994 and 1996 congressional elections as Republicans captured, and then retained control over, both houses of Congress. Led by House Speaker Newt Gingrich, conservative Republicans openly pledged to dismantle the New Deal and Great Society social legislation. This process began with the 1995 implementation of the highly publicized "Contract with America," continued with the passage of welfare "reform" legislation in 1996—with support from some Democrats and

President Clinton—and rolled into the late 1990s, with political pressure building to "save" Social Security through partial privatization schemes.

The consequences of intensified business-driven political lobbying along with increased corporate funding of business PACs included the increasingly transparent conversion of large segments of the Democratic party into a political force reflecting the hegemonic power of superclass-based corporate interests. This trend is apparent in several policy arenas, with, for example, both Republicans and Democrats pledging to reduce the size and power of "big government" (translation: reduce government regulation of business while cutting social programs that benefit workers and the poor). The ascendancy of superclass interests to the top of both Democratic and Republican legislative agendas was further illustrated in 1994 and 1995 by President Clinton's leadership in favor of, and bipartisan congressional passage of, two major corporate-sponsored trade policies: the North American Free Trade Agreement (NAFTA) and the General Agreement on Tariffs and Trade (GATT). As Ralph Nader has said, "Now we have a two-party convergence—one might call it a collaboration or a conspiracy—against the broader political wishes of the American people."[138]

The Economic Dimension of the Class War

At the economic level, superclass corporate elites dictated policies aimed at increasing profits by waging war on workers' wages. Domestically, this has involved the use of government to establish and maintain a hard line against workers' rights and wage demands. Reagan's 1981 firing of the air-traffic controllers established a tough, antilabor policy trend that continued with his appointments of antilabor members to the National Labor Relations Board and with other actions such as his threat to veto the so-called High-Risk bill of 1986–87, which would have mandated government protection for high-risk workers' health.[139]

Internationally, the "globalization strategy" involved the use of technological innovations to facilitate the transfer of manufacturing jobs to Third World nations. During the 1980s and 1990s, credentialed-class corporate managers and professionals designed and executed the increasing use of various new technologies, including satellite communication, computers, standardized production procedures, and containerized shipping, as the technical basis for the globalization of production. These developments accelerated the "capital flight" transfer of production facilities from the United States to nations such as Mexico and Indonesia, which in turn made the use of cheap Third World labor ever more feasible and profitable. Numerous U.S. firms, including General Motors, Ford, Zenith, and Converse, located more and more of their production facilities in Third World nations, and some "U.S." companies, such as Nike (headquartered in Beaverton, Oregon), produce virtually all of their products in Third World nations. In 1994, U.S.-headquartered multinational firms and foreign affiliates controlled by U.S. firms employed more than 25 million workers—many of them in Third World nations.[140]

Although the profits from such practices are spectacular, they can also create corporate public relations headaches. Unions and labor activists concerned with job transfers and the exploitation of Third World workers have publicized these practices. Workers' rights advocates castigate celebrities such as TV personality Kathie Lee Gifford and basketball superstar Michael Jordan for endorsing products and taking shares of profits made by companies that employ child laborers in Third World sweatshops.[141] Sweatshop critics also point out that Third World workers are paid even less than U.S. firms admit. A *Philadelphia Inquirer* sweatshop story, citing Nike as its source, claimed that Vietnamese workers earn $3.37 per pair of shoes selling for $90 in the United States. However, labor activist Jeff Ballinger, using Nike's Vietnam employment and production figures, found that workers received only "57 cents per pair."[142] Despite such criticisms, the corporate economic strategy of globalization continues along with corporate-sponsored domestic economic and political policies, such as plant relocations, concessions bargaining, and prison-based production work. All of these practices are aimed at reducing labor costs—often by breaking or "taming" U.S. unions—and produce constant, intense downward pressures on the wages and benefits of American workers.

The transformation of the manufacturing sector by corporate globalization strategies has accelerated the development of a postindustrial, service-based economy—and hastened the drift toward class polarization. Over the past thirty years the proportion of U.S. workers engaged in manufacturing fell from 33.1 percent in 1970 to a projected 12 percent in 2006. This decline has been paralleled by a sharp increase in service-sector employment, rising from 62.5 percent of all workers in 1970 to a projected 74 percent in 2006.[143] The service economy trend intensifies class divisions because of the corporate-generated, two-tiered labor market that is especially evident in the service sector. This system consists of firms utilizing a small group of high-paid "core" workers, such as managers, professionals, computer programmers, and other "symbolic analysts," and a very large group of moderate- to low-paid "peripheral" workers—viewed as less central to organizational needs and goals.

The differences in pay and benefits for the two groups are closely linked to differences in levels of skill and social capital. Variations in these resources tend to reflect the prestige of the educational credentials workers possess as well as their social ties to organizational leaders (social capital). Thus, workers' possession of these class-based capital resources influence their proximity to corporate and organizational power and their access to the limited number of well-paid positions. Peripheral workers occupy a spectrum of jobs ranging from modestly paid occupations such as teachers and police officers to much lower-paid positions such as data entry clerks, guards, home health aides, and janitors—which are projected to be among the fastest growing occupations of the early twenty-first century.[144] However, even modestly paid service workers find themselves continuously subject to wage and benefit pressures as employers increase contingent-labor staffing policies.[145] At the bottom, the lowest-paid service workers are increasingly linked to large organizations through temporary agencies as contract or contingent laborers who, as noted earlier, now make up as much as 25 to 35 percent of the U.S. labor force.[146]

With superclass interests as a dominant force in the national government, significant features of the welfare state benefiting the working class have been—and are currently being—dismantled. The minimal levels of economic security that national social policies afforded workers and the poor in the past are increasingly disappearing. At the same time, the combination of superclass-sponsored government-corporate attacks on unions, along with the globalization process, has led to a continuous erosion of workers' wages and benefits. These developments have been accompanied by corporate layoff and downsizing policies that have led to the disappearance of many blue- and white-collar middle-income positions. The end result of these class-war-driven policies and practices has been the emergence of the increasingly polarized and hardened new class society.

Copyright © Lloyd Dangle. Reprinted with permission.

BENEATH THE WATERLINE:
CLASS MAINTENANCE AND LEGITIMATION

The second hidden dimension of the class iceberg involves the structures and processes that maintain and legitimate the new class society. Of course, elite classes in stratified societies have always devoted a portion of their considerable resources to legitimating and reinforcing the class system, thereby ensuring their continued possession of disproportionate levels of wealth, power, and privilege. However, the problems of maintaining and legitimating the emerging new class society have been rendered more complex by the extreme inequalities of the system and the tension between these class realities and the relentless, media-driven promotion of the American Dream as a cultural ideal.[147] Thus, the current class maintenance and legitimation strategies, structures, and policies combine sophisticated extensions of approaches used in the past with emerging, innovative forms of control and distraction.

The Class-Power-Network Model

Our perspective on how the new class system is maintained and legitimated is based on an organizational model of class interests and power. It views large firms as repositories of superclass resources and also as dominant sources of power in virtually all sectors of society. According to this approach, privileged-class leaders use corporate-based resources to create, fund, and control extensive, overlapping organizational networks within the economic, political, and cultural social arenas. These networks consist of organizations linked by various connections such as interlocked board members, shared public policy interests, and common goals—including the maintenance and legitimation of concentrated privileged-class power and wealth.

In the economic arena, network examples include superclass-controlled trade associations and peak corporate groups—such as the Business Roundtable. Superclass-funded public policy "think tanks," lobbying organizations, and PACs are examples of organizational networks within the political arena. In the cultural arena, network examples include superclass-funded foundations, civic and cultural organizations, and elite university boards of trustees. We view these interlocked organizational networks as directed by privileged-class leaders who use them to pursue strategies and objectives that reinforce the shared economic, political, and cultural interests of their class. These include legitimating corporate autonomy, power, and profit maximization as well as maintaining the organizational structure of the new class system so as to perpetuate the advantaged positions, interests, and privileges of the superclass and its credentialed-class allies. However, we also believe the organizations within these networks typically present public facades that disguise or deemphasize their privileged-class biases and the ways in which they function as surrogate actors for privileged-class interests.

Although the class-power model views superclass leaders as participating in conscious and deliberate activities to protect privileged-class interests, it is not based on a conspiracy theory of power. We do not view superclass leaders as a group that secretly conspires to promote its interests and maintain class inequalities. Rather, following G. William Domhoff, we view the coordinated, interest-supporting activities of superclass leaders and their credentialed-class allies as grounded in a complex structural system that is populated by a relatively homogeneous group that is similar in many important respects. Privileged-class leaders tend to have similar elite educational backgrounds, to be officers of large, interlocked firms, and to be members of a small number of elite social and cultural organizations. The class-based shared family, business, and social experiences of this group lead to shared common values, worldviews, and commitments to maintaining the status quo.[148] From where privileged-class leaders stand, life is good and the system works. The shared culture of the superclass leads not to conspiracy but rather to an authentic boosterism for the corporate model and the "magic of the market." There's no need for a conspiracy when the most common question among privileged-class leaders is, "Why change what works? (for us!)."

Dominant Class-Power Networks

Figure 2.2 illustrates the main features of our class-power-network model. At the top, the model views the dominant class-power base as grounded in the organizationally active superclass members and their credentialed-class allies (the power elite). This group is centrally involved in directing and coordinating the three overlapping corporate-based dominant power networks. Strategies for class maintenance and legitimation extend downward through four basic social institutions: the national economy, the state and politics, media and culture, and the educational system. The following five chapters consider in detail how the maintenance and legitimation strategies identified by the model are linked to organizational policies and practices directed by privileged-class leadership. And they illustrate how these strategies and related policies serve privileged-class interests—especially by helping to perpetuate and legitimate structured inequalities within the new class society.

By focusing on the top half of the model, we can begin to see how the abstract notion of superclass dominance is channeled through real organizations that collectively merge into powerful networks. From the top down, the dominant power networks pursue superclass interests through corporate-based activities penetrating the four routine institutional structures of society. As we will see, the corporate practices and public policies that emerge from these structural linkages weave legitimation, co-optation, distraction, and coercion into a dense organizational web that sustains the new class system's inequalities.

Members of the new working class find themselves as targets of the dominant power networks depicted by the model. Specific public policies, programs, business practices, and cultural ideas maintaining and legitimating superclass inter-

69

Figure 2.2   Model of Class Power Network

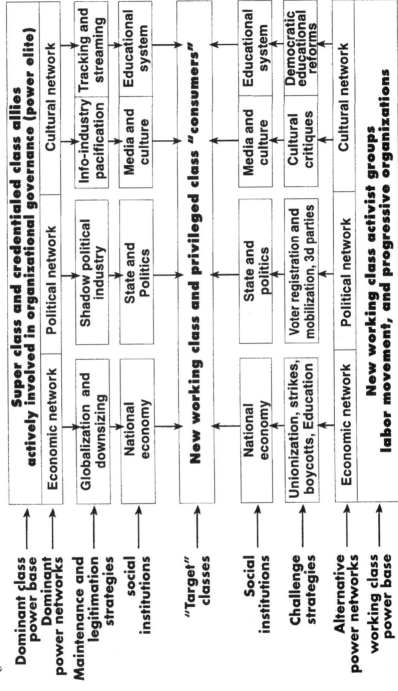

ests, the corporate empire, and class inequalities in the new class system are routinely and repeatedly directed at working-class members (and privileged-class consumers) through the four basic social institutions shown in the model.

For members of the working class, the cumulative effects of social life lived under superclass-dominated social institutions encourage public acceptance of class hierarchies, extensive corporate power, and the inequities associated with these arrangements. Oligopolistic corporate control of the economy (auto and electrical industries), corporate-funded bashing of big government (Rush Limbaugh), and corporate media-sponsored celebrations of the free enterprise system (*Wall $treet Week* on PBS) produce patterns of ideas and experiences that constantly remind the working class that private businesses are "good" and public enterprises are "bad" (or at best inefficient). In short, working-class behaviors and attitudes are shaped in ways that promote public acceptance (ideological legitimation) of class inequalities. Such outcomes ensure that the distribution of capital resources in the new class society remains relatively unchallenged and unchanged—with a small number of highly rewarded positions reserved for members of the privileged-class top diamond and those in the new working-class bottom diamond restricted to positions with much lower rewards.

Superclass-dominated social institutions produce still other effects that maintain and legitimate the new class system. They restrict economic choices for workers and consumers, limit political alternatives, channel social behavior into predictable patterns (e.g., distraction from class inequalities via consumerism and mass culture), diminish the capacity for critical thought, and increasingly organize peoples' time around corporate needs, products, and services. These institutions, especially the corporate-dominated state, also identify and present powerless scapegoats as the "real" sources of social problems (e.g., the poor, illegal immigrants, drug users). And the state serves as a major source of social control threatening working-class members with imprisonment or impoverishment (and often both) as punishment for noncompliance with work, political, intellectual, cultural, lifestyle, and consumer "choices" sponsored by the superclass and designed and regulated by the credentialed-class-managed corporate world.

Alternative Class-Power Networks

Of course, the top portion of figure 2.2 is only part of the story. At the bottom of the figure we find an alternative class-power base grounded in new-working-class activist groups. The labor movement (unions) along with other progressive organizations form the heart of three overlapping alternative power networks. These alternative networks challenge—with varying degrees of vigor and with limited resources—the strategies, policies, and messages of the dominant power networks within the economy, the state, the media, and the schools. The alternative-network dimension of our model underscores the point that we do not equate superclass dominance in the economic, political, and cultural arenas with total control. On one hand, the inequities of the new class society are largely maintained and legitimated by the actions, policies, and ideas orchestrated by superclass-sponsored and credentialed-class-managed organizations within the dominant power networks. But on the other hand, these activities and ideas are subject to challenges by alternative-power-network actors in the economic, political, and cultural arenas, with labor unions serving as the core alternative organizational force.

Our inclusion of trade unions as a key feature of the alternative power networks does not mean that we view unions as speaking with a single voice for workers or that we view all unions as consistent advocates for workers' common class interests. We recognize that the labor movement includes diverse and sometimes contradictory trends and actions. Even so, among organizational alternatives to corporate power, trade unions possess the greatest concentration of human and economic resources and represent the most significant alternative organizational force countering corporate dominance. But this recognition does not diminish the importance of other organizations in the alternative power networks—some of which are linked to leaders and funding sources associated with privileged-class backgrounds. Some of these individuals and groups might—in some sense—be considered "class traitors" by more conventional privileged-class members. Such organizations include public interest groups (e.g., Ralph Nader's numerous organizations), alternative national circulation magazines (e.g., *Nation, Progressive, Mother Jones, In These Times*), progressive research and policy groups (e.g., Institute for Policy Studies), and some religious organizations. These groups, often in conjunction with trade unions, also challenge the strategies, objectives, and policies of the dominant power networks.

BACK TO THE FUTURE:
THE ICEBERG, THE DREAM, AND THE DETAILS

Titanic came around the curve, into the Great Iceberg. Fare thee, Titanic, Fare thee well.

—Leadbelly (H. Ledbetter), "Fare Thee Well, Titanic," 1912

As the Titanic disaster reminds us, icebergs can be treacherous—especially the huge frozen mass below the waterline. Our exploration of the hidden portion of the class iceberg is also fraught with danger, though not of the physical sort. Because of the taboo nature of class, few people venture below the waterline of conventional social analysis. Down there, visibility is limited. The images are murky. The dangers abound of miscommunication, misunderstanding, and charges from "respectable quarters" that it is unproductive or even un-American, to make the trip: better to stick with the dream than explore the iceberg. Even so, we'll take our chances. We think the potential rewards are worth the risks, and we invite you to join us.

The remainder of this book represents a tour of territory that for most Americans is familiar and yet, in many ways, unknown. Our class-power-network model serves as the basic map for exploring the hidden features of the new class society. As we will see, the dominant power networks are not abstract, ivory-tower inventions but real organizational webs of power that we encounter daily. By tracking the interests, strategies, and activities of privileged-class-dominated organizations, the model helps us understand how this class dominates organizations, public policies, programs, ideas, and social behavior in the economic, political, and cultural arenas.

Like a magnifying glass, the model serves as a lens bringing into focus the details of the ways in which the dominant power networks have created and work to maintain and legitimate the new class society. Using this lens, we will discover how the web of power spun by the dominant power networks attempts to control the production and enforcement of ideas about, debates over, attention to, and the enactment of class-relevant laws and public policies as well as the production and distribution of values and beliefs related to personal fulfillment, the mass consumption of goods and services, and the uses of work and leisure time. The cultural dimension of the dominant power networks has become increasingly important to the legitimation process, because the cultural network includes potent organizations (media, schools) that disseminate ideas, information, and images that help legitimate the new class system and also serve as vehicles for distracting public attention away from the many inequalities of the system.

The class-power-network model will also help us see and better understand another important dimension of the class iceberg: the "underdogs" of class conflict. The alternative-power-networks portion of the model provides us with a map for understanding how dominant-power-network strategies, policies, programs, and ideas favoring privileged-class interests are contested and challenged in specific terms by real organizations and real people. These challenges are grounded in an agenda emphasizing fair play, an end to arbitrary class inequalities, and greater opportunities for all Americans to actually achieve the American Dream—and thereby bring about a class-iceberg meltdown.

NOTES

1. See, for example, Seymour M. Lipset and Reinhard Bendix, *Social Mobility in Industrial Society* (Berkeley: University of California Press, 1959); Harry J. Crochett Jr., "The Achievement Motive and Differential Occupational Mobility in the United States," *American Sociological Review* 27 (1962): 191–204; Reinhard Bendix and Frank W. Howton, "Social Mobility and the American Business Elite—II," *British Journal of Sociology* 9 (1958): 1–14.

2. Peter M. Blau and Otis D. Duncan, *The American Occupational Structure* (New York: Wiley, 1967); David L. Featherman and Robert M. Hauser, *Opportunity and Change* (New York: Academic Press, 1978).

3. Beth A. Rubin, *Shifts in the Social Contract* (Thousand Oaks, Calif.: Pine Forge Press, 1996), 7–8; John E. Farley, "What's in the American Dream," in *Sociology* (Englewood Cliffs, N.J.: Prentice-Hall, 1990), 99.

4. George J. Church, "Are We Better Off?" *Time*, January 29, 1996, 37–40.

5. On the 1996 election see, Jonathan Alter and Michael Isikoff, "The Beltway Populist," *Newsweek*, March 4, 1996, 24–27; and Joshua Glenn and Craig Cox, "Nader Wins!" *Utne Reader*, September–October 1996, 22. On the polls, see Kevin Phillips, "Fat City," *Time*, September 26, 1994, 49–56; and "In Fact," *Nation*, August 26–September 2, 1996, 5. On the 1998 election, see Ruth Conniff, "President Wellstone?" *Nation*, May 18, 1998, 11–16; Doug Ireland, "Candidate Wellstone," *In These Times*, June 14, 1998, 12–15; and Doug Ireland, "Left Out in 2000," *In These Times*, February 21, 1999, 4.

6. Marc Cooper, "Harley-Riding, Picket-Walking Socialism Haunts Decatur," *Nation*, April 8, 1996, 21–25.

7. Charles E. Hurst, *Social Inequality* (Boston: Allyn and Bacon, 1995), 308–10.

8. David Elsila, Michael Funke, and Sam Kirkland, "Blaming the Victim: The Propaganda War against Workers," *UAW Solidarity*, April 1992, 11–17.

9. Robert Famighetti, ed., *The World Almanac and Book of Facts, 1997* (Mahwah, N.J.: K-III Reference Corporation, 1996), 290; Ben Bagdikian, *The Media Monopoly* (Boston: Beacon Press, 1997); Scott Sherman, "An Appeal to Reason," *Nation*, March 10, 1997, 15–19.

10. Jonathan Tasini, "Lost in the Margins: Labor and the Media," *EXTRA!*, Summer 1990, 2–5.

11. Bill Turque and Bob Cohen, "Why Clinton Won't Play Class War," *Newsweek*, April 25, 1995, 31–32.

12. Janine Jackson, "We Feel Your Pain," *EXTRA!*, May–June 1996, 11–12.

13. Gregory Mantsios, "Class in America: Myths and Realities," in *Race, Class, and Gender in the United States*, ed. Paula S. Rothenberg (New York: St. Martin's Press, 1995).

14. Howard Fineman, "Extreme Measures," *Newsweek*, March 4, 1996, 20–29.

15. Jim Naureckas, "From the Top: What Are the Politics of Network Bosses?" *EXTRA!*, July–August 1998, 21–22. Also see "Where's the Power: Newsroom or Boardroom?" *EXTRA!*, July–August 1998, 23.

16. Gregory Mantsios, "Media Magic: Making Class Disappear," in Rothenberg, *Race, Class, and Gender in the United States*.

17. See, for example, Michelle Cottle, "The Real Class War," *Washington Monthly*, July–August 1997, 12–16; Donald L. Barlett and James B. Steele, *America: Who Really Pays the Taxes?* (New York: Touchstone, 1994), 93–94; and *Congressional Record, Taxpayer Relief Act of 1997*, June 26, 1997, H4810.

18. David Croteau, "Challenging the 'Liberal Media' Claim," *EXTRA!*, July–August 1998, 4–9.

19. Hurst, *Social Inequality*, 305–12; Harold R. Kerbo, *Social Stratification and Inequality* (New York: McGraw-Hill, 1996), 258–67.

20. G. William Domhoff, *Who Rules America?: Power and Politics in the Year 2000* (Mountain View, Calif.: Mayfield, 1998), 71–123.

21. Thomas Dye, *Who's Running America?: The Clinton Years* (Englewood Cliffs, N.J.: Prentice-Hall, 1995), 215.

22. Hurst, *Social Inequality*, 300.

23. Mantsios, "Media Magic."

24. Richard D. Coleman and Lee Rainwater, *Social Standing in America* (New York: Basic Books, 1978).

25. Kerbo, *Social Stratification and Inequality*, 24; Hurst, *Social Inequality*, 23.

26. Randy Hodson and Teresa A. Sullivan, *The Social Organization of Work* (Belmont, Calif.: Wadsworth, 1995), 165.

27. George Gallup and S. F. Rae, *The Pulse of Democracy* (New York: Simon and Schuster, 1940), 169; Robert W. Hodge and Donald J. Treiman, "Class Identification in the United States," *American Journal of Sociology* 73 (March 1968): 535–47; Mary R. Jackman and Robert W. Jackman, *Class Awareness in the United States* (Berkeley: University of California Press, 1982), 18; Reeve Vanneman and Lynn Weber Cannon, *The American Perception of Class* (Philadelphia: Temple University Press, 1987).

28. Doug Henwood, "American Dream: It's Not Working," *Christianity and Crisis*, June 8, 1992, 195–97.

29. Bennett Harrison and Barry Bluestone, "The Crisis of the American Dream," in *Great Divides*, ed. Thomas A. Shapiro (Mountain View, Calif.: Mayfield, 1998), 179–91.

30. *New York Times, The Downsizing of America* (New York: Random House, 1996), 318.

31. Based on the authors' analysis of fifteen 1997–98 introductory sociology texts.

32. Paul Ryscavage, "A Surge in Growing Income Inequality?" *Monthly Labor Review* (August 1995): 51–61.

33. Lawrence Mishel, Jared Bernstein, and John Schmitt, *The State of Working America, 1996–1997* (Armonk, New York: M. E. Sharpe, 1997), 77.

34. Ibid., 53.

35. U.S. Department of Commerce, Bureau of the Census, *Statistical Abstract of the United States* (Washington, D.C.: U.S. Government Printing Office, 1997), 467.

36. Mishel, Bernstein, and Schmitt, *Working America*, 86.

37. Ibid., 44.

38. Ibid., 140–42.

39. Arthur MacEwan, "Ask Dr. Dollar," *Dollars and Sense*, May–June 1998, 42.

40. Ibid.

41. U.S. Department of Commerce, Bureau of the Census, *Statistical Abstract* (1997), 468.

42. Ibid., 470.

43. Ibid.

44. Michael Parenti, "The Super Rich Are Out of Sight," *Dollars and Sense*, May–June 1998, 36–37.

45. *AFL-CIO*, "Executive PayWatch," <http://www.paywatch.com> (May 4, 1998), 1–4.

46. Jennifer Reingold, Richard A. Melcher, and Gary McWilliams, "Special Report: Executive Pay," *Business Week*, April 20, 1998, 64–70.

47. *AFL-CIO*, "Executive PayWatch," 1–4.

48. For 1973 and 1989 figures, see Mishel, Bernstein, and Schmitt, *Working America*, 227; for 1996, see *AFL-CIO*, "Executive PayWatch," 1–4; for 1997, see Reingold, Melcher, and McWilliams, "Executive Pay," 65.

49. "The Top-Paid CEOs," *Forbes*, May 18, 1998, 229.

50. Reingold, Melcher, and McWilliams, "Executive Pay," 66.

51. Public Citizen Health Research Group, "Health Care Costs: Executive Compensation," *Health Letter*, April 1996, 12; "The Top-Paid CEOs," 229.

52. Michael H. Cimini and Charles J. Muhl, "Twin Cities Nurses Reach Accord," *Monthly Labor Review* (August 1995): 74–75.

53. Mishel, Bernstein, and Schmitt, *Working America*, 138.

54. Ibid., 156, 139.

55. "Percent of Full-Time Employees Participating in Employer-Provided Benefit Plans, 1980–1991," *Monthly Labor Review* (February 1998): 63.

56. Ibid.

57. Jane Bryant Quinn, "Savings at Risk," *Newsweek*, December 11, 1995, 54–55.

58. Mishel, Bernstein, and Schmitt, *Working America*, 159.

59. "Percent of Full-Time Employees," 63.

60. Lawrence Mishel and Jared Bernstein, *The State of Working America, 1992–1993* (Washington, D.C.: Economic Policy Institute, 1993).

61. Paul B. Ginsburg, Jon R. Gabel, and Kelly A. Hunt, "Tracking Small-Firm Coverage, 1989–1996," *Health Affairs* 17 (January–February 1998): 167–71.

62. Anne E. Polivka, "Contingent and Alternative Work Arrangements, Defined," *Monthly Labor Review* (October 1996): 3.

63. Mishel, Bernstein, and Schmitt, *Working America*, 266.

64. Ibid., 268.

65. Ibid., 258, 269.

66. David M. Gordon, *Fat and Mean: The Corporate Squeeze of Working Americans and the Myth of Managerial "Downsizing"* (New York: Free Press, 1996), 225. Also see Andy Neather, "The Temp-ing of America," *UAW Solidarity*, January–February 1995, 11.

67. Mishel, Bernstein, and Schmitt, *Working America*, 249.

68. Richard T. Schaefer and Robert P. Lamm, *Sociology* (New York: McGraw-Hill, 1998), 243.

69. Kerbo, *Social Stratification*, 331–32.

70. Ibid., 334.

71. Greg J. Duncan and Wei-Jun J. Yeung, "Extent and Consequences of Welfare Dependence among America's Children," *Children and Youth Services Review* 17 (1995): 157–82.

72. *New York Times, Downsizing of America*.

73. Michael Golay and Carl Rollyson, *Where America Stands, 1996* (New York: Wiley, 1996), 167–69.

74. Stanley Aronowitz and William DiFazio, "High Technology and Work Tomorrow," *Annals of the American Academy of Political and Social Science* 544 (March 1996): 52–76.

75. Theoretically, downward mobility from the privileged class into the new working class could occur in our model, but we believe it is rare, and the topic would require separate attention. Therefore, we do not address it here.

76. Katherine S. Newman, *Falling from Grace: The Experience of Downward Mobility in the American Middle Class* (New York: Free Press, 1988).

77. Ibid.

78. R. C. Longworth and Sharman Stein, "Middle-Class Muddle," *Indianapolis Star*, September 24, 1995.

79. David Greising, "It's the Best of Times—Or Is It?" *Business Week*, January 12, 1998, 36–38.

80. Aaron Bernstein, "We Want You to Stay. Really," *Business Week*, June 22, 1998, 70.

81. Jeffrey R. Lustig, "The Politics of Shutdown," *Journal of Economic Issues* 19 (1985): 123–59.

82. Gene Koretz, "Downsizing's Painful Effects," *Business Week*, April 13, 1998, 23.

83. Mishel, Bernstein, and Schmitt, *Working America*, 77.

84. Ibid., 44.

85. MacEwan, "Ask Dr. Dollar," 42.

86. Kurt Schrammel, "Comparing the Labor Market Success of Young Adults from Two Generations," *Monthly Labor Review* (February 1998): 3–9.

87. Geoffrey Paulin and Brian Riordon, "Making It on Their Own: The Baby Boom Meets Generation X," *Monthly Labor Review* (February 1998): 10–21.

88. Mishel, Bernstein, and Schmitt, *Working America*, 97.

89. Golay and Rollyson, *Where America Stands*, 167–69.

90. Longworth and Stein, "Middle-Class Muddle."

91. George J. Church, "Are We Better Off?" *Time*, January 29, 1996, 37–40.

92. Longworth and Stein, "Middle-Class Muddle."

93. Robert B. Reich, "Secession of the Successful," *New York Times Magazine*, January 20, 1991, 42.

94. Edward J. Blakely and Mary Gail Snyder, *Fortress America: Gated Communities in the United States* (Washington, D.C.: Brookings Institution Press, 1997), 180.

95. Tim Vanderpool, "Secession of the Successful," *Utne Reader*, November–December, 1995, 32–34.

96. Blakely and Snyder, *Fortress America*, 7–8, 180.

97. Ibid., 6, 74.

98. Evan McKenzie, *Privatopia* (New Haven: Yale University Press, 1994), 105, 186.

99. Charles Murray, "The Shape of Things to Come," *National Review*, July 8, 1991, 30.

100. Robert B. Reich, *The Work of Nations: Preparing Ourselves for the Twenty-first Century* (New York: Knopf, 1991), 140.

101. Ibid., 140–41.

102. Ralph Nader, quoted in Jim Hightower, "Chomp!" *Utne Reader*, March–April 1998, 61.

103. Jerry Adler, "The Rise of the Overclass," *Newsweek*, July 31, 1995, 45–46.

104. Mishel, Bernstein, and Schmitt, *Working America*, 115.

105. U.S. Department of Commerce, *Statistical Abstract* (1997), 469.

106. See, for example, Ben H. Bagdikian, *The Media Monopoly* (Boston: Beacon Press, 1997); Domhoff, *Who Rules America?*; and Dye, *Who's Running America?*.

107. U.S. Department of Commerce, *Statistical Abstract* (1997), 537–38.

108. Dye, *Who's Running America?*, 20–21.

109. Kerry A. Dolan, ed., "The Global Power Elite," *Forbes*, July 28, 1997, 97.

110. Mishel, Bernstein, and Schmitt, *Working America*, 280.

111. David Wessel, "Again, the Rich Get Richer, but This Time They Pay More Taxes," *Wall Street Journal*, April 2, 1998.

112. Mishel, Bernstein, and Schmitt, *Working America*, 115.

113. For examples, see G. William Domhoff, *State Autonomy or Class Dominance?* (New York: Aldine, 1996); Domhoff, *Who Rules America?*; and Michael Useem, *The Inner Circle* (New York: Oxford University Press, 1984).

114. Dye, *Who's Running America?*, 11.

115. Ibid., 175; Domhoff, *Who Rules America?*, 111.

116. U.S. Department of Commerce, *Statistical Abstract* (1997), 345.

117. Mishel, Bernstein, and Schmitt, *Working America*, 65.

118. U.S. Department of Commerce, *Statistical Abstract* (1997), 345.

119. Reingold, Melcher, McWilliams, "Special Report," 64.

120. General Motors "Notice of Annual Meeting of Stockholders and Proxy Statement," May 24, 1996, 17; also see "The Top-Paid CEOs," 236–66.

121. Kerbo, *Social Stratification*, 30–32.

122. Kerry A. Dolan, ed., "The World's Working Rich: United States," *Forbes*, July 6, 1998, 210–15.

123. "The Top-Paid CEOs," 254.

124. "No Sweat?," *UAW Solidarity*, June–July 1997, 9; "The Top-Paid CEOs," 229.

125. Murray L. Wiedenbaum, *Business, Government, and the Public* (Englewood Cliffs, N.J.: Prentice-Hall, 1977), 5–8.

126. Vicente Navarro, "Production and the Welfare State: The Political Context of Reforms," *International Journal of Health Services* 21 (1991): 606.

127. Robert J. Samuelson, "Great Expectations," *Newsweek*, January 8, 1996, 31; also see Mishel, Bernstein, and Schmitt, *Working America*, 71.

128. John B. Judis, "The Most Powerful Lobby," *In These Times*, February 21, 1994, 22–23.

129. Navarro, "Production and the Welfare State," 606.

130. Michael Patrick Allen, "Elite Social Movement Organizations and the State: The Rise of the Conservative Policy-Planning Network," in *Research in Politics and Society*, vol. 4, *The Political Consequences of Social Networks*, ed. Gwen Moore and J. Allen Whitt (Greenwich, Conn.: JAI Press, 1992).

131. Federal Election Commission, "FEC Releases New PAC Count," press release, July 28, 1989.

132. U.S. Department of Commerce, *Statistical Abstract* (1997), 292.

133. Federal Election Commission, "Congressional Fundraising and Spending Up Again in 1996," press release, April 14, 1997, 1–4, 1.

134. Larry Makinson, *The Big Picture: Money Follows Power Shift on Capitol Hill* (Washington, D.C.: Center for Responsive Politics, 1997), 3.

135. Ibid., 16.

136. Ibid., 4.

137. Quoted in Navarro, "Production and the Welfare State," 607.

138. Quoted in Wesley J. Smith, "Nobody's Nader," *Mother Jones*, July–August 1996, 61–63, 61.

139. Earl Wysong, *High Risk and High Stakes: Health Professionals, Politics, and Policy* (Westport, Conn.: Greenwood Press, 1992).

140. U.S. Department of Commerce, *Statistical Abstract* (1997), 561.

141. Nancy Gibbs, "Cause Celeb," *Time*, June 17, 1996, 28–30.

142. "No Sweat over Sweatshops," *EXTRA!Update*, June 1998, 3.

143. Hodson and Sullivan, *The Social Organization of Work*, 264; for projections, see James C. Franklin, "Industry Output and Employment Projections to 2006," *Monthly Labor Review* (November 1997): 40.

144. George T. Silvestri, "Occupational Employment to 2005," *Monthly Labor Review* (November 1995): 79.

145. Steven Hipple and Jay Stewart, "Earnings and Benefits of Contingent and Noncontingent Workers," *Monthly Labor Review* (October 1996): 22–30.

146. Gordon, *Fat and Mean*, 225; Neather, "The Temp-ing of America," 11.

147. Juliet B. Schor, "Keeping Up with the Trumps: How the Middle Class Identifies with the Rich," *Washington Monthly*, July–August 1998, 34–37.

148. Domhoff, *Who Rules America?*, 14–16, 71–123; Richard L. Zweigenhaft and G. William Domhoff, *Diversity in the Power Elite: Have Women and Minorities Reached the Top?* (New Haven: Yale University Press, 1998), 192–94.

3

The Global Economy and the Privileged Class

Unbridled capitalism is an awesome force that creates new factories, wealth, and opportunities that go first to society's risk takers and holders of capital. But unbridled capitalism is also an awesome destructive force. It makes men and women obsolete as rapidly as it does the products they produce and the plants that produce them.

—Patrick Buchanan, *The Great Betrayal*, 1998

On December 1, 1982, an RCA television cabinet-making factory in Monticello, Indiana, closed its doors and shut down production. Monticello, a town of five thousand people in White County (population twenty-three thousand), had been the home of RCA since 1946. The closing displaced 850 workers who were members of Local 3154 of the United Brotherhood of Carpenters and Joiners. Officials at RCA cited high manufacturing costs and foreign competition as key factors leading to the closing.

Reactions of displaced workers from RCA were varied, with most expressing either a general sense of despair or a feeling of confidence that they would survive. One worker was hopeful, stating: "Losing one's job is a serious jolt to your attitude of security, preservation, and well-being. However, I feel strongly that we must look forward to hope and faith in our country and its people. Deep inside I want to believe that tough times won't last, but tough people do. This will mean a lot of sacrifice, determination, and change in those people affected by losing one's job." Less hopeful views are revealed in the following remarks:

We are down to rock bottom and will probably have to sell the house to live or exist until I find a job here or somewhere else. I have been everywhere looking in Cass, White, and Carroll counties. We have had no help except when the electric company was going to shut off the utilities in March and the Trustee [County Welfare] paid that $141. My sister-in-law helps us sometimes with money she's saved back or with food she canned last summer. The factories have the young. I've been to all the factories. (Authors' personal interviews with RCA workers.)

Whether the personal response to the closing was faith, fear, or anger, the common objective experience of the displaced workers was that they had been "dumped" from the "middle class." These displaced factory workers viewed themselves as middle class because of their wages and their lifestyles (home ownership, cars, vacations). Most had worked at RCA for two decades or more. They had good wages, health care benefits, and a pension program. They owned their homes (with mortgages), cars, recreational vehicles, boats, and all the household appliances of the middle class. All the trappings of the American Dream were threatened, and their stable jobs and secure incomes were gone. In the space of a few months these workers and their families would join the growing new working class—the 80 percent of Americans without stable resources for living.

The severity of this jolt to their sense of well-being and their "downward slide" are also revealed in the bleak picture displaced workers have of their future and the future of their children: "I'm afraid it will be years before I get up the courage to buy a car, appliance, or anything on a long-term note, regardless of how good the pay is in a new job"; "I have a National Honor Society daughter with one more year of high school. If she can't get aid there's no way she can go to college." (Authors' personal interviews with RCA workers.)

The experiences of the 850 RCA workers from Monticello, Indiana, were part of a national wave of plant closings that swept across the land a decade ago. Between the late 1970s and mid-1980s more than 11 million workers lost jobs because of plant shutdowns, relocation of facilities to other countries, or layoffs.[1] When these displaced workers found new jobs, it was often in the expanding service sector, where wages were significantly lower than what they had earned and jobs were often part-time and lacked health insurance and other benefits.

During this period, from the mid-1970s to the mid-1980s, the American class structure was being reshaped from the layer-cake "middle-class" society into the double-diamond society described in figure 1.5. The first step in this reshaping was an attack on higher-wage unionized workers, eliminating their jobs in the auto industries, steel mills, rubber plants, and textile mills. The reshaping continued through the late 1980s to mid-1990s, when the strategy changed from plant closings and relocations to "restructuring and downsizing," often directed at eliminating white-collar jobs.

The rush to downsize in some of America's largest and most prestigious corporations became so widespread in the 1990s that a new occupation was needed to handle the casualties. The "outplacement professional" was created to put the best corporate face on a decision to downsize, that is, to terminate large numbers of employees—as many as ten thousand. The job of these new public relations types is to get the general public to accept downsizing as the normal way of life for corporations who have to survive in the competitive global economy. Their job is also to assist the downsized middle managers to manage their anger and to get on with their lives.

The *Human Resources Development Handbook* of the American Management Association provides the operating philosophy for the outplacement professional:

"Unnecessary personnel must be separated from the company if the organization is to continue as a viable business entity. To do otherwise in today's globally competitive world would be totally unjustified and might well be a threat to the company's future survival."[2]

The privileged 20 percent of the population is hard at work telling the other 80 percent about the harsh realities of the changing global economy. "Lifetime employment" is out. The goal is "lifetime employability," which workers try to attain by accumulating skills and being dedicated and committed employees. Even Japan's highly touted commitment to lifetime employment (in some firms) is apparently unraveling, as reported in a prominent feature article in the *New York Times*.[3] It should be no surprise that an elite media organization like the *Times*, whose upper-level employees belong to the privileged class, should join in disseminating the myth of the global economy as the "hidden hand" behind the downsizing of America. The casualties of plant closings and downsizings are encouraged to see their plight as part of the "natural laws" of economics.

This enormous transformation of the U.S. economy over a twenty-year period has been described by political leaders and media as the inevitable and therefore normal workings of the emerging global economy. Some, like former president Reagan, even applauded the changes as a historic opportunity to revitalize the economy. In a 1985 report to Congress, he stated, "The progression of an economy such as America's from the agricultural to manufacturing to services is a natural change. The move from an industrial society toward a postindustrial service economy has been one of the greatest changes to affect the developed world since the Industrial Revolution."[4]

A contrasting view posits that the transformation of the U.S. economy is not the result of natural economic laws or the "hidden hand" of global economic changes but is, rather, the result of calculated actions by multinational corporations to expand their profits and power. When corporations decide to close plants and move them overseas where they can find cheap labor and fewer government regulations, they do so to enhance profits and not simply as a response to the demands of global competition. In many cases, the U.S. multinationals themselves are the global competition that puts pressure on other U.S. workers to work harder, faster, and for lower wages and fewer benefits.

THE GLOBAL ECONOMY AND CLASS STRUCTURE

Discussion about the new global economy generally focuses on three things. First is the appearance of many new producers of quality goods in parts of the world that are normally viewed as less developed. Advances in computer-based production systems have allowed many countries in Southeast Asia and Latin America to produce goods that compete with those of more advanced industrial economies in Western Europe and North America. Second is the development of telecommunication systems that permit rapid economic transactions around the globe and the coordination of economic activities in locations separated by thousands of miles. The combination of advances in computer-based production and telecommunications makes it possible for large firms, especially multinationals, to decentralize their production and locate facilities around the globe. Third is the existence of an international division of labor that makes it possible for corporations to employ engineers, technicians, or production workers from anywhere in the world. This gives corporations great flexibility when negotiating with their domestic workforce over wages and benefits.

These three conditions are often used as evidence of a "new global economy" *out there* constraining the actions of all corporations to be competitive if they hope to survive. One concrete indicator of this global economy *out there* is the rising level of international trade between the United States and other nations. In the 1960s, the United States was the dominant exporter of goods and services, and the imports of foreign products played a small part in the U.S. economy. Throughout the 1970s foreign imports claimed an increasing share, and by 1981 the United States "was importing almost 26 percent of its cars, 25 percent of its steel, 60 percent of its televisions, tape recorders, radios, and phonographs, 43 percent of its calculators, 27 percent of its metal-forming machine tools, 35 percent of its textile machinery, and 53 percent of its numerically controlled machine tools."[5] Imports from developing nations went from $3.6 billion in 1970 to $30 billion in 1980.

Throughout the 1980s, the United States became a debtor nation in terms of the balance between what we exported to the rest of the world and what we import. By 1997, the trade deficit indicated that the import of goods and services exceeded exports by $113.7 billion. This is the largest deficit since the previous high in 1987 of $153.4 billion. But what do these trade figures tell us? On the surface, they appear to be a function of the operation of the global economy, because the figures indicate that we have a $55.7 billion deficit with Japan, $49.7 billion with China, and $14.5 billion with Mexico.[6] It appears that Japanese, Chinese, and Mexican companies are doing a better job of producing goods than the United States and thus we import products rather than producing them ourselves. But is this the correct conclusion? The answer lies in how you count imports and exports.

Trade deficit figures are based on balance-of-payment statistics, which tally the dollar value of U.S. exports to other countries and the dollar value of foreign exports to the United States; if the dollar value of Chinese exports to the United States exceeds the dollar value of U.S. exports to China, the United States has a trade deficit with China. This would appear to mean that Chinese companies are producing the goods being exported to the United States. But that is not necessarily the case. According to the procedures followed in calculating trade deficits, "the U.S. balance of payments statistics are intended to capture the total amount of transactions between U.S. *residents* and *residents* of the rest of the world."[7] If "resident" simply identifies the geographical location of the source of an import, then some unknown portion of the U.S. $49.7 billion deficit with China could be from U.S.-owned firms that are producing goods in China and exporting them to the United States. Those U.S. firms are residents of China, and their exports are counted as Chinese exports to the United States. Thus, the global economy that is *out there* forcing U.S. firms to keep wages low so we can be more competitive might actually be made up of U.S. firms that have located production plants in countries other than in the United States. Such actions may be of great benefit to the U.S. multinational firms that produce goods around the world and export them to the U.S. market. Such actions may also benefit U.S. consumers, who pay less for goods produced in low-wage areas. But what about the U.S. worker in a manufacturing plant whose wages have not increased in twenty years because of the need to compete with "foreign companies"? What about the worker who may never get a job in manufacturing because U.S. firms have been opening plants in other countries rather than in the United States? As the comic strip character Pogo put it: "We have met the enemy and it is us."

American multinational corporations' foreign investments have changed the emphasis in the economy from manufacturing to service. This shift has changed the occupational structure by eliminating high-wage manufacturing jobs and creating a two-tiered system of service jobs. There have been big winners and big losers in this social and economic transformation. The losers have been the three out of four Americans who work for wages—wages that have been declining since 1973; these American workers constitute the new working class (see chapter 1). The big winners have been the privileged classes, for whom jobs and incomes have expanded at the same time that everyone else was in decline. Corporate executives, managers, scientists, engineers, doctors, corporate lawyers, accountants, computer programmers, financial consultants, health care professionals, and media professionals have all registered substantial gains in income and wealth in the last twenty years. And the changes that have produced the "big losers" and "big winners" have been facilitated by the legislative actions of the federal government and elected officials of both political parties, whose incomes, pensions, health care, and associated "perks" have also grown handsomely in the last two decades.

This chapter demonstrates that the privileged classes have benefited at the expense of the working classes. The profits of corporations and stockholders have expanded because fewer workers produce more goods and services for lower wages. The profits of corporations are distributed to executives, managers, and professionals in higher salaries and benefits because they are able either to extract more work from workers while paying them less or to justify inequality, provide distracting entertainment for the less fortunate, or control them, if necessary. The privileged class is able to maintain its position of advantage because its members control the jobs and incomes of other Americans. They also control the mass media and education, which are the instruments of ideological domination. If all of this is not enough, they also control the means of violence (military, national guard, police, and the investigative and security apparatus) that are used to deal with large-scale dissent.

CREATING THE GLOBAL ECONOMY:
THE PATH TO CORPORATE PROFITS

When World War II ended in 1945, all but one of the industrial nations involved had experienced widespread destruction of their industrial system and the infrastructure that is necessary for a healthy economy to provide sufficient food, shelter, and clothing for its people. Although all nations that participated in the war suffered terrible human losses, the United States alone emerged with its economic system stronger than it was at the start of the war.

For nearly thirty years following World War II, the United States dominated the world economy through its control of three-fourths of the world's invested capital and two-thirds of its industrial capacity. At the close of the war, there was concern in the United States that the high levels of production, profits, and employment stimulated by war mobilization could not be sustained. The specter of a return to the stagnation and unemployment experienced only a decade earlier during the Great Depression led to the search for a new economic and political system that would maintain the economic, military, and political dominance of the United States.

The postwar geopolitical-economic policy of the United States was designed to provide extensive foreign assistance to stimulate the recovery of Western Europe. This policy would stimulate U.S. investment in Europe and provide the capital for countries to buy U.S. agricultural and industrial products. The policy was also designed to "fight" the creation of socialist governments and socialist policies in Western Europe, governments that might not be sympathetic to U.S. capital, trade, and influence. The foreign assistance policy known as the Marshall Plan was instituted to provide $22 billion in aid over a four-year period and to bring together European nations into a global economic system dominated by the United States.[8]

This system was the basis for U.S. growth and prosperity during the 1950s, the 1960s, and the early 1970s. By the mid-1970s, steady improvements in the war-torn economies of Western Europe and Asia had produced important shifts in the balance of economic power among industrialized nations. The U.S. gross national product was now less than twice that of the Soviet Union (in 1950 it was more than three times), less than four times that of Germany (down from nine times in 1950), and less than three times that of Japan (twelve times in 1950). With many nations joining the United States in the production of the world's goods, the U.S. rate of growth slowed. As England, France, Germany, and Japan produced goods for domestic consumption, there was less need to import agricultural and industrial products from the United States.

The profits of U.S. corporations from the domestic economy were in a steady decline through the late 1960s and into the 1970s. In the early 1960s the annual rate of return on investment was 15.5 percent. In the late 1960s it was 12.7 percent. In the early 1970s it was 10 percent, and after 1975 it slipped below 10 percent, where it remained.

The privileged classes in the United States were concerned about declining profits. This affected their accumulation of wealth from stocks, bonds, dividends, and other investments. It affected corporate, managerial, and professional salaries indirectly, through the high rate of inflation that eroded the purchasing power of consumption capital (i.e., salaries) and the real value of investment capital (i.e., value of stocks, bonds, etc.). The usual list of suspects was rounded up to account for the U.S. decline. The leading "explanation" was that U.S. products could not compete in the global economy because of the power of organized labor. This power was reflected in the high labor costs that made products less competitive and in cost-of-living adjustments that increased wages at the rate of inflation (which was sometimes at double digits). Union control of work rules also made it difficult for management to adopt new innovations to increase productivity and reduce dependence on labor.

Next on the list was the American worker, who was blamed for a decline in work ethic, resulting in products of lower quality and higher cost. Our workers were seen as too content and secure and as unwilling to compete with the ambitious workers of the rapidly developing economies. The third suspect was the wide array of new regulations on business that had been adopted by the federal government to protect workers and the environment. Corporate executives complained about the increased cost of doing business that came from meeting the workplace standards of the Occupational Safety and Health Administration (OSHA) or the air and water pollution standards of the Environmental Protection Agency (EPA).

These explanations for declining profits, blaming workers and government regulations for making American products less competitive in the global economy, provided the basis for an attack on unions and on workers' wages and helped to justify the plant closings and capital flight to low-wage areas. They also served to put the government on the defensive for its failure to be sensitive to the "excessive" costs that federal regulations impose on business.

What was rarely discussed on the business pages of the *New York Times* or the *Wall Street Journal* was the failure of corporate management in major U.S. firms to respond to the increasing competition to the once U.S.-dominated production of autos, steel, textiles, and electronics. In the early 1960s, imports of foreign products played a small part in the American economy, but by 1980 things had changed. In the early 1960s, imports accounted for less than 10 percent of the U.S. market, but by 1980 more than 70 percent of all the goods produced in the United States were actively competing with foreign-made goods.[9]

American corporations failed to follow the well-established management approach to the loss of market share, competitive advantage, and profits. Instead of pursuing long-term solutions, like investing in more efficient technology, new plants, research and development, and new markets, corporate executives chose to follow short-term strategies that would make the bottom line of profits the primary goal. The way was open for increased foreign investment, mergers, and downsizing.

WHEN YOUR DOG BITES YOU

> With industrial jobs shrinking in the United States, and so much of what we
> buy, from clothing to electronics to automobiles, now made abroad, a common
> perception is that "globalized" production is a primary cause of falling living
> standards for American workers.
>
> —Richard B. DuBoff, *Dollars and Sense*, September–October 1997

While corporate profits from the domestic U.S. economy were declining steadily
from the mid-1970s, investment by U.S. corporations abroad showed continued
growth. The share of corporate profits from direct foreign investment increased
through the 1970s, as did the amount of U.S. direct investment abroad. In 1970,
direct investment by U.S. firms abroad was $75 billion, and it rose to $167 billion
in 1978. In the 1980–85 period it remained below $400 billion but thereafter in-
creased gradually each year, reaching $716 billion in 1994. The one hundred
largest U.S. multinational corporations reported foreign revenue in 1994 that
ranged from 30 to 70 percent of their total revenue: IBM had 62 percent of total
revenue from foreign sources, Eastman Kodak 52 percent, Colgate-Palmolive 68
percent, and Johnson and Johnson, Coca Cola, Pepsi, and Procter and Gamble
each 50 percent.[10]

American multinational corporations sought to maintain their profit margins
by increasing investments in affiliates abroad. This strategy may have kept stockholders happy and maintained the price of corporate stocks on Wall Street, but it
would result in deindustrialization—the use of corporate capital for foreign investment, mergers, and acquisitions rather than for investment in domestic operations.[11] Instead of investing in the U.S. auto, steel, and textile industries, companies were closing plants at an unprecedented rate and using the capital to open
production facilities in other countries. By 1994, U.S. companies employed 5.4
million people abroad, more than 4 million of whom worked in manufacturing.[12]
Thus, millions of U.S. manufacturing workers who were displaced in the 1980s by
plant closings saw their jobs shifted to foreign production facilities. Although
most criticism of U.S. investment abroad is reserved for low-wage countries like
Mexico and Thailand, the biggest share of manufacturing investment abroad is in
Germany and Japan—hardly low-wage countries. The United States has large
trade deficits with Japan and Western Europe, where the hourly wages in manufacturing are 15–25 percent higher than in the United States.[13] This fact challenges
the argument made by multinational corporations that if they did not shift production abroad, they would probably lose the sale of that product.

The movement of U.S. production facilities to foreign countries in the 1980s
was not simply the result of a search for another home where they could once
again be productive and competitive. It appeared as if RCA closed its plant in
Monticello, Indiana, because its high-wage workers made it impossible to compete with televisions being produced in Southeast Asia. Saddened by having to

leave its home of thirty-five years, RCA would now search for another home where, it was hoped, it could stay at least another thirty-five years, if not longer. Not likely: plants did not close in the 1980s to find other homes; the closures were the first step in the creation of the homeless and stateless multinational corporation—an entity without ties to place, or allegiances to people, communities, or nations.

Thus, the rash of plant closings in the 1970s and 1980s began as apparent responses to economic crises of declining profits and increased global competition. As such, they appeared to be rational management decisions to protect stockholder investments and the future of individual firms. Although things may have started in this way, it soon became apparent that what was being created was the *spatially decentered firm*: a company that could produce a product with components manufactured in a half-dozen different plants around the globe and then assembled at a single location for distribution and sale. This global production system was made possible by significant advances in computer-assisted design and manufacturing that made it unnecessary to produce a product at a single location. It was also made possible by advances in telecommunications that enabled management at corporate headquarters to coordinate research, development, design, manufacturing, and sales decisions at various sites scattered around the world.

The homeless and stateless multinational firm is able to move its product as quickly as it can spot a competitive advantage associated with low wages, cheaper raw materials, advantageous monetary exchange rates, more sympathetic governments, or proximity to markets. This encourages foreign investment because it expands the options of corporations in their choice of where to locate, and it makes them less vulnerable to pressure from workers regarding wages and benefits.

The advantages of the multinational firm and foreign investments are also a product of the U.S. tax code. In addition to providing the largest firms with numerous ways to delay, defer, and avoid taxes, corporate profits made on overseas investments are taxed at a much lower rate than profits from domestic operations. Thus, as foreign investments by U.S. firms increased over the last two decades, the share of total taxes paid by corporations declined. In the 1960s, corporations in the United States paid about 25 percent of all federal income taxes, and in 1991 it was down to 9.2 percent. A 1993 study by the General Accounting Office reported that more than 40 percent of corporations with assets of more than $250 million either paid no income tax or paid less than $100,000.[14]

CREATING THE NEW WORKING CLASS

When the large multinational firm closes its U.S. facilities and invests in other firms abroad or opens new facilities abroad, the major losers are the production workers who have been displaced and the communities with lower tax revenues and increased costs stemming from expanded efforts to attract new businesses. But this does not mean that the firms are losers, for they are growing and expanding operations elsewhere. This growth creates the need for new employees in finance, management, computer operations, information systems, and clerical work. The total picture is one of shrinking production plants and expanding corporate headquarters; shrinking blue-collar employee rolls and two-tiered expansion of high-wage professional-managerial and low-wage clerical positions.

Having been extraordinarily successful in closing U.S. plants, shifting investment and production abroad, and cutting both labor and labor costs (both the number of production workers and their wage-benefit packages), major corporations now turned their attention to saving money by cutting white-collar employees. In the 1990s, there were no longer headlines about "plant closings," "capital flight," or "deindustrialization." The new strategy was "downsizing," "rightsizing," "reengineering," or how to get the same amount of work done with fewer middle managers and clerical workers.

When Sears, Roebuck and Company announced that it could cut 50,000 jobs in the 1990s (while still employing 300,000 people) its stock climbed 4 percent on the New York Stock Exchange. The day Xerox announced a planned cut of 10,000 employees, its stock climbed 7 percent. Eliminating jobs was suddenly linked with cutting corporate waste and increasing profits. Hardly a month could pass without an announcement by a major corporation of its downsizing plan. Tenneco Incorporated would cut 11,000 of its 29,000 employees. Delta Airlines would eliminate 18,800 jobs, Eastman Kodak would keep pace by eliminating 16,800 employees, and AT&T announced 40,000 downsized jobs, bringing its total of job cuts since 1986 to 125,000. Not to be outdone, IBM cut 180,000 jobs between 1987 and 1994.

Even the upscale, more prestigious banking industry joined in the rush to become "lean and mean." A total of ten bank mergers announced in 1995 would result in 32,400 jobs lost because of the new "efficiencies" that come with mergers. Even banks that were already successful in introducing "efficiencies" were not immune to continued pressure for more. Between 1985 and 1995, Chase Manhattan's assets grew by 38 percent (from $87.7 billion to $121.2 billion), and its workforce was reduced 28 percent, from 44,450 to 33,500 employees. Yet when Chase was "swallowed" by Chemical Banking Corporation in a merger, both banks announced further reductions, totaling 12,000 people.

Job loss in the 1990s appeared to hit hardest at those who were better educated (some college or more) and better paid ($40,000, or more). Job loss aimed at production workers in the 1980s was "explained" by the pressures of global competition and the opportunities to produce in areas with lower-wage workers. The "explanation" for the 1990s downsizing was either new technology or redesign of the organization. Some middle managers and supervisors were replaced by new computer systems that provide surveillance of clerical workers and data entry jobs. These same computer systems also eliminate the need for many middle managers responsible for collecting, processing, and analyzing data used by upper-level decision makers.

Redesign of organizations was achieved by eliminating middle levels within an organization and shifting work both upward and downward. The downward shift of work is often accompanied by new corporate plans to "empower" lower-level workers with new forms of participation and opportunities for career development. All of this redesign reduced administrative costs and increased the work load for continuing employees.

Investors, who may have been tentative about the potential of profiting from the deindustrialization of the 1980s because it eroded the country's role as a manufacturing power, were apparently delighted by downsizing. During the 1990s the stock market skyrocketed from below three thousand points on the Dow Jones Industrial Average to eighty-six hundred in March 1998—an almost 200 percent increase. The big institutional investors apparently anticipated that increasing profits would follow the broadly based actions of cutting the workforce.

Downsizing is often viewed by corporations as a rational response to the demands of competition and thereby a way to better serve their investors and ultimately their own employees. Alan Downs, in his book *Corporate Executions*, challenges four prevailing myths that justify the publicly announced layoffs of millions of workers.[15] First, downsizing firms do not necessarily wind up with a smaller workforce. Often, downsizing is followed by the hiring of new workers. Second, Downs questions the belief that downsized workers are often the least productive because their expertise is obsolete: according to his findings, increased productivity does not necessarily follow downsizing. Third, jobs lost to downsizing are not replaced with higher-skill, better-paying jobs. Fourth, the claim that companies become more profitable after downsizing, and that workers thereby benefit, is only half-true: many companies that downsize do report higher corporate profits and, as discussed earlier, often achieve higher valuations of their corporate stock. But there is no evidence that these profits are being passed along to employees in the form of higher wages and benefits.

After challenging these four myths, Downs concludes that the "ugly truth" of downsizing is that it is an expression of corporate self-interest to lower wages and increase profits. This view is shared by David Gordon, who documents the growth of executive, administrative, and managerial positions and compensation during the period when "downsizing" was at its highest.[16] Gordon describes bureaucratic "bloat" as part of a corporate strategy to reduce the wages of production workers and increase and intensify the level of managerial supervision. Slow wage growth for production workers and top-heavy corporate bureaucracies reinforce each other, and the combination produces a massive shift of money out of wages and into executive compensation and profits. This "wage squeeze" occurred not only in manufacturing (because of global competition) but also in mining, construction, transportation, and retail trade.[17] Although it is to be expected that foreign competition will have an impact on wages in manufacturing, it should not affect the nontrade sector to the same extent. Thus, the "wage squeeze" since the mid-1970s that increased income and wealth inequality in the United States is probably the result of a general assault on workers' wages and benefits rather than a response to global competition.

Thus, the result of more than a decade of plant closings and shifting investment abroad, and less than a decade of downsizing America's largest corporations, has been the creation of a protected privileged class and a divided working class. The three segments of the working class are core workers, temporary workers, and contingent workers.

Core Workers

These employees possess the skills, knowledge, or experience that are essential to the operation of the firm. Their income levels place them in the "comfort class" described in chapter 1. They are essential for the firm, regardless of how well it might be doing from the point of view of profits and growth; they are simply needed for the firm's continuity. Being in the core is not the same as being in a particular occupational group. A firm may employ many engineers and scientists, only some of whom might be considered to be in the core. Skilled blue-collar workers may also be in the core. Core employees have the greatest job security with their employing organizations and also have skills and experiences that can be "traded" in the external labor market if their firm should experience an unforeseen financial crisis. Finally, core employees enjoy their protected positions precisely because there are other employees just like them who are considered temporary.

Temporary Workers

The employment of temporary workers is linked to the economic ups and downs that a firm faces. When sales are increasing, product demand is high, and profits match those of comparable firms, the employment of temporary workers is secure. When inventories increase, or sales decline sharply, production is cut back, and temporary employees are laid off or fired. The temporary workers' relationship to the firm is a day-to-day matter. There is no tacit commitment to these employees about job security and no sense that they "belong to the family."

A good example of the role of temporary workers is revealed in the so-called transplants—the Japanese auto firms like Toyota, Nissan, and Honda that have located assembly plants in Kentucky, Ohio, Michigan, Illinois, Indiana, and Tennessee. Each of these firms employs between two thousand and three thousand American workers in their plants, and they have made explicit no-layoff commitments to workers in return for high work expectations (and also as a way to discourage unionization). However, in a typical plant employing two thousand production workers, the no-layoff commitment was made to twelve hundred hires at start-up time; the other eight hundred hires being classified as temporary. Thus, when there is a need to cut production because of weak sales or excessive inventory, the layoffs come from the pool of temporary workers rather than from the core workers. Sometimes these temporary workers are not even directly employed by the firm but are hired through an employment firm like Manpower. These temporary workers are actually contingent workers.

Contingent Workers

These workers, as noted above, are employees of an agency that contracts with a firm for their services. It is estimated that about one in four persons in the labor force is a contingent worker, that is, a temporary or part-time worker.[18] These workers can be clerk-typists, secretaries, engineers, computer specialists, lawyers, or managers. They are paid by the temp agency and do not have access to a company's benefit package of retirement or insurance programs. Many of the professionals and specialists who work for large firms via temp firms are often the same persons who were downsized by those same companies. The following experience of a downsized worker is an ironic example of how the contingent workforce is created.

> John Kelley, 48, had worked for Pacific Telesis for 23 years when the company fired him in a downsizing last December. Two weeks later, a company that contracts out engineers to PacTel offered him a freelance job.

"Who would I work for?" Kelley asked.

"Edna Rogers," answered the caller.

Kelley burst out laughing. Rogers was the supervisor who had just fired him. "That was my job," he explained. "You're trying to replace me with myself."[19]

These three groups of workers fit into the bottom part of the double-diamond class structure described in chapter 1, and it is only the core workers who have even the slightest chance to make it into the privileged class. Core workers with potential to move up generally have the credentials, skills, or social capital to have long-term job security, or to start their own business, and therefore the possibility of having substantial consumption capital (a good salary) and capital for investment purposes. Let us now consider how the privileged class holds on to its advantaged position in the double-diamond class structure.

CARE AND FEEDING OF THE PRIVILEGED CLASS

The federal government of 1997 is a very different creature from that of, say, 1977—more egregiously corrupt and sycophantic toward wealth, more glaringly repressive, and even less responsive to the needs of low- and middle-income people.

—Barbara Ehrenreich, *Nation*, November 17, 1997

Most people who are in the privileged class are born there, as the sons, daughters, and relatives of high-paid executives, professionals, and business owners. Of course, they do not view their "achievements" that way. As some wag once said of former president George Bush, "He woke up on second base and thought he'd hit a double." But some members of the privileged class have earned their places, whether by means of exceptional talent, academic distinctions, or years of hard work in transforming a small business into a major corporation. Regardless of how much effort was needed to get where they are, however, the privileged class works very hard to stay where they are. Holding on to their wealth, power, and privilege requires an organized effort by businessmen, doctors, lawyers, engineers, scientists, and assorted political officials. This effort is often cited to convince the nonprivileged 80 percent of Americans that the privileged are deserving of their "rewards" and that, in general, people get out of life in direct proportion to what they put in. This effort is also used to dominate the political process so that governmental policies, and the rules for making policy, will protect and advance the interests of the privileged class.

However, before examining the organized effort of the privileged class to protect their privilege, it is first necessary to examine how members of the privileged class convince one another that they are deserving. Even sons and daughters from the wealthiest families need to develop biographical "accounts" or "stories" indicating they are deserving. This may involve accounts of how they worked their way up the ladder in the family business, starting as a clerk but quickly revealing a grasp of the complexities of the business and obtaining recognition from others of their exceptional talent.

Even without the biographical accounts to justify exceptional rewards, justification for high income is built into the structure of the organizations they join. In every organization, whether an industrial firm, bank, university, movie studio, law firm, or hospital, there are multiple and distinct "ladders" that locate one's position in the organization. New employees get on one of these ladders based on their educational credentials and work experience. There are ladders for unskilled employees, for skilled workers, and for professional and technical people with specialized knowledge. Each ladder has its own distinct "floor" and "ceiling" in terms of what can be expected regarding salary, benefits, and associated "perks." In every organization, there is typically only one ladder that can put you in the privileged class, and this usually involves an advanced technical or administrative career line.

This career line can start at entry levels of $70,000–80,000 annual compensation, with no upper limit beyond what the traffic will bear. These are the career ladders leading to upper executive positions providing high levels of consumption capital and opportunities for investment capital.

Claiming Turf

Many young attorneys, business school graduates, scientists, engineers, doctors, economists, and other professionals would like to get entry-level positions on these upper-level career ladders. In fact, there are probably many people who are qualified for entry positions in terms of their educational credentials and work experiences. So how are people selected from among the large number of qualified applicants for such desirable career opportunities? The answer is simple: Once qualifications and experience are used to define the pool of eligible applicants, the choice of who gets the job depends on the applicants' social capital. In chapter 1, we defined *social capital* as the social ties that people have with members of their college, fraternity or sorority, ethnic group, or religious group. People get jobs through their social networks, which provide them with information about job openings and with references valuable to those doing the hiring.[20] These social networks are usually composed of persons with similar social backgrounds. A recent study examined the social backgrounds of persons in the highest positions in corporations, the executive branch of the federal government, and the military.[21] Although there is increased diversity among leaders today compared with 1950 with respect to gender, ethnicity, and race, the "core group continues to be wealthy white Christian males, most of whom are still from the upper third of the social ladder. They have been filtered through a handful of elite schools of law, business, public policy, and international relations."[22]

A good illustration of how social capital works is found in a study of 545 top position holders in powerful organizations in the United States.[23] Ten institutional sectors were studied, including *Fortune 500* industrial corporations, *Fortune 300* nonindustrial corporations, labor unions, political parties, voluntary organizations, mass media, Congress, political appointees in the federal government, and federal civil servants. Within each sector, fifty top position holders were interviewed—persons who may be considered "elites in the institutional sectors that have broad impact on policy making and political processes in the U.S."[24] Although we have no information on the incomes and wealth of the 545 elites, it is very likely they would fit our definition as members of the privileged class.

Table 3.1 provides some of the findings from this study, which identify the ethnic-religious composition of elites and their distribution across different institutional sectors. As can be seen from the first line of the table, 43 percent of all the elites in the study were WASPs (Protestants with ancestry from the British Isles), 19.5 percent were Protestants from elsewhere in Europe, 8.5 percent were Irish Catholics, 8.7 percent were Catholics from elsewhere in Europe, 11.3 percent

Table 3.1 Ethnic Representation among Elites

	WASPs	Other Protestants	Irish Catholics	Other Catholics	Jews	Minorities	Probably WASPs
1. Overall elite	43.0	19.5	8.5	8.7	11.3	3.9	5.0
2. Men born before 1932	22.9	22.5	4.2	17.2	2.9	14.4	13.4
3. College-educated men born before 1932	31.0	19.8	6.0	15.5	8.9	5.2	10.3
4. Institutional sectors							
Business	57.3	22.1	5.3	6.1	6.9	0.0	2.3
Labor	23.9	15.2	37.0	13.0	4.3	2.2	4.3
Political parties	44.0	18.0	14.0	4.0	8.0	4.0	8.0
Voluntary organizations	32.7	13.5	1.9	7.7	17.3	19.2	7.7
Mass media	37.1	11.3	4.8	9.7	25.8	0.0	11.3
Congress	53.4	19.0	6.9	8.6	3.4	3.4	5.2
Political appointments	39.4	28.8	1.5	13.6	10.6	3.0	3.0
Civil service	35.8	22.6	9.4	9.4	15.1	3.8	3.8

Source: Alba and Moore (1982) table 1.

were Jews, and 3.9 percent were minorities (nonwhites and Hispanics). The second line indicates the percentage of the national population of men born before 1932 from different ethnic-religious backgrounds. The third line indicates the percentage of the national population of college-educated men born before 1932 of each ethnic background. A comparison of line (1) with lines (2) and (3) shows the extent to which each ethnic-religious group may be overrepresented or underrepresented among the elites. Thus, WASPs and Jews are overrepresented among elites relative to their composition in the general population. The elite representation of other Protestants and Irish Catholics is comparable to their representation in the national population; and other Catholics and minorities are underrepresented among elites.

More interesting for our purposes is the overrepresentation and underrepresentation of elites in different institutional sectors. Overrepresentation would suggest the operation of social ties operating to get positions for persons with the same ethnic-religious background. White Anglo-Saxon Protestants are greatly overrepresented in business and in Congress. Irish Catholics are very overrepresented in labor and politics. Jews are sharply overrepresented in mass media, voluntary organizations, and federal civil service. This ethnic-religious overrepresentation indicates that social capital may be used to get access to career ladders leading to the privileged class. Moreover, there appears to be ethnic-religious specialization in the institutional sectors that they "colonize." People help to get jobs for relatives and friends, regardless of whether the job is for a Mexican immigrant in a Los Angeles sweat shop or a young Ivy League graduate in a Wall Street law firm. Parents invest their capital in the Ivy League education for a son or daughter, who now uses the social capital of family or school ties to start on a career line in the privileged class.

Securing Turf

After obtaining positions on career ladders that will make them members of the privileged class, our entry-level managers, attorneys, and faculty become aware of the very high incomes enjoyed by their senior colleagues. One response to these high salaries is to feel that they are unjustified and to exclaim, "Why should the President of the university make $250,000 a year when some of our professors with twenty years' experience are making $60,000?" A second response is to recognize that the president's salary is used to justify the $170,000 salaries of the executive vice presidents, which in turn justify the $120,000 salaries of the deans, which in turn justify the $100,000 salaries of senior professors in selected fields.

The second response is the typical one for people involved in career ladders that promise access to the privileged class. This response might be called symbiotic greed, where the parties are locked together in a mutually beneficial relationship. As the salary of the president rises, so do the salaries of all the others who are on the privileged-class career ladder. The rub is that only a small proportion of all the managers, attorneys, or faculty is on that career ladder, even though they may share the same educational credentials and work experience. This is a form of misguided self-interest, wherein low-level employees support the high salary of their superiors because of the belief that they may one day also have such a high salary.

Now to the organized effort by businessmen, doctors, lawyers, and the like to protect the interests of the privileged class. This effort is revealed in three ways: (1) Members of the privileged class hold upper-level positions in all the major institutions of American society. These institutions control enormous resources that can be used to shape public awareness, the political process, and the nation's policy agenda. (2) The organizations to which the privileged class belong form associations in order to hire lobbyists, contribute to political campaigns, and shape legislation in their interests. (3) The members of the privileged class who are in professional occupations, like medicine and law, are represented by powerful professional associations that protect their members against any efforts by other groups to encroach on their "turf." Thus, the American Medical Association (AMA) makes sure that state legislatures continue to give doctors a monopoly over what they do by preventing nurses, or pharmacists, or chiropractors, or holistic practitioners from providing certain types of care to clients. Similarly, the American Bar Association acts to prevent paralegals from competing with lawyers in handling wills, estates, or certain types of litigation.

Not every segment of the privileged class is unified on all issues. Doctors are not pleased with the actions of attorneys when they vigorously pursue malpractice suits against doctors and hospitals. The AMA has urged Congress to pass legislation limiting the dollar amount of damages that might be awarded in malpractice claims. Lawyers resist such efforts because they make their living from obtaining 30 percent of the damage awards made to persons suing doctors or hospitals. Similarly, the banking industry and the large industrial corporations may differ on whether they would like to see the Federal Reserve Board raise or lower interest rates. Some sectors of the business community may support giving China special trade concessions, while others may be opposed.

Despite the differences and disagreements over specific policies by members of the privileged class, they are unified in their support for the rules of the game as they are currently played: the privileged class is unified in its view of how the political process should operate. Individuals and organizations should be free to lobby members of Congress on matters of interest to them. Individuals and organizations should be free to contribute money to political action committees and to political parties. And above all else, privileged-class members agree that business should be able to operate in a free and unregulated environment and that the country runs just fine with a two-party system.

Then there are the really big policy issues, where the "payoffs" are substantial to almost all segments of the privileged class. The North American Free Trade Agreement (NAFTA) and the General Agreement on Tariffs and Trade (GATT) were supported by Presidents Reagan, Bush, and Clinton and by a bipartisan majority of both houses of Congress. These agreements promise to advance the global economy and the continued pursuit of profits across the globe by multinational corporations.

The privileged class achieved major victories in the 1980s through their efforts to reduce government spending on a variety of social programs that benefit the working class. Using the scare tactics of budget deficits and the national debt, the privileged class supported a balanced-budget agreement that required the president and Congress to reduce spending on welfare, education, Medicare, and Medicaid. In the 1990s, the privileged class turned its attention to the global economy by devising ways to protect opportunities for investment and profit around the globe. The main way to achieve this was to make it easy for large corporations to circle the globe in search of the best opportunities and thereby threaten workers everywhere to keep their wages and benefit demands at low levels. Facing the oft-repeated threat that there are "other" workers willing to do the same work for less money, the American working class has lived with declining earnings and disappearing health benefits and employer-provided pensions. And all this occurred during an eight-year economic recovery and a booming stock market!

During the 1990s, major U.S. and foreign corporations joined forces to lobby Washington policy makers to relax federal policies on international trade. This included granting most-favored-nation trading status to China (with whom we have a high trade deficit) and passing the North American Free Trade Agreement, which eliminated trade barriers between the United States, Canada, and Mexico. Before the passage of NAFTA, the United States had a $1 billion trade surplus with Mexico, but the year following NAFTA that surplus had become a $16.2 billion deficit.[25]

To garner public support free trade, President Clinton frequently pointed out that for every $1 billion in goods and services we export to other countries, we create twenty thousand jobs at home. This may be true, but the problem is that it also works in reverse: for every $1 billion of goods that we import, we lose twenty thousand jobs. And, as indicated earlier in this chapter, in 1997 the United States had a trade deficit of $113.7 billion with overseas companies. Thus, we lose many more jobs than we create with our free-trade policies. But free trade is not about jobs; it is about profits for corporations and the privileged class.

Defending Turf

In February 1998 the *New York Times* published a two-page open letter to the Congress of the United States, entitled "A Time for American Leadership on Key Global Issues."[26] The letter expresses concern about "a dangerous drift toward disengagement from the responsibilities of global leadership." Congress is asked to approve new "fast track" negotiating authority, which would extend NAFTA agreements to other countries in Latin America and around the globe, and to support the International Monetary Fund "bailout" of failed banks in Southeast Asia (although it failed to mention the benefit to U.S. banks and financial institutions that are heavily invested in those economies).

Signatories to this letter include two former presidents (Jimmy Carter and Gerald Ford), forty-two former public officials (secretaries of defense, treasury, commerce, and state; CIA directors and national security advisers; U.S. senators), and eighty-eight corporate presidents and CEOs (of AT&T, Boeing, Amoco, Chase Manhattan Bank, IBM, Time Warner, Bank America, etc.). Many of the former public officials now work as lobbyists for the U.S. and foreign multinationals that "feed at the public trough" via tax loopholes and federal subsidies.

Why would these 132 members of the privileged class spend $100,000 for this two-page ad in the *Times*? Surely not to influence members of Congress. Corporations and the privileged class have more effective ways of doing that, such as the $3 million in campaign contributions by Philip Morris or the $2.5 million that Chiquita Brands CEO Carl Linder gave to both political parties from 1993 to 1996. Perhaps the ad was designed to convince the working class to support "fast track" legislation. Probably not. The circulation of the *New York Times* is about 1.6 million, and very few of those readers are from the working class. The most likely target of the ad was the other members of the privileged class that they wanted to mobilize at the grass roots. The ad was designed to get the millions of privileged doctors, lawyers, journalists, managers, scientists, stock brokers, and media executives to mobilize public opinion through the hundreds of professional and business associations that represent their interests. The privileged class constitutes 20 percent of the population (about 14 million families), and when mobilized, they can be a potent political force.

Opposition to the privileged-class agenda on the global economy is fragmented, with limited resources. Critics of NAFTA and the GATT, like Ralph Nader and Jesse Jackson, can hardly stand up to the National Association of Manufacturers or the U.S. Chambers of Commerce. The opposition to NAFTA and the GATT voiced by Ross Perot and Pat Buchanan, who appeared to be "traitors" to the interests of the privileged class, was dealt with swiftly and sharply by the major media. Perot was given the persona of a quirky, eccentric millionaire who was trying to buy the presidency because he had nothing better to do with his time and money. Buchanan was vilified as a crypto-racist, anti-Semite, and general all-around "loose cannon."

The attacks on Perot and Buchanan by academics and political commentators on media talk shows should not be surprising. Elite universities and the major media are controlled by the wealthy and corporate elite who are at the top of the privileged class. The major networks of ABC, CBS, NBC, and Turner Broadcasting determine what the overwhelming majority of Americans will receive as news and entertainment. Two of the major networks are owned by major multinational firms, and institutional investors control substantial percentages of stock in the networks.

Is it any wonder, therefore, that efforts to attack the status quo are immediately marginalized or co-opted? An example of this process was revealed during the Republican presidential primary in early 1996. Pat Buchanan was making his usual bombastic attacks on immigration, NAFTA, and the GATT when he suddenly started lobbing some grenades at the corporate elite while yelling about "corporate greed." Here are a few samples, from speeches made in February of 1996: "When AT&T lops off 40,000 jobs, the executioner that does it, he's a big hero on the cover of one of these magazines, and AT&T stock soars"; "Mr. Dole put the interest of the big banks—Citibank, Chase Manhattan, Goldman Sachs—ahead of the American People."[27]

When it appeared that Buchanan's attack on the corporate elite was striking a responsive chord among people on the campaign trail, the *New York Times* decided to take the extraordinary step of publishing a seven-part series, called "The Downsizing of America," which ran from March 3 through March 9, 1996. Some might call this a major public service by the *Times*, designed to inform Americans about an important issue. Others might say it was a clever effort to take the issue out of the hands of Buchanan and to shape it and frame it in ways that would deflect the criticisms and attacks on the corporate elite. The *Times* series did not point an accusing finger at corporate America for the loss of millions of jobs. If anything, the series made the reader either feel sorry for everyone, including the "guilt-ridden" managers who had to fire workers ("Guilt of the Firing Squads"), or blame everyone, including downsized workers. In an extraordinary example of blaming the victim, consider the following "explanation" for downsizing. "The conundrum is that what companies do to make themselves secure is precisely what makes their workers feel insecure. And because workers are heavily represented among the 38 million Americans who own mutual funds, they unwittingly contribute to the very pressure from Wall Street that could take away their salaries even as it improves their investment income."[28]

The *New York Times* series did not help its readers to understand who benefits from downsizing, but they did help to defuse the issue and to take it out of the hands of those who might be critical of corporate America. It is an example of the pacification of everyday life (discussed more fully in chapter 7).

THE REAL GLOBAL ECONOMY

In this chapter we have tried to provide a glimpse of the meaning of the "bogey-man" global economy. The term has been used to threaten workers and unions and to convince everyone that they must work harder if they want to keep their jobs. The global economy is presented as if it is "out there" and beyond the control of the corporations, which must continually change corporate strategies in order to survive in the fiercely competitive global economy. There is an aspect of the global economy that is real. More countries today are capable of producing consumer goods that compete with firms producing goods in the United States. The best example of the *real* global economy is the Japanese automobile companies that have captured a major segment of the U.S. auto market. Companies like Toyota, Honda, and Nissan have produced cars (in Japan and in the United States) of high quality and attractive design and have found buyers from among Americans who were used to buying cars from General Motors, Ford, or Chrysler.

The other aspect of the global economy is an accelerated version of what U.S. financial and industrial corporations have been doing since the end of World War II—roaming the globe in search of profits. The big change is that since the 1980s, U.S. firms have found it easier to invest overseas. They have used this new opportunity to attack organized labor and to threaten workers to keep their wage demands to a minimum. In this view, the global economy is composed primarily of U.S. companies investing abroad and exporting their products to the United States (as the largest consumer market in the world) and other countries. These multinational corporations have an interest in creating the fiction that the global economy is some abstract social development driven by "natural laws" of economics, when it is actually the product of the deliberate actions of one hundred or so major corporations.

The real problem posed by the global economy is that it has increased the influence of large corporations over the daily lives of most Americans. This influence is revealed in corporate control over job growth and job loss, media control of information, and the role of big money in the world of national politics. At the same time that this growing influence is revealed on a daily basis, it has become increasingly clear that the major corporations have abandoned any sense of allegiance to, or special responsibilities toward, American workers and their communities.

This volatile mix of increasing influence and decreasing responsibility has produced the double-diamond class structure, where one in five Americans is doing very well indeed, enjoying the protection that comes with high income, wealth, and social contacts. Meanwhile, the remaining four out of five Americans are exploited and excluded.

NOTES

1. Office of Technology Assessment, *Technology and Structural Unemployment* (Washington, D.C.: Congress of the United States, 1986).

2. Joel Bleifuss, "The Terminators," *In These Times*, March 4, 1996, 12–13.

3. Sheryl WuDunn, "When Lifetime Jobs Die Prematurely: Downsizing Comes to Japan, Fraying Old Workplace Ties," *New York Times*, June 12, 1996.

4. John Miller and Ramon Castellblanch, "Does Manufacturing Matter?" *Dollars and Sense*, October 1988, 6–8.

5. Robert B. Reich, *The Next American Frontier* (New York: Times Books, 1983).

6. Richard W. Stevenson, "Trade Deficits for 1997 Hit Nine-Year High," *New York Times*, February 20, 1998.

7. John Pomery, "Running Deficits with the Rest of the World—Part I," *Focus on Economic Issues*, West Lafayette, Ind.: Purdue Center for Economic Education, Fall 1987. (Emphasis added.)

8. For an extended discussion, see Michael Stohl and Harry R. Targ, *Global Political Economy in the 1980s* (Cambridge, Mass.: Schenkman, 1982).

9. Reich, *Next American Frontier.*

10. "The 100 Largest U.S. Multinationals," *Forbes*, July 17, 1995, 274–76.

11. Barry Bluestone and Bennett Harrison, *The Deindustrialization of America* (New York: Basic Books, 1982).

12. Louis Uchitelle, "U.S. Corporations Expanding Abroad at a Quicker Pace," *New York Times*, July 25, 1998.

13. David M. Gordon, *Fat and Mean: The Corporate Squeeze of Working Americans and the Myth of Managerial "Downsizing"* (New York: Free Press, 1996).

14. Richard J. Barnet and John Cavanagh, *Global Dreams: Imperial Corporations and the New World Order* (New York: Simon and Schuster, 1994).

15. Alan Downs, *Corporate Executions* (New York: AMACOM, 1995).

16. See Gordon, *Fat and Mean*, chap. 2.

17. Ibid., 191.

18. Charles Tilly, *Half a Job: Bad and Good Part-Time Jobs in a Changing Labor Market* (Philadelphia: Temple University Press, 1996); Kevin D. Henson, *Just a Temp* (Philadelphia: Temple University Press, 1996).

19. Ann Monroe, "Getting Rid of the Gray," *Mother Jones*, July–August 1996, 29.

20. Mark Granovetter, *Getting a Job: A Study of Contacts and Careers* (Cambridge: Harvard University Press, 1974).

21. Richard L. Zweigenhaft and G. William Domhoff, *Diversity in the Power Elite: Have Women and Minorities Reached the Top?* (New Haven: Yale University Press, 1998).

22. Ibid., 6.

23. Richard D. Alba and Gwen Moore, "Ethnicity in the American Elite," *American Sociological Review* 47 (June 1982): 373–83.

24. Ibid., 374.

25. Richard W. Stevenson, "U.S. to Report to Congress Nafta Benefits Are Modest," *New York Times*, July 11, 1997.

26. *New York Times*, February 11, 1998.

27. Francis X. Clines, "Fueled by Success, Buchanan Revels in Rapid-Fire Oratory, *New York Times*, February 15, 1996.

28. Louis Uchitelle and N. R. Kleinfield, "On Battlefield of Business, Millions of Casualties," *New York Times*, March 3, 1996.

4

The Invisible Class Empire

The way our ruling class keeps out of sight is one of the greatest stunts in the political history of any country.

—Gore Vidal, *Progressive*, September 1986

"The truth is out there." This cryptic tagline from the *X-Files* television series reflects the elusive nature of evidence sought by FBI agents Fox Mulder and Dana Scully. Everyone knows something real is going on, but powerful force fields—emanating sometimes from paranormal phenomena and sometimes from shadowy and sinister human organizations—keep the truth just out of reach.

Like X-Filers, we also believe an elusive truth is out there, but not of a paranormal sort. Our concern is with superclass political power and evidence that reveals the "truth" about this highly charged issue. As Gore Vidal suggests, ruling-class political dominance is a long-standing but typically unacknowledged and unexplored feature of American society. Occasionally it has been candidly recognized—sometimes by writers of elite origins such as Vidal as well as by players at the top of the political game. President Woodrow Wilson once observed that "the masters of the government of the United States are the combined capitalists and manufacturers of the U.S."[1] However, such public candor is rare and may entail negative personal and professional consequences. Vidal, for example, maintains that his public musings on ruling-class political power have earned him undying elite enmity as a class traitor and that as a result, both he and his work have been marginalized and demonized by the privileged-class-controlled mass media.[2]

Superclass elites have long recognized that publicly acknowledged, front-page robber-baron plutocracy is inconsistent with American cultural ideals of democracy and political equality—and dangerous to their interests. Up-front publicity revealing the nature and extent of superclass political dominance would magnify the tensions between democratic ideals and concentrated class-power realities by calling into question the institutional legitimacy of American politics and public policy. For these reasons, superclass leaders prefer to keep the existence of and details about the extent of their class-based power out of sight.

103

THE INVISIBLE EMPIRE AND THE GOLDEN TRIANGLE

The first issue we face in claiming the upper class is a ruling—or governing—
class is that many of its members do not seem to be involved in ruling.

—G. William Domhoff, *State Autonomy or Class Dominance?*, 1996

We believe the superclass preference is for Americans to know less, not more, about "the truth that is out there" concerning the invisible class empire that dominates our national political system. This term refers to the hidden structures and processes through which superclass leaders, along with their credentialed-class allies, penetrate and dominate the American political system. It also refers to the processes used to disguise this reality and the concealed political, economic, and cultural dimensions of superclass power.

It is an empire in the sense that the privileged-class leadership has crafted a far-flung and widely dispersed collection of resources, organizations, and processes into a coherent political force that ensures the perpetuation of its interests. It is invisible in the sense that the class-based dimensions of the resources and control processes that undergird the empire are largely excluded from American public attention. In the political arena, the silence of incumbents, wannabes, and pundits promotes public inattention. In the cultural arena, public inattention grows out of an almost total mass-media blackout of reporting on the empire combined with a nearly total neglect of the subject by the U.S. educational system—at all levels.

As noted in chapter 2, the privileged-class leaders who guide and direct this empire are sometimes referred to as the power elite.[3] At the top, this group consists of superclass members who are active in organizational governance (corporate and political). It shades downward to include a second tier (with respect to class) of semi-autonomous managers and assistants. This junior partner portion of the power elite includes upwardly mobile corporate officers, attorneys, major political office holders, national lobbyists, and other specialists drawn largely from the credentialed class. These groups directly assist the superclass elite or indirectly serve their interests. All of these groups together—with superclass leadership at the center—form a kind of directorate that charts and oversees general economic and political policies as well as routine institutional practices necessary to maintain the class empire.

This chapter begins the process of peeling back the cloak of invisibility that shields the empire by exposing the organizational foundations of what we call the golden triangle of class power. As figure 4.1 illustrates, superclass resources, grounded in the investment capital that members of this class personally hold or control as corporate officers, serve as the basis for financing and controlling two major "industries." The shadow political industry (explored in this chapter) and the information industry (examined in chapter 5) both drive and conceal superclass power. The convergence of these twin structures leads to superclass political dominance. This term refers to the ways in which the routine operation of the two industries promotes superclass domination over major class-relevant public pol-

Figure 4.1   The Golden Triangle of Class Power

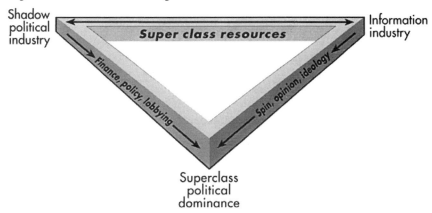

icy outcomes concerning economic and political issues. And it reflects the reality that superclass media ownership provides this class with substantial cultural influence (e.g., shaping popular cultural content), which also has important political and class power implications and consequences.

The shadow political industry extends downward as the left flank of the triangle. It consists of several real-life organizations that provide the political muscle underlying the class empire. This industry parallels—or shadows—the national political- and public-policy-making processes. Created, funded, and dominated by the superclass, this industry consists of three specialized, interrelated organizational groups devoted to (1) political finance—corporate-based individual wealth and political action committees (PACs); (2) policy planning—think tanks, research institutes, policy discussion groups, and foundations; and (3) classwide lobbying—peak corporate groups and corporate-professional group coalitions. Control of politics and government is the primary "products" of this industry. Its goal is to monitor and intervene in the political arena in ways that protect and promote superclass economic and political interests.

The information industry anchors the right flank of the triangle. Grounded in the largest mass media corporations, this industry serves privileged-class leaders' political and economic interests in two ways. First, much of the "news" and editorial commentary disseminated by firms at the heart of this industry help legitimate or conceal the nature and extent of superclass power. Second, large portions of the megaprofits generated through the operations of large media firms are channeled back to superclass owners, with smaller profit shares flowing to credentialed-class, second-tier media executives and managers.[4] This industry operates via three interrelated control processes generating the information, ideas, and images, and the economic, political, and social commentary that reinforce superclass interests. Considered in detail in chapter 5, these include (1) the mainstream ideology process, (2) the public opinion process, and (3) the spin-control process.

The structures and processes of both industries converge at the bottom of the triangle into superclass political dominance. As noted earlier, this term refers to the domination of superclass interests over class-relevant political and economic public policy outcomes as well as its potent influence in shaping cultural content. As we will see, public policy and cultural content outcomes reflect and reinforce superclass dominance by legitimating or disguising (or both) the nature, extent, and consequences of privileged-class power generally. In the political and economic arenas, superclass leaders, along with their credentialed-class allies, are viewed as directing and controlling most major class-relevant national public policy outcomes. Examples of superclass-dominated policy outcomes are considered later in this chapter—especially as the results of classwide lobbying. The concept of superclass political dominance also includes the idea that privileged-class leaders, especially through the information industry, influence the dissemination of news and commentary as well as the entertainment content of popular culture in ways that reinforce superclass interests. These topics are considered at length in chapters 5 and 7.

The triangle model develops selected features of the more general class-power-network model introduced in chapter 2. It does not attempt to address all dimensions or features of superclass power. Even so, it provides a powerful tool for conceptualizing the core of privileged-class economic, political, and cultural power in the United States. By locating superclass power and dominance in organizationally based resources, structures, and processes driven by class interests and unified by a class-based ideology, this concept avoids conspiracy-based theories as the basis for understanding superclass cohesion and power.

Superclass holders of wealth, power, and privilege, as well as their credentialed-class allies, have individual and collective interests in maintaining their advantaged positions. The triangle model (fig. 4.1) zeroes in on the two "industries" that support and sustain privileged-class-based advantages. It also calls attention to the reality that superclass leaders frequently know and interact with one another because they occupy interlocked top positions in large organizations, they control high levels of investment capital, and they participate in overlapping corporate, political, and social arenas. These circumstances, combined with high levels of social, consumption, and skill capital held by superclass members and their credentialed-class allies, serve as the foundation for a widely shared superclass worldview, or political-economy ideology. This idea system blends assumptions grounded in privileged-class interests concerning how the political and economic systems should be organized and function together. In general, it tends to view the economic and political status quo as reasonable, legitimate, and just.[5] The model views the common bonds of economic resources, interests, social identity, and ideology as foundations upon which superclass leaders create, maintain, and justify the linked structures and processes that drive the triangle.

Acting on the basis of a shared worldview and through routine organizational structures and processes, superclass leaders and their credentialed-class allies orchestrate political strategies and media policies aimed at preserving and extending their wealth, power, and privilege. The model views those at the top as holding a strong, shared sense that the "system" works and pursuing concerted, but nonconspiratorial, strategies and tactics that preserve it. Their mantra is, "Why change what works for us?"

THE SHADOW POLITICAL INDUSTRY

Politicians. We Love to hate them. And they make it so easy for us. But should they be the true objects of our scorn? . . . The real power, the men and women who really call the shots, are nowhere to be found on the ballot.

—Michael Moore, *DownSize This!* 1996

Although the shadow political industry is not a totally new development, in the new class society this flank of the triangle has expanded to unprecedented levels of size, complexity, and sophistication. Compared with the recent past, this industry has also become a much more widely shared, class-collaborative project linking superclass leaders with growing numbers of credentialed-class professionals who work—either directly or indirectly—on behalf of superclass interests. These political, legal, and policy-oriented professionals possess specialized legal, lobbying, research, and communication skills and political contacts that are critical to the maintenance of superclass interests and power.

Class collaboration in the shadow industry is particularly evident in the growing numbers of credentialed-class professionals—especially those located in the Washington, D.C., area—who work for superclass-controlled organizations concerned with political finance, policy, and lobbying. In 1997, more than 66,000 attorneys were members of the District of Columbia Bar (compared with 10,925 in 1972).[6] A 1996 study reported that 67,062 people worked in the Washington, D.C., lobbying community—which equals 125 lobbyists for each member of Congress (up from 31 in 1964).[7] This estimate is based solely on the number of lobbyists with offices physically located in Washington and does not include those based in nearby Maryland and Virginia. When these adjacent areas are included, the total Washington-area lobbying community is estimated at more than 100,000.[8]

Most Washington, D.C., members of the growing credentialed-class professional community—including attorneys and lobbyists—are employed (directly or indirectly) by large corporate clients or trade associations representing corporate interests, because these groups have the most money to spend.[9] This is especially evident when we consider that the one thousand largest industrial, financial, and service firms control 75 percent of the sales, assets, and profits in these areas.[10] The links tying D.C.-area credentialed-class professionals—and many others—to superclass-controlled corporate clients form a dense, reciprocal web, weaving together superclass corporate interests, credentialed-class professional skills, and political contacts. These links are cemented by steep-green contracts and salaries typically ranging from $100,000 to $250,000—and occasionally more.[11] Such bonding occurs in part because superclass-controlled organizations represent the main market for the high-paid, specialized legal, lobbying, research, and communication skills possessed by political, legal, and policy-oriented professionals. By their sheer size—corporate-based trade associations and other research and lobbying groups funded by the superclass make up 72 percent of the Washington lobby community[12]—these organizations are the major employers of high-paid professional talent.

The group that generally supervises and controls the shadow industry and drives the market for credentialed-class professionals' services consists of the top twenty-five thousand officers and directors located in the one thousand largest U.S. industrial, financial, and service firms.[13] These top corporate office holders form the privileged-class heart of the institutional power elite, and their firms represent the core of the superclass organizational power base. This group exercises control over enormous levels of investment capital and tends to intersect or overlap with the wealthiest 1 percent of all Americans.[14] The members of this group also either possess or are hardwired into the highest levels of social capital and command extremely high levels of consumption capital. Many members of this group—a third or more—occupy their positions because of inherited wealth from family fortunes.[15]

Some superclass leaders are "newly rich" as a result of entrepreneurial ventures (e.g., Bill Gates) or personal moves up major corporate hierarchies to elite positions—usually from upper-middle-class family origins.[16] This route typically involves assistance from superclass "sponsors." Such individuals act as gatekeepers in identifying and grooming a few rising executives and political operatives from nonelite backgrounds for membership in the power elite—typically, first as junior members and later as full partners. Nonelites who are sponsored in this fashion are usually selected and assisted on the basis of their acquisition of critical social capital (e.g., elite educational credentials) and demonstrated personal qualities such as talent, charm, allegiance to superclass ideology, and organizational effectiveness.[17]

Despite commanding huge resources, great power, and high status, the superclass is still a relatively small group. Its leadership base is too small to attend to the detailed activities necessary to translate general superclass policy preferences into specific public policy outcomes favoring its interests and perpetuating its political dominance. Superclass leaders need junior partners to help ensure that their interests are served and protected in the political and economic arenas. Thus, through their presence on policy-making boards of corporate, cultural, civic, and other organizations, the most organizationally active superclass leaders (the senior power elite) recruit, cultivate, utilize, and generously reward the expertise and assistance of a wide range of professionals who serve superclass interests in the shadow industry. These are the individuals who direct the industry's daily activities. They include high-profile political operatives like James Carville and the now-discredited Dick Morris, along with thousands of lesser-known professionals located in the various superclass-funded political finance, policy-planning, and lobbying organizations that are at the core of the shadow industry.

Largely faceless and unknown to the American public, the shadow industry's professional cadre, along with the staff members they supervise, have an increasingly routine presence in the political life of our society. Their careers are closely linked to the success of the superclass project of controlling U.S. politics and the state. They are the shock troops for and key political allies of the class empire, and they are active participants in the political finance, policy-planning, and classwide lobbying organizations that are central to superclass power and dominance in the United States.

POLITICAL FINANCE: IT'S MONEY THAT MATTERS

Politics [consists of] a series of unsentimental transactions between those who need votes and those who have money . . . a world where every *quid* has its *quo*.

—Don Tyson, CEO Tyson Foods, *National Review*, February 20, 1995

The story of superclass domination of politics and the state through the shadow industry begins with political finance: the relationship between politics and money. Money has always been an important factor in politics, but the increasing use of expensive, high-tech production, communication, and marketing technologies in political campaigns has shifted it to center stage. The effects of these changes on the costs of political campaigns have been dramatic. The expenses involved in winning a seat in the U.S. House of Representatives rose from $200,000 in 1974 to $500,000 in 1994 (in 1994 dollars).[18] In the Senate, the cost of mounting an average winning campaign increased 800 percent from 1976 to 1994,[19] but during that same period the cost of living increased by only 105 percent.[20] In 1996, the cash required to mount a winning political campaign complete with paid staff, computers, polling, consultants, phone banks, direct mailing, and media advertising topped out at $112 million for the presidency (not counting indirect party funding), $4.7 million for a Senate seat, and $673,000 for a House seat.[21] But these are not one-time costs. Each new campaign requires new money. To pay for the next campaign, representatives and senators need to raise $5,000 and $15,000, respectively, *every week* of their terms in office.[22] Being a serious candidate today requires serious money.

The nature of the American winner-take-all political system also helps to drive up the cost of campaigns. Politicians clearly understand the sentiment expressed in Vince Lombardi's well-known sports aphorism: "Winning isn't everything. It's the only thing." In American elections, second place means losing—which is possibly a political "ELE" (extinction-level event). Although large sums of money do not guarantee political victories, they come close. In the 1996 congressional elections, "the candidate who spent the most money won 92 percent of the House races and 88 percent of the Senate races."[23] Even in races where no incumbent was running in 1996, the top spenders won forty-three of the fifty-three open-seat House races and twelve of the fourteen open-seat Senate contests.[24] In a winner-take-all system, increasing the odds of winning requires mountains of money. In 1996 the mountain was $2.4 billion high—the estimated total amount candidates for federal office raised for political campaigns and conventions that year.[25]

So where does the cash come from? The answer is the same for both Democrats and Republicans: primarily from individuals (mostly wealthy) and from PACs (especially corporate and trade PACs). In the 1996 House campaigns, contributions of more than $200 from individuals and from business PACs made up 64 percent of Republican candidates' revenues and 45 percent of Democrats' revenues. In the 1996 Senate races, candidates from both parties raised a total of $167.5 million from individual contributors, with 65 percent of that amount coming from individuals donating more than $200.[26]

Both major political parties and most candidates they field today are primarily financed—in one form or another—by funds from the superclass. Large contributions by wealthy individuals and PACs (typically corporate PACs), often in amounts of $100,000 or more, are legally given to both major political parties in the form of "soft money." Only loosely regulated by federal law, soft money is used by state and national parties to finance party-building activities that assist individual candidates in many ways.[27] In the 1996 elections both major parties together raised a total of $262 million in soft money.[28]

Wealthy individuals and PACs also contribute "hard money" to parties (which is mostly passed along to individual candidates) and directly to candidates.[29] But contributions through these channels are somewhat constrained by federal law establishing maximum amounts of hard money that individuals and PACs may donate to parties and to candidates. "Individuals are allowed to give $20,000 and PACs $15,000 to political parties per calendar year (hence, double the limit per election cycle)."[30] Regarding direct contributions to candidates, individuals are not allowed to donate more than $1,000 per candidate per election and are limited to a $25,000 total for individual donations in a given two-year election cycle. But individuals may also contribute up to $5,000 per year to a PAC. PACs are allowed to contribute $5,000 per candidate per election, which means $5,000 each for the primary and general elections—or a total of $10,000 per candidate. But there are no limits on how many candidates PACs may support—and thus no limits on the amount of money PACs may contribute in any election.[31]

Despite these regulations, the amounts raised are staggering. In 1996, candidates for federal offices raised a total of $1.6 billion in hard-money contributions from large and small donors and from PACs.[32] Candidates from both major parties running for the House in 1996 received 65 percent of their hard-dollar campaign funds from individuals contributing more than $200 and from PACs. Of course, these are two groups that typically have vested interests in public policy decisions. By contrast, only 20 percent of hard-dollar contributions for House candidates came from small donors (i.e., contributors of less than $200).[33]

Individual Contributions: Top of the Class

Although PACs receive the most media attention, the primary sources of campaign funding for winning candidates in the 1996 House and Senate elections were individual contributions—most often in amounts of more than $200.[34] Contributions from individuals to congressional candidates totaled $444 million in 1996. Senate candidates received a total of $167.5 million from individuals, of which more than two-thirds was in amounts of $200 or more and more than one-third was from donations of $750 or more. House candidates received $276.5 million, of which $176 million was in amounts of more than $200.[35]

Individual contributions of more than $200 made up the single largest source of funding for candidates in the 1996 congressional races, averaging 36 percent of all contributions.[36] Sometimes the candidates and the wealthy contributors were the same people, because in several congressional races, wealthy candidates legally financed their own campaigns. In 1996, congressional candidates contributed or loaned $106.6 million to their campaigns (Senate, $57.6 million; House, $49.8 million),[37] with 149 giving themselves more than $100,000.[38] This practice is especially common among incumbent U.S. senators, who are among the wealthiest national office holders, with thirty of the one hundred members of the Senate reporting net assets of more than $1 million in 1995.[39]

Aside from personally wealthy politicians, who are the people making large political donations? The short answer is, a tiny minority of Americans—mainly privileged-class members, and especially those in the superclass. Few people make political contributions, and the ones who do, especially those who contribute more than $200, are almost entirely upper-income members of the privileged class. During the 1995–96 election cycle, 630,000 Americans (one-quarter of 1 percent of the U.S. population) gave direct contributions of $200 or more to federal candidates, totaling nearly $600 million. The contributions from this tiny group made up 45 percent of the $1.3 billion donated by all individuals to all candidates running for federal offices in 1996.[40] The pattern of wealthy contributors dominating campaign funding also extends to the state level. In 1994, 70 percent of campaign contributions to gubernatorial candidates came from donors who gave $500 or more. A 1992 Maine study estimated that only one-half of 1 percent of the state population gave $50 or more to a candidate for state office. This means that in a state with 1.2 million people, only 6,000 "pay to play."[41]

People with family incomes above $75,000 are more than one hundred times likely to contribute to candidates than those with family incomes below $15,000.[42] But even $75,000 incomes are far below the amounts earned by the 235,000 Americans who, in amounts of $1,000 or more, gave an estimated $477 million to candi-

dates and political parties in 1995–96. This group, representing one-tenth of 1 percent of the U.S. population, actually contributed a total of $638 million in political
donations in 1995–96—including their gifts to PACs and soft money accounts.[43]

Where do these wealthy contributors live? The short answer is, mainly large eastern cities. Wealthy residents (those contributing $200 or more) of New York City,
the Washington, D.C., metro area, and Boston combined for a total of $64.3 mil-
lion in campaign donations in 1995–96. The Hollywood glamour connection was
weaker than many people might imagine, with the wealthy of the Los Angeles-Long
Beach area contributing "only" $13.2 million in 1995–96—which was $1.4 million
less than the $14.6 million contributed by wealthy Chicagoans in the same year.[44]

A 1997 study of the four hundred top individual political contributors identified
a range that stretched from $661,000 (Bernard L. Schwartz, CEO of New York-
based Loral Space and Communications) to $77,300 (Michael A. Goldberg, CEO of
Aerolease International, a cargo-plane leasing company).[45] A 1996 study of the
same group found that half of the donors were either corporate heads or lawyers,
and many appeared on the *Forbes* magazine list of America's wealthiest individuals.
Their contributions were made to individual candidates, political parties, and PACs
that in turn give money to candidates that support their interests. Slightly more
than half (50.25 percent) gave to Democrats, slightly less than half (47.25 percent)
gave to Republicans, and a small minority (2.5 percent) gave to both. According to
the 1996 study, "the majority are bankers, lawyers, investors, or other businessmen
with a big financial stake in the outcome of [federal] legislation."[46] In short, the top
four hundred are superclass members, superclass wannabes, or credentialed-class
agents representing superclass clients. In each case the strategy is the same: the top
four hundred invest in politics to protect privileged-class interests.

Corporate PACs: Another Class Act

In the 1996 congressional races, PACs donated $106.7 million to Republicans and
$93.9 million to Democrats, which made PACs the second largest source of can-
didate funding, averaging 25 percent of all contributions.[47] But this second-place
pattern varied depending on the office and the candidate. In 1996, PAC contributions accounted for 16 percent of the receipts for Senate candidates and 31 percent for House candidates.[48] However, for winning candidates, PAC donations
represented 22 percent of Senators' receipts ($1.1 million on average) and 40 per-
cent of Representatives' receipts ($288,000 on average).[49]

Corporate PACs combined with corporate-dominated trade and membership
associations and health PACs are of special importance to reinforcing superclass
political dominance for three reasons. First, these PACs collect, control, and disburse a majority of all PAC money. Second, they are almost exclusively organized
and administered by committees of upper-level corporate managers from large
corporations who share a common business-based worldview that reflects superclass interests. Third, corporate PACs consistently reflect classwide business unity

Copyright © Tom Tomorrow. Reprinted with permission.

growing out of shared interests and the effects of federal limits on PAC donations. These factors lead to contribution patterns whereby most corporate PAC contributions flow to politicians who endorse policies that protect and extend the wealth and power of large corporations and the superclass elites who control them.

In the 1995–96 election cycle a total of 4,528 PACs disbursed $429 million, but the 1,836 corporate PACs plus the 896 trade and membership associations and health PACs (most with close corporate links) accounted for $235.9 million—

55 percent of that total.[50] Despite the huge sums they control today, corporate PACs as campaign-funding vehicles are relatively new. Following the Watergate-related revelations of secret corporate political donations to the Nixon campaign, it first appeared that corporate campaign contributions would be severely limited. However, in 1975 the Federal Election Commission (FEC, established by federal law in 1971) ruled, by a vote of four to three, that the Sun Oil Corporation PAC could solicit funds from both stockholders and employees. After the so-called SUN-PAC decision, the number of corporate PACs increased from 89 in 1974 to 433 in 1976 and has continued to increase since then.[51]

The political power of the 2,732 corporate and corporate-dominated PACs (in 1996)[52] rests in the hands of corporate PAC committees that are almost exclusively composed of privileged-class corporate managers and officers. These committees bring together superclass members and upwardly mobile credentialed-class corporate professionals. The two groups are closely linked through their shared involvement with and concern for shaping corporate policies that favor superclass and corporate interests and through a shared political worldview. The political unity, consensus, and cohesion typically found among corporate PAC managers are based on "a set of underlying material relations—loans from the same banks, sales and purchases from each other, interlocking boards of directors, common interests in accumulating capital and avoiding government regulations that might restrict their power."[53] These material and social relations reinforce PAC managers' interpretations of, and decisions and actions on, both politics and business—in favor of superclass interests. Thus, the millions of dollars that corporate PACs raise, control, and disburse tend to be directed by PAC committees to those candidates most favorable to shared, superclass-based business interests.

Although corporate PAC contributions are sometimes disbursed in ways that appear to reflect efforts by competing firms or economic sectors to promote their narrow interests at the expense of other firms or sectors, such patterns are not the norm. More often, corporate PAC contributions tend to be mutually supportive. Convergent patterns of corporate PAC giving indicate classwide business unity on a wide range of regulatory and labor policy issues—rather than hard-ball competition. Superclass unity is especially evident in cases of policies affecting corporate control over labor markets—including issues such as working conditions and unionization campaigns.[54]

Corporate PAC contribution patterns of classwide unity also reflect the influence of federal law limiting PAC donations to $5,000 per candidate per election. Under this rule, superclass leaders recognize that only by acting together can the corporate community have a major impact on the political process in ways that protect and serve their common class interests. The $5,000 PAC limit means that individual competing PACs would have very limited power because several small, cross-purpose PAC contributions would cancel out one another's influence. By contrast, a classwide strategy of mutually supportive, convergent patterns of campaign funding magnifies corporate PAC power over the political process. This strategy serves the interests of the superclass power elite who occupy and control the top positions in corporate America. Thus, the legal incentives for PAC collaboration combined with corporate PAC officers' experiences with their peers results in a shared network of contacts, information, and reciprocal patterns of gift giving to those candidates most supportive of shared superclass and corporate interests.[55]

Studies of corporate PAC contributions consistently document the pattern of classwide business unity rather than competition or conflict in the political arena as the dominant reality. Although a few examples of competing business PACs can be found, "opposed to this [behavior] are literally dozens of examples of companies that 'hate each other,' are 'suing each other all of the time,' and are each other's major competitors but that nonetheless work well together in Washington. They cooperate in promoting the same policies, sponsoring joint fundraisers [for candidates], and in general behaving as a unified bloc." One study of corporate PAC donations found business to be unified in three out of four political races, giving, on average, nine times more money to one candidate than to the other. Moreover, "PAC officers may disagree with their counterparts at other corporations, but the unstated rules forbid public disputes, and only reluctantly will one business directly oppose another."[56] The superclass leadership of the corporate community recognizes that only by acting together can business PACs use their combined resources to exert substantial, sustained power over the campaign-funding dimension of the political process.

Connecting the Dots

Of course, corporate PACs are not the only players in the campaign funding game, but compared with their most obvious competitors such as organized labor and public citizen groups, they are by far the largest and best-funded groups. The centrality of corporate PACs to funding the political process, the superclass bias of PACs, and corporate PAC links to both major parties are key features of the political finance process. Consider the following "dots":

- Corporate PACs, 1,836; labor PACs, 358. In 1996, corporate PACs outnumbered labor PACs by six to one.[57]
- Business PACs, 11; labor PACs, 1. Combining PAC and large individual contributions for the 1995–96 elections, business contributed eleven times more than labor.[58]
- Representation of the privileged-class, 100 percent; representation of non-privileged class, 0 percent. Of the eleven hundred PACs that gave $20,000 or more to congressional candidates during the 1994 elections, none represented poor people, unemployed workers, toxics victims, or small banking depositors and borrowers.[59]
- PAC contributions to Democrats, $65 million; PAC contributions to Republicans, $62 million. In the 1994 congressional elections, Democratic candidates actually received more business PAC money than Republicans.[60]

If we connect the corporate PAC and superclass-funding "dots," we begin to see a pattern. Superclass-driven campaign funding represents more than just the pooled resources of another interest group. Corporate PAC dollars combine with wealthy donor contributions to create a powerful political force field dominating both major political parties and the entire political process. Although the Republican Party has long been perceived as the party of superclass and business interests in American politics, these same groups also have a long record of channeling substantial funds to the Democratic Party and Democratic candidates.

Since 1980, superclass support for the Democratic Party and Democratic candidates generally—especially for national offices—has increased dramatically. This conclusion is supported by FEC records showing that more than 70 percent of the contributions to the Democratic and Republican Parties come from corporations. From 1991 through 1994, the Republican Party raised $95 million in soft money, with more than 90 percent of the large donations, more than $20,000 each, coming from business interests including corporations, executives, trade associations, and lobbying firms. During the same period, the Democratic Party raised $75 million in soft money, with more than 70 percent coming from corporate donors.[61] The period since 1980 has witnessed continued superclass dominance of the Republican Party combined with a virtually complete takeover of the Democratic Party as well. One researcher summarized the effects of the increasing penetration of the Democratic Party by the class empire through superclass funding in these terms: "Fifteen years ago when the Democrats became more adept in attracting corporate money, a *Wall Street Journal* article stated that 'Business already owns one party and now has a lease, with an option to buy, on the other.' The disregard for labor by centrist Democrats has less to do with ideology, analysis, or changing demographics. It's simply a reflection of Democrat dependence on corporate money."[62]

The combination of wealthy contributors and corporate PAC money tilts the political playing field into a perpendicular configuration with the high end only accessible to elite players with steep-green chips. Preliminary information on the 1998 congressional elections indicates a continuation of this pattern. Candidates for 1998 U.S. House and Senate seats raised $232.9 million and spent $112.1 million during 1997. With receipts up by $48 million compared with the same period in the 1996 election cycle (an increase of more than 26 percent), these amounts broke all previous FEC records as the 1,037 congressional candidates entered the 1998 election year with a total of $207.1 million cash on hand. Federal Election Commission records indicate wealthy individuals and PACs retained their respective first- and second-place locations as the primary sources of campaign cash for 1998—as in the recent past.[63]

As we have shown, the political campaign dimension of the class empire rests on a dense web of financial connections whereby funds donated and controlled by the superclass become the dominant financial resource that underwrites the political process—for both major political parties. The evidence supporting our contention that the magic mountain of superclass-controlled, politically targeted cash affords this class an iron grip over U.S. politics is more than circumstantial. "Judge for yourself. The evidence . . . [is] enough to convict our political system of serving the interests of the wealthy. Whether the subject is health care reform, environmental regulation, farm subsidies, weapons production, or trade policy, it is difficult to even get a hearing in Washington without spreading around a lot of dough."[64]

POLICY PLANNING: THE BIG PICTURE

> The policy-planning network is . . . the programmatic political party for the upper class and the corporate community.
>
> —G. William Domhoff, *State Autonomy or Class Dominance?*, 1996

Is big government the source of our most pressing national problems today? Are vampire-like "greedy geezers" sucking the financial lifeblood of the younger generation—pushing Social Security and Medicare toward bankruptcy? Do we need to slash and burn the funding of social programs to ease the national deficit? Are welfare, drugs, and crime eroding America's moral fabric? The short answer to these questions is yes—at least according to many of the organizations that are part of the superclass-funded national policy-planning network.[65]

The Policy-Planning Network

The policy-planning network consists of several superclass-dominated organizations, including think tanks, research institutes, policy discussion groups, and foundations.[66] Grounded in superclass resources and institutions, this network is dedicated to setting the national policy agenda, establishing policy priorities, and shaping public policy outcomes. It is based on a superclass worldview—shared by credentialed-class professionals who implement routine network functions—that sees the existing economic and political reward, opportunity, and power structures as the most legitimate and the preferred national organizational arrangement (especially compared with more egalitarian alternatives).[67] The network functions through a variety of organizations and processes that collectively promote superclass interests by sustaining the economic and political status quo—or slight variations thereof.

The links between this network and superclass political dominance are tied to the reality that "policy planning in the United States takes place largely outside of government, in private policy-planning organizations funded by private corporations and foundations."[68] This means that the organizations in the superclass-funded policy-planning network generate most of the research, ideas, and policy discussions that dominate and shape the national policy agenda, priorities, debates, and most legislative or regulatory "solutions." The multifaceted input from this network to the national government is clearly tilted in favor of policies that support and extend existing class-based wealth, income, and power inequalities and thereby reinforce superclass economic and political interests. Although it may be argued that divisions exist within the superclass on some policies and issues, there is also a clear consensus in favor of policies that support "economic growth, a stable business cycle, incentives for investment, economy and efficiency in government, a stable two-party system, and maintaining popular support for political institutions."[69]

Network Members: Naming Names

Think tanks and research institutes are typically nonprofit organizations that provide settings where experts from academic disciplines and former public office holders discuss a wide range of contemporary social problems and consider alternative policies for dealing with them.[70] Although the classification of specific organizations as think tanks or research institutes is contested terrain in the social sciences, researchers generally agree that the policy-planning network core consists of a very short list of five superclass-connected and politically influential "centrist" organizations. The Business Roundtable, the Brookings Institution, and the RAND Corporation are key players in the formation of U.S. domestic policies, and the Council on Foreign Relations (CFR) and the Trilateral Commission play similar, central roles in the establishment of American foreign policies.[71] In addition to the five core players, five other major centrist groups also play important roles in the policy-planning network: the Business Council, the U.S. Chambers of Commerce, the Committee for Economic Development (CED), the Conference Board, and the National Association of Manufacturers (NAM).[72]

Parallel with the major centrist organizations is an increasingly influential cluster of conservative think tanks. The ten most prominent organizations in this group include the Hoover Institution, American Enterprise Institute, Heritage Foundation, Center for Strategic and International Studies, Institute for Contemporary Studies, Institute for Foreign Policy Analysis, National Strategy Information Center, Manhattan Institute, Institute for Research on the Economics of Taxation, and the Pacific Research Institute.[73] Over the past twenty-five years these organizations have emerged as important contributors to the policy formation process as the political climate has shifted to the right. "In the mid- to late 1970s, business began its own [political] counter-mobilization. . . . Money was shifted out of liberal and moderate think tanks and policy organizations (the Brookings Institution, Council on Foreign Relations, and Committee for Economic Development) to newly founded or reinvigorated conservative equivalents (the American Enterprise Institute, Hoover Institution, and Heritage Foundation) . . . [By] 1980 the conservative organizations spent substantially more than the moderate ones."[74]

Policy-discussion groups are often affiliated with think tanks and research institutes, but these groups have somewhat different goals and function in ways that are distinct from think tanks. They serve as important meeting grounds where super-class corporate elites and their professional allies from various venues come to-gether. The purpose of these informal weekly or monthly meetings is partly to share ideas but also to allow superclass leaders opportunities to identify, recruit, and groom talented individuals from the professional ranks for top leadership positions within government and other key organizations in the policy-planning network. The meetings also help to legitimate the organizations and their activities by por-traying both in altruistic terms and by emphasizing the nonprofit, "independent" status of the organizations.[75] The key organizations that serve as policy-discussion groups (or facilitate such activities) often overlap with think-tank organizations and include the NAM, the U.S. Chambers of Commerce, the Conference Board, the CFR, the CED, the American Assembly, and the Brookings Institution.[76]

Foundations and Board Interlocks

As we saw earlier, campaign funding is a central feature of superclass influence over the political process. The same basic principle also applies to policy planning, but instead of wealthy individual donors and corporate PACs, superclass-dominated foundations serve as the major financial engines providing much of the funding for the policy-planning network.[77] These tax-exempt, nonprofit organizations are often the creations of corporate entrepreneurs and wealthy families who founded them in part to reduce their own taxes and to use them as vehicles for encourag-ing policies favorable to their class interests.[78]

The resources controlled by foundations are staggering. The 1998 *Foundation Directory* lists 8,642 foundations with assets of at least $2 million or that gave at least $200,000 in annual distributions. This group's combined assets totaled over $247 billion, which represented 88.8 percent of all foundation assets. Just the one hundred largest foundations (by assets) held more than $124 billion in assets, ac-counting for more than 45 percent of all foundation assets. This elite group in-cludes many well-known corporate names with asset levels placing them in the top ranks of the top one hundred, including Ford (no. 1, $8.1 billion), Kellogg (no. 2, $7.5 billion), Lilly (no. 5, $6.8 billion), and Kresge (no. 13, $1.8 billion).[79]

Foundations are managed by boards of directors or trustees composed primarily of members from the superclass and closely allied members of the credentialed class. One study of the top foundations found that 50 percent of the directors and trustees were members of upper-class social clubs.[80] The top fifty foundation boards include a total of 402 director positions that are filled mainly by men (85 percent) who attended Ivy League or other prestigious universities.[81] Moreover, many Rockefellers, Mellons, Lillys, Danforths, and members of other wealthy fam-ilies (such as the Waltons of Wal-Mart fame) sit on the boards of directors of their family foundations and also often serve on corporate boards of several other firms.[82] For example, recent Rockefeller foundation trustees have included John D. Rockefeller III; Richard H. Jenrette, chairman of Equitable Life Insurance; Arthur

Levitt, chairman of the American Stock Exchange; Frank G. Wells, former CEO of Walt Disney; and Harold Brown, a director of AMAX, CBS, and IBM and former U.S. secretary of defense.[83]

Foundation budgets come mainly from dividends received through their ownership of large blocks of corporate stock. These organizations spend their annual budgets on a variety of activities, but support of policy-planning network organizations is a consistent funding priority. For example, the Brookings Institution, a mainstream, centrist think tank with a staff of 250 and an annual budget of $20 million,[84] received a total of $5,661,475 in foundation grants during 1993–94.[85] Over the years Brookings has also benefited from both foundation and corporate funding, attracting, for example, 24 foundation and 150 corporate "sponsors" during the mid-1980s.[86]

Top foundations have historically provided substantial support to a variety of large, mainstream, politically centrist policy-planning organizations like the Brookings Institution. The Ford Foundation, for example, has been one of its most important financial supporters.[87] Another example of a mainstream policy-planning group benefiting from financial support by top foundations is the Council on Foreign Relations. Over the years it has received substantial funding from the Ford, Lilly, Mellon, and Rockefeller foundations.[88] More recently, smaller, conservative policy-planning think tanks have also benefited from foundation support. For example, between 1977 and 1986, twelve foundations (including Pew Memorial, Adolph Coors, Lilly, and nine other smaller foundations) provided more than $63 million of the $88 million in grant funds received by the ten conservative policy-planning think tanks noted earlier.[89]

In recent years less well known conservative foundations have increased their involvement in funding conservative think tanks, university programs, media groups, and other organizations linked to the policy-planning network. Their goal is to promote a more conservative policy agenda extolling the virtues of the "free market" and the dangers of government regulations.

A recent study by the National Committee on Responsive Philanthropy found that from 1992 to 1994, twelve "core" conservative foundations (Lynde and Harry Bradley, Smith Richardson, Sarah Scaife, Carthage, Philip McKenna, John M. Olin, Henry Salvatori, Charles G. Koch, David H. Koch, Claude R. Lambe, Earhart, and J. M. [Milbank]) donated $210 million to promote conservative activities. More than $80 million went to conservative think tanks and other organizations that explicitly advocated unregulated "free markets," such as the Heritage Foundation ($8.9 million), the American Enterprise Institute ($6.9 million), the Cato Institute ($3.9 million), the Hudson Institution ($3.3 million), and the Manhattan Institute ($2.1 million). Large portions of the remaining $130 million went to academic centers, legal groups, and media outlets that promote the "free market" cause. Examples include support for conservative scholarships, endowed chairs, and "research" centers, such as the $3 million donated to the Institute for Humane Studies and $2.1 million for the Center for the Study of Marketing Processes. Both promote "free market" principles and are located at George Mason University in Fairfax, Virginia.[90]

In addition to foundation funding, superclass members also influence policy planning by serving as directors on think tank boards. Mainstream policy-planning organizations' boards of directors are especially likely to reflect close ties with the superclass. For example, all the 220 members of the Business Roundtable are CEOs of some of the largest banks and industrial firms in the United States, including Citicorp, General Motors, and Exxon.[91] The trustees of the Brookings Institution and the CFR average four corporate directorships each, and only 6 percent of the trustees for these two organizations were not members of corporate boards. Moreover, more than two-thirds of the directors of the CFR, the Business Roundtable, and the Brookings Institution graduated from just twelve prestigious universities.[92]

CLASSWIDE LOBBYING: INVESTING IN PRIVILEGE

> On Capitol Hill, it is the lobbyists who have the clout. They speak for the vested interests.... And they have been extraordinarily successful in blocking ... law[s] that would be detrimental to the privileged as well as in preserving [laws] that benefit the few at the expense of the many.
>
> —Donald L. Barlett and James B. Steele, *America: What Went Wrong*, 1992

In American politics, lobbying has two faces: special-interest competition and classwide practices. The former is familiar and widely reported, but the latter, consistent with the class taboo, is seldom the topic of media attention or public discussion. Lobbying's special-interest face has been the subject of increased media attention following the passage of the Lobbying Disclosure Act of 1995, which took effect January 1, 1996.[93] A joint Associated Press (AP) and Center for Responsive Politics analysis of disclosures required by the law found that in 1997, corporations, trade groups, unions, and other special-interest lobbying groups spent $1.17 billion trying to influence the federal government—up from about $800 million spent in a comparable period in 1996.[94] The 1997 figure means that publicly disclosed lobby expenditures—through registered agents at the national level—now average about $100 million per month.[95] But even this staggering sum is only part of the lobby story. A 1996 study of all forms of lobbying estimated that "$8.4 billion is spent each year in Washington to lobby the federal government."[96]

The AP/Center for Responsive Politics study, as well as most media reports on lobbying, typically emphasize that although lobbying is a big business, it is also a highly competitive enterprise involving intense rivalries among powerful forces and organizations contending with one another to promote their own narrow agendas and interests. The joint study's analysis illustrates this focus. It identifies the American Medical Association (AMA) and Philip Morris as among the top-spending lobbyists in the first half of 1997, reporting expenditures of $8.5 and $5.9

million, respectively.[97] In a related mainstream newspaper report, Philip Morris is identified as a firm that "wants to limit its legal liability on cigarettes," and the AMA is said to be interested in health care issues such as "urging caution on reform of the Food and Drug Administration."[98] It is easy to infer from the context of the report that Philip Morris is lobbying to *prevent* tighter controls on tobacco products, and the AMA is working, in part, to *promote* the strength of a federal agency (the FDA) that is likely to play a major role if tobacco is regulated as a drug.

Mainstream media accounts of lobbying tend to leave readers and viewers with the impression that although lobbying is not necessarily fair to poorly funded groups, the high-stakes, special-interest competition among "heavy hitters" leads to a rough balance of power. In fact, such stories often imply that competition among the "big boys" combined with the spotlight of media attention act as a kind of checks-and-balances system limiting the most egregious excesses of undue government influence among well-heeled lobby groups. Although we would agree that special-interest competitive lobbying is an important feature of our political system, we contend it is of secondary importance compared with the political-influence dealing and policy-shaping power of lobbying's other face.

Classwide lobbying is very different from the competitive, special-interest face of political lobbying most often presented in the media. It is supported by a wide array of superclass-dominated organizations acting in concert to promote legislative and regulatory policies supportive of superclass interests. The next four sections describe and illustrate classwide lobbying. First, we provide a brief overview of the classwide lobbying community. Second, we illustrate how classwide coalitions have produced policy outcomes favoring superclass interests in the areas of worker health and safety, free trade, and health care "reform." Third, we examine recent policy contests concerning NAFTA expansion and labor funding of political campaigns that illustrate that classwide political domination does not equal total control of policy making. Finally, we summarize how superclass-crafted national taxation and spending policies benefit this class—and the credentialed class—at the expense of the working class.

We could have chosen many examples to illustrate the nature, extent, and consequences of classwide lobbying, but we believe our choices exemplify how superclass unity and political dominance are reflected in classwide lobbying campaigns and policies. The examples illustrate that classwide campaigns organized and funded by the superclass typically dominate public policy making and produce policy outcomes that serve the economic and political interests of this class (at the expense of the working class). Even so, groups within the alternative power networks do challenge and contest superclass dominance—and sometimes they win.

The Classwide Lobby Community

The classwide lobby community comprises a core of peak business groups, which are mainly nonprofit trade associations consisting of several individual corporate members with shared views and policy objectives. Depending on the issues, peak groups can and do participate in both classwide and special-interest lobbying, and some also serve as members of the policy-planning network. Peak groups tend to be organized around groups of top corporate leaders from large firms (e.g., CEOs) and specific industries (e.g., oil, electronics) as well as general, shared business interests (e.g., commerce and trade). Historically, peak groups have formed the organizational core of classwide lobbying efforts. On a number of issues that have reached congressional legislative or regulatory reform policy contests, a small number of peak groups has consistently been at the center of lobbying activities representing the interests of the business community as a whole as well as the class interests of wealthy elites.

Among the most influential classwide lobbying groups are the CEO-dominated organizations, including the Business Roundtable, the Committee for Economic Development, and the Conference Board.[99] Specific, industrywide peak groups that frequently play leadership roles in promoting, coordinating, and supporting classwide lobbying campaigns include the National Association of Manufacturers (NAM), the Chemical Manufacturers' Association, the American Petroleum Institute, the American Mining Congress, the Health Insurance Association of America (HIAA), the Pharmaceutical Manufacturers' Association (PMA), and many others. More general shared business interests are represented by peak groups such as the U.S. Chambers of Commerce and, for smaller firms, the National Federation of Independent Business (NFIB).

Classwide Coalitions and Policy Outcomes

Industrywide and CEO-headed peak groups have historically taken the lead in creating ad hoc coalitions to promote classwide business unity and to spearhead lobbying campaigns aimed at influencing legislative outcomes on policies where superclass and corporate interests are at stake. In the mid-1980s, the NAM created and led the Coalition on Occupational Disease Notification that helped defeat the labor-supported High-Risk Occupational Disease Notification Act.[100] In 1993, the Business Roundtable organized the USA*NAFTA business coalition that helped secure passage of the North American Free Trade Agreement.[101] The Business Roundtable also led the fight against health care reform in 1993–94 with help from the insurance industry, including the Alliance for Managed Competition (created by the "Big Five": Aetna, Prudential, Travelers, CIGNA, Metropolitan Life, and the HIAA).[102]

Classwide lobbying campaigns draw upon resources provided by a variety of corporate-oriented, law, lobbying, and public relations firms. In the political battle over NAFTA, for example, the USA*NAFTA coalition hired the Wexler Group, a Washington lobbying firm headed by Anne Wexler—a former Carter White House aide with strong ties to the Clinton administration—to promote the bill.[103] USA*NAFTA, with donations from firms such as Exxon, DuPont, General Electric, and Dow Chemical, spent more than $4 million to promote NAFTA's passage, with money flowing to lobbyists as well as to public relations firms that crafted numerous pro-NAFTA ads that ran in newspapers, magazines, and on television.[104]

The utilization of lobbying and public relations firms was also evident in the classwide lobbying campaign against health care reform. For example, the HIAA paid $1 million to a Des Moines-based public relations firm, CMF&Z PR, to help create a "grassroots" Coalition for Health Insurance Choices and also spent $7 million on the "Harry and Louise" TV campaign—both efforts aimed at killing health care reform.[105]

In addition to utilizing high-dollar, professional "hired guns" in the legal, lobbying, and public relations communities, classwide lobbying campaigns also rely on the resources of corporate-dominated professional associations. Many of these organizations can be counted on as dependable "class allies" and lend their "scientific expertise" in support of classwide lobbying efforts. For example, the American Industrial Hygiene Association and the American Occupational Medical Association worked on behalf of corporate interests in the classwide campaign to defeat the High-Risk legislation in the mid-1980s.[106] Professional groups are valuable allies because they lend legitimacy to classwide lobby efforts. They provide a patina of scientific respectability to what might otherwise appear to be purely superclass, "wealth- and privilege-protection" lobbying campaigns. Together with law and public relations firms, the expertise of professional associations helps to maximize the effectiveness of superclass-driven policy-intervention lobbying campaigns.

Challenging Classwide Lobbying and Superclass Dominance

In the late 1990s, two classwide lobbying campaigns organized and funded by superclass sponsorship were defeated by labor-led alternative power network coalitions. The first issue involved superclass efforts to win fast-track status for a trade agreement to expand NAFTA to Chile, Brazil, and other Central and South American nations. "Fast track" is a legislative device that increases the U.S. president's power to negotiate terms of foreign trade pacts and then allows him to submit such agreements to Congress for up or down votes—no amendments allowed. The second issue involved superclass support for federal and state legislation that would have required labor unions to "obtain written permission from union members every year before spending money on politics."[107] This effort was part of a superclass backlash in response to the relative success of the AFL-CIO's Labor '96 campaign, which supported prolabor candidates through a $35 million union-provided election fund.[108]

In August 1997, President Clinton used his national radio address to press the case for fast track. At about the same time, the Business Roundtable sent a letter to hundreds of corporate heads asking for donations to support "a multi-pronged fast-track lobbying campaign."[109] The letter said, "We believe we need to raise a minimum of $3 million in order to insure that the voice of the business community is heard." It was signed by the CEOs from Boeing, Caterpillar, Chrysler, TRW, General Motors, and Procter and Gamble—and each of these firms had already agreed to donate $100,000 to the cause.

The letter also outlined a strategy involving a "grassroots campaign" that included "aggressive use of [a] 1-800 number to generate congressional communications from company employees, suppliers, and constituents." And it promised the "distribution of fast-track lobbying kits to companies for congressional visits." These efforts would be supported by a "Washington campaign relying on use of corporate offices of Roundtable companies and CEO communication with legislators."[110] Despite this well-funded superclass effort, the fast-track campaign failed to win public support and failed in Congress. The labor-led, anti-fast-track coalition won the public opinion battle as polls showed 56 percent of Americans opposed the fast-track effort.[111] In October 1997 the legislation barely passed the Republican-controlled House Ways and Means Committee—but only four of sixteen Democrats on the committee supported it.[112] On November 10, 1997, President Clinton and Republican congressional leaders withdrew the bill after it failed "to get the votes needed to pass it."[113]

In 1998 a major classwide superclass-funded lobbying campaign was aimed at members of Congress as well as state voters (especially in California) as part of an effort to reduce union funding of prolabor political candidates and policies. In Congress, Republicans introduced the deceptively titled Worker Paycheck Protection Act, and in California (and in other states) superclass-funded organizations placed propositions on ballots for statewide votes.[114] In both cases the goal was the same: to pass federal and state legislation that would force unions to "obtain advance, written, annual permission from members to use dues money for 'political purposes.' "[115]

Superclass supporters of these efforts included the "usual suspects" and raised a huge war chest estimated at $149 million.[116] The Business Roundtable raised $20 million to support federal and state efforts to legislate "paycheck protection" laws. This amount was augmented by an $18.75 million pledge from the NAM to support the legislative campaigns and also by the support of the U.S. Chambers of Commerce, whose president, Thomas Donahue, promised, "You're going to see us everywhere."[117] These core groups' efforts were reinforced by Americans for Tax Reform (who contributed $10 million and field coordination responsibility), the National Right to Work Committee ($10.5 million), and the American Legislative Exchange Council (which provided model legislation).[118]

The federal "paycheck protection" legislation was stopped by a filibuster led by prolabor senators in early 1998, which also had the effect of shifting the battle to California.[119] There, the AFL-CIO and California-based unions mounted a major campaign to defeat Proposition 226 (the title of the proposed law on the June 2, 1998, California ballot). Through the efforts of three hundred union field organizers, thousands of volunteers, and a budget of some $20 million, Prop 226 was defeated by a 53- to 47-percent margin. As a result, "plans by conservatives to take a similar measure to dozens of other states evaporated."[120]

These two campaigns illustrate that superclass political dominance does not equal absolute control over all class-relevant policy contests. Even so, these were not stake-through-the-heart losses for the superclass. Despite setbacks in these two battles, the superclass war against workers continues on the issues of free trade and the political balance of class power. The historical record reveals that when superclass economic and political interests are at stake, the organizations representing this class are persistent, resourceful, and often victorious—even after sustaining initial defeats.[121]

One recent example of superclass policy resilience occurred in 1994, when a Republican-led Senate filibuster killed a bill that would have stopped employers from hiring permanent replacement workers to take the jobs of striking employees (a practice legalized by a 1938 Supreme Court decision).[122] Although a similar bill had passed the House in June 1993, a concerted classwide, corporate-funded campaign against the legislation led to its eventual demise in the Senate.[123] Thus, initial superclass policy "losses" do not necessarily equal defeat—especially where classwide superclass and corporate interests are at stake. The fast-track and paycheck protection battles may well represent only temporary setbacks for superclass interests. The policy-making process is still in motion on these issues, and the jury of history is still out.

Classwide Lobbying: Federal Taxation and Spending Policies

The jury is not out on the issue of superclass dominance over federal tax and spending policies. However, these are two areas where classwide and special-interest lobbying sometimes intersect and overlap—thereby at times obscuring classwide campaigns and superclass dominance. Journalists often focus on special-interest lobbying and point out that the political contributions of individual firms or industry PACs often appear to lead to specialized tax breaks or federal subsidies for specific firms or industries. Although such policy outcomes are often both obvious and outrageous, they are actually of secondary importance to classwide lobbying. The cumulative effects of classwide campaigns dating from the 1960s aimed at shaping federal (as well as state and local) tax and spending policies to further advantage privileged-class interests are evident in current federal, state, and local laws. Classwide tax campaigns in 1985–86 and 1996–97 provide two examples of efforts that produced major changes in tax rates benefiting the wealthy and corporations.

Classwide Campaigns and Tax Reform: 1986

The list of companies and trade associations that lobbied Congress as key committees considered and crafted the Tax Reform Act of 1986 and the 1997 Budget Reconciliation Act includes the "usual suspects" involved in classwide lobbying campaigns—plus a few new groups. The record of the 1985 House tax reform hearings fills nine volumes and more than nine thousand pages, and the vast majority of the nearly one thousand witnesses who appeared represented corporate interests. Although many corporate representatives were seeking specialized benefits for individual firms or industries, some of the most potent corporate players advocated preserving and extending corporate tax breaks that would promote the classwide advantages and interests of wealthy corporate owners and officers. This message was evident in testimony from witnesses representing the Business Roundtable, the NAM, the U.S. Chambers of Commerce, the NFIB, and many others.[124]

Even coalitions that appeared to represent specialized corporate interests secured results that on closer inspection had classwide implications. The 1985 coalition known as the Alliance for Capital Access, formed with contributions from 120 financial companies, illustrates this point. The alliance, with close connections to Michael Milken (the "junk-bond king" of the 1980s) and Carl Lindner (CEO of Chiquita Brands International), spent $4.9 million from 1985 through 1990 to help preserve the tax deduction for interest paid on corporate debt—an effort in which they succeeded. The Tax Reform Act of 1986 left the deduction intact.[125] This provision benefited not only the "junk-bond" industry but the entire corporate community as well, and since the bill's passage corporations have increasingly turned to debt rather than issuing more stock as a preferred means of financing corporate operations and expansion.

House hearings held in 1990 on the impact, effectiveness, and fairness of the Tax Reform Act of 1986 generated seventy-six statements for the record. Of this number, forty-nine came from corporations or trade associations, with most praising various features of the 1986 act. Many of these statements were submitted by the same classwide organizational advocates that had supported the legislation in 1985. The few critics submitting statements in 1990, such as the AFL-CIO and the American Federation of State, County, and Municipal Employees (AFSCME), pointed to problems that the 1986 tax law had created as a result of reducing tax rates for corporations and very wealthy individuals. The critical testimony of these witnesses called attention to the classwide benefits and costs embedded in the 1986 act—extensive financial benefits for superclass and many credentialed-class members—and to the substantial costs that were passed along to the entire working class.[126]

Classwide Campaigns and Tax Reform: 1997

In the spring of 1997 the "same old gang" came forward to lobby for further reductions in corporate taxes, federal capital gains taxes, and federal inheritance taxes. In the context of an expanding economy, political pressures to balance the budget, Republican control of the Congress, and a compliant president, the issue was not whether taxes would be cut—that was a foregone conclusion. The real issues involved which taxes would be cut and how the cuts would be distributed.

During the 1997 budget negotiations, Deputy Treasury Secretary Lawrence H. Summers remarked that "the interests pushing for a cut in estate taxes were motivated by 'selfishness.' " He emphasized that "the overall tax package has to have as its thrust helping middle-class America."[127] Summers was immediately attacked by congressional Republican leaders and by a variety of conservative groups and pundits for "promoting class warfare" and favoring "socialism." Two days after his remarks, he was "forced to issue a public apology."[128] Summers had violated an important dimension of the class taboo: "[He] acknowledged that all tax cuts do not benefit all Americans equally and that class is very much the defining issue."[129]

The tax cuts mandated by the Budget Reconciliation Act of 1997 primarily benefited privileged-class members and their wealth-producing machines called corporations. As the details of the tax bill were being crafted, members of Congress again—as in 1986—listened closely to lobbyists from the NAM, the U.S. Chambers of Commerce, and the NFIB, who coordinated their efforts to win business tax cuts—ostensibly to improve fairness, investment, and productivity (and not just to juice profits).[130] This corporate-focused lobbying effort to reduce taxes was reinforced by classwide coalitions seeking cuts in the capital gains and estate taxes. In all three instances the lobbying campaigns were aimed at tax cuts that would primarily produce classwide benefits for wealthy Americans.

The lobbying effort to reduce the capital gains tax was led by a coalition of conservative groups that publicly focused attention on the need for Congress to use "tax revenue windfalls" created by a rapidly growing economy "for tax cuts for all Americans."[131] The precise kinds of tax cuts favored by these groups were not always publicly specified. But the coalition included several groups fronted by well-known conservative political and business leaders that have long favored cuts in capital gains taxes: Jack Kemp, of Empower America; Lewis K. Uhler, of the National Tax Limitation Committee; David Keating, of the National Taxpayers Union; Steve Forbes, of Americans for Hope, Growth, and Opportunity; Matt Kibbe, of Citizens for a Sound Economy; and Harrison Fox, of Citizens for Budget Reform.[132]

The estate-tax-reduction campaign was led by a coalition of 105 lobbying groups backed by privileged-class members with financial interests in passing family fortunes intact (tax free) to the next generation.[133] And federal estate tax rates are not a trivial issue for the rich. Estates are taxed at federal rates of 18 percent on the first $10,000, 37 percent for assets of more than $500,000, and 55 percent for estates valued in excess of $3 million.[134] Although the estate tax cut was claimed by its supporters to benefit all Americans, few parents amassed estates above the pre-1997 $600,000 federal exemption ($1.2 million for married couples) to pass along to their heirs. In 1996, 69,772 estates with assets in excess of $600,000 filed forms with the Internal Revenue Service, but after allowable deductions and exemptions, only 31,918 estates paid federal estate taxes—just 1.2 percent of all estates.[135]

The congressional Joint Committee on Taxation estimates that over the next eight years the percentage of estates subject to federal taxes will rise from 1 to 2.8 percent. Several politically powerful baby boomers are on the cusp of inheriting family enterprises worth an estimated $10 trillion over the next twenty years.[136] Is it any wonder that a classwide lobby campaign against federal estate taxes sought changes as the 1997 tax deal was being crafted?

The 1997 classwide tax-reduction campaigns paid off for the privileged class. The Budget Reconciliation Act of 1997 cut capital gains taxes from 28 to 20 percent. The minimum corporate tax was eliminated, and the federal estate (inheritance) tax exemption was raised from $600,000 to $1 million ($1.3 million for family farms and businesses).[137] The 1997 tax act distributed three-fourths of individual tax cuts to people with annual incomes of more than $100,000. And "over one-third of all tax breaks will go to the wealthiest 1 percent who will end up with more tax relief than the bottom 80 percent." At the same time, "changes in the Alternative Minimum Tax (AMT) . . . lowered the tax burden for corporations by $18.3 billion over 10 years."[138]

Copyright © Lloyd Dangle. Reprinted with permission.

The tax act did not come close to the high priority Deputy Treasury Secretary Summers placed on restructuring the tax code so as to help "middle-class America." Instead, the richest 5 percent of American families will get 83 percent of the benefits from cuts in the capital gains tax, the elimination of the minimum corporate tax, and the near doubling of the estate tax exemption.[139] Families in the top 20 percent income group will get annual tax breaks of more than $1,000, but those in the top 1 percent will "be paying $16,157 less per year."[140] This amount includes average tax cuts of $7,939 in capital gains, $6,313 in estate taxes, and $2,353 in corporate taxes, minus small increases ($451 on average) in excise taxes. Families in the middle 20 percent income group receive a tax break of only $153 per year, and families in the lowest and second-lowest income groups will see either no tax cuts or a slight tax increase.[141] Final tax-savings score: privileged class, billions of dollars; new working class, chump change.

Taxploitation and Spendsploitation

As we noted earlier, the new working class comprises some 80 percent of Americans with limited capital resources and with a share of total economic output that is small and declining. As the history of federal tax and spending policies illustrates, not only does this group have little influence in the shaping of national policies, it is increasingly exploited by policies governing how taxes are collected on individuals and corporations and by the ways in which government spends tax revenues.

Of course, the policies directing how government taxes and spends do not have to be exploitative. For example, tax rates could be used to remedy the high levels of income and wealth inequalities in the United States today by levying higher tax rates on corporations and wealthy individuals. The money raised by such policies could be spent on public goods that improve opportunities for, and the economic well-being of, the nonprivileged. Better schools, national health insurance, government-financed higher education, reconstruction of public infrastructure facilities, and job creation, training, and placement are all examples of public goods that could be financed by funds raised through higher taxes on the privileged class. As it now stands, goods that potentially could be publicly funded, such as health care and higher education, must be purchased by most Americans from their earnings, but most of the nonprivileged can barely afford these goods. Thus, tax and spending policies in the United States do not function to redistribute wealth and income but rather extend their maldistribution and concentration.

In the United States today national (as well as state and local) tax laws and spending policies are dictated by the wealthy and powerful through both class-wide and interest-group lobbying. As we have seen, these lobbying efforts are very effective, because they are driven by the same groups that are centrally involved in the financing of most political campaigns. Thus, the ways that tax dollars are collected and distributed are not only not redistributive, but they collect an increasing share of taxes from the nonprivileged and spend the money in ways that disproportionately benefit the privileged. We should think of superclass-dominated national tax and spending policies as examples of *taxploitation* and *spendsploitation*—two types of exploitation that compound the more general levels of wealth and income inequality.

We illustrate these forms of exploitation with three figures depicting "American pies." The basic idea of the "wealth pie" shown in figure 4.2 was introduced in our chapter 1 discussion of wealth inequalities in the United States. It shows that only two of ten Americans (20 percent) control 92 percent of the financial wealth of the country, meaning ownership of stocks, bonds, and commercial real estate. The other eight out of ten Americans (80 percent) hold the remaining 8 percent of total wealth.[142] This means that about 80 million families, or about 216 million people, work every day throughout their entire adult lives producing wealth that goes largely to others, while they receive a few "crumbs" from the pie themselves. The extraordinary extent of wealth inequality in the United States could be reduced if the wealthy were required to pay higher tax rates on their incomes and assets and if they were prevented from transferring their wealth to their children. But that is not the way that U.S. tax and inheritance laws have been written.

The "tax pie" (figure 4.3) illustrates the share of total taxes paid by individuals and corporations. In 1999 the share of federal tax revenues paid by corporation income taxes is estimated at 11.4 percent. This figure is down sharply from the 26.5 percent share corporations paid in 1950. By contrast, in 1999 taxes paid by individuals (individual income taxes plus Social Security and Medicare taxes)

Figure 4.2   The Wealth Pie, 1999

92%

8%
Working-class share

Privileged-class share

The national financial wealth share owned by 20 of 100 Americans

The national financial wealth share owned by 80 of 100 Americans

Source: Wolff, 1996, 67.

Figure 4.3   The Tax Pie, 1999

**Share of total taxes   Share of total taxes
paid by corporations   paid by individuals**

Source: Office of Management and Budget, 1998, 29–30.

Note: The amounts shown in the diagram do not total 100 percent because other forms of taxes were collected. However, these other forms include taxes (such as excise) that are typically paid by individuals. Thus, the individual share shown in the diagram is lower than the actual share paid by individuals.

made up an estimated 80 percent of federal tax revenues. This figure is up sharply from the 51 percent share paid by individuals in 1950.[143]

But as we have already noted, not all individual taxpayers get the same breaks from federal tax policies. Take the case of Social Security. All American workers pay about 7.7 percent of the first $68,400 in annual earnings to the Social Security fund.[144] By the late 1990s, more than 90 percent of all American workers earned less than $68,400 annually, so they pay taxes on 100 percent of their earned incomes.[145] Privileged-class Americans who earn $200,000 or $2 million annually also pay Social Security taxes, but only on $68,400 of their income. So the non-privileged pay taxes on all of their income, and the privileged pay taxes on a small percentage of their income. But at payout time, the rich still collect their full Social Security checks, even though they are likely to still have incomes in the range of hundreds of thousands of dollars.

The U.S. Tax Code is filled with ways for rich individuals and corporations to reduce their taxes (often to less than zero), while working-class Americans make up for these lost taxes. The reason for this is simple: the tax code is written by the privileged class and for the privileged class, who justify their advantaged status with the widely shared ideological aphorism, "When the rich do well, everyone does well." Why would this be the case? Because, as the rest of the story goes, the rich invest their money, which in turn creates more jobs and more wealth shared by all Americans. This fairy tale—akin to the former Divine Right of kings myth—was invented by the superclass, seconded by the credentialed class, widely believed by the working class, and turned into law by Congress. Congress is receptive to this tale because most of its members are either already among the rich or are on the make, and they are provided with huge contributions to influence their votes on taxes.

The crash-and-burn reality of this fairy tale propagated by the privileged class is evident every year at tax time, when thousands of corporations and wealthy individuals escape taxes. For 1994 (the most recent year available), "of the 1,109,498 income tax returns with AGI [adjusted gross income] of $200,000 or more, 1,137 . . . showed no U.S. income tax liability." Another 10,662 Americans in this highest income bracket (more than $200,000) paid less than 10 percent of their incomes in taxes. It is true that 70.8 percent of taxpayers with incomes in excess of $200,000 pay tax rates of between 20 and 30 percent; but these levels are not much above the rates paid by average wage earners.[146] Families in the $30,000 to $40,000 income range paid an average of 19.7 percent of their earnings in 1996 in federal payroll taxes (income, Medicare, and Social Security).[147]

How are these tax inequities possible? Quite simply, the rich enjoy a variety of special exemptions, deductions, and other favored rules written into the tax code by our generous and understanding legislators. One final example: In 1991, a total of $44.3 billion was received by U.S. taxpayers in the form of tax-exempt interest income—most often from bonds issued by state and local governments. Most of this annual untaxed income subsidy goes to the very wealthy. In 1991, just thirty-two thousand Americans with personal incomes in excess of $1 million collected $4.8 billion in tax-exempt income—an average of $150,000 per millionaire![148] This income tax subsidy to the rich has survived over several decades despite repeated efforts by some lawmakers to close this "loophole."

The final figure presents two "redistribution pies," which provide vivid illustrations of how the largely privileged-class members of Congress choose to spend the tax dollars that are collected. However, before we look at figure 4.4, we should note that large chunks of federal spending are legally mandated and are not subject to annual congressional review. For example, Social Security payments to retired Americans (now under attack) and interest payments on the national debt (never under attack) are forms of entitlement spending that cannot be avoided. But in recent years, discretionary spending on "welfare programs" such as Aid to Families with Dependent Children (AFDC) and foodstamps has come under attack by both Democrats and Republicans.

In 1996 a majority of both parties in both houses of Congress voted to "end welfare as we know it." This effort culminated in President Clinton's signing of the Personal Responsibility and Work Opportunity Act in August 1996. The new law ended the AFDC program and replaced it with the Temporary Assistance to Needy Families (TANF) program. Among other things, the 1996 law ended the federal guarantee of cash assistance to poor families, set time limits on how long families can receive assistance from TANF funds (sixty months), mandated 22 percent cuts in foodstamps and Supplemental Security Income (SSI) over the next six years, and instituted penalties to states that do not force substantial portions of their adult TANF recipients into narrowly defined work programs.[149]

Although AFDC was the primary federal "welfare program" of last resort providing cash assistance to the poorest of poor American families, it accounted for less than 1 percent of annual federal expenditures. The TANF program that re-placed AFDC will cost taxpayers about $16.5 billion in 1999—which also amounts to less than 1 percent of the total $1.7 trillion federal budget. It is instructive to compare the political attacks on and the media attention devoted to "welfare de-pendency" to almost exact opposite reactions where the U.S. defense budget of $271 billion (in 1999) is concerned.[150]

Figure 4.4 illustrates the relative size of federal "wealthfare" (defense) versus federal welfare (TANF) spending in 1999. Of course, some portion of defense spending is legitimate on the grounds of protecting U.S. national security (though how much is open to debate). But large chunks of defense spending exist prima-rily to juice the profits of military contractor firms and to feed the hundreds of thousands of high-paid scientists, engineers, and civilian employees who work in government, industry, and university research and administration units through-out the "national security state."[151] In short, the superclass and their credentialed-class allies are the principal beneficiaries of much of the defense spending. Con-sequently, we do not see political attacks or hear media complaints about the "dependency" induced by defense spending.

There is no national debate over the defense "wealthfare" for the privileged class (or other forms of wealthfare), because this group has strong lobbies in Washing-

Figure 4.4   The Redistribution Pie, 1999

Note: TANF: (Temporary Assistance to Needy Families) is the current federal pro-gram providing cash assistance to poor families. In 1997 it replaced the previous Aid to Families with Dependent Children (AFDC) federal program.

ton and its members control the major media and educational institutions. But no one lobbies for the poor. As Bob Dole once said, poor people don't have a PAC. All they do is irritate the rich by their presence—and sometimes serve as a convenient scapegoat to blame for the fading fortunes of the working class. But poor people do not vote and they have no political clout, so their program is cut while defense spending continues to grow—even in a post-Cold War world.

It is clear that classwide lobbying helps juice federal spending in ways that ensure the privileged class gets large shares of the American pie. True, as Ringo Starr once sang, "You know it don't come easy." Keeping the federal cash spigot open requires that the superclass funnel millions of dollars to prime the congressional pump. Classwide political-campaign-financing and classwide lobbying practices are expensive. But for the superclass and its credentialed-class allies, the tax and spending payoffs are huge.

SUPERCLASS INTERESTS, POLITICAL POWER, AND LEGITIMACY

> The power elite has the economic and political resources to continue its domination of the federal government . . . and most people are likely to accept the current arrangements as long as they can make their lives work.
>
> —G. William Domhoff, *Who Rules America?*, 1998

The superclass has always had critical interests in controlling politics and government. These political interests are logical extensions of its economic interests. Superclass control over great wealth has historically provided this group with a critical resource for influencing the selection and election of political candidates, the electoral process, and policy formation, implementation, and enforcement. As we have seen, superclass funding of candidates leads to powerful influence over elected lawmakers and helps ensure superclass dominance over the formation and implementation of laws and public policies as well as major appointments to the state bureaucratic apparatus. Under this system, the state becomes a vehicle for legitimating existing class-power relationships and the production and distribution of wealth. Laws governing incorporation, corporate rights, taxes, and the regulation of labor markets ensure the dominance and legitimacy of large corporate enterprises in the economy. The stamp of state legitimacy combined with ancillary laws and regulations affords corporations effective control over workers' terms of employment and control over the production and distribution of wealth for elite owners. Completing the circle of power, corporate-generated wealth provides superclass members with the economic resources they need to access and dominate the political process and the state.

Although economic wealth and the shadow political industry provide the superclass with the structural foundation facilitating its domination of politics and government, this arrangement is inconsistent with American democratic ideals. Superclass domination of the political and economic arenas is contradicted by widely shared democratic values and equal opportunity ideals. Left unaddressed, these contradictions could lead working-class members to call into question the legitimacy of the U.S. political and economic systems. However, superclass-owned organizations that make up the information industry have developed control processes that help obscure—and thereby reduce—the tensions generated by the clash between economic and political realities and cultural ideals. These control processes help minimize the prospects of a "crisis of legitimacy" for superclass-controlled economic and political institutions. The next chapter explores the role played by the information industry in maintaining the legitimacy of superclass power.

NOTES

1. Quoted in Vicente Navarro, "Medical History as Justification Rather than Explanation: A Critique of Starr's *The Social Transformation of American Medicine*," *International Journal of Health Services* 14 (1984): 516.

2. Gore Vidal, "The End of History," *Nation*, September 30, 1996, 11–18.

3. G. William Domhoff, *State Autonomy or Class Dominance?* (New York: Aldine de Gruyter, 1996), 25; G. William Domhoff, *Who Rules America?: Power and Politics in the Year 2000* (Mountain View, Calif.: Mayfield, 1998), 2.

4. Ben H. Bagdikian, *The Media Monopoly* (Boston: Beacon Press, 1997), 13; Robert W. McChesney, "The Global Media Giants," *EXTRA!*, November–December 1997, 11–18.

5. Maynard S. Seider, "American Big Business Ideology: A Content Analysis of Executive Speeches," *American Sociological Review* 39 (1974): 802–15; Alan Neustadtl and Dan Clawson, "Corporate Political Groupings: Does Ideology Unify Business Political Behavior?," *American Sociological Review* 53 (1988): 172–90; Richard L. Zweigenhaft and G. William Domhoff, *Diversity in the Power Elite: Have Women and Minorities Reached the Top?* (New Haven: Yale University Press, 1998), 192–94.

6. District of Columbia Bar, *1996–1997 Annual Report* (Washington, D.C.: Bar D.C. 1997), 1–10, 3.

7. Office of Congressman Dick Armey, "Washington's Lobbying Industry: A Case for Tax Reform—Executive Summary," June 19, 1996, 1–4, 1.

8. Kevin Phillips, "Fat City," *Time*, September 26, 1994, 51.

9. Allan Shuldiner and Tony Raymond, *Who's in the Lobby? A Profile of Washington's Influence Industry* (Washington, D.C.: Center for Responsive Politics, 1998), 7–19.

10. Dan Clawson, Alan Neustadtl, and Denise Scott, *Money Talks* (New York: Basic Books, 1992), 182.

11. Phillips, "Fat City," 52.

12. Kay L. Schlozman and John T. Tierney, *Organized Interests and American Democracy* (New York: Harper and Row, 1986), 77.

13. Clawson, Neustadtl, and Scott, *Money Talks*, 182.

14. Domhoff, *Who Rules America?*, 103–11.

15. Chuck Collins, "Horatio Alger, Where Are You?" *Dollars and Sense*, January–February 1997, 9; S. M. Miller, "Born on Third Base: The Sources of Wealth of the 1996 *Forbes* 400," *United for a Fair Economy*, February 1997, 5–6.

16. Thomas Dye, *Who's Running America?: The Clinton Years* (Englewood Cliffs, N.J.: Prentice-Hall, 1995), 175; Domhoff, *Who Rules America?*, 111.

17. Domhoff, *Who Rules America?*, 111–15; Domhoff, *State Autonomy or Class Dominance?*, 1996, 25. Also see Harold R. Kerbo, *Social Stratification and Inequality* (New York: McGraw-Hill, 1996), 348.

18. Marc Breslow, "Congress for Sale," *Dollars and Sense*, July–August 1996, 43.

19. D. Stanley Eitzen and Maxine Baca Zinn, *In Conflict and Order* (Boston: Allyn and Bacon, 1995), 401. Also see Ellen Miller and Randy Kehler, "Mischievous Myths about Money in Politics," *Dollars and Sense*, July–August 1996, 23.

20. "Consumer Price Indexes (CPI-U), by Major Groups: 1960–1994," doc. 761, in U.S. Department of Commerce, Bureau of the Census, *Statistical Abstract of the United States* (Washington, D.C.: U.S. Government Printing Office, 1995), 492.

21. Larry Makinson, *The Big Picture: Money Follows Power Shift on Capitol Hill* (Washington, D.C.: Center for Responsive Politics, 1997), 5–6.

22. Bob Schiff, "Bogus Comparisons," *Public Citizen*, Spring 1996, 15.

23. Makinson, *The Big Picture*, 6.

24. Ibid., 6–7.

25. Ibid., 1.

26. Federal Election Commission (FEC), "Congressional Fundraising and Spending Up Again in 1996: Contributions from Individuals by Size of the Contribution," press release, April 14, 1997, 4, 1–1.

27. Clawson, Neustadtl, and Scott, *Money Talks*, 11.

28. Makinson, *The Big Picture*, 3.

29. Marty Jezer, "Soft Money, Hard Choices," *Dollars and Sense*, July–August 1996, 30.

30. Ibid.

31. Clawson, Neustadtl, and Scott, *Money Talks*, 11.

32. Makinson, *The Big Picture*, 1.

33. Figures cited are based on calculations using data from FEC, "Congressional Fundraising and Spending Up: Contributions from Individuals," 4, 1–1; and FEC, "Congressional Fundraising and Spending Up Again in 1996: PAC Financial Activity, 1995–1996," press release, April 14, 1997, 4, 1–1.

34. FEC, "Congressional Fundraising and Spending Up: Contributions from Individuals," 4, 1–1.

35. Ibid.

36. Ibid.

37. Ibid., 2.

38. Makinson, *The Big Picture*, 7.

39. Jonathan D. Salant, "Financial Reports Show Members Still Take Lobbies' Free Rides," *Congressional Quarterly Weekly Report*, June 17, 1995, 1709.

40. Makinson, *The Big Picture*, 2.

41. David Donnelly, "Maine Leads the Way," *Dollars and Sense*, July–August 1996, 34.

42. Ellen Miller and Randy Kehler, "Mischievous Myths about Money in Politics," *Dollars and Sense*, July–August 1996, 23.

43. Makinson, *The Big Picture*, 2.

44. Ibid., 77.

45. Rachel Burstein and Larry Makinson, "The *Mother Jones* 400," *Mother Jones*, May–June 1997, 40–62, 72–75.

46. Ted Gup, "The *Mother Jones* 400," *Mother Jones*, March–April, 1996, 43.

47. FEC, "Congressional Fundraising and Spending Up: Contributions from Individuals," 3.

48. Ibid., 2.

49. Makinson, *The Big Picture*, 3.

50. FEC, "Congressional Fundraising and Spending Up: PAC Financial Activity," 4, 1–1.

51. Clawson, Neustadtl, and Scott, *Money Talks*, 32–33.

52. FEC, "Congressional Fundraising and Spending Up: PAC Financial Activity," 4, 1–1.

53. Clawson, Neustadtl, and Scott, *Money Talks*, 161.

54. Ibid., 140–41.

55. Ibid., 181.

56. Ibid., 176, 160.

57. FEC, "Congressional Fundraising and Spending Up: PAC Financial Activity," 4, 1–1.

58. Makinson, *The Big Picture*, 4.

59. Miller and Kehler, "Mischievous Myths about Money in Politics," 22.

60. Breslow, "Congress for Sale," 43.

61. Charles Lewis, "The Buying of the President," *Dollars and Sense*, July–August 1996, 28, 41.

62. Jezer, "Soft Money, Hard Choices," 30.

63. FEC, "1998 Congressional Candidates Raise $233 Million," press release, March 6, 1998, 1–3.

64. Marc Breslow, "Government of, by, and for the Wealthy," *Dollars and Sense*, July–August 1996, 23–24.

65. Jeff Cohen and Norman Solomon, *Adventures in MediaLand* (Monroe, Maine: Common Courage Press, 1993), 28. Also see Dean Baker, "Generation Excess," *EXTRA!*, March–April 1996, 12–13; and *Ageism on the Agenda*, special issue, *EXTRA!*, March–April 1997.

66. Domhoff, *Who Rules America?*, 125–69.

67. Dye, *Who's Running America?*, 215. Also see Michael Dolny, "What's in a Label?," *EXTRA!*, May–June 1998, 9–10; David Croteau, "Challenging the 'Liberal Media' Claim," *EXTRA!*, July–August 1998, 4–9.

68. Thomas R. Dye, "Organizing Power for Policy-Planning: The View from the Brookings Institution," in *Power Elites and Organizations*, ed. G. William Domhoff and Thomas R. Dye (Newbury Park, Calif.: Sage, 1987), 185–86.

69. Ibid., 188.

70. Domhoff, *Who Rules America?*, 134.

71. Dye, *Who's Running America?*, 222–27.

72. Val Burris, "Elite Policy-Planning Networks in the United States," in *Research in Politics and Society*, vol. 4, *The Political Consequences of Social Networks*, ed. Gwen Moore and J. Allen Whitt (Greenwich, Conn.: JAI Press, 1992), 115–20.

73. Michael Patrick Allen, "Elite Social Movement Organizations and the State: The Rise of the Conservative Policy-Planning Network," in Moore and Whitt, *Research in Politics and Society*, vol. 4, 95.

74. Clawson, Neustadtl, and Scott, *Money Talks*, 139.

75. Domhoff, *State Autonomy or Class Dominance?*, 34.

76. Ibid., 38.

77. Ibid., 29–32.

78. Kerbo, *Social Stratification and Inequality*, 180–81. Also see Domhoff, *Who Rules America?*, 134.

79. Elizabeth H. Rich, ed., *The Foundation Directory, 1998 Edition* (New York: Foundation Center, 1998), vii–xi.

80. Kerbo, *Social Stratification and Inequality*, 180.

81. Dye, *Who's Running America?*, 11, 171.

82. Ibid., 135.

83. Kerbo, *Social Stratification and Inequality*, 180. Also see Dye, *Who's Running America?*, 135.

84. Sandra Jaszczak, ed., *Encyclopedia of Associations*, 31st ed., vol. 1 (Detroit: Gale Research, 1996), 2265.

85. Linda G. Tobiasen, ed., *The Foundation Grants Index, 1996* (New York: Foundation Center, 1995).

86. Dye, "Organizing Power for Policy-Planning," 183.

87. Ibid.

88. Dye, *Who's Running America?*, 225.

89. Allen, "Elite Social Movement Organizations and the State," 96–97.

90. Robert Parry, "Who Buys the Right?" *Nation*, November 18, 1996, 5–6.

91. John B. Judis, "The Most Powerful Lobby," *In These Times*, February 21, 1994, 22–23.

92. Dye, *Who's Running America?*, 236–37.

93. Peter Nye, "Lobbying and Gift Reform Shines Sunlight on Influence Peddling," *Public Citizen*, January–February 1996, 1, 3.

94. Jonathan D. Salant, " '97 Lobbying Topped $1 Billion Mark," *Indianapolis Star*, July 8, 1998.

95. Jim Drinkard, "Lobbying Costs Hit $100 Million a Month," *Indianapolis Star*, March 7, 1998.

96. Office of Congressman Dick Armey, "Washington's Lobbying Industry: A Case for Tax Reform—Executive Summary," June 19, 1996, 1–4, 1.

97. Allan Shuldiner and Tony Raymond, *Who's in the Lobby?: A Profile of Washington's Influence Industry* (Washington, D.C.: Center for Responsive Politics, 1998), 7.

98. Drinkard, "Lobbying Costs Hit $100 Million a Month."

99. Domhoff, *Who Rules America?*, 150–59. Also see Clawson, Neustadtl, and Scott, *Money Talks*, 180.

100. Earl Wysong, *High Risk and High Stakes: Health Professionals, Politics, and Policy* (Westport, Conn.: Greenwood Press, 1992), 59.

101. Judis, "The Most Powerful Lobby," 22–23.

102. Joel Bleifuss, "Money Talks, Democracy Walks," *In These Times*, May 16, 1994, 12–13.

103. Gabriella Boyer, "Corporate America Stacks the NAFTA Debate," *Public Citizen*, July–August 1993, 26.

104. Joan Claybrook, "Why It's Their NAFTA, Not Ours, Not Yours," *Public Citizen*, November–December 1993, 2, 15.

105. Bleifuss, "Money Talks, Democracy Walks," 12–13.

106. Wysong, *High Risk and High Stakes*, 102–10.

107. "Phony Paycheck Protection: It'll Cost You More than You Think," *UAW Solidarity*, March–April 1998, 10–11.

108. Russ Davis, "AFL-CIO Unveils Program to Revitalize Labor Movement," *Labor Notes*, March 1997, 1, 14.

109. Ken Silverstein and Alexander Cockburn, "Our Little Secret: Life on the Fast Track," *CounterPunch*, September 1–15, 1997, 2–3.

110. Ibid.

111. "Fast Track Media Misperceptions," *Extra!Update*, February 1998, 1.

112. "Fast Track Falters in Major House Vote; UAW Steps Up Drive," *UAW Solidarity*, October 1997, 9.

113. "Fast Track Sidetracked," *UAW Solidarity*, November 1997, 7.

114. "Paycheck Deception Act: Don't Let Them Fool You," *AFSCME Public Employee*, March–April 1998, 7–19.

115. "What Is the 'Paycheck Deception Act'?" *AFSCME Public Employee*, March–April 1998, 10–11.

116. "Paycheck Deception Act," 7.

117. Ibid.

118. Ibid.

119. "Phony 'Paycheck Protection,'" 10–11.

120. Marc Cooper, "Labor-Latino Beat in CA," *Nation*, June 29, 1998, 5–6.

121. Domhoff, *Who Rules America?*, 266–81.

122. David Masci, "Senate Rejects Striker Bill; More Action Unlikely," *Congressional Quarterly*, July 16, 1994, 1936.

123. Jill Zuckman, "Senate Foes Ready to Block Striker Replacement Bill," *Congressional Quarterly*, June 19, 1993, 1579. Also see David Masci, "Senate Foes Likely to Derail Striker Replacement Bill," *Congressional Quarterly*, July 9, 1994, 1873.

124. U.S. Congress, House of Representatives, *Comprehensive Tax Reform*, Committee on Ways and Means, 99th Congress, 1st sess., serial 99–41, 1985, Washington, D.C.: U.S. Government Printing Office.

125. Donald L. Barlett and James B. Steele, *America: What Went Wrong?* (Kansas City: Andrews and McMeel, 1992), 207.

126. U.S. House Committee on Ways and Means, *Impact, Effectiveness, and Fairness of the Tax Reform Act of 1986*, 101st Cong., 2d sess., 1990, serial 101–92.

127. Michelle Cottle, "The Real Class War," *Washington Monthly*, July–August 1997, 12.

128. Ibid.

129. Ibid., 13.

130. *Congressional Record, Alternative Minimum Tax Reform Act: Chamber of Commerce of the United States of America*, and *Alternative Minimum Tax Reform Act: Statement of National Association of Manufacturers*, May 8, 1997, S4237; *Congressional Record, The Small-Business Capital Gains Enhancement Act of 1997*, May 15, 1997, S4588–91; *Congressional Record, Amendment no. 519*, June 26, 1997, S6449–51.

131. *Congressional Record, Pro-Taxpayer Groups Urge Congress to Act Now on Future Tax Cuts*, June 27, 1997, S6678–79.

132. Ibid., S6679.

133. Cottle, "The Real Class War," 15.

134. John Miller, "More Wealth for the Wealthy: The Estate Tax Giveaway and What To Do about It," *Dollars and Sense*, November–December 1997, 26.

135. Ibid., 26–27.

136. Cottle, "The Real Class War," 15.

137. John Miller, "Tax Cuts: Clinton and Congress Feed the Wealthy," *Dollars and Sense*, November–December 1997, 43; Miller, "More Wealth for the Wealthy," 26.

138. "The Rich Get a Good Return on Their Campaign Investments," *Sanders Scoop*, Winter 1998, 1.

139. Miller, "Clinton and Congress Feed the Wealthy," 43.

140. Ibid.

141. Ibid.

142. Edward N. Wolff, *Top Heavy* (New York: Twentieth Century Fund, 1996), 67.

143. Office of Management and Budget, "Historical Tables," *Budget of the United States Government: Fiscal Year 1999* (Washington, D.C.: U.S. Government Printing Office, 1998).

144. Cottle, "The Real Class War," 17.

145. U.S. Department of the Treasury, Internal Revenue Service, *Statistics of Income, 1995: Individual Income Tax Returns*, Publication 1304 (Washington, D.C.: U.S. Government Printing Office, 1997), 13.

146. U.S. Department of the Treasury, Internal Revenue Service, *The Statistics of Income (SOI) Bulletin*, Winter 1997–98, 32, 89.

147. David Wessel, "Again, the Rich Get Richer, but This Time They Pay More Taxes," *Wall Street Journal*, April 2, 1998, 1.

148. Donald L. Barlett and James B. Steele, *America: Who Really Pays the Taxes?* (New York: Touchstone, 1994), 116.

149. Randy Albelda, "Farewell to Welfare but Not to Poverty," *Dollars and Sense*, November–December 1996, 17.

150. Office of Management and Budget, *Budget of the United States Government: Fiscal Year 1999* (Washington, D.C.: U.S. Government Printing Office, 1998), 10, 149, 224.

151. Joel Bleifuss, "Warfare or Welfare," *In These Times*, December 9, 1996, 12–14.

5

The Information Industry

The concentration of media power means that Americans increasingly get their information from a few sources who decide what is "news."

—Oliver Stone, *Nation*, June 3, 1996

In the mid-1990s the *National Catholic Reporter* published a story criticizing the Briggs and Stratton engine company's decision to eliminate two thousand high-wage union jobs in the Milwaukee, Wisconsin, area.[1] The article suggested the layoffs were not in keeping with the Catholicism of some of Briggs' top executives. Briggs and Stratton officials refused to be interviewed for the story, but after it ran, the company filed a $30 million libel and invasion-of-privacy lawsuit against the *Reporter* (which has fifty thousand subscribers). Briggs vice president George Thompson was quoted in the *Wall Street Journal* as saying, "My religious up-bringing . . . has absolutely nothing to do with the basic economic decisions made by the company."[2] As the media-watch journal *EXTRA!* pointed out, Thompson's comment "is exactly what *National Catholic Reporter* was talking about."[3]

This episode reveals several important features of the relationship between superclass-based corporate power and the media. First, contrary to what some conservatives imagine to be the case, media critiques of superclass corporate power and policies are extremely rare.[4] Media accounts of corporate power in America seldom include the kind of critical edge found in the *Reporter* story. Second, when the agents of superclass power are stung by media critiques, they have enormous resources at their disposal to punish offenders. The $30 million lawsuit serves as a chilling reminder to all editors and reporters of the risks they face if they challenge superclass corporate power and policies. This high-dollar punitive legal action has certainly been noted across all media outlets, giving writers, editors, and broadcast producers pause as they consider story lines on corporate issues.

The episode also illustrates that when media critiques of corporate power and policies do appear, they are extremely unlikely to be found in mainstream media outlets. Rather, such reports are far more likely to appear in small, alternative media sources like the *Reporter*. This is the case because the mainstream media are themselves large corporations that in turn are increasingly owned by even larger conglomerate firms. The managers, editors, producers, and writers who work for the giant information industry have no interest in corporate critiques. Their concerns are mainly with bottom-line financial issues. For them, media content is simply a means of delivering readers and viewers to advertisers' messages. Corporate critiques are not conducive to establishing the kind of media ambience that makes readers and viewers receptive to corporate advertising. The information industry prefers media content that will keep it light, keep it bright, and keep it moving.

THE MAINSTREAM CORPORATE MEDIA

A specter now haunts the world: a global commercial media system dominated by a small number of super-powerful . . . transnational media corporations.

—Robert W. McChesney, *EXTRA!*, November–December 1997

The information industry consists of giant interlocked electronic and print-media corporations that are largely owned by superclass members and managed by a small number of superclass leaders in conjunction with credentialed-class junior partners.[5] These firms disseminate information, ideas, and images about, and interpretations of, national and global economic, political, and social news and issues to national and international audiences. The industry can be viewed as part of an even larger enterprise that some critics have termed the "culture industry" or the "national entertainment state."[6] Such labels suggest that in addition to generating news and commentary (largely consonant with superclass interests), the industry also serves as a major conduit for disseminating most forms of mass entertainment, corporate public relations propaganda, product ads, promotional campaigns, and paid political advertising.

The content of the news and information delivered by the electronic and print-media arms of the information industry is not neutral in terms of viewpoints conveyed or class interests served. But the news media are also not liberal in the sense of being critical of mainstream economic and political institutions or policies—as many conservative pundits, such as Rush Limbaugh, claim. Studies of media content do reveal consistent biases—but of a probusiness, pro-privileged-class sort. News story lines and accompanying images typically begin with probusiness sources, such as superclass-funded think tanks.[7] And the commercial media most often "favor style and substance that [are] consonant with their corporate [economic] interests."[8] The information industry consistently delivers news and information that effectively reinforce superclass and corporate interests—at the expense of working-class interests in an informed citizenry and participatory democracy. "It is a disaster for anything but the most superficial notion of democracy—a democracy where, to paraphrase John Jay's maxim, those who own the world ought to govern it."[9]

Although polls suggest deep public skepticism exists concerning news media credibility, the information industry nevertheless dominates national attention to current affairs, with most Americans getting most of their news about such events from mass media outlets.[10] A 1998 national survey found 61 percent of Americans reported they get most of their news from television. Newspapers were reported as a distant second news source (24 percent) followed by radio (8 percent), internet or on-line services (2 percent), and magazines (1 percent).[11] These findings indicate that TV and newspapers are the primary news sources for 85 percent of the public. This means the leading sources of information in the United States today are the major television networks (ABC, CBS, NBC, CNN), national circulation newspapers (*New York Times, Washington Post, USA Today, Wall Street Journal*), the three major news magazines (*Newsweek, Time,* and *U.S. News and World Report*), the fifteen largest newspaper chains (accounting for more than half of the total newspaper circulation in the United States, led by Gannet, Knight-Ridder, and Newhouse), and the Associated Press wire service,[12] which in 1996 supplied most national news to the 1,533 U.S. daily newspapers.[13]

Although the preceding list of news sources appears to be rather diverse, it is important to recognize that the core of the information industry consists of several large, interlocked news media firms that include both electronic and print divisions. Moreover, most large, multidimensional news media firms have, for the most part, merged with giant nonmedia corporations.

In the late 1990s, four corporate giants control increasingly large shares of the largest media firms that run major news operations: (1) General Electric (GE) owns NBC, which runs NBC Network News and also owns several television stations, portions of TV cable channels (e.g., Court TV, A&E, the History channel), half of the Microsoft-NBC interactive news service (MS/NBC), and a book publishing firm (Romance Classics) and influences radio markets through NBC Radio (owned by Westwood One). (2) Time-Warner (TW) owns Turner Broadcasting—which runs CNN News. TW also owns a large group of magazines (e.g., *Time, Fortune, Sports Illustrated, Money*), book-publishing houses (e.g., Time-Life Books, Book-of-the-Month Club, Little, Brown), and cable television operations (e.g., HBO and Cinemax). TW is also interlocked with Tele-Communications, Inc. (TCI), Seagrams, and Capital Group Companies. (3) Disney owns ABC, which, in addition to running ABC Network News, also owns several major-market TV stations covering 24.5 percent of U.S. households. Disney's media holdings also extend to several newspapers and magazines (through its Fairchild and Chilton Publications subsidiaries) and cable TV (Disney Channel, ESPN, ESPN2, ESPNews and holdings in the Lifetime, A&E, and History channels).[14] (4) Westinghouse "changed its name to that of the [CBS] network it swallowed."[15] CBS (Westinghouse) owns Group W Satellite Communications (satellite distribution of TV programming) and runs CBS Network News, several major-market TV stations, CBS Radio (which operates 21 FM and 18 AM stations and disseminates CBS news programming to 450 stations), and TV cable operations (Country Music Television, TNN, and Home Team Sports).[16]

The four large parent firms and the diverse media holdings they control, plus most of the other mass media firms outside of the four corporate giants, are largely owned or controlled by the same twenty-five thousand officers and directors of the one thousand largest firms that supervise and control the shadow political industry.[17] Thus, the electronic and print mainstream mass media are almost exclusively composed of large corporate firms whose policies, personnel, and reporting practices reflect superclass and corporate interests.[18] However, this outcome should not be surprising since "the truth about the news industry has always been that rich businessmen (and a few rich women) own it."[19] And although news media ownership today more often takes a corporate rather than patriarchal form, the top news media CEOs are structurally bound to policies that advance elite-class interests.[20] Thus, superclass-based ownership and management patterns and related media policies have produced a kind of "corporate ministry of information." As one media critic put it, "It is normal for all large businesses to make serious efforts to influence the news, to avoid embarrassing publicity, and to maximize sympathetic public opinion and government policies. Now they own most of the news media that they wish to influence."[21]

Corporate interlocks linking the boards of directors of mass media firms to nonmedia companies illustrate how the web of superclass owners and employers cuts across the top levels of corporate America. One example of media-corporate links replicated many times over in the United States begins with the *Washington Post* (which also owns *Newsweek* magazine). In 1992, the *Post*'s board of directors included several "outside" members based in the larger corporate community: Donald R. Keough (CEO, Coca-Cola), Anthony J. F. O'Reilly (CEO, H. J. Heinz, and a director of GE and the New York Stock Exchange), James E. Burke (former CEO, Johnson and Johnson), and Richard D. Simmons (president, *International Herald Tribune*, and director of J. P. Morgan and Union Pacific).[22]

In addition to general media-corporate interlocks, superclass linkages also extend downward to media-firm management levels, where news content and editorial policy decisions are made. This pattern is illustrated by the *New York Times* editorial board: in 1993 it included Donald M. Stewart (director, Principal Financial Group), George B. Munroe, Richard L. Gelb, and George L. Shinn (directors, New York Life Insurance Company), and Louis V. Gerstner (director, Bristol-Myers Squibb). Such a membership roster may make it easier to understand why the *Times* consistently editorialized in favor of "managed competition" health care "reforms" favored by large insurance and financial firms in the early 1990s while reporting infrequently and most often negatively on "single-payer, Canadian-style" health care reform proposals.[23]

Corporate interlocks that tie media firms' news operations with superclass interests of political control and profits lead to interesting contradictions. As a cultural ideal, news is supposedly delivered by "objective" media sources free from biases. In practice, as we have glimpsed and as we will see in more detail later, this is never the case. The stakes are too high. For superclass members and their credentialed-class allies to maintain their positions of wealth, power, and privilege, the working class must be persuaded that the economic and political status quo and the institutions that comprise and sustain them are legitimate. This means the news media must provide those who are not members of the privileged class with ideas, information, and interpretations that support a superclass worldview while ignoring or discrediting alternative views. Thus, news and editorial content trend heavily in the direction of reports and interpretations of events that legitimate the status quo, thereby protecting the interests of superclass members at the top of the class structure.

Of course the existence of dominant, prosuperclass media reporting trends does not mean oppositional trends, views, or interpretations are totally absent from the media. They do exist—mainly as fragmented and minority positions—but our focus here is on superclass dominance of the mainstream mass media. The following sections explore three major control processes that operate through the information industry. The mainstream ideology, opinion-shaping, and spin-control processes function in ways that promote superclass domination of economic and political thinking in the United States and also help conceal the operation and effects of both the shadow political and information industries.

THE MAINSTREAM IDEOLOGY PROCESS

> The ideology process consists of the numerous methods through which members of the power elite attempt to shape the beliefs, attitudes and opinions of the underlying population.
>
> —G. William Domhoff, *The Powers That Be*, 1983

The mainstream ideology process is the most general of the three control practices operating as part of the information industry. But before we discuss this process, the term *ideology* needs a bit of clarification. This concept may seem like a remote, abstract reference. In fact, ideology is quite simple. It refers to idea systems that organize our thinking on various subjects. If we think sex is pleasurable—or disgusting—or that sports are fun—or boring—it is because of the idea systems we have learned that surround those topics and color our experiences with them. Our sex and sports ideologies include assumptions and conclusions about these subjects as well as selected "facts" (gleaned from personal experiences or conveyed to us by credible sources) that "prove" that our views are right and those held by others are wrong.

In the economic and political arenas, idea systems exist that have the same basic features as our sex and sports idea systems. Political-economy ideologies consist of assumptions about how power and wealth are (or should be) organized and distributed along with selected "facts" that "prove" that the views people hold on these topics are "correct." Political-economy ideologies are most often referred to as ranging from "left" to "center" (or middle of the road) to "right." These labels can take on many meanings, but leftist ideologies are basically grounded in the view that democratic government can and should serve as an agent promoting political, economic, and social justice for all citizens. By contrast, ideologies on the right today tend to publicly portray "big government" as an enemy "of the people" (although they support government subsidies to businesses). But right-wing views see nothing wrong with the development of powerful private concentrations of wealth and power—as in the case of large corporations.

Whether we know it or not, most Americans have little experience with leftist ideologies but lots of experience with centrist and rightist ideologies. This situation reflects the ongoing socialization of the working class to economic and political ideas and views that promote and reinforce superclass economic and political interests. Such training occurs through several social institutions, including schools and the mass media, with the latter serving, in part, as a major conduit for the ideology process.

The *mainstream ideology process* refers to the powerful, indirect influence that the superclass has, especially through the mass media, upon the political-economy ideological views held by most Americans—including those in the new working class. It refers to the numerous ways that superclass-supported procorporate, free-market, individual-choice, "government is bad" (or at best inefficient) ideas get woven into and subtly dominate the content of mass-media-disseminated news and commentary. As a result of this process, public debates and discussions on political and economic issues and policies tend to reflect superclass ideological views, preferences, and interests.

Credible evidence exists that supports our view that the superclass shares a rather uniform political-economy ideology that in turn dominates public thought via the mainstream ideology process. We also believe that the operation of the process whereby superclass ideological views dominate news and information content delivered to working-class members via the mass-media-based information industry can be illustrated by an examination of four key topics. These are (1) the corporate media-management structure, (2) the influence of corporate interests and advertising on media content, (3) the deep structural ideological foundation of the media, and (4) classroom penetration by media-produced materials.

Superclass Political-Economy Ideology

The mainstream ideology process is grounded in superclass leaders' ownership of and control over the mainstream media and their shared economic and political ideas, which comprise a dominant "ideological umbrella" ranging across a short, neoliberal-centrist-conservative spectrum. Of course, it would be an oversimplification to argue that all superclass members share the same political-economy ideology. But the apparent emerging consensus among superclass leaders favoring domestic austerity policies in the United States, Europe, and elsewhere in the world, as well as corporate-mediated international trade, suggests widespread superclass support for the "neo-liberal agenda of privatization, deregulation, and 'free trade.'"[24] Differences in superclass leaders' ideological views appear to be matters of nuance, emphasis, and degree across the dominant ideological umbrella rather than fundamental differences in values and policy directions.[25] Thus, the core values underlying the superclass ideological spectrum emphasize free enterprise, competition, equal opportunity, individualism, and minimal government involvement in business activities.[26] These values and principles reinforce what is claimed by privileged-class leaders to be a superior (compared to the alternatives) and preferred (for all citizens) political and economic status quo.

With the information industry owned and controlled by the same core of superclass leaders who direct the shadow political industry, it is hardly surprising that the political-economy ideological preferences of this group cover a short spectrum. Research on this topic reveals that mass media CEOs are typically economic conservatives interested in profits and markets and that they use the media to promote corporate values consistent with their interests.[27] As one researcher put it, "Media moguls—from Rupert Murdoch to Katherine Graham to Laurence Tisch to the executives of General Electric—may not exactly be 'movement' conservatives. But neither are they 'liberals.'"[28]

A recent study of CEOs who head the firms controlling the four major TV networks characterized their political views as conservative. Moreover, three of the four—Jack Welch (GE/NBC), Michael Jordan (CBS/Westinghouse), and Rupert Murdoch (News Corporation/Fox Television)—were described as taking actions aimed at influencing news and commentary content in their media divisions in support of conservative political causes or neoliberal-conservative corporate economic policies (e.g., aggressive downsizing and opposition to government regulation). Michael Eisner (Disney/ABC), described as a Democratic Party centrist, was viewed as holding views that were not much different from those of the first three. Eisner has supported former New Jersey Senator Bill Bradley, "a pro-Contra Democrat," and he "boasts of the apolitical nature of his company's products."[29]

The Corporate Media-Management Structure

Although conservative superclass corporate leaders control enormous media resources, as a group they are too few in number to supervise the details necessary for the translation of their shared ideological views into routine media policies and content. Dependable corporate media managers who hold compatible views are recruited by superclass-dominated corporate boards to handle those tasks. These upper-tier, credentialed-class professionals operate under a supervision and reward structure that ensures procorporation content standards are met—along with high profits and bonuses for superclass owners and upper-level media management.[30]

Top corporate media managers extend the superclass ideological "food chain" downward. They recruit and richly reward their immediate subordinates and top media professionals such as network TV-news anchors, producers, reporters, writers, and commentators for performing three important tasks: (1) structuring media content that will, for the most part, reflect superclass ideological views and principles, (2) attracting the largest possible audience (with the right demographics—usually young, affluent adults), and (3) not offending corporate advertisers. The latter issue is not inconsequential, because most media profits come from advertising revenues. In 1994, *Advertising Age* estimated that corporations spent $150 billion on national advertising,[31] and that figure rises to $1 trillion if all forms of corporate marketing are included.[32]

Corporate Interests, Advertising, and Media Content

As the news divisions of media firms have emerged as major profit generators in recent years, media managers, producers, and reporters are under increasing pressure to produce media content that conforms to procorporate views. For members of this group, the result is a collection of news media policies, practices, traditions, and personal experiences that favor bland, noninvestigative news reporting and toothless commentary. This style of news frequently lapses into corporate cheerleading ensuring that media ad revenues are not interrupted by negative news stories or controversial, critical commentary concerning high-spending corporate advertising clients.[33]

Soft news reporting practices are shaped sometimes by covert links between corporate interlocks and media reporting practices and sometimes by direct corporate pressure on the media. Both types of influence result in corporate censorship of the news—in one form or another. The covert influence source is illustrated by an *EXTRA!* (a media-watch publication) reporter's observation concerning the power of subtle internal corporate pressures on news reporting: "Most people who work for large corporations understand without being told that there are things you should and should not do. The *Today Show* producer who declined to include an anti-GE campaign in a segment on consumer boycotts probably wasn't thinking of an official memorandum when she said, 'We can't do that one. Well, we could do that one, but we won't.'" [34]

Outside, direct corporate pressure to change or kill news stories is also directed at media firms—but obviously the most successful attempts are those the public never hears about. One recent public case illustrating this practice occurred in 1997 and continued in 1998. It involved television reporters Jane Akre and Steve Wilson, Fox TV station WTVT in Tampa, Florida, and an investigative news series. The reports focused on the genetically engineered recombinant bovine growth hormone (rBGH) drug Posilac sold by the Monsanto Corporation. Questions were raised about how the drug was tested for safety, possible negative health effects of the drug on cows, and possible health hazards people might face by consuming milk from cows injected with the drug (which increases milk production by up to 30 percent).[35]

As a result of legal pressures brought by Monsanto against Fox News, the investigative series was never broadcast. An attorney representing Monsanto in a February 21, 1997, letter to Fox News CEO Roger Ailes warned that "enormous damage can be done by the reckless presentation of unsupported speculation as fact."[36] The letter was forwarded to the WTVT station and promoted a series of internal discussions and reviews of the series. The reporters stood by their story, but the station management decided not to run it. As the station manager told the reporters, "We paid three billion dollars for these television stations. We'll tell you what the news is."[37]

The reporters said Fox News tried to buy their silence, offering them a settlement "which amounted to nearly $200,000."[38] But in return they would have to sign a gag order "promising never to discuss the rBGH story, Monsanto's involvement, and how Fox responded." They refused and were fired in December 1997. Since then, they have established a website (<http://www.foxBGHsuit.com>) where they have learned of horror stories similar to their own, and they have filed a lawsuit against Fox Television "seeking redress under a Florida law designed to protect whistle-blowers." As the reporters have said, "We didn't leave journalism, it left us."[39]

This case and others, such as the widely reported 1997–98 "mad cow" lawsuit brought against TV talk-show host Oprah Winfrey, illustrate that corporate efforts to directly influence (or silence) news media content are both real and powerful. Oprah's case was somewhat different from the Akre and Wilson episode because she was sued for civil damages by the National Cattlemen's Beef Association (NCBA). The NCBA claimed that Howard Lyman, a guest on Oprah's TV show, made comments "disparaging" beef (while discussing "mad cow disease") that were in violation of a Texas "food disparagement" statute, but a Texas jury disagreed and ruled in favor of Oprah.[40]

Although these cases illustrate direct corporate actions aimed at shaping media content, such efforts are probably less important than more routine business-media connections. A more common route of corporate influence over media content occurs through the informal clout businesses have as a result of their massive expenditures for mass-media advertising. Some sense of the extent of this clout was evident in a 1997 survey of 241 members of the group Investigative Reporters and Editors working at commercial television stations. "Nearly three-quarters of the respondents reported that advertisers had 'tried to influence the content' of news at their stations." A majority also reported that advertisers had tried to kill stories. Forty percent said their stations had caved in to advertiser pressures, 43 percent said they had not, and 59 percent said there was pressure from within their stations "*not* to produce stories that advertisers might find objectionable."[41]

In the print media, the *Wall Street Journal* reports that large corporate advertisers demand to know magazine content in advance to ensure that their ads do not appear in publications with "offensive content." As an illustration, "Colgate-

Palmolive Co. sends its agencies guidelines forbidding them from running ads in magazine issues with 'offensive' sexual content or material the company 'considers antisocial or in bad taste.' Michael Samet, media director at Colgate's lead agency, Young & Rubicam Advertising, says the agency has a 'protocol' . . . to make sure every magazine carrying Colgate's ads honors its rules."[42]

According to the *Journal*, the practice of corporate advertisers demanding control over magazine content is widespread and involves large firms and entire industries. In one instance *Esquire* magazine editor Edward Kosner killed a short story centered around gay men after being warned by his publisher that Chrysler Corporation would pull four pages of ads if the story ran. Other large firms demanding advance knowledge of or control over magazine content include Ford Motor Company, Ameritech, and American Brands. Industrywide involvement in these practices is evidenced by the long-standing policy of tobacco and alcohol advertisers demanding advance warnings from publications about any articles that deal with people who abuse or who have been harmed by their products.[43]

As the *Journal* notes, "Big advertisers have always tried to influence the contents of magazines, and every other medium." Such practices are not new, not illegal, and not even unethical: "The American Society of Magazine Editors . . . [does not have] any policy to prevent magazines from giving advertisers advance warnings about stories."[44]

Deep Structure

Conscious corporate efforts influencing media content to ensure a favorable advertising climate are paralleled by a deeper and more pervasive penetration of media organizations by superclass and corporate ideological views and values. *Deep structure* refers to the institutionalization of superclass-based political-economy views and values in the training and reward structures of, and working conditions experienced by, most mass media professionals. In part, this concept is similar to what media critic Ben Bagdikian has termed "internalized bias"—the unstated and taken-for-granted understanding that journalists working for mainstream media develop concerning what constitutes "acceptable" (to corporate interests) reporting topics, practices, and news content.[45]

The deep-structure linkages between superclass members' views and media content are often indirect, and the connections tend to operate in ways that are both subtle and sometimes covert. For example, it would be difficult to trace the informal policy pathways through which media CEOs' ideological values and news preferences get translated into routine reporting practices. As an illustration, consider events that transpired in 1995 at a series of closed-door political-media meetings sponsored by the conservative Heritage Foundation. The meetings brought together Republican members of the House Commerce Committee and CEOs from nearly all major U.S. media and telecommunications firms, including Fox, ABC, NBC, CBS, Time-Warner, Turner Broadcasting, Tribune Company, and

Gannett. At one point, Time-Warner CEO Gerald Levin reportedly asked Newt Gingrich "what he and other media owners could do to make coverage of the House Speaker more 'fair.' 'Get Your children to behave,' Gingrich reportedly replied."[46] Who knows how—or if—this exchange was translated into informal company reporting policies? The simple fact that they asked the question indicates that superclass media CEOs have specific interests in news content—and reporters are very likely to know it.

Deep structure acts as a kind of hidden context. It is the vehicle through which superclass-favored values and beliefs are woven into the organizational hierarchies, management policies, print and programming decisions, and daily reporting practices of the mainstream media. And these are the firms that generate most of the electronic and printed news and commentary in the United States. Like a transparent fishbowl shaping and bounding the water world of fish, deep structure imposes constraints and patterns on media policies and practices that are nearly invisible—unless its configurations are consciously perceived.

The deep structure of superclass ideological influence in the electronic media is reflected in many ways, but it is especially evident in how resources are granted or withheld in programming decisions. Corporate-media managers routinely select, showcase, and lavishly support conservative, "free-market" corporate cheerleaders. Examples include Rush Limbaugh, Louis Rukeyser (host of *Wall $treet Week* on PBS television), and GE-sponsored "news" programs: *The McLaughlin Group* (PBS),[47] *This Week* (ABC), *Crossfire* (CNN), and *Money Matters* (National Public Radio).[48] By contrast, the same media managers closely scrutinize and often quickly ax the few corporate critics or progressive commentators that typically find short-lived mass media exposure.

One example of the latter practice would be the experience of radio talk-show host and frequent corporate critic Jim Hightower, whose program, *Hightower Radio*, was dropped by ABC.[49] A second example would be Michael Moore's difficulties in keeping his sometimes corporate-biting television program, *TV Nation*, on the air. Moore's show ran briefly in the summer of 1994 on NBC but was quickly dropped by the network. It was picked up in 1995 by the Fox Network, only to be quickly dropped again.[50] The problems these shows have in staying on the air illustrate that the combination of corporate sponsorship and informal censorship leads to a very narrow range of neoliberal-centrist-conservative, probusiness news, information, and commentary disseminated by virtually all mass media outlets.[51] This reality is in sharp contrast to the frequently repeated charge (most often by conservative pundits) that a "liberal bias" exists in mass media news reporting.[52]

Classroom Penetration

Superclass ideological views are not only disseminated to the public by the information industry, but also to schools as well. Classroom programs and educational discounts made available to schools and colleges by the major newsmagazines (*Time, Newsweek, U.S. News and World Report*) ensure that superclass-compatible views and interpretations of national and world events reach high school and college age groups in the guise of "educational materials." Where schools are concerned, the information industry frequently works hand-in-glove with the public relations industry (examined in more detail in the section on spin control). Together, these industries create and promote "educational materials" for the U.S. Chambers of Commerce, NAM, and other corporate-sponsored groups that disseminate free, procorporate teaching materials to teachers and professors. As media critic Ben Bagdikian points out,

> Free classroom materials are produced by 64 percent of the 500 largest American industrial corporations, 90 percent of industrial trade associations, and 90 percent of utility companies. . . . The publication *Media Decisions* estimated that as much as $3 billion in corporate money goes into all methods of promoting the corporation as hero and into "explanations of the capitalistic system," including massive use of corporate books and teaching materials in the schools, almost all tax deductible.[53]

These information and public relations industry products are always represented as educational aids and tools. The content is never described for what it is: mainstream-ideology corporate propaganda promoting the interests of the superclass.

Mainstream Ideology Results

The results of an information industry dominated by superclass ownership, political-economy ideological values, procorporate managers, and co-opted journalistic professionals are threefold. First, the superclass-approved "pluralistic" model of political power is promoted at several levels and in a variety of forms through the major media firms that make up the information industry. Second, political-economy views that differ from superclass views—and the groups that promote them—are ignored, marginalized, or demonized by the information industry. Third, working-class members are encouraged to embrace superclass values and views as their own and to accept the economic and political status quo as the most desirable institutional arrangement.

"Pluralism" Promoted

The extensive promotion of a "pluralism model" of politics and government by the information industry is evident by the ideas and imagery used by nearly all mass media where political reporting is concerned. This model rests on an interest-group interpretation of politics in America. A wide range of interest groups is claimed to exist, but the model argues that no one group is dominant in the political process. Such a view of the nature of politics in America is a constant refrain in media reports and commentary throughout the information industry and effectively neutralizes or excludes alternative perspectives on the nature of U.S. politics and political power.[54]

Media accounts of corporate PAC money and political influence typically reflect—at an implicit level—pluralist interpretations. Political reporters typically point out that a wide array of "special-interest" PACs exist and then go on to explain that this situation actually promotes democracy. Such a reporting focus reinforces the view that American politics consists of competing, interest-based "veto groups" that check one another's power. From this viewpoint, politics and public policies are seen as a kaleidoscopic swirl of pluralistic confusion with a multitude of PACs and individual donors competing for political influence in a kind of rotating King-of-the-Hill game of governance. According to pluralist imagery, corporate PACs are simply one of many PAC types, and they are typically presented in media reports as fragmented interest groups more often competing than cooperating with one another for narrow gains in the political process. This comforting view reinforces the notion that the U.S. political system ensures that no single interest group can corrupt or capture the democratic process.

Corporate PAC donations receive extensive media coverage as potential sources of political influence, but reporters typically look only at specific PAC donations to specific candidates. The idea is to detect evidence connecting the policy-interest "fingerprints" of specific PAC contributors with the actions of specific elected officials. When such connections are found, they are used by reporters as evidence that the media is an effective watchdog providing the public with tough investigative reporting.

Of course, the problem with "pluralist-based" reporting on corporate PAC money as a source of political influence is that the focus on divided interest-group power—rather than upon unified superclass power—in effect calls attention to the trees while ignoring the forest. Pluralist-based reporting leads readers to the conclusion that no single group dominates the political process—and thereby disguises the nature of superclass political power and the operation of the shadow political industry.

Marginalization of Alternatives

In addition to promoting pluralist-based reporting, the mainstream ideology process also encourages media marginalization and demonization of economic and political views or groups disfavored by the superclass. For example, trade union PACs are subject to media attacks as efforts by "union bosses" to manipulate and control the political process.[55] In fact, virtually all organizations, ideas, and public policies or programs promoting working-class interests are often subject to negative mass media reporting.[56] The negation of alternative worldviews is a necessary part of superclass efforts to control the terms of economic and political discourse in the United States. The reality of conflicting class interests means that the experiences, policy priorities, and legislative preferences of the working class are not the same as those of the superclass (or their credentialed-class allies). The consequences for the superclass of allowing the working class to translate its shared interests and experiences into legitimate political discussion, debate, and coherent policy alternatives without the benefit of "ideological coaching" from the information industry would be to risk the growth of class consciousness and class politics. The mainstream ideology process is part of superclass efforts to prevent these prospects from becoming reality.

Embracing Superclass Values?

Superclass ideology legitimates centrist-conservative politics, predatory corporate business practices, and the existing class system—including the wide array of advantages and privileges it provides for the superclass and its credentialed-class allies combined with extensive inequalities for the working class. As a result of our exposure to the mainstream ideology process, most of us tend to take the way the world is organized politically and economically—including the whole catalog of extensive class inequities—for granted. We assume that it is sort of natural and that there is not much we can do about it, so we tend to accept it—perhaps with some grousing and complaining—and go on. In fact, what this attitude reflects is our familiarity with only one ideological perspective: the superclass view. This is the case because it is the one that is subtly and powerfully woven into much of what we see, hear, and read in mass-media-provided news and commentary via the mainstream ideology process.

Unfortunately for superclass leaders, their political-economy ideological foundations are problematic because the public principles they espouse are often at odds with the routine business practices pursued by the large firms they control. For example, superclass leaders claim to favor the ideals of free enterprise, competition, and equal opportunity. But in practice, the large firms, owned largely by the superclass, clearly prefer to dominate markets and maximize profits through monopolistic or oligopolistic practices that exclude the existence of competitive free enterprise or equal opportunity. Also, although corporate executives pay lip service to individualism, they clearly prefer a labor force tightly regimented by unchallenged corporate rule and a consuming public manipulated and dominated by mass advertising. Finally, whereas large firms oppose government regulation of business as well as government policies that would expand the "social wage" (economic programs that would increase the income and economic security of working-class Americans), they typically support the existence and expansion of government programs that channel tax dollars into business revenues and profits. As we will see later in this chapter, reducing the tensions between publicly promoted superclass ideological values and contradictory corporate practices is a major concern of the information industry—often pursued via the opinion-shaping and spin control processes.

THE OPINION-SHAPING PROCESS

> Media conglomerates . . . share values and perspectives that guarantee cloned information. . . . There is no real choice where media concentration narrows the terms of debate and thinking. Thus, the legitimate consent necessary for representative democracy is manufactured.
>
> —Nolan A. Bowie, *Nation*, June 3, 1996

The mainstream ideology process morphs seamlessly into the opinion-shaping process. The two processes overlap in many ways, but the key difference is that whereas the former promotes general neoliberal-centrist-conservative ideological values and principles, the latter involves their detailed infusion into the specifics of news programming, content, and commentary. The opinion-shaping process is most evident through the information industry's consistently favorable treatment—through images, reports, and interpretations—of superclass-dominated ideas, organizations, and policies. Two widespread media practices help create and reinforce public opinion favorable to superclass interests: deck stacking and selective reporting.

Deck Stacking

"Deck stacking" refers to the overwhelming preponderance of prosuperclass and procorporate media managers, editors, commentators, and reporters within the information industry. One way for superclass media owners and their credentialed-class top-level media managers to subtly achieve this result is through staffing and pay practices that distance upper-tier media professionals from average workers' experiences and pay levels and link them more closely to the interests (and views) of elite owner and managers. A 1990 study of editors and reporters covering workers' issues highlighted the gap between workers' experiences and the people who report on their lives and concerns. As workers struggle with declining real wages and as the labor force becomes increasingly diverse, media professionals remain a relatively uniform and well-paid group of mainly white males from middle- and upper-middle-class backgrounds.[57] A 1998 survey of 444 journalists based in Washington, D.C., listed in the *News Media Yellow Book* found that 52 percent of the 141 respondents reported annual household incomes of more than $100,000 and 14 percent reported incomes of more than $200,000 per year.[58]

At the highest reaches of the media hierarchy are elite professionals earning millions who can be counted on to express views consistent with their superclass owner-employer bosses. High-profile examples of media star salaries from the mid-1990s included *ABC News'* Diane Sawyer ($6 million) and Ted Koppel ($5 million), and on radio, Rush Limbaugh ($12 million).[59] Top media professionals continued to command serious money in the late 1990s, with NBC's *Today Show* coanchor Katie Couric reportedly signing a four-year contract in 1998 worth $28 million ($7 million per year), which put her salary close to that of NBC anchor Tom Brokaw.[60] Also in 1998, NBC's *Dateline* coanchor Jane Pauley was reported to have signed a multiyear contract worth $5.5 million annually.[61]

The uniform staffing of information industry management and reporting personnel leads to an ideological filtering and opinion-shaping system generating news content and commentary that consistently parallels and reflects but virtually never challenges superclass ideological views. This situation begins with built-in structural biases grounded in corporate ownership of the media, leading to owners' hiring and rewarding of managers and editors who reflect prosuperclass and procorporate values and views. Acting as gatekeepers, these groups in turn hire and reward reporters who share their views—or who are willing to self-censor their work to conform with the ideological boundaries imposed by the corporate structure and enforced by editorial oversight.[62]

Ongoing, informal social events promoted by top media management linking media professionals with superclass leaders in congenial settings help reinforce a shared worldview and promote cordial media-business ties. In the mid-1990s, *Time* magazine spent $3 million to "fly dozens of corporate chiefs around the world for nine days . . . [escorted] by *Time's* top managers and editors."[63] The firms represented included Lockheed Martin, General Motors, Rockwell, Philip Morris, and Mitsubishi, and the executives met with heads of state from India, Hong Kong, Vietnam, Russia, and Cuba. In a comment on this event, *EXTRA!* asked, "How eager will *Time's* . . . reporters be to scrutinize the firms their bosses have wined and dined across the globe?"[64]

Poll results regarding media professionals' views on labor and their ideological orientations illustrate the nature and extent of deck stacking in the press. A *Los*

Angeles Times poll found 54 percent of editors side with business in labor disputes, and only 7 percent side with labor. A survey, sponsored by the United Auto Workers (UAW), of the one hundred largest daily newspapers found that 60 percent opposed union positions on minimum-wage increases, trade regulations, and plant-closing laws.[65] A Brookings Institution study of Washington, D.C., journalists found that 58 percent identified themselves as either conservative or middle of the road.[66] A more recent (1998) survey of Washington-area journalists found that 66 percent characterized their political orientation as center or right on social issues, but on economic issues 83 percent characterized their political orientation as center or right.[67]

Deck stacking extends across all media formats and is especially evident in the lopsided spectrum of viewpoints presented by television news programming and by nearly all nationally syndicated electronic and print commentators. In 1998 all of the leading political-opinion talk shows on national commercial or public television had centrist or conservative hosts and moderators: *Face the Nation, Meet the Press, The McLaughlin Group, Crossfire, Firing Line, One-on-One, Tony Brown's Journal,* and *Damn Right!*[68]

ABC's *Nightline* illustrates the nature of deck stacking in television "news" shows. *Nightline* routinely hosts two guests debating contemporary political and social issues, giving the appearance that a wide range of viewpoints is being expressed. In fact, *Nightline* most often provides a spectrum of political opinion that extends from the center to the right. A study of the show's regular guests reveals that the vast majority are white, male, and conservative. Moreover, "Nightline almost never airs left-wing analysis that critically questions the basic underlying assumptions of capitalism."[69]

CNN's *Crossfire* news program has the same general format and ideological uniformity as *Nightline*. As the media-watch group Fairness and Accuracy in Reporting (FAIR) points out, the results are predictable: "Although it presents itself as a debate between both ends of the spectrum, usually it ends up as a confrontation between an aggressive advocate for conservative ideology and a more tentative defender of Washington's status quo. True advocates for the left—people who actually push for progressive social change and identify with left-of-center activists—are almost invisible on TV.[70]

Syndicated columnists writing for the print media reflect a pattern of centrist-conservative thought similar to television news and commentary programming. This reality has even been acknowledged by the conservative American Enterprise Institute: "Despite the image of a media dominated by liberals, the reality is much different. The most widely syndicated columnists are conservatives."[71]

Selective Reporting

"Selective reporting" refers to unstated but routine news-reporting policies and practices that produce a preponderance of flattering (virtue-exaggerating) news media coverage of superclass-favored and superclass-sponsored issues, organizations, activities, policies, or people and ignore or play down the merits or significance of topics that threaten superclass interests. Selective reporting is especially evident in news media treatment of business and labor issues.

Business Good, Unions Bad

Selective reporting begins with much greater chunks of media time and space devoted to covering business topics as against labor and union issues. A study of national news television broadcasts found that business and economic reporting receives double the amount of time devoted to workers' issues. Moreover, workers are virtually never interviewed or portrayed as "experts"; and no worker has ever been selected as "Person of the Week" by *ABC World News Tonight*—although many corporate executives are often chosen for this feature.[72] A recent study of local television news broadcasts found that stations devote fewer than 2 percent of news time to labor issues.[73] In addition to imbalanced television news coverage, there are also many specialty business television programs (e.g., *Wall $treet Week, The Nightly Business Report*) and mass-circulation national business publications (e.g., *Wall Street Journal, Business Week, Forbes*) that have no parallels among worker or labor union audiences.

The largely positive media portrayal of business interests, corporate actions, and company executives—including the corporation-as-hero theme—is another feature of selective reporting. This tendency stands in sharp contrast to complaints by some corporate officials that the media often treat businesses harshly.

Copyright © Tom Tomorrow. Reprinted with permission.

However, the evidence overwhelmingly supports the conclusion that "the standard media—mainstream newspapers, magazines, and broadcasters—have always been reliable promoters of the corporate ethic."[74] This is illustrated by a survey of CEOs from the one thousand largest industries in the United States, which revealed that two-thirds believe media treatment of their companies is good or excellent and only 6 percent feel it is poor.[75]

When the mainstream media do present what appear to be negative accounts of corporate actions, a closer look at such stories typically reveals a different truth: "When news shows like *60 Minutes* or *20/20* do segments on 'big business versus the little people,' they usually define the problem in terms of the greed of one group of executives or the excesses of a single company. They never seriously address the nature of capitalism and the structural factors that often lead companies to harm the 'little people.' "[76]

Many mid-1990s reports in the mainstream media on economic trends and disparities gave the appearance of being critiques of corporate practices and power. Two high-profile examples were the 1996 *New York Times* special series, "The Downsizing of America," and *Newsweek*'s sensationalistic cover story on the same topic, titled "Corporate Killers."[77] Both reports seem, to the casual reader, to "dis" the system and criticize the greed of corporate executives. However, a close reading of these reports—and others similar to them—makes it clear that neither corporations nor corporate leaders were presented as villains. In the *Times'* series, the dislocation of workers resulting from corporate downsizing was actually presented as being in the long-term best interests of everyone.

The issue of corporations or corporate leaders acting as instruments of conflicting class interests was never addressed in either piece. Moreover, the *Newsweek* story profiled several examples of corporate "good guys" and provided a long sidebar by former Scott Paper CEO Al Dunlap explaining how corporate downsizers function much like doctors treating disease. Such accounts hardly represent media demonization of corporations. "What these superficially critical stories really make clear is that, though reporters may tug heartstrings from time to time over workers' economic troubles, there's little room in mainstream debate for progressive ideas on what to do about them."[78]

In contrast with corporate media treatment, when unions are the subject of media reporting, they are most often depicted in negative terms: as outdated, confrontational, out of touch with global economic realities, selfish, and corruption riddled.[79] A UAW study identified six negative myths about unions repeatedly cited in the mass media, including these especially damning notions: "Unions have been slowly strangling American business. Workers and unions demand the moon and make consumers pay for it. Unions can't do anything to reverse the falling fortunes of workers. Unions might have once been valuable, but now have too much power and need to be weakened or eliminated."[80] Despite the reality that these myths are easily refuted by accurate information, the study found such information is seldom reported in the mainstream media.

A university study entitled "Media Portrayals of Organized Labor" also reported a pattern of negative media depictions of unions. This study found unions were frequently portrayed by reporters according to eight negative stereotypes that paralleled the myths identified by the UAW study.[81] These findings are consistent with media critic Ben Bagdikian's observations regarding corporate power and media reporting on corporations and unions: "The result of the overwhelming power of relatively narrow corporate ideologies has been the creation of widely established political and economic illusions in the United States. . . . [One is] that labor-union-induced wages are a damaging drag on national productivity and thus on the economy. [It is] false but [it has] been perpetuated by corporate-controlled media for decades."[82]

The negative treatment of unions extends beyond the media to related kinds of firms that are also supposedly in the business of promoting the free exchange of ideas. In October 1996, Michael Moore, author of *DownSize This!*, was informed by the Borders Bookstore chain that his book-signing promotional tour involving Borders stores had been canceled. Borders' management banned him from speaking or signing books at any Borders store in the country. Why? Moore explained: "My book was doing well. It has been on the *New York Times* best-seller list for a month and was the number two best-selling Random House book for the entire Borders chain. I've been banned, I found out, because I made the mistake of uttering a five-letter word, the dirtiest word in all of corporate America—'union.'"[83]

Actually, Moore's "offense" was slightly more complicated. When his book tour hit the Philadelphia Borders store in September, Moore found about one hundred people picketing in support of a former employee who had been fired after a union-organizing drive she had led at the store failed. Moore explained to Borders representatives that he did not cross picket lines and asked if the demonstrators could come inside. They agreed, and the result was a congenial exchange of views, a talk by the fired employee, and record noontime booksales for an author at the Philadelphia Borders store. Following this event, Moore reported that Borders' upper management decided that allowing him to invite the demonstrators inside was a mistake, and the company subsequently canceled the book signing and speaking tour scheduled for October 30.[84] (The lessons here?: Unions are bad! Silence criticism!)

Greedy Geezers

Selective reporting also applies to specific issues and results in one-sided media presentations that attempt to sway public opinion in the direction of superclass interests and public policies that would serve those interests. Illustrating this practice is the growing media reporting trend in the middle and late 1990s depicting senior citizens as "greedy geezers" endangering the federal budget. "Geezer bashing," the portrayal of the aged as "greedy or spoiled, and unwilling to sacrifice," emerged as a growth industry in the mainstream media.[85] These depictions were part of a superclass-based attack on federal entitlement programs, particularly Social Security and Medicare, which were claimed by many politicians (in both parties) and much of the mass media to be on the verge of "bankruptcy."[86]

The superclass interests involved with these issues are twofold. First is money. If just 5 percentage points of Social Security taxes were privatized, $150 billion would be channeled through investment firms.[87] Management fees and administrative charges on privatized, individual retirement accounts would juice Wall Street profits to the tune of millions of dollars. Similar results would occur with the privatization of Medicare. The second issue is political. Reductions in the "social wage"—material benefits provided through the state to citizens as a "right"— increase the economic insecurity of the working class and thus strengthen the political and economic power of the superclass. If workers are confronted with a future that does not include state-funded programs to secure health care and pensions for them in old age, they are rendered even more vulnerable to whatever wage levels and working conditions superclass-controlled employer organizations impose on them.[88]

Social Security and Medicare have long been opposed by conservative elites who would prefer to privatize parts or all of them as a way of diverting funds to profit-making insurance and investment firms. However, in recent years what was once the conservative position on Social Security and Medicare has moved increasingly to the political center as President Clinton and many Democrats have also embraced the "need" for restructuring both programs. The media, owned and controlled by the superclass and corporate America, have been active partners in making the case for cutting so-called budget-busting programs benefiting "greedy geezers."

One media practice encouraging attacks on seniors has been selective reporting on "generational accounting." This term refers to the idea that people born in recent years will pay enormous tax rates to finance federal funding of entitlement programs for the aged and also to service the growing national debt incurred to support these programs. High-profile media reports on this topic appeared in the mid-1990s in the *New York Times* and the *Washington Post*, on ABC's *Nightline*, and in many other national media.[89] At the same time, schemes for privatizing Social Security and controlling Medicare costs through "private-sector efficiencies" also received increasing media attention.

The case for privatizing Social Security was the subject of a 1995 *Time* magazine cover story.[90] Later that year, the *New York Times* ran an op-ed piece by Senators Robert Kerry (D-Nebr.) and Alan Simpson (R-Wyo.) proposing that Social Security could be saved by allowing individuals to invest part of their Social Security taxes in the stock market.[91] The Social Security offensive continued in 1996 as seven of the thirteen members of President Clinton's Social Security Advisory Council proposed some form of privatization and the media continued to parrot superclass claims for the need to cut or privatize Social Security (or both).[92] In 1998 and 1999, Social Security "reform" continued as a center-stage political topic, with most major political players in both parties—including President Clinton—as well as major print and electronic media outlets favoring at least partial "privatization" of the system.[93]

Media attacks on Social Security in the 1990s were paralleled by similar stories and commentary on the need to "reform" Medicare. As one media critic observed, "By focusing narrowly on the conflict between President Clinton and congressional Republicans over the depth of cuts, most reporting has obscured the elite consensus on the need to cut Medicare spending and accelerate the privatization of the program."[94] The "privatize and cut" reporting themes were supported by numerous mainstream commentators such as *Newsweek*'s Robert J. Samuelson, who argued that Clinton needed to take the lead in transforming both Medicare and Social Security by making "a policy reversal that will be blessed by history."[95]

The blessing of history may be in doubt, but there is no doubt that the policy of cutting and privatizing Social Security and Medicare has the blessing of superclass-controlled Wall Street investment and insurance firms. Biased media reporting on the need to cut and privatize these programs to save the nation from "greedy geezers" has led to a virtual media blackout on the class-based forces driving such policies.

The only exceptions to be found are primarily in the alternative media. Three high-profile examples were cover stories on Social Security in *Mother Jones* in 1996, the *Nation* in 1997, and the *Progressive* in 1999. These reports documented how superclass-controlled organizations were driving the campaign to privatize Social Security and undermine public confidence in it.[96] Following the money and naming names, *Mother Jones*, *Nation*, and *Progressive* reporters illustrated the powerful influence of Washington, D.C., insider lobby groups on the Social Security policy debate and on mass media coverage of it. The pro-privatizer groups identified in these reports read like a list of the "usual suspects" who routinely promote superclass interests: the NAM, the U.S. Chambers of Commerce, the American Council of Life Insurance, and think tanks like the conservative Cato Institute.[97]

Mother Jones reported that the Cato Institute had amassed a $2 million corporate-donated budget to convince the media, the public, and members of Congress that "Social Security is headed for a crisis."[98] The *Nation* and the *Progressive* pointed out the effectiveness of the superclass-funded media campaign. From the *New York Times* and the *Washington Post* to other large city newspapers, in the mid- to the late 1990s, the op-ed pages and news columns were often filled with Cato and Concord Coalition-cloned copy. Dean Baker, an economist with the liberal Economic Policy Institute, observed that "the media have closed off discussion. . . . They think everyone agrees Social Security is a basket case and has to be overhauled."[99] The effects on public opinion of the nearly unanimous mass media reports in favor of "reforming" Social Security were consistent with superclass interests. In 1997 a *Wall Street Journal/NBC News* poll reported that "an overwhelming 83 percent of Americans now accept that changes are needed in Social Security."[100]

Articles critical of efforts to "reform" Social Security and Medicare continued in 1999, but only in alternative media such as *Dollars and Sense*, *EXTRA!*, *In These Times*, *Mother Jones*, the *Nation*, and the *Progressive*. Such reports stand in stark contrast to the prosuperclass content of most mainstream media reports on Social Security, Medicare, and other entitlement programs for the aged and the poor. But the limited resources of the alternative media make it difficult for reports grounded in reality to counter mass media accounts grounded in superclass-generated propaganda.

Think Tanks (Again!)

Selective reporting on a wide range of topics is reinforced through extensive media reliance on information derived from superclass-funded "official sources" such as think tanks. A 1998 study of 1997 media references to major think tanks according to their ideological orientations found an overwhelming reliance on conservative and centrist organizations. Using a Nexis database search of major newspapers and radio and TV transcripts for 1997, the study found a total of 14,623 media references to think tank sources. There were 7,733 references (53 percent) to conservative think tanks such as the Heritage Foundation and 4,623 references (32 percent) to centrist organizations such as the Brookings Institution. By contrast, the study found only 2,267 references (16 percent) to progressive think tanks such as the Institute for Policy Studies (172 references).[101]

Given extensive superclass funding of and media firm links to conservative-centrist think tanks, the results of the study should not be surprising. For example, the Heritage Foundation, the conservative think tank most widely cited by the U.S. media in 1997 (1,813 citations), collected $29.7 million in contributions in 1995, with much of the money coming from conservative sources such as the Olin and Bradley foundations.[102] The conservative Cato Institute (1,286 media citations in 1997) now has annual funding of $8 million (double that of 1992), with contributions coming from "drug, medical device, biotechnology, and tobacco manufacturers and their corporate foundations."[103] Also, Cato's board of directors includes two major media CEOs: News Corporation (Fox TV) owner Rupert Murdoch (who also sits on the Philip Morris board of directors) joined the Cato board in 1997, and John C. Malone (CEO of Tele-Communications Inc., the largest U.S. cable operator) has been a Cato board member since 1995.[104]

THE SPIN-CONTROL PROCESS

The whole topic [of propaganda in U.S. culture] is vastly understudied for pretty obvious reasons.

—Noam Chomsky, *Nation*, November 18, 1996

The "spin-control process" refers to a wide array of propaganda-driven media practices. It involves media owners, managers, reporters, pundits, and commercial and political advertisers using the information industry as a platform for disseminating news, commentary, images, and advertising with a prosuperclass and pro-corporate slant. The objectives of spin control include ideological justifications of the economic and political status quo and the commercial marketing of products, services, and corporate images as well as media-based marketing of political candidates, public officials, and public policies. Spin control involves a symbiotic linkage between the information industry and the public relations industry, a $10 billion corporate enterprise based on the twin goals of manipulation and deception. Using the information industry as a platform, the public relations industry provides a wide array of services—mainly to superclass, corporate, and political clients—ranging from conventional press releases to commercial and political advertising campaigns to "the hiring of spies, the suppression of free speech, and even the manufacture of 'grass roots' movements."[105]

The spin-control process operates at two levels. The first involves interpretation: it consists of information-industry-channeled news reporting and commentary that is "shaded"—through media professionals' choices of value-laden terms, images, references, context, and illustrations—in directions that reflect positively on superclass-favored ideas, policies, organizations, and interests and negatively on topics disfavored by elites. The second level involves propaganda, deception, and calculated manipulation. It consists of all forms of advertising and public relations strategies and tactics aimed at manipulating target populations' opinions, attitudes, tastes, and behaviors (mainly those of the working class) on behalf of goals established most often by superclass-controlled corporate and political clients.

Spin control is an extremely complex topic with many facets extending beyond the scope of this book. The purpose of this section is simply to highlight, through illustrative examples, how each spin-control level furthers superclass interests, often in ways that conceal the nature and extent of these interests and of superclass power as well.

Spin Control: Interpretation

As noted earlier in this chapter, tensions between superclass ideological assertions that the U.S. economic and political systems are the best in the world and routine corporate practices producing a variety of negative economic and political consequences for the working class are problematic for elites. Efforts to reduce or reconcile these tensions are a routine focus of the spin-control process. Mainstream media reporters and pundits typically address these tensions with interpretive news reports and commentary that represent U.S. economic, political, and social problems as resulting from a host of non-class-based causes. Most often these "causes" are represented as various individual-level flaws (often psychological or biological), subcultural pathologies, governmental meddling, and temporary, unavoidable, but good-for-everyone-in-the-long-term consequences of large-scale "natural laws." These latter forces often include the wonderful and mysterious "free market" or the equally magical "global economy." One important effect of media interpretations of these factors as causal forces driving social problems is that it distracts audiences from the problematic effects of superclass domination and control of the media and indeed of most other institutions in the society.

Superclass to Media: Downsize, But Don't Kill The Dream!

Some of these themes were evident in the mid-1990s as the mainstream media focused briefly on economic changes negatively affecting nonelite workers and their families: downsizing, job losses, global trade, and declining real income. In 1996 two major U.S. newspapers ran reports on the trend of growing economic inequalities. The *New York Times* series, "The Downsizing of America," explored some of the human costs of downsizing and was later expanded and published as a book-length report.[106] The *Philadelphia Inquirer* series "Who Stole the Dream?" was more starkly descriptive of growing class inequalities than the *Times* series and focused more directly on how government policies had contributed to growing economic polarization.[107]

Despite their seemingly critical focus, both series actually came equipped with built-in spin-control interpretative schemes. Although the *Times* series did report on the human face of downsizing, the accounts steered clear of exploring the role of superclass and corporate interests as critical forces driving the downsizing trend. Instead, the articles essentially advised workers to drop their "floating anger," sharpen their skills, and "learn to live with layoffs."[108] The *Inquirer* series described growing class-polarization trends in pointed terms but primarily invoked public policies—rather than superclass- and corporate-based power and practices—to account for growing economic inequalities.[109] In this sense, the series fit into a long-standing mainstream media tradition of viewing government (especially the federal government) as the problem. Rather than exploring how and why government policies facilitating economic inequalities have been shaped by superclass and corporate power channeled through the shadow political industry and government officials and agencies, this tradition simply views big government as the villain.

Although there was a total absence of any real critique of superclass and corporate power in either series, big spin-control guns were quickly rolled out to blunt even implied criticism of the American economic system. The *Inquirer* series was too much for the *Seattle Times*. The paper first decided to reprint the series "but canceled it after just one installment—and apologized to readers for running that one."[110] Both series were critiqued by Robert J. Samuelson, economic columnist for the *Washington Post* and *Newsweek*. Using labels such as "junk" and "shoddy journalism," Samuelson dismissed both series as products of ignorance on the part of the journalists and their editors. He also took care to praise a more balanced series (in his view) from the *Los Angeles Times* that profiled "the gains that economic change creates as well as the trauma it inflicts."[111] Another spin-control effort came from Mike Meyers of the Scripps-Howard News Service.

Using information from the National Association of Business Economists, Meyers' syndicated report headlined, "No Doom and Gloom, Americans Better Off." He quoted business economists and the American Enterprise Institute to make two points: (1) negative media reports on the U.S. economy are wildly misleading because "more Americans are better off than at any other time in the nation's history"; and (2) reporters may be economic dunces, but they know that bad news gets more attention than good news.[112]

Also in 1996, the *Washington Post* weighed in with a thinly veiled spin-control series highlighting public ignorance on basic economic realities. This three-part effort zeroed in on comparisons between public knowledge and attitudes about the U.S. economy (based on a poll of 1,511 adults) and economic reality as viewed by economic experts (based on a survey of 250 Ph.D. economists). Although it was presented as an objective investigation into a major public policy issue, the main thrust of the series was in the direction of discrediting negative public views about the economy as based on ignorance, not on facts.[113] Barely any reading between the lines was necessary to see the series for what it was: a sharp attack on mainstream media accounts of the economy for including what could be interpreted by nonelites as negative information—such as the *Times* and *Inquirer* series. The *Post* series spin clearly implied that such accounts help create false negative public perceptions about the economy, thereby complicating the efforts of our fine economic experts in their quest to develop "sound" (superclass-friendly) public economic policies.

A high-profile spin defense of the American economic system appeared early in 1996, preceding the major "critical" media reports that ran later in the year. A *Newsweek* cover story ("Cheer Up America! It's Not as Bad as You Think") treated readers to a lengthy excerpt from Robert J. Samuelson's new book with extensive tables and charts "proving" two main points: (1) by virtually any measure, Americans are better off today than ever; and (2) the major problem in America today stems from unrealistic expectations owing mainly to an "entitlement mentality" driven by—what else?—government promises. Getting to the heart of the matter, Samuelson wrote, "People expect government to solve all of their grievances.... By now, it's obvious we can't have it all."[114] He went on to counsel Americans to revise their expectations and recognize that when it comes to the American economy, job opportunities, security, and wages as well as consumer prices are actually much better than they seem to be—or as they are sometimes portrayed in the media.

These examples represent a few of the many cases in the 1990s in which the information industry invoked spin-control to defend the American economic system in the face of growing economic inequalities and to attack reports viewed as critical of "the system." This pattern continued through the late 1990s. Critics of "negative" media reports on American businesses had a spin field day when the *Cincinnati Enquirer*'s investigation into alleged wrongdoing by Chiquita Brands International (owned by superclass bipartisan political donor Carl H. Linder) crashed and burned—big time. As a result of finding that the reporter allegedly used stolen voice-mail messages and engaged in other alleged reporting irregularities, in 1998 the *Enquirer* fired the reporter, ran three days of front-page apologies, and agreed to pay Chiquita Brands $10 million—supposedly to avoid a lawsuit.[115]

Conservative critics saw this episode as a vindication of their belief that the "liberal media" were antibusiness. And they used it (along with cases of journalistic fabrication that came to light in 1998) as a spin platform to discredit "institutional liberalism" (claimed to permeate the media) and "the first principle of liberalism [which] is that big business is bad."[116] Regardless of conservative pundits' comments, the lesson for media managers and reporters from this episode was likely to be, Avoid corporate criticism! Yet, following the settlement, Chiquita's business practices were still being investigated by the Securities and Exchange Commission, and the government of Honduras was reviewing possible bribery charges against the firm.[117]

Demonizing Critics

Switching from positive to negative spin-control modes is routine in the information industry when it comes to individuals and groups viewed as critics of the economy—or of the superclass-credentialed-class power elite that runs it. One example occurred in early 1996 when Labor Secretary Robert Reich, commenting on corporate policies and decisions negatively affecting workers, their families, and communities, called for "a new corporate citizenship" and encouraged business leaders to "do some soul searching" and "size up their responsibilities to America." In reporting on his comments, the *Washington Post* spin referred to the "strident tone" of Reich's "barrage" and sarcastically described his efforts as a "crusade" for corporate responsibility. As FAIR pointed out, "When the *Post*'s news reporters refer to such measured comments as 'strident,' it's evidence that there's a need for more *journalistic* responsibility."[118]

Similar negative spin control is routine when the information industry reports on organized labor. In late 1995, the AFL-CIO's contested presidential election served as a brief focus of media attention—and illustrated how the media routinely lace labor stories with pejorative terms and imagery to generate negative spin control where unions are concerned. As one media critic pointed out, "The election coverage . . . drew heavily on corporate-owned media's stock images of organized labor as disruptive yet marginal, both aggressive and moribund."[119]

Media accounts of the AFL-CIO presidential election in the *Washington Post*, the *New York Times*, and the *Chicago Tribune* included a number of negative value-laden terms and images aimed at discrediting the views, goals, and tactics of unions. The *Post* story described eventual presidential winner John Sweeney's supporters as "shock troops," used the terms "militant" or "militancy" seven times, and speculated about labor's return to "bare knuckle tactics." The *Times* reported (falsely) that Sweeney would "blockade the economy," and the *Tribune* editorialized against "confrontation by unions." In these cases and others, "media accounts made the appeals by workers and labor advocates for more assertive, proactive leadership sound like a call for armed insurrection."[120]

Spin Control: Propaganda

The public relations industry is the major force driving explicit, calculated spin control through the use of advertising, propaganda of all sorts, and newer techniques such as the creation of "grassroots" movements to support any given client's interests, as well as the conscious manipulation of journalists. The industry is led by large firms, such as Hill and Knowlton, Burson-Marsteller, and Ketchum PR, and employs "150,000 people (20,000 more than all the reporters in the U.S.)," and influences "an estimated 40 percent of what Americans now see and read."[121] Propaganda-based spin control comes in many forms, but three are especially important to protecting and concealing superclass and corporate interests and power: corporate-image advertising, astroturf campaigns, and journalistic manipulation.

Corporate Image Advertising

Corporate advertising to promote the ideology and image of corporations represents at least a half-billion-dollar-a-year enterprise today.[122] Ads attesting to the altruism and benevolent good works of corporations such as Dow, DuPont, Mobil Oil, Phillips, and others are routinely published in national magazines and aired on network television. Meanwhile, "on so-called 'public TV,' a dozen big corporate polluters—including BASF, Goodyear and Mobil—polish their images by underwriting nature shows."[123] The head of a large advertising agency described the purpose of corporate advertising thus: "It presents the corporation as hero, a responsible citizen, a force for good, presenting information on the work the company is doing in community relations, assisting the less fortunate, minimizing pollution, controlling drugs, ameliorating poverty.[124]

The point of corporate advertising is to create favorable public opinion regarding corporate ideas, motives, and actions. This helps maintain the legitimacy of corporations—and by extension helps protect not only their business interests but also the economic and political interests and power of superclass corporate owners.

Astroturf Campaigns

Corporations may be able to count on the built-in procorporate biases of commercial journalism, but these leanings do not necessarily guarantee favorable media coverage for any specific firm or industry—especially where sensitive health, safety, or environmental issues are concerned. However, corporations have discovered that "astroturf campaigns" organized by the public relations industry can be very useful in generating positive press coverage, public opinion, and favorable treatment by policy makers and the courts. Indeed, this form of lobbying, whereby citizens are used as pawns in pseudograssroots, corporate-sponsored public relations offensives, "has ballooned into a half-billion-dollar PR sub-specialty."[125] It typically involves the use of "industry-generated 'citizens' groups who can be relied upon to lobby government and speak eloquently to [the] media."[126]

The most successful examples of astroturf campaigns—from a corporate perspective—are not publicly known because they are the ones whose true nature and purposes were never discovered or revealed. However, recent examples that have come to light illustrate such how campaigns serve corporate interests via the spin-control propaganda process.

Beginning in the 1980s and continuing into the 1990s, Dow Corning Corporation became the target of lawsuits filed by women claiming health problems caused by silicone breast implants made by Dow Corning. Moreover, in 1990 some women began appearing on TV complaining not only that Dow Corning implants had made them ill but also that the company knew it but did not care. The publicity surrounding this issue prompted an investigation into the matter by the Food and Drug Administration. For Dow Corning, the issue was very serious for both financial and corporate-image reasons. As Dan Hayes, the CEO at Dow Corning, wrote in a 1991 confidential internal memo, "Obviously this is the largest single issue on our platter because it affects not only the next 2–3 years' profitability of DCC but ultimately has a big impact on the long-term ethics and believability issues. . . . What is at risk here is somewhere between $50 million and $500 million."[127]

For assistance with its image and financial problems, Dow Corning hired the Burson-Marsteller public relations firm—an organization with experience in developing "astroturf campaigns." One facet of the public relations strategy crafted by Burson-Marsteller involved the creation of pro-silicone-implant "grassroots" patient groups to speak out favorably on behalf of silicone breast implants. "According to a confidential letter . . . Burson-Marsteller's strategy for DCC involved identifying patients who could be trained as spokespeople, making corporate grants to appropriate organizations, and providing day-to-day media support for the group." The idea was to recruit and train women (including celebrities) to deliver "testimony written for them to . . . Congressional committees. The public relations goal was to get 'women angry about having the right to make their own decision about implants taken away from them.'"[128]

The "pro-choice" position regarding silicone implants was articulated in several public forums by numerous groups and spokespersons including Sharon Green, executive director of the national breast-cancer organization, Y-ME. On September 27, 1995, Green appeared on the *Oprah Winfrey Show*, and in 1996 she was quoted in *MS. Magazine* (the March–April issue) and interviewed for a WBBM-TV science segment on breast implants on February 2. She also testified before Congress in 1995 on the implant issue. However, the fact that Y-ME is funded in part by Dow Corning, Bristol-Myers Squibb (another silicone implant manufacturer), and the Plastic Surgeons' Associated was not revealed in any of Green's appearances.[129]

Burson-Marsteller was also the force behind the creation (with funding from Philip Morris) of a "grassroots" group known as the National Smokers Alliance to promote smokers' rights.[130] In fact, many tobacco firms were involved in astroturf campaigns in the 1990s to help protect their economic interests in the $45 billion industry. For example, RJR Nabisco helped create and hired the Ramhurst Corporation public relations company in 1993. This firm "combines 'grassroots lobbying' with inside-the-Beltway influence peddling."[131] But more recently, "grassroots" campaigns created and promoted by the tobacco industry have shifted their focus: "Smokers' rights groups have given way to more effective—and more covert—coalitions with anti-tax groups."[132] As one investigative reporter put it, "'Grassroots' coalitions have become a vital tool for tobacco's survival because of the industry's increasingly negative public image."[133]

The Dow Corning and tobacco industry astroturf spin efforts illustrate the tip of a corporate iceberg involving phony "grassroots" campaigns. The public relations industry's expanding use of these campaigns on behalf of corporate clients was the subject of a mid-1990s book, and the issue is frequently covered by the media watch publication *EXTRA!*.[134] These campaigns traffic in calculated deception but translate into favorable media coverage, political influence, and economic gains for corporate clients, public relations firms, and their superclass owners.

The net effects of such campaigns extend beyond single-corporation or industry gains. Astroturf campaigns can (and are) used on behalf of entire clusters of firms and industries to promote classwide policy outcomes favorable to superclass interests. The fact that such campaigns strike at the heart of representative democracy is irrelevant to corporate clients. Superclass astroturf campaign clients understand that it is possible to combine the sentiments of National Football League coach Vince Lombardi's well-known cliché and singer-songwriter Randy Newman's song title into a single line: "It's Winning and Money That Matter in the U. S. A."

Journalistic Manipulation

Since the public relations industry's mission essentially involves serving the interests of wealthy clients, it has an ongoing concern with developing practices that will generate media spin control in directions desired by its clients. To maximize media influence and control on behalf of wealthy clients, some public relations firms now specialize in "compiling dossiers on [reporters] so . . . corporate clients will know how to manipulate individual members of the media." One such firm called TJFR Products and Services, founded by former *Wall Street Journal* reporter Dean Rotbart, had six thousand reporters' biographies in its computerized files in 1993. These files are for sale to corporate clients. As Rotbart says, "If at any point you get a call from a journalist and don't know who it is, call us up and we will fax you that bio within an hour."[135]

Other public relations firms track specific issues and prepare reports on the journalists who cover them. For example, Rowan and Blewitt, headquartered in Washington, D.C., was retained by the dairy industry to analyze media coverage of the recombinant bovine growth hormone (rBGH) issue. The CARMA International public relations firm was also hired to track the same issue and "ranked individual reporters based on whether their stories were 'favorable' or 'unfavorable' to rBGH."[136]

Public relations firms also provide media manipulation spin skills to corporate public relations representatives by hiring real journalists to take part in training exercises. For example, Robert J. Meyers and Associates of Houston hired three journalists to help ARCO Petroleum "practice its PR plan for handling the news media following environmental disasters." According to one of the journalists involved, the reporters were assigned to play the role of the "predatory press" while professional actors were hired to play the part of environmentalists. For the Meyers firm this was not an isolated event. In the past six years the company has conducted more than four hundred similar training drills.[137]

These examples of journalistic manipulation illustrate one of the many ways in which it is possible for the public relations industry to "spin" so much of what Americans read, see, and hear in the media in prosuperclass and procorporate terms. They also underscore the point that these kinds of services are provided mainly on behalf of wealthy corporate clients to further their economic and political interests—and those of their superclass owners. Finally, they call attention to the lamentable dearth of "counterspin" agents and practices working on behalf of working-class interests and power.

THE INFORMATION INDUSTRY: CONCLUSIONS

"Help FAIR Spread the Word about Journalists' Addiction: Corporate Control Is the Problem."

—FAIR solicitation letter, October 1997

The mainstream ideology, opinion-shaping, and spin control processes are driven not by a superclass conspiracy but rather by superclass media ownership, a shared ideology that views the economic and political status quo as the best possible world, in accordance with common classwide interests and routine business practices. These factors thread superclass preferences and ideological biases into the fabric of virtually all news reporting, commentary, and advertising generated by the information industry. The industry consistently tilts reporting and commentary on events, institutions, personalities, and policies relevant to superclass interests in directions consistent with those interests. Of course, the three processes operating through the information industry may not always lead to a uniform, superclass-blessed "corporate ministry of information party line" on all issues and topics. But they clearly produce a lopsided presentation of ideologically infused news and commentary that trends in the direction of privileged-class interests on most issues, most of the time.

Root, Root, Root for the Home Team?

Media-based "ideological coaching" may not always lead the working class to share the views and policy preferences of superclass-sponsored opinion shapers. However, it clearly predisposes public opinion among working-class members in those directions—at least on some critical class-based issues such as legitimating the accumulation of private wealth and the importance of reducing the federal deficit. Poll data illustrate superclass successes in shaping public opinion on these issues. As the United States was emerging from the Great Depression in 1939, a Roper poll found only a minority—24 percent—agreeing that there should be a law limiting the amount of money a person could earn in a year. By 1992, with economic inequality accelerating, that number had shrunk to a tiny 9 percent.[138] Also, although the "balanced budget" movement is recognized by many progressives as a superclass-driven smoke screen for dismantling more social programs,[139] a sizable portion of the American public has been convinced of the need for the government to "balance its checkbook"—just like average folks. In the mid-1990s, a Gallup poll reported 82 percent of Americans said "significant" deficit reduction should be the top or a high priority for the incoming Congress.[140]

A further effect of the control processes operating via the information industry relates to the political awareness of and choices made by the working class. By restricting the expression of alternative perspectives, superclass-based media control leads to confusion among working-class members over how the shadow political industry is both driven by and serves superclass resources and interests. It also leads to circumscribed, sterile politics and fatalistic or de facto support among workers for the economic and political status quo. The lopsided ideological spectrum and stunted political debate presented in the media "leaves most citizens without a coherent view of politics . . . [and] a population unable to select alternative patterns of power sustains the status quo."[141]

The Persistence of Resistance?

The preceding section suggests working-class members frequently share superclass favored views, but other evidence indicates that significant divisions also exist on some issues. The opposing nature of superclass and working-class views is evident in the results of a 1996 poll conducted by the *Nation* and the Institute for America's Future, surveying average Americans and political donors who contributed $5,000 or more to federal political candidates during the November 1993 through March 1996 period. The poll shows that whereas average Americans are concerned with growing economic insecurity and corporate power, elite donors are not. For example, 83 percent of average Americans agree (almost three-fifths strongly agree) that "average working families have less economic security today, because corporations have become too greedy and care more about their profits than about being fair and loyal to their employees." By contrast, a majority of large donors disagree with the statement.[142]

Other recent polls of average Americans also reveal views hostile to superclass interests and control. A 1996 poll of eight hundred Americans, sponsored by the Preamble Center for Public Policy, found that 70 percent believe corporate greed, not the global economy, is behind corporate downsizing. Moreover, 46 percent believe corporate greed is the biggest obstacle to middle-class living standards, compared with 28 percent who see government waste and inefficiency as the main problem. Also, 76 percent support "living-wage laws" and 82 percent favor congressional action for "setting standards for responsible corporate behavior" and lowering taxes on companies that comply.[143]

The results of such polls illustrate that despite the superclass biases inherent in the information industry, working-class members are not always passive vessels filled with superclass-generated information and propaganda. Instead, such results indicate resistance among nonelites to the massive dissemination through the information industry of information and commentary that preponderately supports the status quo. It is apparent that increasing experiences with and knowledge about class-based inequalities among the nonprivileged is fostering a growing awareness of and concerns about the nature and extent of superclass interests, motives, and power in the economic and political arenas.

The Stealth Industries

Despite the size, power, and record of success in promoting superclass interests, most features of the information industry—including details concerning superclass funding and control of its operations—are seldom reported by the mainstream media.[144] The scant media and public attention paid to superclass control of this industry as well as its control of the shadow political industry reveals their stealthlike qualities: They're there, but they do not register on media radar screens or generate much public attention. Why not? We believe the answer has three parts.

First, these industries are cloaked in the same powerful political force field that drives the class taboo: the mass media's avoidance of reporting on class issues—based in and funded by the superclass and its corporate domain—including the absence of serious inquiries into the organizational foundations of class inequities.[145] Second, the information and shadow industries consist of numerous legitimate organizations with extensive resources and payrolls. Their links to major corporations, the mainstream mass media, and the national government make them a routine part of society—a nonstory, by mainstream media standards. Third, when either industry does become the focus of media reports or books, the "pluralist-special-interest group" model typically organizes and drives these accounts.[146] Viewers and readers are left with the impression that both industries consist of a diverse collection of competing organizations and sectors. No mention is made of the existence or importance of the superclass to funding, organizing, and coordinating the activities of these industries.

These factors help ensure that for each industry, the superclass-based political control structures and processes as well as the class consequences of their actions are largely shielded from media reporting and public attention. The result is the "stunt" Gore Vidal described in the opening of chapter 4: superclass political dominance vanishes behind the unreported, widespread business-as-usual routines and legitimacy accorded to most features of the information and shadow political industries. In effect, the organizational foundations of the class empire and the results of its activities are hidden—in plain sight.

NOTES

1. Robert A. Sirico, "The Capitalist Ethic: True Morality," *Forbes*, December 2, 1996, 85.

2. Timothy D. Schellhardt, "Are Layoffs Moral? One Firm's Answer: You Ask, We'll Sue," *Wall Street Journal*, August 1, 1996.

3. "Soundbites," *EXTRA!*, September–October 1996, 5.

4. Peter Hart and Steve Rendall, "Meet the Myth Makers," *EXTRA!*, July–August 1998 26–27.

5. Robert W. McChesney, "The Global Media Giants," *EXTRA!*, November–December 1997, 11–18. Also see Jim Naureckas, "From the Top: What Are the Politics of Network Bosses?," *EXTRA!*, July–August 1998, 21–22.

6. Mark C. Miller, "Free the Media," *Nation*, June 3, 1996, 9–15.

7. Sam Husseini and Norman Solomon, "The Right-Leaning Rolodex," *EXTRA!*, July–August 1998, 13.

8. David Croteau, "Challenging the 'Liberal Media' Claim," *EXTRA!*, July–August 1998, 9.

9. McChesney, "The Global Media Giants," 11.

10. Evan Thomas and Gregory L. Vistica, "Fallout from a Media Fiasco," *Newsweek*, July 20, 1998, 25.

11. Ibid.

12. Thomas Dye, *Who's Running America?: The Clinton Years* (Englewood Cliffs, N.J.: Prentice-Hall, 1995), 112–13.

13. Robert Famighetti, ed., *The World Almanac and Book of Facts, 1997* (Mahwah, N.J.: K-III Reference Corporation, 1996), 290.

14. Mark C. Miller, "The National Entertainment State," *Nation*, June 3, 1996, fold-out map. Also see Johnnie L. Roberts, "Mergers' Main Men," *Newsweek*, July 29, 1996, 42–48; and McChesney, "The Global Media Giants," 15.

15. Naureckas, "From the Top," 21.

16. Miller, "The National Entertainment State," fold-out; Roberts, "Mergers' Main Men," 42–48.

17. McChesney, "The Global Media Giants," 11–18.

18. Ben H. Bagdikian, *The Media Monopoly* (Boston, Mass.: Beacon Press, 1997), 6–8, 15–16.

19. Robert Parry, "The Right-Wing Media Machine," *Extra!*, March–April 1995, 7.

20. Naureckas, "From the Top," 21–22. Also see "Where's the Power: Newsroom or Boardroom?," *EXTRA!*, July–August 1998, 23.

21. Bagdikian, *The Media Monopoly*, 26.

22. Dye, *Who's Running America?*, 115.

23. Vicente Navarro, "The Politics of Health Care Reform in the United States, 1992–1994: A Historical Review," *International Journal of Health Services* 25 (1995): 185–201.

24. Janine Jackson, "Let Them Eat Baguettes," *EXTRA!*, March–April 1996, 14–15.

25. Dye, *Who's Running America?*, 196.

26. G. William Domhoff, *Who Rules America?: Power and Politics in the Year 2000* (Mountain View, Calif.: Mayfield, 1998), 175.

27. Bagdikian, *The Media Monopoly*, 6.

28. Parry, "The Right-Wing Media Machine," 7.

29. Naureckas, "From the Top," 21–22.

30. Bagdikian, *The Media Monopoly*, 85–86.

31. Miller, "The National Entertainment State," 12.

32. Eyal Press, "Spin Cities," *Nation*, November 18, 1996, 30.

33. Bagdikian, *The Media Monopoly*, 159–61.

34. Jim Naureckas, "Corporate Censorship Matters: The Case of NBC," *EXTRA!*, November–December 1995, 13.

35. Sheldon Rampton and John Stauber, "This Report Brought to You by Monsanto," *Progressive*, July 1998, 22–25.

36. Jane Akre, "We Report, They Decide: Fox TV Censors Series on Milk Hazards," *National News Reporter*, June 1998, 13.

37. Ibid.

38. Rampton and Stauber, "This Report Brought to You by Monsanto," 24.

39. Akre, "We Report, They Decide," 13.

40. Sheldon Rampton and John Stauber, "Oprah's Free—Are We?," *EXTRA!*, May–June 1998, 11–12. Also see Ralph Nader, "Product Libel," *Public Citizen News*, May–June 1998, 4.

41. Lawrence Soley, "The Power of the Press Has a Price," *EXTRA!*, July–August 1997, 11–13.

42. G. Bruce Knecht, "Hard Copy: Magazine Advertisers Demand Prior Notice of 'Offensive' Articles," *Wall Street Journal*, April 30, 1997.

43. Ibid.

44. Ibid.

45. Bagdikian, *The Media Monopoly*, 218.

46. Jim Naureckas, "Editor's Note: The Media-Republican Complex," *EXTRA!*, March–April 1995, 2.

47. Parry, "The Right-Wing Media Machine," 6–10.

48. Gail Dines, "Capitalism's Pitchmen," *Dollars and Sense*, May 1992, 20.

49. Edward S. Herman, "The Media Mega-Mergers," *Dollars and Sense*, May–June 1996, 8–13. Also see "Action Alert," *EXTRA!*, December 1995, 4.

50. Chris Lehmann, "Michael and Me," *In These Times*, October 14, 1996, 39–40.

51. "Field Guide to TV's Lukewarm Liberals," *EXTRA!*, July–August 1998, 14–17.

52. Joseph Perkins, "Caught in the News Media's Liberal Bias," *Indianapolis Star*, July 18, 1998. Also see "'The 89 Percent Liberal Media,'" *EXTRA!*, July–August 1998, 10; and Parry, "The Right-Wing Media Machine," 6–19.

53. Bagdikian, *The Media Monopoly*, 51, 58.

54. Kevin Phillips, "Fat City," *Time*, September 26, 1994, 49–56.

55. Janine Jackson, "Major Player or Big Bully?," *EXTRA!*, January–February 1997, 9–10. Also see "Don't Let Them Fool You!," *AFSCME Public Employee*, March–April 1998, 6–11.

56. Dines, "Capitalism's Pitchmen," 18–20.

57. Jonathan Tasini, "Lost in the Margins: Labor and the Media," *EXTRA!*, Summer 1990, 4.

58. Croteau, "Challenging the 'Liberal Media' Claim," 8.

59. "Lifestyles of the Rich and Fatuous," *EXTRA!Update*, April 1994, 2.

60. Rick Marin and Yahlin Chang, "The Katie Factor," *Newsweek*, July 6, 1998, 53.

61. Robert J. Samuelson, "Down with the Media Elite!?," *Newsweek*, July 13, 1998, 47.

62. George Seldes, "Is the Entire Press Corrupt?," *EXTRA!*, November–December 1994, 26–27.

63. "CEOs Play Reporter," *EXTRA!Update*, February 1996, 2.

64. Ibid.

65. David Elsila, Michael Funke, and Sam Kirkland, "Blaming the Victim: The Propaganda War against Workers," *UAW Solidarity*, April 1992, 11–17.

66. Martin A. Lee and Norman Solomon, "Does the News Media Have a Liberal Bias?," in *Taking Sides*, ed. Kurt Finsterbusch and George McKenna (Guilford, Conn.: Duskin, 1996), 28.

67. Croteau, "Challenging the 'Liberal Media' Claim," 4.

68. "Field Guide to TV's Lukewarm Liberals," 14–17.

69. Dines, "Capitalism's Pitchmen," 20.

70. "From the Left: More Than a Figure of Speech?," *EXTRA!Update*, February 1996, 1.

71. Elsila, Funke, and Kirkland, "Blaming the Victim," 12.

72. Tasini, "Lost in the Margins," 2–6.

73. Jennifer Gonnerman, "Media Watch," *In These Times*, December 25, 1995, 9.

74. Bagdikian, *The Media Monopoly*, 52.

75. Ibid., 57.

76. Dines, "Capitalism's Pitchmen," 18.

77. *New York Times, The Downsizing of America* (New York: Random House, 1996). Also see Allan Sloan, "The Hit Men," *Newsweek*, February 26, 1996, 44–48.

78. Janine Jackson, "We Feel Your Pain," *EXTRA!*, May–June 1996, 12.

79. Janine Jackson, "Moribund Militants: Corporate Media on (Re)Organized Labor," *EXTRA!*, January–February 1996, 6–7.

80. "Media Myths and Facts," *UAW Solidarity*, April 1992, 17.

81. Jonathan Tasini, "Media Stereotypes about Unions," *EXTRA!*, Summer 1990, 4.

82. Bagdikian, *The Media Monopoly*, 44.

83. Michael Moore, "Banned by Borders," *Nation*, December 2, 1996, 10.

84. Ibid.

85. Jeff Cohen and Norman Solomon, *Adventures in MediaLand* (Monroe, Maine: Common Courage Press, 1993), 28.

86. *Ageism on the Agenda*, special issue, *EXTRA!*, March–April 1997.

87. Trudy Lieberman, "Social Insecurity: The Campaign to Take the System Private," *Nation*, January 27, 1997, 12.

88. Marc Breslow, "Death by Devolution," *Dollars and Sense*, January–February 1996, 20–22, 38.

89. Dean Baker, "Generation Excess," *EXTRA!*, March–April 1996, 12–13.

90. George J. Church and Richard Lacayo, "Social In-Security," *Time*, March 20, 1995, 24–32.

91. Bob Kerrey and Alan K. Simpson, "How to Save Social Security," *New York Times*, May 23, 1995.

92. "The Illusory Crisis," *In These Times*, January 6, 1997, 2. Also see Bill Turque, "Picking a Fight about the Future," *Newsweek*, December 9, 1996, 30–31.

93. Mike McNamee, "Social Security Reform: Ready for Prime Time?," *Business Week*, January 19 1998, 33; Fred J. Solowey, "Selling Social Insecurity," *EXTRA!*, March–April 1998, 22–23; "Social (In-)Security," *Nation*, June 1, 1998, 3–5; James Weinstein, "Social Security versus Securities," *In These Times*, June 28, 1998, 1; Paul Wellstone, "The People's Trust Fund," *Nation*, July 27–August 3, 1998, 4–5; David D. Kallick, "Saving Social Security (From Its Saviors)," *In These Times*, March 7, 1999, 10–13; Ruth Conniff, "Will Democrats Abandon Social Security?," *Progressive*, March 1999, 19–23.

94. John Canham-Clyne, "When Elites Say 'Cut Medicare,' Press Debates 'How Much?,'" *EXTRA!*, January–February 1996, 12.

95. Robert J. Samuelson, "Can Clinton Do a Nixon?," *Newsweek*, December 9, 1996, 32.

96. Robert Dreyfuss, "The End of Social Security as We Know It?," *Mother Jones*, November–December 1996, 50–58. Also see Lieberman, "Social Insecurity," 11–18; and Conniff, "Will Democrats Abandon Social Security?," 19–23.

97. Dreyfuss, "The End of Social Security as We Know It?," 50–58.

98. Ibid., 56.

99. Lieberman, "Social Insecurity," 15.

100. "Washington Wire," *Wall Street Journal*, January 31, 1997.

101. Michael Dolny, "What's in a Label?," *EXTRA!*, May–June 1998, 9–10.

102. Norman Solomon, "The Media's Favorite Think Tank," *EXTRA!*, July–August 1996, 10.

103. Norman Solomon, "Media Moguls on Board," *EXTRA!*, January–February 1998, 19–22.

104. Ibid.

105. Press, "Spin Cities," 32.

106. *New York Times, Downsizing of America.*

107. Donald L. Barlett and James B. Steele, "America: Who Stole the Dream?," *Indianapolis Star*, September 22–29, 1996.

108. Jackson, "We Feel Your Pain," 11.

109. Barlett and Steele, "America: Who Stole the Dream?."

110. Janine Jackson, "Economic Pack Journalism," *EXTRA!*, November–December 1996, 12.

111. Robert J. Samuelson, "Confederacy of Dunces," *Newsweek*, September 23, 1996, 65.

112. Mike Meyers, "No Doom and Gloom, Americans Better Off," *Kokomo Tribune*, September 12, 1996.

113. Richard Morin and John M. Berry, "Reality Check: The Economic Perception Gap," *Washington Post*, October 13–15, 1996 (lead page each day).

114. Robert J. Samuelson, "Great Expectations," *Newsweek*, January 8, 1996, 31.

115. Richard Turner and Peter Annin, "Leaving Messages, Sending Messages," *Newsweek*, July 13, 1998, 64–65.

116. Perkins, "Caught in the News Media's Liberal Bias."

117. Douglas Frantz, "Chiquita Scrutiny Continues despite Paper's Retraction," *Indianapolis Star*, July 19, 1998.

118. "Soundbites," *EXTRA!*, May–June 1996, 5.

119. Janine Jackson, "Moribund Militants," 6.

120. Ibid.

121. Press, "Spin Cities," 30.

122. Bagdikian, *The Media Monopoly*, 58.

123. Cohen and Solomon, *Adventures in MediaLand*, 45.

124. Bagdikian, *The Media Monopoly*, 58.

125. Press, "Spin Cities," 32.

126. Laura Flanders, "Is It Real . . . Or Is It Astroturf?," *EXTRA!*, July–August 1996, 6.

127. Ibid.

128. Ibid.

129. Ibid.

130. Ken Silverstein, "Manufactured News," *EXTRA!*, January–February 1997, 23–24.

131. Peter H. Stone, "The Nicotine Network," *Mother Jones*, May–June 1996, 50.

132. Ted Gup, "Fakin' It," *Mother Jones*, May–June 1996, 54.

133. Stone, "The Nicotine Network," 50.

134. John Stauber and Sheldon Rampton, *Toxic Sludge Is Good for You: Lies, Damn Lies, and the Public Relations Industry* (Monroe, Maine: Common Courage Press, 1996).

135. John Stauber and Sheldon Rampton, "Watching the Watchdogs: How Corporate PR Keeps Tabs on Reporters," *EXTRA!*, May–June 1996, 22.

136. Ibid.

137. Ibid.

138. Todd Gitlin, "Unum versus Pluribus," *Nation*, May 6, 1996, 32.

139. "Balance This," *In These Times*, May 13, 1996, 4–5.

140. Michael Golay and Carl Rollyson, *Where America Stands, 1996* (New York: Wiley, 1996), 16.

141. Bagdikian, *The Media Monopoly*, 206.

142. Robert L. Borosage and Ruy Teixeira, "The Politics of Money," *Nation*, October 21, 1996, 21–22.

143. "In Fact," *Nation*, August 26–September 2, 1996, 5.

144. Parry, "The Right-Wing Media Machine," 6–10. Also see Dolny, "What's in a Label?," 9–10.

145. Parry, "The Right-Wing Media Machine," 6–10.

146. Phillips, "Fat City," 49–56.

6

Educating for Privilege: Dreaming, Streaming, and Creaming

> The educational system is an integral element of the reproduction of the prevailing class structure of society.
>
> —Samuel Bowles and Herbert Gintis, *Schooling in Capitalist America*, 1976

Nick Caradona and Arnie Seebol were an unlikely pair to become good friends in high school. They were from different parts of the city and from widely different ethnic and religious traditions—one Italian and a nominal Catholic, the other from a Jewish family with practicing parents and recalcitrant kids. Nick's and Arnie's paths would never have crossed if they had not both passed a citywide exam to get into an "elite" science-oriented high school. Most of the kids in the high school were college bound, but the idea of college had never occurred to Nick or Arnie, or to their parents, for that matter.

Nick's and Arnie's parents had a tough time making ends meet, because of their unstable low-income jobs. Only one of the four parents claimed a high school diploma. Nick's parents were separated. When Nick was five years old, his father went to Washington, D.C., to look for work; he drove a cab in D.C. for the rest of his working years, but he never returned to his family. Nick's mother worked as a domestic until he was twelve years old and then took a job as a clerk in a laundry. Arnie's father drove a truck for the *New York Daily News*, and his mother did "home work" for shops in the garment district. Nick and Arnie were both urged by their junior high teachers to take the exam for admission to the select high school, and after being admitted they both enrolled.

At first, the bond between Nick and Arnie was based on the extremity of their shared differences, focusing on the "dirty secrets" of their elders and their ethnic cultures, namely, the disparaging terms and put-downs they had heard used against members of the in-group and the out-group. Arnie taught Nick the fine points of distinction between a *putz* and a *schmuck*. Nick also learned to smack himself in the head and exclaim "goyisha kopf" whenever he did something stupid. Arnie told him that Jews would use this routine whenever they did something foolish, exclaiming with the phrase that they were acting like Gentiles. It reminded Nick of his grandfather's frequent practice of referring to someone as an American in broken English ("you must be 'Merican"), pronounced in such a way that it sounded very much like "merde de cane," which Italians would understand literally as "shit of the dog." It was an unschooled double entendre, which Nick taught Arnie to use against other kids in school.

Arnie and Nick soon discovered other bonds. They both liked baseball (Nick a Yankee fan, Arnie a Dodger fan), and both had a flair for "hustling," as they were both always short of money. They took bets in school from other students, who would choose three baseball players whom they expected would get a total of six hits in that day's ball games. The odds on each bet were three to one. Thus a kid would bet a nickel that his three favorite players would get a total of six hits that day. If the three players scored the six hits, the bettor won fifteen cents; if not, Nick and Arnie won the nickel. The odds were always with the "bookmaker" as long as there were a sufficient number of bettors. Many kids had favorite ball players who rarely got more than one hit a game, but they bet on them nonetheless. Nick and Arnie would also "pitch pennies" and play cards during the lunch hour. Their high school was huge (five thousand students), so there was always plenty of "action" for Nick and Arnie.

Late in their senior year, Nick started to have problems, academically and otherwise. He went "on the hook" too many times and faked letters of excuse from his mother. In the midst of these problems, he quit high school a month before the end of term, failing to take any final exams. He went to work as a "runner" for a bookmaker and was soon "promoted" to a "writer" in a betting room where men assembled to talk about horse racing and to make bets on races at a number of tracks in New York, New Jersey, and the New England area. Off-track betting was illegal, but it was carried out openly with the paid-for cooperation of local police.

Arnie graduated on schedule and went to work for his uncle in his dry cleaning store. Arnie would learn all about the business, and he hoped one day to own his own store or several stores.

Several things should be noted in this little vignette. Nick and Arnie are kids who showed some talent in elementary school. Their teachers had a "dream" that they were worthy of moving into an educational tracking system that gave talented kids a chance to "make it" in the opportunity contest—meaning a chance to go to college. But Nick and Arnie themselves did not have the dream, and they never gave any thought to the track that could lead to a college education and beyond. It was partly because the cost of college-going was beyond the means of Nick's and Arnie's parents. But it also required Nick and Arnie to forgo the income they would earn from working and the claim to adult status that comes with the end of schooling. Many of Nick and Arnie's classmates were middle class and college bound from years of anticipatory socialization. They were "hot-house" kids who had been cultivated for years in an environment of controlled feeding and sunlight. They did not yearn for the freedom of adult status, for their sense of self was fused with the wishes held for them by their parent cultivators.

Nick and Arnie were working-class kids from low-income working-class families, and their parents were working too hard to be involved in the school activities of their children. The opportunity provided by their admission to an elite high school does not exist in a vacuum. In Nick and Arnie's case, it existed within the working-class culture that was their everyday reality. Thus, if all the poor kids in East St. Louis were suddenly enrolled in a school with good teachers, facilities, and programs, it would be great for the kids; but only so much can be expected to follow from an enriched educational experience. The kids will still be poor, as will their parents and friends. Their educational system and experience is contained within a context, a class structure that shapes events that extend far beyond the classroom.

AMERICAN EDUCATION SYSTEM

In effect, if not by design, the American education system functions primarily to transmit advantage and disadvantage across generations. This assertion flies in the face of a powerful and dominant ideology that permeates all levels of society, namely that education is the great equalizer. Education is what brought Abe Lincoln from a log cabin to the highest office in the land. Education is what gave millions of poor but aspiring immigrants in the United States throughout this century the chance to be whatever they were willing to work for. This is the ideology of the American Dream. The dream is so powerful that parents will fight "tooth and claw" to control local schools, so that their programs, teachers, and curriculum will serve the interests of their children. In the dream, education is the passport to a future that exceeds (if you are poor) or matches (if you are privileged) the economic situation of your parents.

For the dream to become a reality, schools have to be organized to meet the aspirations of the dreamers. In schools in which all the kids are from professional families, only one kind of education is needed—a college preparatory program. But when the kids in school come from diverse economic backgrounds, a system must be devised to provide not only the best education to the college-bound children from professional families and to some of the poor kids who, based on probabilities alone, would be able to compete with the college bound, but also a quality educational experience for those who are not heading to college. The idea behind this system is that the educational experience should be designed to meet the "needs of the child."[1] The system is called *tracking and streaming*.

Tracking seems to be a very progressive idea. Does it make sense to identify students who are headed to college, white-collar employment, or mechanical trades and provide them with the particular knowledge and skills that will be most useful—vocational and shop courses for the young men and women going to work in factories, keyboarding and word processing for those who would be clerks and secretaries in corporate bureaucracies, and literature, languages, mathematics, and the sciences for those headed toward colleges and universities? The problem with this theory of education is that students' vocations need to be identified fairly early in their young lives to make use of this system. Of course, this is no easy task, but the ideology of the American Dream states that with the help of "objective" testing, student's strengths can be identified and tracked to make the best use of their abilities.

Tracking was needed when schools were heterogeneous in terms of the economic backgrounds of their students. If a school had the children of professionals, white-collar clerks, and unskilled workers, tracking was necessary to meet the needs of the child. But today, schools are much more homogeneous in terms of the backgrounds of students and their educational plans. Children from the corporate and managerial classes are generally either in private schools or in suburban schools limited to members of their social class. Virtually all of these students are college bound; so what would be the point of tracking? At the other end of the class-structure spectrum we have poor rural schools or inner-city schools filled with children from the bottom one-third to one-half of the economic system. The closest thing you might have to tracking in these schools is the effort of dedicated teachers to reach out and identify those with the greatest potential and to groom them for college, hoping that they might have a chance to attend.

In the case of these homogeneous schools today, they are involved in streaming, not tracking. *Tracking* is a competitive metaphor, implying a contest among entrants in a race where all the "runners" have an equal chance to win. *Streaming* is a noncompetitive metaphor, implying that participants are "carried along" to their destination without any appreciable effort ("competition") on their part. If you go to the right private schools or the better suburban schools, college attendance is the assumed outcome for all involved.

An excellent example of the streaming metaphor is revealed in the following remarks made by the dean of the Harvard Law School when greeting a new class of students at the orientation session.

> The fact is that you are not competing with each other. Your life at the school and your life as a lawyer will be happier and more satisfying if you recognize that your goal is to become the best possible lawyer so that you can serve your clients and society with maximum skills. Although you will experience frustrations from time to time, I think that rather than the *Paper Chase* you will see the school as much closer to the image involved in a letter we received some years ago from a Japanese lawyer who had just been admitted: "Dear Sir: I have just seen the movie *Love Story* with Ryan O'Neal and Ali McGraw and I am looking forward to a very romantic time at the Harvard Law School."[2]

Compare this "laid-back" welcoming speech with the prototype competitive welcome offered by the dean or professor at a less "prestigious" program: "Look at the person on your right and the person on your left. At the end of the first year, only one of you will still be in the program." Those in the privileged classes attempt to create an elementary and high school educational structure that is characterized by streaming, so that their children are "guaranteed" good grades, high test scores, an enriched curriculum, extracurricular activities, and advising that will get them admitted to the country's most elite schools. Privileged classes work to develop these "guarantees" at the same time they support the myth of the dream, extolling the virtues of equality of opportunity as the hallmark of American society.

THE POWER OF THE DREAM

> If kids go to college because high school jobs are so terrible, they may wind up with these jobs anyway. We won't slow our rising inequality just by jamming more and more kids into college.
>
> —Thomas Geoghagen, *New York Times*, 1997

The myth of the American Dream is a powerful force in American life, and it is based on two distinct beliefs: First, that everyone can aspire to levels of success that exceed their starting points in life, because where a person starts life is an accident that can be remedied; and second, that there is equality of opportunity to reach one's goals, and that the game has a set of rules that are fair and capable of producing the desired success goals.

The dream can be a source of inspiration for the young and a source of hope for parents who push their children to better themselves. It also serves to legitimate the great inequality in society in wealth, power, and privilege. It leads to the belief that those who receive high rewards are deserving because they have contributed more in terms of effort and hard work. The dream is a comfort to the privileged and a heavy burden for the less fortunate.

The dream is so pervasive in our culture, so embedded in our family rituals and significant celebrations, that we often follow its logic without examination. It is a kind of cultural reflex leading us to continually search for evidence of the dream in action, and to urge it on others as a guide for living. Consider the following obituary, which the writer, with little or no evidence, chooses to frame within the myth of the dream. The headline reads, "B. Gerald Cantor, Philanthropist and Owner of Rodin Collection, Is Dead at 79."

This headline, in half-inch type, is accompanied by an almost full-page story reporting the achievements of the deceased. The story begins,

> B. Gerald Cantor, who started out as a boy selling hot dogs at Yankee Stadium, became a wealthy financier and philanthropist, amassed the world's most comprehensive collection of Rodin sculpture in private hands, and gave much of it away to dozens of cultural institutions, died on Wednesday in Los Angeles after a long illness. . . .
>
> Mr. Cantor, who was raised in modest circumstances in the Bronx, and his wife Iris, who grew up three blocks from the Brooklyn Museum, came to be widely known in New York for their generosity to the Metropolitan Museum of Art, the Brooklyn Museum, and to medical institutions in the city. . . .

Before he was 15, Bernie Cantor became a vender at Yankee Stadium. "I only worked during Sunday double headers," he recalled, because "you could sell more things" in the delay between the two games. . . .

He graduated from DeWitt Clinton High School and went on to study law and finance at New York University from 1935 to 1937. He originally planned to become a lawyer, but he changed his mind when he spotted a lawyer friend who had to take a job working with a pickax on a construction project of the Works Project Administration."[3]

This fifty-five paragraph story about a well-known philanthropist manages to create, for the casual reader, the clear impression in its opening sentence, and in the first few paragraphs, that we are dealing with yet another personification of the "rags to riches" American Dream.[4] Poor boy works hard—selling hot dogs, no less, at Yankee Stadium (a double dose of the dream being played out in the playground of dreams)—achieves phenomenal success, and gives all his money back to the "people" (actually to museums, hospitals, and at least a half-dozen universities).

But before we can make sense of Cantor's life, we need to know what it means to be raised in modest circumstances. We also need to know how these "modest circumstances" carried him to New York University during the height of the Depression. The point of these questions is neither to ignore Cantor's achievements nor to diminish his generosity. The point is to show the ease with which the cultural production industry of newspapers, TV, films, et cetera, creates the powerful myth of the American Dream. Even this straightforward story of one person's life and achievements was "torqued" to feed into the myth. The story not only pumps up the dream, but it also legitimates the wealth of multimillionaires by first saying they "did it themselves, with hard work and dedication," and by then dwelling on how many millions they "gave back."

It is precisely because of such obituaries, *Forrest Gump*-genre films, and other "rags-to-riches" cultural products that most Americans appear to accept the myth of the American Dream. Figure 6.1 reports the results of a national survey in which Americans were asked to rate the importance of various factors in "getting ahead in life." Almost nine out of ten Americans report that a good education and hard work are the keys to "getting ahead," whereas only six out of ten say the same about natural ability. In contrast, only two out of ten surveyed say that being from a wealthy family and having political connections are very important. The other factors involving social capital (knowing the right people or having well-educated parents) are considered very important by four out of ten Americans.

Americans put their faith in education and hard work as the keys to success. In answering the survey questions, respondents did not have to make a choice between a wealthy family and a good education. They could have chosen both as being very important. The power of the American Dream is not only that it defines the paths to success (education and hard work) but it also defines what is not related. The dream can not tolerate a simultaneous belief in the value of education—which makes great sense in a credentialing society—and the advantage that

Figure 6.1   Factors of Success

Hard work — 89%
A good education — 84%
Natural ability — 59%
Knowing the right people — 40%
Well-educated parents — 39%
Being from a wealthy family — 20%
Political connections — 16%

Source: Davis and Smith, 1989.

Note: Figures given are percentages of respondents who rated various factors as very important in "getting ahead in life."

comes from wealth. The myth creates facts that do not exist ("You can be whatever you want to be") and denies facts that do exist (the chances for a poor child to rise to the privileged class are very slim).

The dream is manufactured in the popular culture, and the main vehicle for achieving it is the school system. Equality of opportunity for all, regardless of accidents of birth, is the official ideology of American education. Education is the great equalizer, providing skills and knowledge, attitudes and values. The dream was not always located in the school system. The Horatio Alger success stories popular around the turn of the century describe the poor boy who "makes it" because of his virtues of thrift, honesty, and hard work.[5] The path to success traveled not through the classroom but through the workplace, where the street urchin turned stock boy came to the attention of the boss because of his virtues. The secular myth of Horatio Alger was consistent with the times, in that preparation for the world of work involved acquiring skills and training in the workplace. Even the so-called knowledge-based professions of law, medicine, and the ministry were open to entry through apprenticeship preparation.

At the turn of the century, about 72 percent of the U.S. population, aged five to seventeen years, were attending public elementary and secondary schools. In 1960, the figure was 82 percent, and by the mid-1990s it reached 92 percent—nearly all elementary-age children are now registered in school. More telling is the fact that in 1900, 6.4 percent of seventeen-year-olds graduated from high school; that figure rose to 68 percent in 1960 and to 71 percent in 1995. At the highest end of the educational process, in 1900 about 29,000 Americans received college degrees; this figure climbed to 485,600 in 1960 and to 1,677,000 in 1995.[6]

This virtual explosion in America's enrollment at different levels in the educational system probably does not owe simply to love of learning. Increasingly in this century, and especially after World War II, good jobs have been linked to educational credentials. First, it was the high school diploma, then the bachelor's degree, and finally the specialized professional degree. Some analysts believe that the strong connection between education and jobs is the result of major technological advances that have changed the skill requirements of jobs. As the proportion of jobs requiring high levels of skill has increased, there has been increased reliance on the formal educational system to provide the required knowledge and skills. However, it is also possible that the increase in educational requirements for jobs is a way that privileged groups protect their access to those jobs that provide the greatest rewards.[7]

As more people enrolled in elementary schools, the high school diploma became the credential for many jobs that were formerly held by people with an eighth-grade education. Then, as enrollments in high school increased, the bachelor's degree became necessary for many jobs formerly held by people with a high school diploma. And so it goes. With expansion of higher education and 1.5 million graduates a year, the new credential derives from *where* you get your bachelor's degree. The privileged classes that control the major corporations and universities keep moving the goalpost whenever too many of the nonprivileged class start to get access to the valued educational credential.

RALL Copyright © Ted Rall. Reprinted with permission of Universal Press Syndicate. All rights reserved.

Once schools became established as the place where peoples' futures were determined, their programs, activities, and curricula took on a larger significance. Schools became the models of a "small society" where the things that were learned formally and informally were relevant for the larger society. Schooling is carried out on a very rigid schedule, starting and ending at a predetermined time. Weekends are free, and there is an established schedule of vacations. Tardiness and absences must be explained, and if they are excessive they will be punished. The school has established authority figures who must be followed without question. The Pledge of Allegiance, acceptance of God and country all serve to reaffirm the legitimacy of the established order. The daily activities and classes are built around respect for rules, self-discipline, grades, and performance according to externally imposed standards.

Within this "small society" framework, there is variation among schools, usually reflecting the class composition of its students. Schools for the privileged usually provide students with more opportunities for creativity, autonomy, and self-directed activities, whereas schools for the nonprivileged are more concerned with discipline, obedience, and job-related skills. Pressure for these different emphases often comes from parents. Parents who know their children are going to college emphasize enrichment in the arts, music, and cultural activities; those who know their children are headed for jobs emphasize the need for job-related activities.

In addition to the social and technical skills learned at school, students are also prepared for their futures as citizens of a political and economic system. Does schooling have a "liberating" effect on students, calling upon them to question the political-economic order and to play an active role in promoting change or reform? Or does schooling lead students to accept things as they are, believing that they are living in the best of all possible worlds? Several studies of the schooling experience indicate that schooling has a conservative effect on students and that there are important class differences in this experience.[8]

Students in elementary and high school are encouraged to think about themselves as members of society primarily in courses on government and civic education. A content analysis of civics textbooks in "working-class" and "middle-class" schools indicates that students learn very different things about their government and economy and about their responsibilities as citizens. Moreover, interviews with school administrators, teachers, PTA officials, and leaders of community civic groups indicate that they have very different views of how the political process should be presented in the school's civic education program. The main findings from this research follow.

1. Civics textbooks in the working-class school (compared with those in lower-middle- and upper-middle-class schools) are particularly bland, containing more descriptive material about the political process and less attention to power, influence, and intergroup conflict. Textbooks in the upper-middle-

class school give the most attention to the use of power as the main ingredi-
ent resolving political struggles.

2. Community influentials in the upper-middle-class school are more likely to
   endorse the inclusion of "realistic" political themes in the civics programs.
   They view politics "as a process involving the resources of politicians and
   power, and the conflict-alleviating goal of politics." These views tend to reinforce the content found in the upper-middle-class civics textbooks. Community influentials from the lower-middle- and working-class communities
   tend to ignore or avoid "realistic" themes, thereby reinforcing the bland content found in civics textbooks in their schools.

3. Measures of the political attitudes of students taken before and after they had
   taken civic education classes indicate that only the attitudes of upper-middle-
   class students change in the direction of supporting greater awareness of
   power and conflict in the political process. Students from lower-middle- and
   working-class schools show little change, suggesting that in their schools and
   communities "politics is treated and learned as a formal, mechanistic set of
   governmental institutions with emphasis on its harmonious and legitimate
   nature, rather than as a vehicle for group struggle and change."[9]

These findings indicate that students at these three socioeconomic levels are
being socialized to play different roles in the political system, and this is done in a
way that legitimates the existing system of economic and political inequality. Children from working-class and lower-middle-class communities are being prepared
to continue the low levels of political participation exhibited by their elders.
Moreover, they are prepared for a passive role in the political process because they
have been taught that the institutions of government work for the benefit of all
citizens. Students from the privileged upper-middle-class community are clearly
being prepared to participate in and influence the political agenda. The privileged
are made aware of the role of power, influence, and conflict in public affairs,
whereas nonprivileged are encouraged to work together in harmony.

Other research on the effects of schooling indicates that students' early socialization leads them to develop positive and trusting orientations toward the symbols and institutions of political authority.[10] Moreover, schools transmit the idea
that government is the main center of power in society, thereby neglecting the role
of large corporations and the conflict that exists among competing political and
economic interests.[11] This shaping of students' attitudes toward the economic and
political order tends to bring them into conformity with the dominant ideology
that serves the interests of the privileged class. The longer students are in school,
the greater is their exposure to the dominant ideology. In a study of elementary
and secondary students from urban schools in the southwestern United States,
two-thirds of third graders supported government intervention in the economy
through assistance for those out of work and for the poor. The same level of support was found among sixth graders; but less than one-third of the ninth- and

twelfth-graders supported an active role for government. Student attitudes toward private ownership of major industries became increasingly positive across the four grade levels, with 16 percent of third graders being positive compared to 63 percent of twelfth graders. Finally, attitudes toward trade unionism became increasingly negative as they progressed across grade levels. Third graders were least negative toward unionism (17 percent) and twelfth graders were most negative (59 percent).[12]

There may be naiveté and poorly formed attitudes among students (especially third-graders), but it is clear from this research that the ideology that benefits the privileged gains greater strength in the minds of students as they move from the third to sixth to ninth to twelfth grade. Students do not necessarily start school supporting the ideas of private property, government restraint, or antiunionism, but that is clearly where they wind up at high school graduation. Schools function to affirm the legitimacy of the dominant political and economic order and perpetuate the myth of equality of opportunity. In so doing, they serve the interests of the privileged class.

TRACKING AND STREAMING

> The objective of primary and secondary education, as enunciated by the legislators, educators, and community leaders who control it, is to propagate a devotion to the dominant values of the American system.
>
> —Michael Parenti, *Power and the Powerless*, 1978

One of the main concerns of members of the privileged class is to protect their advantage and to transmit it to their children. In a society where educational credentials are used by the privileged to justify their rewards, it is critical that the rules of the game are designed to give advantage to the children of the privileged class. Of course, others can also play by these rules if they choose, but it may be comparable to poker players who try to draw to an inside straight—a risky bet.

Tracking and streaming are two ways in which the rules of the game are used to give advantage to children of the privileged class. In order to understand how these strategies work, it is important to remind ourselves how precollege public education is financed in the United States. Funds for public education are drawn primarily from local property taxes (state and federal governments also provide funds). The amount of money raised through property taxes depends on the tax rate applied to the assessed value of homes and businesses. Communities with newer and more expensive homes and a strong business community will be able to generate more tax revenue for use in paying salaries of teachers and providing educational resources for students. They can often do this with a lower tax rate than that of poorer communities, because the aggregate value of their homes and businesses is larger. Because property taxes and mortgage interest are deductible from federal income tax, the privileged classes receive a larger indirect subsidy for the education of their children than that received in poorer communities.

Evidence from recent research on the effects of school expenditures indicates that higher per pupil expenditures for instruction are associated with higher levels of student achievement.[13] Higher student achievement comes from smaller class size and a higher ratio of teachers to students. The more money a school can spend on instruction, the more teachers they can hire and the more money they have to pay experienced teachers. The presence of more teachers and better-paid teachers also improves the social environment of the school, as lighter work loads both improve teacher morale and enable teachers to get to know students better. This research also reports the interesting finding that some types of school spending are a "dead end" for student achievement: capital outlays for building improvements and school-level administration had no impact on student achievement. Spending additional money on more and better teachers is the way to improve education, but such money is often not available in poor school districts.

In heterogeneous school districts, where children of the privileged and nonprivileged are in the same school, there is a single pool of money to fund that school. That money is used to get the best teachers, the most up-to-date books, the best laboratory equipment, films, computers, and other educational resources. In order to give an advantage to the privileged children, it is necessary for the school to develop programs that allocate the best teachers, the most computers, and the best resources to programs that are most likely to be taken by the privileged class. The money is not given to the children of the privileged class, but to programs in which they are more likely to enroll. Thus, tracking is invented—a system that allocates resources to programs that are tied to distinct outcomes—a college preparation or a vocational preparation. Tracking is a form of inequality within schools.

In homogeneous school districts, where almost all the children are from the privileged classes or almost all are from lower classes, there is no need for tracking. In the rich schools, at least nine out of ten children are headed for college, and in poor schools, one out of ten children is going to college. When the percentage attending college in poor schools exceeds one in ten, it is usually because of special circumstances like a local state college or a community college enabling poor students to work or live at home while attending school. However, the rich schools will have more money to spend on schooling because of the higher value of assessed property in their school districts. With more money, these schools hire better teachers, purchase better equipment, provide more extracurricular activities and better guidance and counseling, and thereby provide a better all-around education. In poor schools with less money to spend, the quality of education suffers in all areas of the schooling experience. Streaming is a form of inequality between schools.

Tracking, despite its official noble intentions, is a process of separating the winners from the losers. It is estimated that about 85 percent of public schools use a system of tracking[14] to provide different and unequal education for those believed to be college bound and those believed to be heading directly to the labor market.

And these beliefs are powerful self-fulfilling prophecies. Track placement is directly and indirectly related to the class background of students. The direct effects are a result of the expectations that teachers and administrators have of children from higher-class backgrounds.[15] The indirect effect occurs because less-privileged children may express less interest in college, receive less parental and peer encouragement to go to college, and lack the achievement scores to be selected for placement in the college track. There are sharply different views of tracking. Some see it as a way of providing opportunities for students who might otherwise be ignored, others see it as a way of reproducing social inequality. Although many factors influence how schools choose students for track placement, there is substantial evidence that class background is important.[16] This choice, however, is crucial to a student's future in terms of academic achievement, high school graduation, and college attendance.[17]

Inequality between schools (i.e., streaming) is revealed most sharply in the differences between suburban and inner-city schools. Per pupil expenditures in 1988–89 in the Chicago area ranged from a high of $9,371 in the suburbs to $5,265 in the inner city. In Camden, New Jersey, suburban spending was $7,725 per pupil, compared with $3,538 in the city. A comparison of six districts in the New York City area revealed a high of $15,084 in the suburbs and a low of $7,299 in the central city.[18] National data for 1994 indicate that urban school districts spent $4,500 per pupil, compared with $5,066 in nonurban districts. The spending gap between urban and nonurban districts in major cities like New York was about $4,300 per student.[19] Wealthy suburban schools that spend nearly twice as much per pupil are able to have better teachers, better facilities, smaller classes, and a variety of enriching activities and programs. Such advantages will never find their way into inner-city schools as long as school funding is based on property taxes.[20]

The one large consequence of tracking and streaming is their effect on college enrollment. Students who are in vocational tracks or in high schools composed primarily of students from low-income families are at a great disadvantage. Their educational aspirations are reduced because they receive little encouragement from peers and parents in their social milieu. Even students with high academic achievement and potential are less likely to think about college as a goal.[21] In contrast, students whose friends are the children of doctors, lawyers, and other professionals are likely to receive continual encouragement for college attendance.

Ample research evidence indicates that even students with high academic achievement and high measured intelligence are not likely to enter college if they are from lower economic groups. One study reports that 91 percent of students with high intelligence and high-social-class backgrounds attend college, compared to 40 percent of students with high intelligence but low-social-class background.[22] The combination of money to pay for college and the encouragement of peers and parents results in 84 percent of all students from higher-class backgrounds attending college, compared with only 21 percent of all students from lower-class backgrounds.

The advantages of going to college include better chances for higher-prestige jobs and higher incomes. In 1979, a male college graduate received almost 50 percent more income than a high school graduate. In 1992, the advantage of the college graduate increased to 83 percent more income.[23] In short, access to high positions and high income are more closely related to educational credentials today than was the case several decades ago.

Evidence from the past thirty years indicating how education is linked to better jobs and higher earnings has led many to jump on the education bandwagon and to propose more and better education as the solution to many of society's problems. Workers displaced by new technology or plant closings are told that they must improve their skills to find work in the high-tech economy. Young men and women from the poorest groups are encouraged to get a high school degree and to think about going to college, even if only a community college. Politicians love to talk about legislation to increase financial aid to students. President Clinton has proposed a $1,500 tax credit for college to help pay for the first two years of college. He has also proposed a $5,000 tax deduction for college education or job training.[24]

It is hard to argue with the call for more education—it has certainly worked for those members of the privileged class who have converted their credentialed skills into high-paying positions in business, finance, and the professions. In 1975, about 40 percent of the young men and women from the richest one-quarter of the population earned college degrees. This was about seven times greater than the 6 percent of high schoolers from the poorest one-quarter who went to college. By 1994, eight out of ten sons and daughters from the richest quarter of the population earned a college degree, doubling the rate from twenty years earlier. In contrast, college attendance for the poor increased to a meager 8 percent from the 6 percent of twenty years earlier.[25]

Clearly, the rich got the message about the changing global economy in the mid-1970s and the increased importance of credentialed skills in that economy. The privileged class has in recent years sent almost all its children to college, as did many families of better-paid blue-collar workers and middle-income groups. But they did not all go to the same type of college, they did not major in the same fields, and they did not enjoy the same rewards in later years.

PRINCETON VERSUS PODUNK: GETTING "CREAMED"?

It is often asserted that new technologies will equalize learning opportunities for the rich and poor. It is devoutly to be wished for, but I doubt it will happen."

—Neil Postman, *Nation*, October 9, 1995

Up to this point, we have demonstrated the strong influence schooling has on the reproduction of class inequality. Contrary to the beliefs contained in the American Dream, education is not the means for providing equality of opportunity to all Americans regardless of their social position at birth. Schooling serves to reproduce inequality through the power of the myth of the American Dream and through the effects of tracking and streaming as the way to deny equal access to the means for upward mobility. We now continue our analysis of schooling by examining the question of who goes to college and where they go.

As noted earlier in this chapter, rates of college attendance have increased dramatically in the past fifty years. In 1940, 216,000 degrees were awarded by American colleges and universities. By the mid-1990s, some 1.5 million degrees were being awarded. A total of 14,306,000 students were enrolled in 3,494 higher education institutions in 1993. These institutions consist of 2,106 four-year institutions, and 1,388 two-year institutions.

The expansion in college enrollments has had the effect of introducing greater diversity into the college environment. It is probably safe to assume that in the era

Copyright © Lloyd Dangle. Reprinted with permission.

of small enrollments, the college population was composed of persons with similar social and economic backgrounds. Only the sons and daughters of the most privileged classes attended college. But what are we to say about a time when 14 million young people are in college? Although they do not represent all of those persons from lower economic backgrounds who would go to college but cannot afford to, it must surely contain some of them. Perhaps what we have is a modified form of the American Dream, where at least some persons from the nonprivileged classes do get access to equality of opportunity. Perhaps.

The main argument of this section is that although the expansion of enrollments at the college level has resulted in larger proportions of nonprivileged youth attending colleges and universities, there has been at the same time movement toward a more rigidly class-based system of inequality within the framework of higher education. This more subtle and less visible form of inequality is reflected in the schools that privileged and nonprivileged students attend and in the areas in which they choose to specialize. The consequences of a class-based system of inequality within higher education are as serious in terms of wasted human resources as the class-based system of tracking and streaming that determines who goes to college.

Let us begin with the approximately thirty-five hundred institutions of higher education that are available to serve the needs of America's aspiring youth. Approximately 40 percent of those institutions are two-year colleges that students typically attend either because they lack the academic credentials to be admitted to a four-year institution or because they lack the money to pay for tuition, room, and board. Some enrollees at two-year colleges are nontraditional students who are already employed and are trying to improve their credentials and career opportunities.

The remaining 60 percent, the twenty-one hundred four-year institutions, are also highly differentiated. About two hundred of these institutions are the larger and more prestigious research universities that award almost all the professional and advanced degrees in the United States. These institutions graduate the doctors, lawyers, engineers, scientists, economists, and managers that populate the privileged class. These two-hundred "top" universities can be further subdivided into the Ivy League (Brown, Columbia, Cornell, Dartmouth, Harvard, Pennsylvania, Princeton, and Yale), the so-called Big Ten (Illinois, Indiana, Iowa, Michigan, Michigan State, Minnesota, Northwestern, Ohio State, Penn State, Purdue, and Wisconsin), and other state universities. And then there are the small "elite" liberal arts colleges that provide high-quality education, strong social ties (the basis of social capital), and very high tuition (Amherst, Bates, Bowdoin, Clark, Colby, Franklin and Marshall, Hamilton, Haverford, Hobart, Oberlin, Reed, William Smith, Swarthmore, Tufts, etc.).

The point of this little exercise (aside from the fact that we have probably misclassified many schools) is to indicate that higher education is highly differentiated, with a small number of schools that are very selective about their admissions and consistently rated among the elite colleges and universities. The number of elite schools in the United States that confer great advantages on their graduates probably numbers about thirty, or less than 1 percent of all the colleges and universities in the country. If you are admitted to one of these thirty elite schools, after graduation you will be able to be admitted to one of the elite graduate or professional schools. And when schooling is completed, the graduates of elite schools will assume high-level positions in the major institutions of American society and join the privileged class. Students admitted to the "elite 1 percent" are getting "creamed," which is the positive meaning of this term used at the beginning of this section. Those who rise to the top in this system will enjoy the "good life" with all of its material and psychological benefits.

Students who are enrolled at the 1,388 community colleges, and at most of the 2,100 nonelite schools, are getting "creamed" in the negative meaning of the term—that is, they are getting "clobbered." Most of these students are caught between a rock and a hard place. They choose to go to college because it is their only hope for getting a decent job. The absence of good jobs for people with only a high school diploma drives most into college. Their parents cannot really afford to cover the costs of college, and so students work and take out loans in the hope that all the debt and sacrifice will pay off in the end. They forgo income for four years and incur debt, yet when they graduate, all they may find is a job paying $6–$10 an hour, or $12,000–21,000 a year. The median starting salary for 1993 college graduates was $22,968 (about $19,000 for education majors and $31,000 for computer science and engineering majors). About 40 percent of these graduates reported that the job they held did not require a college degree (only 17 percent of engineering graduates said this, but about 50 percent of graduates in humanities and social sciences said a college degree was not required for their current job).[26] To be sure, there is a small minority of graduates of the 2,100 nonelite schools that do better. They are usually graduates in engineering or business or those with teaching certificates who have the skill capital and credentials to command better incomes. But they will not be joining the privileged class.

This two-tiered system of schooling for privilege is summarized in figure 6.2. On the extreme left of the figure is the secondary school system that was described in the section on tracking and streaming. The children of the most wealthy members of the privileged class enter the stream in the elite prep schools that prepare students primarily for Harvard, Princeton, and Yale. The remaining children of the privileged class are being educated in the resource-rich suburban high schools that are homogeneous in terms of the economic class of their students and are well funded from their property taxes. These students from the privileged class compete among themselves for admission to a small number (about fifty) elite universities and liberal arts colleges. They are elite because they are well endowed by financial contributions from wealthy alumni and because their admissions procedures are highly selective (i.e., they get applications from many more students than they can ever admit). Some of the graduates of these elite schools go on to the elite schools of law, medicine, business, and engineering, and most of the rest go into entry-level positions in America's major corporations.

Figure 6.2   Two-Tiered System of Schooling for Privilege

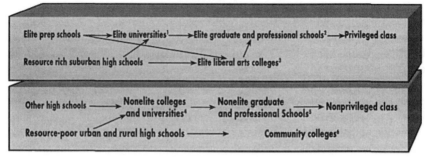

Note: [1] Elite universities: Approximately 20, including Harvard, Yale, Princeton, Chicago, Stanford, Northwestern, California-Berkeley, Michigan, Wisconsin, UCLA, North Carolina, Columbia, Duke, Pennsylvania.

[2]Elite graduate and professional schools: Approximately 15, including Harvard, California-Berkeley, Yale, Chicago, Wisconsin-Madison, Michigan, Columbia, Stanford, Princeton, Cornell, Illinois-Urbana, Pennsylvania.

[3]Elite liberal arts colleges: Approximately 30, including Amherst, Bates, Bowdoin, Brown, Bryn Mawr, Reed, Swarthmore, Tufts, Colgate, Smith, Wellesley, Williams, Oberlin, Hamilton, Franklin and Marshall, Wesleyan of Connecticut, Barnard, Brandeis, Mount Holyoke, Haverford, Hobart, Skidmore, Union.

[4]Nonelite colleges and universities: there are approximately 2,100 schools in this group.

[5]Nonelite graduate and professional schools: there are approximately 200 schools in this group.

[6]Community colleges: there are 1,388 schools in this group.

The lower panel of figure 6.2 is where most students are located. In 1994, 2.5 million students graduated from high school, of whom about 300,000 graduated from private schools. Enrollments in the fifty elite colleges and universities are a small fraction of the millions enrolled in higher education, with the overwhelming proportion of students enrolled in the 2,100 nonelite colleges and universities and the 1,388 community colleges. A very small percentage of these students "escape" their nonprivileged paths and are admitted to elite schools, usually owing to their academic achievements and their performance on the Scholastic Aptitude Tests (SAT) that are used with all applications for college.[27] A study of Harvard's admission process indicates that the school does attempt to admit a small number of "working-class" students and "students of color" who have academic merit, based on scores on the SAT and other achievement tests.[28] This possibility of "moving up" describes the small amount of "creaming" from the bottom tier of figure 6.2 into the schooling streams of the privileged class.

The interesting thing about this two-tiered system of schooling for privilege is that the way it works has not changed very much in the past forty years. Graduates of the elite colleges and universities have always obtained better jobs (in terms of prestige, opportunities, and income) than graduates of the nonelite schools, and this is true independent of merit. The prestige of the degree-granting institution has an effect on postcollege jobs and incomes over and above the ability of their individual graduates.

In the 1950s, research compared the incomes of graduates from Ivy League schools, prestigious "technical" schools (e.g., Cal Tech, Carnegie, MIT), elite private colleges, the Big Ten, other midwestern colleges, and other eastern colleges. The findings indicated that the median incomes of male graduates are directly related to the prestige ranking of the schools, and this pattern was found across different fields of study. The following summary from the researchers is important for its historic value, given that this was a period before higher education became as differentiated by prestige as it is today.

> Although we have noted that good grades may at least sometimes lead to good incomes, it develops that even the poorest students from the Ivy League share in the general prosperity—and do better than the best students from other schools. Of the Ivy Leaguers who just got by—the C and D students—42 percent had reached the [highest income] level. Of the A students from the Big Ten, only 37 percent had hit that mark, and only 23 percent of the A students from "all other Midwest" colleges. Even the great financial disadvantage of a general education, rather than a specific one, does not seem to hold back the Ivy Leaguers. Of the Ivy League humanities majors, 46 percent had reached the [highest income] bracket, and of the social scientists 50 percent. But even among the Big Ten's engineering graduates, with their highly specific training and all the advantages that go with it, only 23 percent had reached the [highest income] level. [At the time of this study, the "highest income" was about three times the median income for all U.S. men. A comparable "highest income" figure in 1998 would be $108,000.]
>
> What all this amounts to is that the differences in earning power between graduates of rich and famous schools and those from small obscure schools are so great that they override everything else. Earning power rises steadily with each increase in wealth and prestige of the school. At the extremes, the Ivy League graduates do best of all financially even when they make poor grades and take a general rather than specific course, both of which are ordinarily handicaps—while the graduates of the smallest schools do not get up to the averages even when they make fine grades and take the type of specific courses which ordinarily produce the biggest incomes.[29]

The pattern of advantage for graduates of elite schools observed more than forty years ago is still in operation today. Students from privileged-class backgrounds are more likely to enroll in the most prestigious schools, and they choose programs of study that have the greatest potential for high income.[30] In fact, the effects of privilege on who goes where to college may be greater today than they were forty years ago. Sons and daughters of the privileged class go to better high schools (if not private schools) and are provided with an educational experience that is geared to satisfy entrance requirements at the most selective elite colleges. And if that is not enough, privileged-class families have the money to help their children prepare for college entrance exams.

The final barrier for even the brightest working-class high school graduate is the cost of attending an elite college. How can a family earning the median national income of $34,000 a year afford to pay $27,000 a year for tuition, room, and board? Lacking funds, such students go to state colleges with lower costs, and they obtain financial aid and work to cover expenses. Choosing a major is often driven by practical considerations, such as the need to get a job after graduation. This can lead to vocationally oriented programs such as education, nursing, and technology degree programs, which assure jobs after the baccalaureate degree but allow limited opportunities for achieving high income or for accumulating wealth.

Findings such as those reported above indicate a clear lack of correspondence between the expectations derived from the American Dream and the actual experiences of college graduates. Ability and merit are important for a person's success after college, but where one goes to school is also important.

In the 1960s, there was growing interest in the science-based professions, such as engineering, as examples of a profession that was open to talented people, regardless of their social and economic origins. In the professions of medicine and law it is possible that a graduate's family background could influence postcollege success by providing the money to start a practice or the social contacts for attracting wealthy clients. But engineers work in large corporations where their scientific and technical expertise determines their movement up the corporate ladder. An engineer's social and economic background should have less significance for his or her success than might be the case in medicine or law.

Once again, contrary to the myth of equality of opportunity and the belief that engineering is a career open to talent, engineering graduates from higher social origins (based on their father's occupation) were more likely to hold engineering positions that provided greater prestige, power, and income.[31] This finding was based on a study of the graduates from a single university of moderate prestige, not part of the elite schools. When the research was expanded to a national sample of engineering graduates, it was found that engineers with upper social origins earned more money and held more-responsible positions than engineers from lower social origins. Moreover, this class difference was found to be true even among engineers who had the highest grades in college and had attended the most selective engineering schools.[32] Thus, even when working-class high school graduates are "creamed" (i.e., are recruited to elite universities), their final rewards of income and position may not put them in the privileged class.

THE FUTURE: CONTINUING INEQUALITY AND CORPORATIONS IN THE CLASSROOM

Corporations and their foundations have become sacred cows to university administrators. Few professors are willing to jeopardize their standing in universities by publishing research articles critical of these donors.

—Lawrence C. Soley, *Leasing the Ivory Tower*, 1996

The main argument of this chapter is that the American educational system operates in a way that reproduces the existing structure of inequality in the larger society. It achieves this end, first of all, by promoting an ideology that proclaims schooling to be the great equalizer and the main avenue for upward mobility. Second, inequality is perpetuated through a multitiered system of education made up of elite schools, average schools, and horrible schools. The different quality of these schools is directly linked to the social- and economic-class level of their students. The quality of the educational experience in primary and secondary schools helps to determine a student's chances for attending college.

The inequality in primary and secondary schools that is linked to the social-class position of students is likely to be reinforced and extended in the years ahead. The most notable innovations in public education that are currently on the public agenda are the voucher system and the charter school. The voucher system provides families each school year with a voucher ($2,000 to $4,000) that can be used to enroll their children in nonreligious private schools. There have been attempts to extend the use of vouchers to religious schools, but such efforts have been blocked by lawsuits. Charter schools enable groups of parents, teachers, and community members to propose a new way of providing education for their children. For example, they might wish to emphasize self-paced learning, cross-disciplinary education, or traditional back-to-basics programs. Such groups apply for a charter from the local school board or state Board of Education to create the new school, and, if approved, they receive public funding on a per pupil basis similar to funding for public schools.

Vouchers and charter schools are attractive ideas because they appear to empower parents who have become frustrated with the public school system's failure to educate their children. Many parents in low-income inner cities have come to view these new ideas as the only way to provide their children with a better education. Unfortunately, only a fragment of inner-city families will be able to take advantage of vouchers or charter schools. Charter schools are not obligated to take all students who apply, and the ability to use a voucher may be dependent on the availability of transportation and other resources to get children to schools outside of their neighborhood. The main impact of vouchers and charter schools will be to siphon money away from public schools, leaving those left behind with even poorer facilities. The more affluent will take advantage of vouchers to move to private schools, leading to greater segregation in schools.

Students from resource-rich schools receive the kind of preparation that enables them to compete for admission to elite colleges and universities. Students from resource-poor schools are more likely to drop out or to terminate their education with the high school diploma. Those who do go to college attend community colleges and a wide variety of average to good state colleges and universities.

Based on everything we know today about the U.S. economy and the actions of corporations (as discussed in chapter 3), the inequality described above will not only continue, but in all likelihood, it will get worse. Students from families in the bottom of the double-diamond class structure will find it increasingly difficult to pay the costs of attending college. Moreover, it will become increasingly apparent that large numbers of college graduates will be unable to find any but the lowest-level jobs available in the service sector. It will become apparent that there is a significant mismatch between the kinds of jobs that colleges prepare students to enter and the kinds of jobs that are actually available.

In addition to continuing inequality in schooling, we expect greater involvement of private sector corporations in the educational system at all levels. At the primary and secondary levels, there will be continuing interest in alternative ways of "delivering" education to the young. The current antiunion, antibureaucracy, antigovernment climate will stimulate proposals to "privatize" education. Private-sector firms, perhaps in cooperation with universities, will attempt to provide higher-quality education and at lower costs. The CEOs from *Fortune 500* firms have become involved in school reform efforts at the state and national levels.[33] Since these business leaders are used to thinking in terms of the "bottom line," productivity, and efficiency, their involvement gives one pause as to the kind of educational "reforms" that may appear on the nation's agenda. In addition to "for-profit" private schools, we should expect great attention to new educational technology that will reduce the need for teachers and increase dependence on telecommunications-based instruction.

Corporations have already recognized the potential for advertising commercial products to the millions of school children who are today's consumers as well as consumers of the future.[34] Classroom films, television, and weekly papers are owned by large corporations, and the products developed for schoolroom use are accompanied by corporate logos and advertising material.[35]

Many of the proposals to bring corporate expertise and technology into the classroom are based on the assertion that the telecommunications revolution will be available to rich and poor alike. Schooling will therefore be able to deliver on its promise as the "equalizer," as all students will have access to the same educational resources, the same information, and the same master teachers, on the information superhighway. Once again, a technological fix to the problem of class inequality. This is reminiscent of the problem of Nick and Arnie, whom we met at the beginning of this chapter. Nick and Arnie had the chance to go to one of the best schools in the city and to be exposed to other talented kids who were college bound. But it did not take, because they lived in another world outside of the school. The life experiences of class inequality will not disappear because of the information superhighway.

Finally, we need to consider corporate penetration of higher education.[36] Private firms are no stranger to higher education. Corporate CEOs are prominent as trustees of most major universities but especially the elite schools. Such representation helps to encourage corporate-university relations that result in corporate funding of research and a variety of university programs. In return, corporations get access to the latest knowledge that can be converted into patents on products and processes that benefit the corporations providing the funding. Often, corporations that provide funds for research by faculty or graduate students are able to obtain agreements guaranteeing that the results of the funded research will remain secret for an agreed-upon period of time. The doctoral dissertation in biomedical engineering or pharmacology of a student whose research has had corporate funding can be kept from public disclosure until such time as the corporation that funded the research can realize its expected benefits. Students and professors may not be able to publish the results of such research until given permission to do so by the corporation. This practice of secret or confidential research may have started during the Cold War era, when the Department of Defense funded research that involved national security interests. Today, the private corporations can prevent publication because of private financial interests.

Many faculty members at major research universities are active participants in corporate-university relations. Those whose work may have commercial possibilities are actively pursued by corporations with substantial research grants or consulting fees. Some faculty members are able to double their incomes through their consulting agreements, especially in several fields in engineering, science, and the business schools. Those faculty with a more entrepreneurial bent often start their own firms in a research park near the university while retaining their academic positions and salary. Faculty at large research universities may receive e-mail messages from their research offices with titles such as "Leveraging Your Research by Starting a Business." This "call-out" to faculty, staff, and students is an attempt to stimulate interest in starting a business by offering information on university guidelines for faculty-owned businesses and discussions of where to find capital. These cyberspace messages are supplemented with hard-copy slick brochures with announcements like the following: "The climate for starting technology-based businesses has never been better. Owing to steady or dwindling budgets, coupled with increasing demand of and competition for funds, government support for university research projects is harder to secure. University research programs are seeking alternative funding sources, such as funneling research ideas with commercial potential into start-up businesses. The bottom line: becoming an entrepreneur is not only 'in' but is encouraged."[37]

Universities generally look the other way when confronted with the active corporate pursuit of faculty. They usually have regulations stipulating that faculty may be involved in "outside activities" for one or more days per week or month, depending on the university. There is no stipulation as to how much they may earn as consultants, and no requirement that the university must be reimbursed for the time taken away from university responsibilities. Universities encourage these relationships in part because they hope to increase the flow of dollars from the private sector into the university's budget.

In recent years there has been a decline in federal money coming to universities for their research programs. This money often comes with agreements to cover overhead costs that allow universities to support other activities. In addition to the decline of federal dollars, many public universities have not been able to obtain more state funds or raise tuition. The only source for new money has been the private sector, which has been only too willing to help—but at a price. The price might be confidential research (as noted above). Private-sector funding might give the corporation the right to select researchers for projects and define the research topics to be pursued. It might even give corporations a voice on matters of promotions and tenure of faculty who work on corporate projects.

And it is also possible that corporate penetration of academe will have a chilling effect on those faculty in the liberal arts whose inclinations or disciplines tend to raise questions about corporations in American life, about the relative merits of capitalism versus socialism, or about the impact of unrestrained technology on the environment and our communities. Just as downsizing and plant closings serve to depress wages and discourage unionization, corporate penetration of academe could serve to create a climate of "corporate correctness" that will dominate the minds of students and faculty alike.

NOTES

1. Michael B. Katz, *The Irony of Early School Reform*, Cambridge: Harvard University Press, 1968).

2. Robert Granfield and Thomas Koenig, "Pathways into Elite Law Firms: Professional Stratification and Social Networks," in *Research in Politics and Society*, vol. 4 *The Political Consequences of Social Networks*, ed. Gwen Moore and J. Allen Whitt (Greenwich, Conn.: JAI Press, 1992), 325–51.

3. Eric Pace, "B. Gerald Cantor, Philanthropist and Owner of Rodin Collection, Is Dead at 79," *New York Times*, July 6, 1996.

4. The *Chicago Tribune* published a much abbreviated eight-paragraph story about Cantor obtained from the *New York Times* News Service. The *Tribune* story started with the same lead sentence used in the fifty-five-paragraph *Times* story, revealing the extraordinary appeal of the rags-to-riches story, even when it may not be true in its substance.

5. R. Richard Wohl, "The 'Rags to Riches Story': An Episode of Secular Idealism," in *Class, Status, and Power*, ed. Reinhard Bendix and Seymour M. Lipset (New York: Free Press, 1966), 501–26.

6. U.S. Department of Education, National Center for Educational Statistics, *Digest of Educational Statistics*, 1997, NCES 98-015, ed. Thomas D. Snyder, Charlene M. Hoffman, and Clair M. Geddes (Washington, D.C.: Government Printing Office, 1997).

7. For a discussion of these two different views of why educational requirements for many jobs have increased, see Randall Collins, *The Credential Society* (New York: Academic Press, 1979); and Randall Collins, "Functional and Conflict Theories of Educational Stratification," *American Sociological Review* 36 (1971): 1002–19.

8. Edgar Litt, "Civic Education, Community Norms, and Political Indoctrination," *American Sociological Review* 28 (February 1963): 69–75.

9. Ibid., 72, 73.

10. Dean Jaros, *Socialization to Politics* (New York: Praeger, 1973); Edward S. Greenberg, *Political Socialization* (New York: Atherton, 1970).

11. Alan Wolfe, *The Seamy Side of Democracy* (New York: David McKay, 1973); Ira Katznelson and Mark Kesselman, *The Politics of Power* (New York: Harcourt, Brace Janovich, 1975).

12. Scott Cummings and Del Taebel, "The Economic Socialization of Children: A Neo-Marxist Analysis," *Social Problems* 26 (December 1978): 198–210.

13. Harold Wenglinsky, "How Money Matters: The Effect of School District Spending on Academic Achievement," *Sociology of Education* 70 (July 1997): 221–37.

14. Christopher Jencks, Marshall Smith, Henry Acland, Mary Jo Bane, David Cohen, Herbert Gintis, Barbara Heyns, and Stephan Michelson, *Inequality: Reassessment of the Effect of Family and Schooling in America* (New York: Harper and Row, 1972).

15. Robert Rosenthal and Lenore Jacobson, *Pygmalion in the Classroom* (New York: Holt, Rinehart and Winston, 1968).

16. Sally Kilgore, "The Organizational Context of Tracking in Schools," *American Sociological Review* 56 (1991): 189–203.

17. Karl Alexander, Martha Cook, and Edward McDill, "Curriculum Tracking and Educational Stratification," *American Sociological Review* 43 (1982): 47–66.

18. Jonathan Kozol, *Savage Inequalities: Children in America's Schools* (New York: Harper, 1991).

19. Noreen Connell, "Underfunded Schools: Why Money Matters," *Dollars and Sense*, March–April 1998, 14–17, 39.

20. Ibid.

21. William A. Sewell, A. O. Haller, and G. W. Ohlandorf, "The Educational and Early Occupational Status Attainment Process," *American Sociological Review* 35 (1970): 1014–27.

22. William A. Sewell and Vimal Shah, "Parents' Education and Children's Educational Aspirations and Achievements," *American Sociological Review* 33 (1968): 191–209.

23. Robert Kominski and Rebecca Sutterlin, *What's It Worth? Educational Background and Economic Status*, U.S. Bureau of the Census, Household Economic Studies, P70-32 (Washington, D.C.: U.S. Government Printing Office, 1992).

24. Thomas Geoghagan, "Overeducated and Underpaid," *New York Times*, June 3, 1997.

25. Thomas Mortenson, of the National Council of Educational Opportunity Associations, Washington, D.C., reported in Karen W. Arenson, "Cuts in Tuition Assistance Put College beyond Reach of Poorest Students," *New York Times*, January 27, 1997.

26. U.S. Department of Education, National Center for Education Statistics, *The Condition of Education, 1996*, NCES 96-304, ed. Thomas Smith (Washington, D.C.: U.S. Government Printing Office, 1996).

27. James Hearn, "Academic and Nonacademic Influences on the College Destinations of 1980 High School Graduates," *Sociology of Education* 64 (July 1991): 158–71.

28. David Karen, "Toward a Political-Organizational Model of Gatekeeping: The Case of Elite Colleges," *Sociology of Education* 63 (1990): 227–40.

29. Ernest Haveman and Patricia Salter West, *They Went to College* (New York: Harcourt, Brace, 1952), 180.

30. Scott Davies and Neil Guppy, "Fields of Study, College Selectivity, and Student Inequalities in Higher Education," *Social Forces* 75 (1997): 1417–38.

31. Robert Perrucci, "The Significance of Intra-Occupational Mobility," *American Sociological Review* 26 (1961): 874–83.

32. Carolyn Cummings Perrucci and Robert Perrucci, "Social Origins, Educational Contexts, and Career Mobility," *American Sociological Review* 35 (1970): 451–63.

33. Douglas D. Noble, "Schools as 'Instructional Delivery Systems,'" *In These Times*, November 30, 1992, 28–29.

34. Marianne Manilov, "Channel One, Joe Camel, Potato Chips, and ABC," *EXTRA!*, July–August 1996, 18–19.

35. Luke Mines, "Globalization in the Classroom," *Nation*, June 1, 1998, 22–24; William Hoynes, "News for a Captive Audience: An Analysis of Channel One," *Extra!*, May–June 1997, 11–17.

36. For an expanded discussion, see Lawrence C. Soley, *Leasing the Ivory Tower: The Corporate Takeover of Academia* (Boston: South End Press, 1996).

37. Purdue Research Foundation, *Home for High-Tech Business* (West Lafayette, Ind.: Purdue Research Park, 1998).

7

The Pacification of Everyday Life

The strongest is never strong enough to be master, unless he transforms his strength into right, and obedience into duty.

—Jean-Jacques Rousseau, *The Social Contract*, 1782

As the twentieth century spiraled to a close, American popular culture witnessed a surge of interest in UFOs, aliens, and paranormal phenomena. The 1999 George Lucas film, *Episode I: The Phantom Menace*, seems likely to propel this trend into the twenty-first century. It reinforced the public's appetite for science-fiction story lines that had been fueled not only by the earlier *Star Wars* trilogy but also by a wave of popular science-fiction films from the late 1990s. The 1998 hit list included the conspiracy-laced *X-Files: Fight the Future* and end-of-the-world grabbers *Deep Impact* and *Armageddon*. Hits from 1997 like *Men in Black* and *Contact* also racked up huge ticket sales, as their release coincided with current events fueling public interest in extraterrestrials and space exploration. One such occurrence was the fiftieth anniversary of the Roswell incident—the alleged UFO crash in July 1947 near Roswell, New Mexico. Also, on July 4, 1997, in a kind of real-life variation of the 1996 *Independence Day* film, the U.S. Pathfinder space probe landed on Mars and sent live pictures back to earth. The heightened popularity of sci-fi movies as the century ended was both preceded and paralleled by a dramatic growth of science fiction and paranormal-oriented TV programming, video-games, and internet websites. As we enter the twenty-first century, it is clear that the culture industry has shifted into warp speed to create—as well as fill and magnify—public interest in UFOs, extraterrestrials, and the paranormal.

American fascination with space aliens is not a new trend in popular culture. Many earlier films, TV series, books, and magazines have plowed this same ground. But as the window of this century closes, the intensity of public interest in such topics appears to be reaching higher and more sustained levels than in the past. Of course, this cultural trend does not erase public unease over growing economic inequalities and insecurities. And it has not displaced popular enthusiasm for the optimistic sentimentalism of *Forrest Gump* or for the romantic tragedy of *Titanic*. But it does underscore the culture industry's tendency to channel mass entertainment in directions that distract public attention from class-based issues. It reminds us that the culture industry is more about distraction and pacification than it is about inspiration or instruction—especially where class inequalities are concerned. But sometimes even the culture industry can surprise us.

From the perspective of social-class analysis, one of the more interesting sci-fi movies dates not from the late 1990s but from the late 1980s. *They Live!*, a 1988 John Carpenter film, explicitly links extraterrestrial aliens with social-class inequalities and superclass dominance. The movie portrays creepy reptilian aliens—who mingle with the general population in human form—as forming a secret alliance with an elite group of ruling-class humans. In league together, these two groups dominate the nonelite human population through hedonistic consumerism, subliminal mass media-based manipulation and thought control, and—as needed—coercive force.

The secrets of this dark alliance are revealed to the audience through an unemployed laborer who accidentally finds a special pair of sunglasses produced by a growing human resistance movement. Wearing these "shades," the actor walks the streets of an ordinary community—but he views the people and events from a totally new perspective. The audience sees through the eyes of the actor and his special sunglasses. We see aliens who have assumed human forms and the "real" text of disguised messages embedded in mass media content reinforcing alien and ruling-class control of nonelite humans: Submit, Conform, Consume, Inform, Reproduce, and above all, Do Not Question Authority!

They Live! was not a huge box-office success. It barely made a blip on the radar screen of popular culture and quickly dropped from sight. Its theme of an alliance between aliens and the human ruling class was not repeated in the story lines of popular science-fiction films or TV programs running through the late 1990s. Certainly the film could be critiqued on many grounds—including its tendency to reinforce a conspiratorial view of rich and powerful elites dominating nonelites. Despite its weaknesses, the unusual (by movie standards) class-based features of the film help call attention to how the routine and seemingly "invisible" practices of mainstream social institutions perpetuate privileged-class dominance and at the same time legitimate and reproduce social-class inequalities—especially at the level of everyday life. *They Live!* illustrates that the culture industry sometimes produces films with class themes woven into story lines that call attention to and help illuminate the nature of the process that is the central focus of this chapter—the pacification of everyday life.

PACIFICATION: THE HOMETOWN FILES

> How do you prevent people who are fed up with the way they are being treated from doing anything about it? It's simple: deprive them of any sense that people have ever fought back.
>
> —David Reynolds, *Democracy Unbound*, 1997

Pacification refers to the transformation of potentially disruptive social situations or restive populations into serenity: passive, peaceful, and calm—as dramatically illustrated in *They Live!* In the context of conflicting class interests, pacification also implies the manipulation and control of subordinate classes by dominant classes (but not necessarily in a conspiratorial sense). By linking pacification with everyday life, the title of this chapter is meant to call attention to how the class-related consciousness of average people going about their day-to-day routines is shaped.

In this chapter we consider how the power and advantages of the privileged class are exercised, reinforced, and legitimated at the level of everyday life. To bring this complex process down to earth, we focus first on two case studies, involving community development and drug education. These cases link national trends with local activities and illustrate how privileged-class-dominated organizations promote control of consciousness, ideological domination, and the legitimation of class inequalities among the nonprivileged class. These cases also illustrate how privileged-class power and ideas are embedded in taken-for-granted institutional routines and practices through which the pacification of everyday life occurs. Following the two cases, we return to the culture industry and consider how this industry—especially through television and movies directed at hometown consumers—reinforces the pacification process.

Our first case study considers the story of how Japanese automobile assembly plants came to be located in several midwestern communities. It calls attention to the way the privileged class creates local crises, demands local sacrifices, legitimates these sacrifices, and benefits from "solutions" to the problems it created. It shows how citizens' awareness of local class-related issues is shaped by the interests of the privileged class (often called "community leaders") through local media in the form of local decisions on taxes, bond issues, and financial incentives for business. Average citizens are typically provided by community newspapers with only one way to think about important local decisions—unless they happen to belong to groups with alternative points of view (e.g., taxpayer associations, labor unions, environmental groups).

The second case focuses on the Drug Abuse Resistance Education (DARE) program as a form of symbolic politics. The DARE story calls attention to how, despite its record of ineffectiveness in preventing youth drug use, this school-based drug prevention program, which came out of the "War on Drugs," has expanded into a cultural and political force serving the economic, political, and ideological interests of the privileged class. We show how DARE grew and how it boosts the careers of its supporters, serves the public relations and political interests of corporate sponsors, and encourages unquestioned acceptance of privileged-class-controlled authority structures. In each instance our focus is on showing how DARE contributes to public distraction from class issues and to the legitimation of class inequalities.

The concluding section follows up on themes and trends introduced in the opening section of this chapter. Here we focus on the electronic media dimension of the culture industry—especially television and the movies—to illustrate how this industry helps legitimate the new class society. We document the massive size, scope, and largely class-free content of the electronic media arm of the culture industry to show how it effectively dominates public consciousness and discourages critical thought and reflection. Using this informational and conceptual framework, we illustrate how the routine operation of the industry marginalizes class issues, distracts public attention from class inequalities, and generally contributes to the pacification of everyday life.

GROW OR DIE: THE PRIVILEGED-CLASS THREAT TO SMALL-TOWN AMERICA

A move by a major corporation can have a devastating impact on a local growth coalition. . . . The net result is often a "race to the bottom" as rival cities offer tax breaks, less environmental regulation, and other benefits to corporations in order to tempt them to relocate.

—G. William Domhoff, *Who Rules America?* 1998

As we have seen, the privileged class has been very successful in keeping the largest shares of income and wealth for itself. We have also seen that this outcome does not come easy—or cheap. It requires the constant care and feeding of the shadow political and information industries by the superclass. Moreover, shaping and delivering politics and policies favorable to privileged-class interests do not stop at the national level. They continues in states, cities, and towns throughout the United States.

We have to recall that the privileged class consists of some 20 million families, and they do not all live in New York, Washington, or Los Angeles. Although members of the superclass are more likely to live in exclusive urban gated enclaves, the more numerous credentialed class of highly paid professionals is scattered across the country in small communities with names not usually associated with wealth and power. Consider, for example, obscure small towns like Marysville, Ohio; Smyrna, Tennessee; Lafayette, Indiana; Normal, Illinois; Flat Rock, Michigan; and Georgetown, Kentucky. With populations ranging from sixty-five hundred to eighty-five thousand, these small towns shared the experience in the 1980s of becoming the "hometown" of a large Japanese automobile assembly plant. Each city and state was the "winner" in a multistate competition to attract foreign investment. The story behind these "winners" reveals how the privileged class in America creates crises and then benefits from solutions to the problems they created.

Picture a small town with about twenty thousand to thirty thousand people. The city has a couple of large companies employing about a thousand workers each, a dozen mid-size firms each with two hundred or so employees, and hundreds of small retail and service businesses in the downtown area and on the outer edges of town. One day, out of the blue, one of the large companies announces that it plans to shut down and move to another location. The company "spin" is often that the plant is rather old, and, based on a cost-benefit analysis, it would cost too much to upgrade its production line and improve other parts of its support system.

The mayor of the city immediately begins talks with corporate executives about what it would take to make them reconsider. The union representing the workers starts to talk with management about a new contract with wage concessions, productivity-linked benefits, and greater flexibility concerning plant work rules. The threat of eliminating a thousand jobs in a small community sends ripples of anxiety throughout the community. The loss of one thousand workers each earning, on average, $25,000 annually would take a lot of buying power out of the community. And the loss of payroll taxes and property taxes on plant and equipment would significantly reduce the city's revenue. The plant and its employees also have traditionally made sizable annual contributions to the United Way and to local churches, to say nothing of volunteer work performed by workers and their families in a variety of community organizations.

Before the city can begin to digest this unanticipated crisis, the local business community starts to pressure the mayor and the city and county councils to spend more money on community development activities. Maybe they need to hire a development professional and print some special brochures outlining the attractive qualities the town has for new corporations. Of course, all this will cost money, at a time when revenue is declining. To make matters worse, some of the other businesses start to remind the city and county about their own increased costs of doing business. Several would like to expand and employ more people but question the wisdom of such a move at this time. Perhaps, they suggest, a waiver of taxes on new expansion might be helpful. The city has given tax abatements before, but doing so now would mean fewer dollars for schools, fire and police protection, city services, and, of course, the new push for a professional community development office.

Some of what is described in this story about a hypothetical small town sounds a bit like extortion, blackmail, and bribery—although these activities are not called by those terms in political and business circles. And it is not just a hypothetical story. This story line reflects the basic outline of what has happened—and is still happening—in hundreds of small communities across the United States over the past twenty years.

From the mid-1970s through the late 1990s, millions of high-wage jobs in the manufacturing industries were lost as a result of waves of plant closings in the auto, steel, rubber, electronics, and textile industries. As we saw in chapter 3, thousands of U.S. plants closed down and moved their operations to lower-wage foreign production centers. The waves of plant closings and resulting high levels of unemployment had devastating effects on many states and communities faced with the sudden loss of revenue from payroll taxes and corporate property taxes. These losses were magnified by increased demands for public services to assist the unemployed as well as development expenditures aimed at trying to strengthen local economies. The intersection of structural change in the U.S. economy, plant closings, and increased unemployment resulted in heavy pressure on national and state governments to cut spending. As the federal government tried to save money by cutting assistance programs to states, state and local problems were compounded even further.

Rust Belt states like Michigan, Illinois, and Ohio were hard hit by plant closings involving major corporations and were drawn into "regional wars"[1] of competition for new businesses. And how do communities attract new industries? The short answer is by providing attractive "incentives." In 1991 the fifty states gave $16 billion to businesses to relocate plants in their states. Sometimes the money would lure a corporation to close a plant in one state and move to another state—as in the case of Mack Truck, which moved its production plant from Pennsylvania to Winnsboro, South Carolina, in the late 1980s.[2] And sometimes the money was used to attract foreign corporations to come to the United States.

State "incentive packages" for large foreign industrial firms typically highlight a powerful "language hook": FREE! (translation: taxpayer subsidized). The list of freebies often begins with land and also usually includes site preparation (roads, water, sewer lines), worker training, and property tax waivers—with the total incentive package value often reaching $200 million or more. In 1985 the state of Kentucky gave Toyota $12.5 million for land, $20 million to prepare the land for construction, $47 million for road improvements, $65 million for worker training, and $5.2 million to meet the special educational needs of Japanese managers' children. These breaks were all part of the incentive package to attract the firm to Kentucky. When the cost of bond interest payments is added to the "up-front" incentives, the total cost to Kentucky taxpayers reaches $350 million.[3] And the beat goes on. When Toyota decided to expand its production to include more light trucks, Indiana landed the new truck plant in 1996 by providing an incentive package of $75 million.[4]

Other nations have also gotten in on the incentive package action. In the 1990s two German firms, BMW and Mercedes, announced plans to open assembly plants in the United States. When the dust from the state bidding wars settled, South Carolina landed the BMW plant (opened in 1994 in Spartanburg) and Alabama was awarded the Mercedes plant (opened in 1997 in Vance). South Carolina taxpayers kicked in $150 million in direct and indirect subsidies to BMW, and Alabama taxpayers provided Mercedes with a $250 million incentive package.[5]

Of course, the purpose of the incentives is to attract a company that would bring new jobs to the state and stimulate fading local economies. But the cost in incentives represents an increasingly high price tag for economic growth. In the 1980s the incentive packages amounted to $50,000 for each job in the Japanese transplants and continued to climb in the 1990s to $79,000 per direct job at the BMW plant and then to a staggering "sticker-shock" level of $167,000 per direct job at the Mercedes plant.[6] These price tags are typically covered by increased state taxes—most often levied on nonprivileged-class members—in the form of more sales, property, and income taxes.

The Privileged Class Comes Calling: Pacification in the Heartland

Narrowing our focus to just the decade of the 1980s, we find the states of Michigan, Tennessee, Ohio, Illinois, Kentucky, and Indiana chipping in a total of more than one billion "incentive package" dollars to land Japanese auto assembly plants. Honda built a plant in Ohio; Nissan located in Tennessee; Mazda went to Michigan; Mitsubishi set up shop in Illinois; Toyota chose Kentucky; and Indiana got Subaru-Isuzu. For the one thousand to two thousand workers who would get jobs in the new plants, the money for the incentives would be seen as well spent. And it would certainly be seen as a good idea by the business community that benefits from growth—especially the banks, lawyers, and realtors who would facilitate the new growth-related business transactions. But most residents in the cities and counties where the plants were located (probably 90 percent) would not join in the benefits. Instead, they got to pay higher taxes to cover the multimillion-dollar incentive packages. They also "won" increased traffic congestion, higher housing costs (for rental units and new homes), and more municipal spending to cover school costs for children who would accompany their parents to the jobs created by the "growth boom."

Obviously there are economic benefits associated with growth, but benefits for whom? The costs are real, both in terms of dollars in taxes and in the more intangible "quality of life" changes that occur when a town grows quickly. But perhaps more important is the fact that nobody asked people in the towns whether or not they thought it was a "good deal" to spend more than $50,000 of taxpayers' money for each new job that would be created. No one asked local citizens if they would prefer to spend the tax money in different ways, such as helping local small businesses expand in the city or providing new educational and recreational facilities for existing families. There were no public referendums on the question of growth or of growth at what cost. The deals were made between the managers of incoming corporations and state and local members of the privileged class (political, business, and professional leaders), and the deals were then sold to the people in the affected communities.

The privileged class typically develops economic projects that it wants and that will serve its interests and then presents the projects to the nonprivileged class as if they will serve the general good. This happens all the time at the national level. It is often so transparent that virtually anyone can recognize how privileged-class interests drive such deals and also generate a "common-good" justification incorporated into the media "spin" on stories about these deals.

A high-profile case in point was the 1997 "balanced-budget agreement" negotiated by President Clinton and Republican congressional leaders. As part of the deal, both sides agreed to changes in federal tax laws that would reduce the tax on capital gains. This meant that investors would pay lower taxes on the "paper-profit" gains they make when stocks, bonds, commercial real estate, and other investments go up in value compared with what they paid for them. The cut in the capital gains tax primarily benefited members of the privileged class, who are the

principal owners of most investments affected by the tax changes. But the justification presented by politicians who supported the tax cut, and the one reported
almost without critical examination in the media, was that people who get to keep
more of their capital gains will invest or spend the money in ways that stimulate
the economy. And when the economy grows, there is a need for more workers to
produce the goods and services being purchased by the new dollars available to
the privileged from the capital gains tax cut.[7] In short, the capital gains deal was
justified by a recycled version of "trickle-down" economic theory—a familiar fairy
tale left over from the Reagan era. For average Americans, it was "deja vu all over
again," but the privileged-class-controlled media treated the deal like a great creative leap forward for the good of all mankind.[8]

A similar story line is used at the local level. The taxpayer-provided incentives
for the industry transplants are presented as spending packages that will benefit
all residents of the communities. That is the "spin" at the heart of the transplant
stories, and it is used to justify the millions of dollars in incentives given to foreign corporations. This story is told locally by the electronic and print media.
Local newspapers are especially important in telling this story because they are institutions with long-standing reputations of journalistic objectivity and civic responsibility. Although local newspapers are known to have political biases (to be
conservative or liberal, to support Republicans or Democrats), they are often seen
as having broad community interests in mind when reporting on issues such as
new community-financed construction of schools, libraries, roads, and recreational facilities. These kinds of projects spend public money raised through
taxes, and when newspapers examine the pros and cons of public projects, their
stories are framed in such a way that the newspaper is presented as seeking outcomes consistent with the community's best interests.

But we must recall that newspapers are, first and foremost, businesses. They are
expected to make profits for their owners and stockholders, just like any other
business. Some money may be made by expanding circulation, but the sale of advertising space is the engine that drives newspaper profits. Thus, newspapers in
the transplant cities have a vested (but typically hidden and unacknowledged) interest in growth, which they share with bankers, realtors, attorneys, construction
firms, and the Chamber of Commerce. So when newspapers in the cities competing for transplants tell the story about incentives and transplant benefits for communities, it is a story spun by card-carrying members of the privileged class.

Local Spin: All the News That's Fit to Print?

We examined newspaper stories written in conjunction with the process of locating Japanese transplant firms in three midwestern communities by three different
hometown newspapers—one in each community where the transplants would be
located. The period of coverage for each newspaper was thirteen months, beginning
with the first newspaper story that mentioned the possibility of a Japanese auto

plant moving to the city or state. The purpose of the analysis was to see how local newspapers dealt with the complex task of assessing the potential costs and benefits of competing for and having a new, large manufacturing firm come to their community. Each of these projects had the potential of producing opposition from a variety of community groups such as environmentalists, organized labor, and concerned taxpayers, who might have viewed the plant as imposing unreasonable tax increases to cover the costs of the incentives and services to the plant and their employees and families. Given the potential for public controversy and community conflict, we were interested in how the local newspapers presented the story and shaped community thinking on this issue. Because local newspapers are dominated by privileged-class interests, we wondered if the content of news stories about the coming of the transplants might objectively reflect community tensions and divisions related to this story, or, on the contrary, would be more of the same of what we often saw at the national level: corporate and privileged-class propaganda masquerading as news. That is, would local news accounts reflect a progrowth spin aimed at soothing potentially disruptive local fears and concerns and defusing potential opposition? In short, we wanted to see if local newspaper coverage of the transplant story might represent an example of the pacification of everyday life— cooling out the locals while protecting the interests of the privileged class.

The three newspapers and time periods analyzed were the *Lafayette* (Indiana) *Journal and Courier* (December 1986–September 1987), the *Murfreesboro* (Tennessee) *Daily News Journal* (September 1980–September 1981), and the *Lexington* (Kentucky) *Herald Leader* (December 1985–December 1986). In all, 490 transplant stories were written by the three newspapers in the time periods we examined. All stories were read and analyzed to answer the question, Who speaks on the transplants? We ask this question because newspapers make choices about the people and organizations that will be asked to express their opinions about the transplants, incentive money, and what it will mean for the community.

In the 490 stories from the three newspapers, 1,769 persons were named and their points of view about the transplants presented. A single event could be written up under the headline, "Auto Plant Dredges Up Ill Will" or "Auto Plant: A Plan Comes Together." These stories would incorporate the views of different persons to create an impression of divided opinion, conflict, harmony, and agreement, or a mixture of costs and benefits to the community. The journalists creating these stories often knew in advance the point of view of the people they interviewed for the story. When they interviewed the city's mayor or a representative of a community development agency, they could expect a favorable attitude toward the transplant, because these community leaders had been involved in developing the package of incentives to attract the new business. On the other hand, when interviewing a labor official they were likely to get a more critical view of the transplants, because of the strong antiunion bias of the Japanese.

When we examined who the 1,769 persons were who spoke through the news stories, we found that 36 percent were from business and industry (corporate executives, representatives of the Chamber of Commerce, attorneys) and 50 percent were local or state elected officials (mayors, state representatives, congressional representatives) or officials of state or local government agencies. Only 13 percent of the 1,769 interviewees were outside of the business-political sectors, such as labor leaders, educators, and social welfare services. This meant that almost nine out of ten opinions on the transplants expressed in news stories came from persons who would be expected to be probusiness, progrowth, or to have protransplant interests. In effect, representatives from the privileged class did most of the talking in the newspaper stories. This outcome hardly reflects an effort by newspapers to provide balanced information and analysis to their readers.

When we examined the content of the 490 stories on the transplants and the amount of space devoted to positive or negative accounts about the transplants, the evidence indicated a clear preference for a positive "spin" on the transplant projects. The 490 stories made up a total of 19,331 square inches of space in the three newspapers, and only 17 percent of this space was devoted to stories that could be called "negative" or "critical" of some aspect of the transplant projects. The negative stories were largely clustered around four issues. These included (with sample headlines):

1. the high cost of the financial incentives ("Two Join Suit over Toyota Plant Financing")
2. environmental issues ("Toyota Jobs vs. Environmental Impact Debates")
3. citizens' loss of property ("Path to Auto Plants Cuts across Yards")
4. legal challenges to the state's right to give land to a private corporation ("State's Plan to Give Toyota Land May Be Unconstitutional")

The other 83 percent of the total square inches written about the transplants we characterized as variations of three positive themes. These were (also with sample headlines):

1. blatantly positive ("Auto Plant Gets Community Support")
2. passively positive ("Nissan Decision Opens New Era for County")
3. human-interest positive—descriptive stories of the positive effects of the plants for people directly involved in the projects ("Japanese Family Enjoys New Life in Greater Lafayette")

The overall impact of the newspaper coverage of the transplants was unequivocally positive and supportive of the total idea of providing financial incentives to a private corporation. Rather than being objective, neutral providers of balanced information and opinion, the newspapers acted as cheerleaders for economic growth and the transplant projects. Their coverage and biased story lines concerning the transplants were consistent with the profit-oriented, privileged-class interests of the newspaper owners, publishers, and editors.

The overwhelming representation of progrowth views in local newspapers illustrates the domination of state and local credentialed-class members in framing economic issues with class-based implications and consequences for local communities. In the case of the transplants, the actions of local credentialed-class members had the effect of reinforcing and reproducing at the local level the interests of the national superclass of corporate and political elites. As the transplant cases illustrate, many communities are caught in a corporate squeeze that starts with multinational corporations closing plants and shipping jobs overseas. Faced with fiscal crises brought on by unemployment and declining tax revenues, these communities are forced to compete with other towns and states facing the same squeeze for the "privilege" of handing out more than $200 million in taxpayer money in "incentives" to lure corporations to bring new jobs to their towns.

The New Catch-22: Private Profits, Public Costs

The all-too-familiar scenario of plant closings followed by competition for the transplants illustrates how a new kind of "Catch-22" is built into the double-diamond class structure. The essence of the catch is this: profits are private, costs are public, and both are largely underwritten by the working class. Because the profits from doing business are private, they flow largely intact back to members of the privileged class—with few dollars skimmed off by ever lower corporate and capital gains tax rates. But the social costs of plant closings, such as increased unemployment, higher welfare costs, more family violence, increased crime, and higher rates of mental and physical illness, as well as the tax-funded costs of financial incentives to attract new businesses, are public. And both kinds of costs are primarily paid for by members of the working class. The routine business practices of corporations controlled by the privileged class create social problems while generating private profits, but the working class pays—in one form or another—most of the costs associated with the corporate system. Most obviously this includes higher taxes for the working class, but it also includes absorbing most of the human costs associated with corporate-generated social problems: the pain of unemployment, the confusion of disrupted lives, and the frustration of diminished community services. The double diamond leads to a double deal: A winning hand for the privileged class, a raw deal for the working class.

This new Catch-22 of the new class society provides useful insights into the contradiction between class benefits and class burdens where corporate practices and public policies are concerned. But as we have seen, newspaper accounts of the coming of the transplants do not acknowledge the existence of such a "catch." The win-win vocabulary that dominated much of the local reporting on the transplants helped obscure the existence of conflicting class interests and coaxed local populations into accepting the deals as being in the best interests of all parties concerned. In a sense, the newspapers were an important part of a community-wide, street-level pacification project aimed at winning the "hearts and minds" of

Copyright © Lloyd Dangle. Reprinted with permission.

the working class in favor of the transplant projects. No conspiracy was necessary. The routine operation of privileged-class-dominated institutions, as the newspaper coverage illustrates, was sufficient to ensure local pacification. This outcome was evidenced by the absence of significant or sustained local opposition to the transplants in the chosen communities.

DARE: BRINGING THE DRUG WAR HOME

It's a proven program which I believe has been well received nationwide. The way they train their officers they become real role models for the kids.

—Howard Safir, New York City Police Commissioner,
quoted in *Kokomo Tribune*, October 7, 1996

Symbolic politics describes the political strategy of choosing and using safe political issues and public policies on the part of political elites to advance their interests and those of their privileged-class supporters. This approach is safe in that it involves a focus on issues and programs that appear to address social problems—but in ways that do not threaten privileged-class interests and also have wide appeal among the working class. Symbolic politics are typically associated with at least three levels of symbolic action. First, to promote their own political interests, public-office holders often "construct threats" to public well-being. This means political leaders—with the help of superclass sponsors and media attention—select social conditions widely perceived as undesirable and transform them, by policy pronouncements and the mobilization of political resources, into high-priority public "threats" requiring public policy intervention. Second, public-office holders can invoke a "scapegoating strategy" whereby social conditions publicly viewed as problematic or "constructed threats" are explicitly or implicitly linked with unpopular or stigmatized groups, which encourages public perceptions of these groups as the source of the problems or threats. Third, political leaders can propose programmatic interventions that they claim will ameliorate problematic conditions or "constructed threats" and which will also reassure voters that public institutions are responding appropriately to these dangers.[9]

DARE as Symbolic Politics

Although the 1990s provided many examples of symbolic politics (e.g., gay rights, abortion, TV ratings, the V-chip, pornography on the internet, family values, declining civility), we view the so-called War on Drugs as a classic example of these concepts in action. Growing out of a high-profile, politically constructed "threat" (the "drug plague"), the drug war resulted in numerous multifaceted government programs with national and local class-related implications and consequences—such as the DARE (Drug Abuse Resistance Education) program. DARE represents a safe, programmatic example of symbolic action claiming to address a threat to the public well-being at the community level. Organized and promoted by members of the privileged class, DARE is a powerful but unadvertised and unnoticed part of the everyday cultural routines that reinforce privileged-class interests, help legitimate class inequalities, and thus contribute to the pacification of everyday life.

On the surface, it appears that DARE has everything to do with preventing youth drug use and nothing to do with social-class inequalities. But as in the film *They Live!*, peering beneath surface images can open our eyes to a very different reality. What we find beneath DARE's surface is a drug education program of questionable effectiveness that over the past decade has become an institutionalized cultural and political force serving the economic, political, and ideological interests of the privileged class. Although there is no evidence that DARE was deployed as part of a conscious, privileged-class conspiracy to distract public attention from growing class inequalities and related social problems, there is evidence that the DARE program does help produce this and other outcomes that serve privileged-class interests.

What Is DARE?: A Really Brief History and Overview

DARE is a standardized, copyrighted, school-based drug prevention program that began in Los Angeles in 1983–84 as a joint effort involving the Los Angeles Police Department (LAPD) and the Los Angeles Unified School District. Following former president Reagan's launching of his antidrug "crusade" in 1986, DARE expanded rapidly. This expansion was facilitated by DARE America, a nonprofit, tax-exempt corporation formed in 1987 to promote and coordinate DARE. By the late 1990s, DARE was taught in more than half of all U.S. local school districts in all fifty states and in several foreign countries.[10]

The DARE core curriculum is designed for fifth- and sixth-graders and consists of seventeen weekly lessons approximately forty-five to sixty minutes each in length. All DARE classes are taught by uniformed police officers who have undergone eighty hours of specialized training. Classroom activities are scheduled during the regular school day, and the program encourages student involvement in exercises such as "question and answer [sessions], group discussions, and role-play[ing] activities." DARE's "major goal . . . is to prevent substance abuse among school children"; it strives to accomplish this goal by teaching students "the skills for recognizing and resisting social pressures to experiment with tobacco, alcohol, and drugs." The DARE lessons focus on enhancing students' self-esteem, decision-making, coping, assertiveness, and communication skills and "teaching positive alternatives to substance use."[11] In addition to classroom instruction, the program also can involve other activities such as the use of selected high school students as DARE "role models" in the elementary grades, informal officer-student contacts, teacher orientation, parental education, and community presentations.

Although DARE's basic goals and curriculum structure have remained relatively constant since its inception, over the years DARE has also changed in several ways. During 1992–94, revisions were made in the core curriculum. Materials were added to place "greater emphasis on the prevention of tobacco use . . . normative beliefs, and on violence prevention and conflict resolution." The presentation format was also changed to make the program more interactive. The revised curriculum was phased in during 1993–94 and was fully implemented after January 1, 1995.[12] More recently, DARE America has promoted an expansion of the curriculum into a multistage sequence, partly as a response to researchers' findings that DARE has no long-term effects on student drug-use rates. Using a kind of medical vaccine-inoculation model, DARE America now recommends that school children be exposed to the DARE program three times before they graduate from high school (in the fifth, seventh, and tenth grades). In 1997 this full DARE program was claimed to be in place in about 25 percent of schools nationwide.[13]

Despite changes in the program, DARE's objectives regarding student drug use still embrace the same "zero tolerance/no use/drug-free" orientations that have guided national drug policies over the past several years. DARE also implicitly embraces "free will" and "user accountability" principles. This means that all forms of drug use are viewed as being driven by free-willed, individual choices, and users are held strictly accountable for their choices. The DARE program assumes it provides students with the information and life-skills resources necessary to guide them into making the "right" choices. If after DARE exposure, individuals still choose to use illicit drugs, such choices are viewed as free-willed criminal acts to be condemned and punished by the legitimate application of all available legal sanctions. This logic holds despite the acknowledgment of DARE's curriculum that structural factors such as mass media advertising (like the $6 billion tobacco and alcohol ad budgets) contribute to public demand for drugs.

DARE makes no distinction between legal and illegal drugs and advocates total abstinence as the only acceptable approach to all types and categories of drugs. Moreover, it makes no distinction between experimental and frequent drug use. An unstated assumption of DARE appears to be that experimental use of any drug (including legal—for adults—"gateway drugs" such as tobacco) constitutes "drug abuse" or will inevitably lead to problematic drug use. More realistic approaches to drug use, such as "responsible use" or "harm reduction"—as used in drug education programs in other nations such as the Netherlands—are excluded and have no place in the DARE program.

DARE: Hometown Drug Prevention or Pacification?

In 1987, DARE came to Kokomo, Indiana, a midwestern auto factory town with a population of forty-five thousand. In fact, Kokomo was the first Indiana city to adopt the DARE program. The process that led DARE to Kokomo began in 1986, when the mayor and chief of police learned about the program while attending a conference—about the same time the "war on drugs" transformed the "drug problem" into a hot-button political issue. By late 1986, local political, educational, and law enforcement leaders had decided to implement DARE in the Kokomo schools.

We were invited by school and police officials to assess DARE's effectiveness in Kokomo. Our efforts began in 1987, and by the mid-1990s we had completed several short- and long-term studies of the program. Our most comprehensive project was a seven-year study of DARE's long-term effectiveness in preventing or reducing adolescent drug use. Based on a series of comparisons between the 214 high school seniors exposed to the DARE program in the fifth grade and the 331 high school seniors not exposed to DARE, we found no significant differences in the self-reported drug-use rates of the two groups. Moreover, when we talked to seniors from both groups in focus group interviews, we heard the students saying in their own words what our questionnaire data revealed: DARE was not effective in keeping kids off drugs. Our findings paralleled those of other researchers across the United States and seemed to present us with a contradiction: although DARE was ineffective as a drug-prevention program, throughout the nation it continued growing rapidly in size, scope, and popularity. We had to wonder why.

When we consider DARE's role in the class-based pacification of everyday life, we can see that our research findings and DARE's resilience and popularity are not at all contradictory. When viewed as a political and cultural force serving privileged-class interests, DARE's expansion and popularity make perfect sense. The following sections describe DARE's emergence as a political and cultural force and describe how the program serves the political, material, and ideological interests of the privileged class.

DARE: A Political and Cultural Force

National interest in the "drug problem" among the political leaders of both major parties crystallized in 1986 with President Reagan's televised "War on Drugs" address to the nation and the subsequent passage of the "Anti-Drug Abuse Act of 1986." Once set in motion, the drug war remained a popular focus of political and media attention through the 1990s.[14] It was also transformed into a complex and multifaceted political and organizational force.[15] The "Anti-Drug Abuse Act of 1988" systematized the drug war under the Bush and then Clinton administrations into a "national drug control strategy" aimed at controlling both the supply of and demand for illicit drugs in the United States.[16] The latter dimension of this strategy included an emphasis on developing "demand reduction" programs of all types, including drug education. As the drug war generated more public support for antidrug programs, political interest in and federal funding for drug education programs—including DARE— increased substantially throughout the 1980s and 1990s. Federal funding for youth-targeted antidrug education grew from $230 million in 1988 to $660 million in 1995 to more than $1 billion in 1997.[17] By 1998, all forms of federal funding aimed at reducing youth drug use had risen to $1.7 billion and was projected to be more than $2 billion through 2003.[18]

Increased federal funding for drug education combined with drug-war-driven popular support for such programs led to the emergence of direct and indirect "DARE stakeholder" groups. For the most part, these groups consist of privileged-class individuals and organizations with material, political, and ideological interests in DARE's continuation and expansion.[19] Direct stakeholders are those groups and individuals with explicit links to DARE in terms of direct involvement in supporting and implementing the program—such as DARE America officials and program administrators in schools and law enforcement agencies. By contrast, indirect stakeholders are those groups and individuals only loosely coupled and only indirectly involved with DARE—such as political leaders and corporate sponsors who publicly support or contribute to the program. Both groups benefit from the reflected approval, legitimacy, and widespread public support associated with a program linking a popular cause with traditional authority structures, symbolized by the involvement of schools and law enforcement agencies.

At the national level, DARE emerged as a bipartisan favorite of political leaders in the late 1980s, and strong political support for the program continued through the 1990s. Powerful members of Congress allied with former president Bush ensured passage of a 1990 amendment to the 1986 Drug-Free Schools and Communities Act (DFSCA) mandating federal funding for DARE. As amended, the DFSCA requires that 10 percent of DFSCA "governor's funds" (30 percent of federal funds made available each fiscal year to states for drug prevention programs) be used to fund programs "such as Project Drug Abuse Resistance Education."[20] DARE was the only drug education curriculum specifically targeted for federal funding by the DFSCA, which gave the program a tremendous boost.

Over the years, national political support for DARE has included various high-profile events including several joint congressional-presidential "DARE Day" proclamations applauding DARE's contributions to the national campaign against drugs.[21] Perhaps even more important is the explicit reauthorization of federal funding for DARE through 1999. The latter action is part of the $12.7 billion congressional reauthorization of the 1965 Elementary and Secondary Education Act in 1994, including the 1986 DFSCA, reauthorized as Title IV, Safe and Drug-Free Schools and Communities Act (SDFSCA).[22] The popularity of DARE among national political leaders was clearly evident in the House debate on the reauthorization bill, during which many House members repeatedly praised DARE and worked to include provisions that would ensure continued federal funding for the program.[23]

These highly visible federal actions represent the tip of an iceberg of links between national, state, and local politicians and the DARE program. Federal resolutions and funding support, along with similar actions at the state and local levels, link political leaders to the program as indirect DARE stakeholders, who boost their own popularity by being identified with the popular program. At the same time, their political support further legitimates the DARE program and enhances its funding prospects, thereby benefiting individuals and organizations directly involved with its operation and expansion.

DARE's direct and indirect stakeholders have collaborated to embed the program within a complex organizational support structure that helps ensure a continuing flow of resources to sustain its survival and growth. An important feature of this structure is DARE America, a nonprofit corporation organized in 1987 as a 501(c)(3) tax-exempt organization to promote and coordinate the DARE program. Information from DARE America's 1996 federal tax return provides a sense of the organization's financial stake in the drug war, and it illustrates the financial interests of DARE America's top credentialed-class officers in the continuation of the program. In 1996, DARE America reported total revenues of $218,287,639 and total expenses of $217,528,310. The organization's president, Glenn Levant (former LAPD assistant police chief), was paid $232,948. Two deputy directors earned $90,000 each, and three specialized directors earned $80,000, $64,000, and $63,750, respectively.[24]

DARE America has been a potent organizational advocate for the DARE program. It has aggressively worked to expand the program by pursuing goals that include "the adoption of DARE in all states and communities . . . support [for] a national DARE instructor training program . . . [and] coordinat[ing] national fund-raising for DARE."[25] The organization has also successfully recruited numerous corporate, political, and entertainment elites, such as TV personality Arsenio Hall and singer Ted Nugent, to serve as DARE spokespersons and fund raisers.[26] The DARE America Board of Directors consists of well-known national business, political, law enforcement, educational, sports, and entertainment figures. For example, in 1996, the thirty-five-person board included Thea Adelson, Rosey Grier, Alice King, Helen Mars, Diane Disney Miller, and Willie L. Williams.[27]

Another dimension of DARE's organizational support structure consists of a network of ties linking DARE programs to various federal, state, and local government agencies. The Bureau of Justice Assistance (BJA, an agency within the U.S. Department of Justice) serves as a major organizational link tying DARE programs to the federal government. This connection dates to 1986, when former LAPD chief Daryl Gates succeeded in arranging a BJA grant of $140,000 to the LAPD "to share [the] unique DARE Program with other communities throughout the United States."[28] Bureau of Justice Assistance involvement with DARE expanded in the late 1980s and led to agency funding of five regional DARE training centers. The BJA also appoints five of the fifteen members who make up the DARE Training Center Policy Advisory Board, which is responsible for overseeing the training of DARE officers. Other federal agencies with ties to DARE include the National Institute of Justice and the National Institute on Drug Abuse, which have funded DARE evaluation research. The U.S. Department of Education also provides some program funding through the DFSCA, and the U.S. Department of Defense has adopted DARE for use in the schools it operates for dependents of U.S. military personnel. Government linkages also extend down to the state and local levels and involve law enforcement agencies, schools, and community groups.[29]

In addition to extensive public-sector support, there are numerous links tying DARE to corporate sponsors at the national, state, and local levels. DARE America has been especially instrumental in recruiting national corporate sponsors. For example, in 1995, Kimberly-Clark contributed $401,505 to DARE America, and Citibank, First Interstate Bancorp, Packard Bell, Simon and Schuster, and Western Union each contributed $100,000 (or more). Other corporate contributors include Kentucky Fried Chicken, McDonald's, Toys "R" Us, Warner Brothers, and Zenith. Corporate support at the state and local levels involves hundreds of large and small firms contributing to the program.[30]

DARE: Stakeholder Interests and Pacification

Although direct and indirect DARE stakeholders have different types and levels of interest in the program, the preceding section suggests that both groups have shared and overlapping concerns in several areas including economic, political, and ideological interests. Among direct stakeholders, DARE benefits the material interests of credentialed-class members. This is the case because like many other programs devised to address social problems, DARE is largely administered, supported, and delivered by members of this class. The top DARE America officials represent one obvious example of how credentialed-class members benefit from public and private resources allocated to fund the program. Other examples are credentialed-class members who administer and coordinate DARE through the BJA-funded DARE regional training centers, the Department of Defense, and local school districts. Also, top credentialed-class administrators in all DARE-connected organizations benefit directly from DARE's popular public image. As one local DARE official confided to us, "DARE is a great PR program for the schools and the police." DARE even serves as a career booster for lower-level law enforcement officers. A police colonel from Washington state testified during congressional hearings that "a lot of DARE officers are being promoted across our state. . . . [We are] continually looking for officers to train other officers . . . because they end up getting promoted."[31]

Indirect DARE stakeholder groups, such as national political leaders and superclass corporate sponsors, have a number of class-based political and ideological interests that are served by DARE's emphasis on individuals, drugs, and authority. These features of DARE help promote privileged-class interests, legitimate class inequalities, and reinforce the pacification of everyday life in several specific ways.

First, DARE promotes the acceptance of individual-level explanations for and solutions to social problems. Second, it encourages a continuing public focus on drug-war issues while distracting public attention from social-class inequalities as sources of social problems. Third, DARE reinforces uncritical acceptance of and deference to privileged-class-controlled authority and power structures including, at the community level, the schools, the police, and corporate program supporters. Fourth, it assists in the "demonization of drugs" and helps rally public unity against a common enemy. Fifth, DARE helps legitimate a punitive law enforcement, antidrug model and harsh sanctions that are used to control drug use as well as other forms of deviance viewed as stemming from free-willed choices or "bad attitudes."

DARE's ideologically loaded lessons promote privileged-class interests because the indoctrination of working-class students, parents, and citizens to these ideas distract people from class inequalities, defuse class tensions, constrain the development of class consciousness, and reinforce the legitimacy of privileged-class-dominated social control agencies. The latter feature is especially relevant to DARE's social effects because as one arm of the larger war on drugs, the program helps legitimate that war. And as Ken Silverstein and Alexander Cockburn point out, "Domestically, the 'drug war' has always been used as a pretext for social control. . . . Essentially, the drug war is a war on the poor and dangerous classes, here and elsewhere. How many governments are going to give up on that?"[32]

Although it is a national program, DARE acts as a franchiselike operation bringing the symbolic politics, actions, distractions, and other features of the drug war relevant to privileged-class interests down to the community level. Even most "DARE-less" communities have some variation of drug education in their schools, not to mention high-profile state and local drug laws in place, so the political and cultural dimensions of the drug war have become permanent fixtures in every community. And although DARE has been subject to some criticism on the basis of its costs and effectiveness and as promoting a kind of "Big Brother is watching" mentality, few communities have dropped DARE, and more are signing up— about four hundred more each year, including New York City in 1996.[33]

As noted earlier, we do not view DARE's pacifying effects as the result of some dark superclass conspiracy. Even so, there is little doubt that DARE's individual-level prevention focus and symbolic messages concerning the drug threat, respect for authority, and condemnation of deviance are consistent with privileged-class interests. They are also consistent with the privileged-class-supported, Rush Limbaugh-like conservative ideology regarding the causes of and "cures" for a wide range of social ills in America today. According to a number of conservative political leaders, pundits, and radio talk-show hosts, most current problematic social conditions—from poverty to joblessness to drug use—are essentially "attitude problems."[34] The routine "cure" prescribed by this group consists of a short "attitude adjustment" course (sometimes combined with a kick in the pants). DARE represents a neat fit with the conservative model of the causation of social problems. DARE's match with privileged-class interests and conservative ideology illustrates how a program seemingly far removed from the issue of class inequalities is actually not so far removed after all. By helping to keep public attention focused on winning the drug war—and not on a truly explosive issue like starting a "class war"—in hometowns across the United States, DARE contributes to the pacification of everyday life.

THE CULTURE INDUSTRY AND PACIFICATION

> The United States' global industrial pre-eminence may be slipping, but the domestic output and international sale of one of its manufactures is booming— packaged consciousness.
>
> —Herbert I. Shiller, *Nation*, June 3, 1996

The transplant and DARE cases illustrate how projects set in motion by and for the privileged class can dominate public awareness about economic and social issues and confine policy debates to a narrow range of options endorsed by privileged-class-controlled organizations. The effects of issue framing, agenda setting, and policy making by the privileged class in these cases include deflecting public attention away from class inequalities while promoting acceptance of the status quo. These outcomes are also reinforced by the culture industry, which, as the opening of this chapter suggests, disseminates electronic entertainment "products" that typically have the effect of distracting public attention from class issues rather than calling attention to them.

The culture industry was briefly mentioned in chapter 5 as part of our introduction to one of its major subdivisions—the information industry. As we noted then, the culture industry encompasses far more than the dissemination of information. It is a complex enterprise composed of large multimedia firms that are increasingly interlocked with even larger industrial and service corporations, advertising agencies, and nominally nonprofit groups (such as the Public Broadcasting Service). The heart of this industry consists of large firms that produce and disseminate a wide range of entertainment, information, and advertising "products" through television, radio, recorded music, movies, books, newspapers, magazines, and most recently, personal computers. This industry is too large and complex to be considered in detail here—but that is not our purpose. Rather, our goal here is to present a brief overview of the scope and content of the electronic-media segment of the industry—especially television and films—to provide a sense of how it contributes to the pacification of everyday life.

The massive scope and everyday reach of the electronic media are evident in the huge distribution networks that disseminate culture-industry products such as TV and radio programming, sporting events, movies, videotapes, audio tapes and CDs, videogames, and computer website materials to thousands of communities and millions of homes and consumers. In the late 1990s the "wiring of America" provided electronic links between various media firms and sixty-six hundred hometown movie theaters, 98 percent of households with TVs, 81 percent of TV households with VCRs, and 63 percent of TV households with TV cable or satellite service.[35] By the late 1990s, several computer firms were providing on-line services to 50 percent of the 40 million U.S. households with personal computers (out of 100 million total U.S. households in 1997).[36] One result of this extensive penetration of communities and homes by media networks has been that Americans are spending more and more time as passive consumers of electronic media products.

Time spent by individuals on noncommercial activities such as informal socializing or critical reflection and writing produces no benefits for culture-industry profits. Only time devoted to the consumption of products generated by culture-industry firms (TV programming, movies, software, commercial websites, videogames, etc.) juices market shares, sales, and profits. The industry has an interest in channeling more and more consumer time into its commercial products. And it is succeeding. In 1988, the average American spent 1,751 hours consuming various electronic media products (TV was no. 1, at 1,490 hours, followed by recorded music, home videos, and theater movies), with a total of 3,310 hours devoted to all forms of media consumption (including newspapers, magazines, and books).[37] By 2000, total American media consumption is projected to increase to 3,540 hours per person, with 3,190 of those hours devoted to all forms of electronic media (including TV, again no. 1, at 1,650 hours, followed by radio, recorded music, home videos, theater movies, home video games, and internet access).[38] This means Americans—for a variety of reasons—are devoting more and more discretionary time to media consumption—and especially to electronic media consumption.

The Colonization of Consciousness

To the extent that the awareness and limited free time of nonprivileged-class members are dominated by ideas, programs, activities, and events created by the superclass-owned and credentialed-class-managed culture industry, it means that their consciousness is, in a sense, captured—or colonized—by an outside force. This privileged-class-directed "media force" is driven by class interests that are quite different from those of nonprivileged consumers. For us, then, the colonization of consciousness refers to the ongoing invasion by the culture industry—especially through electronic mass media entertainment and advertising content—of ever larger shares of peoples' time, interests, and imagination. This process is driven by many techniques, including the electronic media firms' constant tracking and linking of popular cultural trends with media content. It also involves the media's use of compelling imagery (in TV programming, movies, advertising, video games, web search-engine graphics) and its constant barrage of cleverly produced ads emphasizing the prestige and novelty features of mass, niche, and (upscale and downscale) consumer products.[39] Although this process results in a number of consequences, including increases in culture-industry profits, from our perspective, the reduction in time available to individuals for all other activities outside of media consumption is among the most important. Of particular importance in this regard is how the colonization of consciousness contributes to the marginalization of class-related issues and interests in individuals' everyday thoughts and discussions as more time and "thought space" are devoted to media products.

Although we may live in a "24-7" world (twenty four hours a day, seven days a week), each of us can claim only about sixteen waking hours a day—or about 5,800 hours per year. If we subtract the time devoted to work (about 2,000 hours per year), family and personal obligations, and the 3,190 hours spent on electronic media consumption, we find very little time remains each year for nonprivileged-class members to read, think, or talk about public issues—including class inequalities. Moreover, given the taboo nature of class in America and the interests of superclass culture-industry owners, we would not expect to find class-based themes, issues, or interests routinely included in the movie and television content "inserted" in consumers' minds as the colonization of consciousness process unfolds.

Movies: Class-Free Content?

Class-related issues and themes are rarely presented in movies, as revealed by a content analysis we conducted of large samples of dramas (699), science-fiction films (750), and documentaries (263) drawn from the *1995 Movie/Video Guide*. In this study we found that only about 5 percent of the films in each category (thirty-five dramas, forty science fiction films, fifteen documentaries) included story lines or themes that could be interpreted as critiques of elite-class power or as providing sympathetic portrayals of working-class individuals or organizations (e.g., labor unions).[40] Our short list of thirty-five critical dramas that addressed working-class interests and grievances or critiqued elite-class-dominated institutions included "classics" (from the 1940s on) as well as recent films.

In many respects the findings from our study parallel what movie historian Steven J. Ross found in his review of class themes in the movies. With a focus primarily upon silent films, Ross found that a substantial number of films sympathetic to working-class interests were produced in the United States prior to World War I. However, he points out, the advent of talkies led to the demise of such movies. In a brief discussion of the contemporary period, he notes that class-critical films with "labor-capital" themes have virtually disappeared from the American cinema—reinforcing what we found in our study.[41]

The *Grapes of Wrath* (1940), starring Henry Fonda, was a high-profile, classic film from our list that we viewed as important because it helped establish and legitimate a kind of critical, sympathetic movie treatment of class underdogs in the contemporary era. Bringing the Steinbeck novel of the same title to the screen exposed millions of Americans who had not read the book to its heartbreaking portrayal of the Joad family. Tracing the family's experiences as it migrated from the Dust Bowl during the Great Depression, the movie provides a compelling and sympathetic account of how the Joads and people from similar working-class families were brutalized by the American economic and class structures of the 1930s.

Only a very small number of high-profile dramas from the recent past has followed in the class-critique, sympathy-for-the class-underdog film tradition and also featured well-known Hollywood stars. Four recent titles illustrate and also virtually exhaust the list of recent films with both qualities.

1. *Norma Rae*: This 1979 film starring Sally Field compassionately portrays the title character's transformation from passive worker to union activist in a southern textile plant.
2. *Reds*: Warren Beatty and Diane Keaton star in this 1981 film that presents a sympathetic account of American radical journalist Jack Reed's career, including his reporting on the Russian Revolution.

3. *Remains of the Day*: This 1993 film starring Anthony Hopkins powerfully depicts how the British class system of the 1930s stunted and distorted servants, masters, and human relationships.
4. *Bulworth*: Warren Beatty produced and stars in this 1998 "political farce" that, although flawed in many respects, includes scenes that voice powerful critiques of current American class and race inequities.

A smaller number of less well known recent dramas has also followed in the class-critique, sympathy-for-the-class-underdog tradition, but with much less star power. Two examples include *Matewan* and *The Killing Floor*. The former is a 1987 film directed by John Sayles that sympathetically depicts the union side of the West Virginia "coal wars" of the 1920s. The latter title is a 1993 film that presents a historically informed account of how Chicago meatpacking firms in the early 1900s resisted unionization by exploiting racial and ethnic divisions and tensions among the workers.

Although more titles could be added to the examples listed, the entire group of class-critique dramas identified in our study makes for a very short list. Few movies in the genres we reviewed provided critiques of elite-class power or sympathetic accounts of the economic, political, social, and personal grievances of the working class. Dramas reflecting the class-critique tradition as well as science-fiction films including overt critiques of ruling-class power (such as *They Live!*) are infrequently made, narrowly promoted, and seldom viewed by mass audiences. Moreover, they are notable exceptions to the non-class-based, escapist themes and action story lines routinely depicted in most mainstream American films. In fact, we are likely to see even more escapist action movies in the future. A 1996 study by *Variety* concluded that films with budgets of more than $60 million generate more profits than cheaper films. And action films combine the lowest risks with the greatest (financial) rewards—especially as Hollywood films are distributed worldwide and often earn more money overseas than in the United States. According to one media executive, "Kicking butt plays well everywhere."[42]

As butt-kicking action films become ever more common, class themes are likely to appear even less often in movies than in the past. The film formula of the future seems to be more action equals more distraction. Speaking to the effects of movie content on culture and class consciousness, film historian Ross maintains that "American filmmakers have helped create a culture whose citizens either no longer view class as an important part of their lives or define the middle class so broadly that class no longer seems to matter."[43]

TV and ABC

So what's on TV? For openers, try advertising. A typical thirty-minute TV-network program includes at least seven minutes of advertising. Local programs have even more. American television networks now broadcast six thousand commercials per week, up 50 percent since 1983.[44] From 1989 to 1996, advertisers increased their spending on all forms of television advertising from $27 billion to $40 billion.[45] This 67 percent increase reflects not only the increase in broadcast time devoted to advertising but also advertisers' faith in the power of TV to sell more stuff.

What kinds of programming do the ads support? Or what else besides ads do we find on TV? The really short answer is ABC: Anything but Class. If we set aside TV news as being part of the information industry (chapter 5), we find TV advertising supports a wide range of programming that for the most part ignores class issues and trends heavily toward distraction. A tour of recent *TV Guide* daytime and evening listings reveals recurring programming patterns, particularly for network TV. Mornings are devoted mainly to newsmagazine and talk shows. Afternoons bring soap operas and more talk shows. Evening programming is more diverse and includes paranormal *X-Files*-like series, "reality"-based crime shows, sporting events, comedy series staples, Gen-X nighttime soaps (e.g., *Melrose Place, Pacific Palisades*), more newsmagazine shows, and more talk shows. Cable, satellite, PBS, syndicated programs, and movies add diversity to daily programming, but studies of TV content reveal a striking absence of programs that depict the lives or concerns of working-class Americans or that deal with class-based inequalities in ways that might promote critical reflection among viewers.

One study of four decades of TV entertainment (from 1946 to 1990) found that of 262 domestic situation comedies, only 11 percent featured blue-collar, clerical, or service workers as heads of households. By contrast, the vast majority of the series, 70.4 percent, portrayed "middle-class" families with incomes and lifestyles that were more affluent than those of most middle-income American families. In fact, in 44.5 percent of the comedy series studied, the head of the household was a professional.[46]

Another study of thirteen TV situation comedies from the 1990s found the issue of social mobility across class lines is sometimes used as a source of comic tension and moral instruction. On the rare occasions when characters in the series studied aspired to or encountered upward mobility, the outcomes reminded viewers that "achieving inter-class mobility is rare, and the rewards of any substantial social movement will likely be bittersweet." The study concluded that TV situation comedies send mixed and paradoxical messages where social mobility is concerned. On one hand, these programs typically reinforce the myth of America as a land of opportunity where hard work and persistence pay off. On the other hand, on the rare occasions when characters actually encounter social mobility, their experiences tend to be portrayed as disruptive and often undesirable.[47] The net result is the subtle reinforcement of existing class divisions, structures, and locations as normal, natural, and preferred—to the disruptive effects of social mobility.

In the late 1990s, only four prime-time network television comedy series sometimes portrayed working-class characters, families, issues, or problems in sympathetic or positive terms, and two of these were animated programs. The four included *Roseanne* (starring Roseanne Barr—canceled after the 1996-97 season),

Grace under Fire (starring Brett Butler), *The Simpsons* (created by cartoonist Matt Groening), and *King of the Hill* (devised by *Beavis and Butthead* creator Mike Judge and Greg Daniels—formerly of *The Simpsons*). By contrast, there were many near-prime-time syndicated tabloid-style TV "newsmagazines" that virtually never reported on working-class issues or concerns. Programs such as *Inside Edition, Hard Copy,* and *American Journal* routinely traffic in high-energy celebrity profiles and gossip about the stars—especially reports concerning sex, drugs, deviance, and opulent lifestyles. Such titillating stories appear designed to deliberately appeal to nonelite viewers by providing vicarious thrills and voyeuristic gratification. They seem to say, Maybe you can't afford it or do it, but you can watch others own it and do it—Right here! Right now!

The themes of titillation and distraction are also staples of most daytime TV talk shows. The summer of 1998 saw the following sampling of shows and topics: *Jerry Springer* on incest between twins, *Ricki Lake* on unfaithful mates, *Montel Williams* on betrayal of trust, *Maury Povich* on phobias, and *Jenny Jones* on people who have renounced their race.[48] Other, more "prestigious," daytime TV talk shows have adopted formats that frequently mix glitzy topics with celebrity interviews (usually TV, movie, or sports stars or the suddenly famous or infamous promoting their movies, books, or careers). A typical 1997 summer week of *Oprah Winfrey* reruns included a show on female celebrities as well as interviews with Tiger Woods, Sarah Ferguson, Mark Fuhrman (former LAPD detective from the O. J. Simpson case), and Madonna (enough said?). The same summer week of *Rosie O'Donnell* reruns saw interviews with Penny Marshall, John F. Kennedy Jr., Jason Alexander, Jennifer Aniston and Kim Coles, and one show that combined Sylvester Stallone, Annabella Sciorra, Ray Liotta, and Peter Berg.[49] The pattern of TV talk-show hosts interviewing celebrities also extends to nighttime TV talk shows—with talk-show hosts often interviewing the celebrity hosts of other TV talk shows![50]

ABC and the Oprahfication of the Mind

In situation comedies, talk shows, newsmagazines, and other programming formats, ABC—Anything but Class—is what's on TV. "ABC" is an important factor contributing to the colonization of consciousness; and the "ABC" focus and content of most TV programming—especially talk shows and newsmagazines—contribute to another phenomena involved in the pacification process: the Oprahfication of the mind. This term refers to how the electronic media—especially television "infotainment" (superficial information presented in "information" or "news" formats but whose primary value is as entertainment)—contributes to the demise of critical thinking about current and past social, cultural, and political events and issues.

High-profile media stars (e.g., Oprah Winfrey) projected through powerful TV media platforms help establish a pop-culture conceptual framework that blends current events, celebrity, and social issues into short, seamless entertainment packages. As a result, working-class TV viewers are encouraged to concentrate on only the most glamorous or sensationalized personalities and issues: Lady Di (forever), the O. J. Simpson trial, Oklahoma City bombing, Woodward au pair, and Theodore Kaczynski trials, TWA flight 800, serial-killer sprees, millennial-doom prophecies, Michael Jordan, Jeff Gordon, NASCAR fever, septuplets, billionaire Bill Gates, millionaires next door, and the long-running Wall Street drama. They are coached to conceptualize and think about such topics largely in terms of the most immediate, superficial, and individualized case details. Any sense of how social-class inequalities or wider historical or cultural contexts may be linked to current issues is lost to Oprahfication.

American TV viewers are also encouraged to think about social, political, and economic issues through a superficial popular cultural lens that brings into dazzling focus "SGP" (shock, glamour, and the perverse) topics while blurring the field of vision where serious issues like working-class interests, grievances, or inequalities are concerned. As our review of TV-talk-show content suggests, the SGP focus of these shows (and many TV newsmagazines) routinely ranges across topics like sexual orientations, practices, and abuse, body piercing, satanic rituals, tattoos, racial strife, and the latest fashion or hair-style trends.

The SGP focus is reinforced by increasingly common "socialization to novelty" experiences among TV viewers and consumers of popular culture generally. Mass media advertising often encourages consumers to devalue stability and continuity in products, packaging, entertainment, and lifestyle trends. Much of the content and many of the commercials in the electronic media reinforce the idea that routine is boring and changes—especially fast-paced novel changes—are good. Viewers are encouraged to think that "been there, done that" experiences equal boring repetition and are to be avoided. Consumers are encouraged to pursue and prefer novel products, experiences, and activities because novelty is presented as the source of fulfillment and fun.[51] Preferences for novel products, images, and activities are driven by the mass media's recognition that speed, action, color, change, and novelty juice viewer interests as well as TV and merchandise-marketing profits.

The combination of SGP programming and repeated viewer exposure is a key factor leading to the Oprahfication of the mind. Oprahfication is a kind of truncated and compartmentalized cognitive style that not only erodes peoples' capacity for critical thinking but also diminishes even the legitimacy of critical thought. Oprahfication reduces (1) the likelihood that people will think of social issues or current events in terms of class analysis (too boring!); (2) peoples' ability to think in such terms (they have too little practice or experience); and (3) peoples' ability to understand or appreciate a class-based analysis of problematic social conditions if it is presented to them (too confusing!). Colonization and Oprahfication are major elements in the pacification of everyday life through the culture industry.

PACIFICATION AND PROVOCATION: TWO SIDES OF EVERYDAY LIFE

As we have shown, the pacification of everyday life is a pervasive, complex, and powerful process. The illustrations presented in this chapter suggest that it promotes privileged-class interests through a variety of institutionalized routines and practices that for the most part legitimate and reproduce existing class inequalities and at the same time distract working-class members from these issues. However, it is also important to recognize that pacification does not proceed as an unopposed process, nor is it a seamless, one-dimensional force without internal contradictions.

As we noted in chapter 2, alternative class-power networks essentially operate in ways that call attention to, challenge, and contest the pacification process. The provocation efforts of these networks typically operate outside the organizations and structures that dominate the pacification process—but not always. Some branches or substructures of mainstream organizations that drive the pacification process sometimes deliberately include people and ideas from the alternative power networks. For example, public (and on occasion commercial) radio and television broadcasters sometimes include alternative power network members on some programs typically as a means of legitimating their image as providers of "open forums" for discussions of public issues. Whatever the motives of gate-keepers controlling privileged-class-dominated organizations, whenever labor leaders, consumer advocates, or elite-power critics (e.g., AFL-CIO President John Sweeney, Ralph Nader, Gore Vidal) testify at congressional hearings or appear on TV or radio talk shows and newsmagazines, their messages challenging the pacification process are heard and seen by the working class.

Perhaps more important than token mainstream appearances by alternative power network members are the effects that occur as a result of internal contradictions that arise from institutional imperatives associated with the routine practices of the organizations that drive the pacification process. At the same time that privileged-class-dominated organizations produce pacifying "products" such as the policies, programs, and entertainment described in this chapter, some features of some products also result in paradoxical effects. That is, some products produced in the routine course of the pacification process may highlight or even challenge class inequalities rather than legitimate them. When this occurs, these features of the pacification process may actually contribute to contradictory outcomes—such as increased class tensions and resentment or even heightened class consciousness.

One illustration of how class provocation and pacification can occur at the same time as a result of routine organizational imperatives and practices can be found in the political arena. As we have seen, candidates for office are largely financed by superclass-provided funds. However, candidates must also appeal to working-class voters. The latter reality can sometimes lead even superclass-funded candidates to take public positions on some issues that appear to reinforce working-class interests at the expense of the privileged class. In the 1996 presidential election Patrick Buchanan was accused by mainstream media pundits of promoting "class war" because of his speeches denouncing corporate greed, NAFTA, the loss of American jobs, and the growth of economic insecurity among American workers. He may have been insincere, but these campaign themes illustrate that the routine operation of a political system that generally reinforces the pacification process has the potential to generate contradictory messages—at least temporarily and episodically.

The electronic media also illustrate how institutional imperatives can produce contradictions in pacification products. As we have seen, although most media products help to distract public attention from class issues and serve to legitimate class inequalities, mass media firms are fundamentally money-making businesses. Because TV and movie corporations are driven by profit-maximization concerns, they must deliver a constant stream of novel products to attract viewer attention so as to increase sales and profits. In the absence of explicit censorship and in the routine course of producing creative and marketable products, some movies and TV programs are produced that include content critical of class inequalities or privileged-class interests. Some may even turn out to be popular "hits" and perhaps inspire the creation of similar product lines (as illustrated by the 1999 movie *A Civil Action*, starring John Travolta, concerning the health effects of toxic waste and a possible sequel, with Travolta, focusing on the "Gulf War Syndrome").

As we saw earlier, few movies focus on class inequalities. However, the ones that do often encourage viewers to empathize with exploited working-class underdogs or to be outraged by exposés of elite-class arrogance and power abuses. These themes are included in classic hits like *Grapes of Wrath* and they are also woven into more recent big- and low-budget films critical of elite classes, such as *Bulworth*, *They Live!*, and Michael Moore's 1998 film, *The Big One*.[52] Although we would agree that most movies are much more likely to have pacifying rather than provocative effects where class issues are concerned, the routine operation of the pacification process still produces some films that inject critical class-based themes and ideas into popular culture.

Like the movies, television is also most closely associated with pacifying effects. However, even routine television products can produce paradoxical outcomes. For example, some TV newsmagazines and talk-show forums have reported on topics that do not necessarily serve privileged-class interests, such as soaring CEO pay levels, plant closings, sweatshops, campaign finance reform, capital gains tax cuts for the rich, and ethical lapses among professionals (e.g., physicians and attorneys). Such programming has the potential to fuel class tensions and resentment, increase public cynicism about mainstream institutions (especially corporations and government), and even increase class consciousness. These effects are revealed by public opinion polls: in a 1995 Gallup poll, 58 percent of Americans said major corporations have "too much power," and 76 percent agreed "the government is pretty much run by a few big interests looking out for themselves."[53] Also, a 1995 *New York Times* poll found that 55 percent of Americans now identify themselves as members of the "working class."[54]

Sometimes regularly scheduled TV programs include content that heightens some forms of class consciousness among nonprivileged-class viewers. During the 1994 (NBC) and 1995 (FOX) summer seasons, Michael Moore's *TV Nation* garnered high ratings and won awards while often featuring entertaining reports that were critical of class inequalities and privileged-class interests.[55] (Of course, the series was canceled.) *Grace under Fire* sometimes combines entertainment with subtle critiques of class inequalities and privileged-class members' arrogance. As an illustration, in an early episode of the series, working-class Grace was treated in condescending and patronizing terms by an upper-middle-class mother who first encouraged and then discouraged Grace's daughter from competing in a largely upper-middle-class beauty pageant for six-year-olds. As a clever exposé of "classism," the episode combined humor, outrage, warmth, compassion, and entertainment while increasing viewers' class consciousness.

The parade of examples illustrating the flip side of the pacification process could go on and on, but the point is that there is another side. The everyday, routine functioning of mainstream social institutions like local newspapers, drug education programs, movies, and TV programs does, for the most part, serve to distract nonprivileged groups from class issues, defuse class tensions, and legitimate class inequalities. But at the same time, the daily routines and practices of mainstream institutions occasionally can and do subvert the pacification process. On those infrequent occasions, chunks from the dark mass of conflicting interests from beneath the waterline of the class iceberg churn to the surface and produce transient episodes of inconvenience, embarrassment, and even anger for privileged-class members. Fortunately for them, such "provocations" are usually isolated and quickly smoothed over by the powerful and predictable privileged-class-controlled institutional routines that on a daily basis reinforce the pacification of everyday life. However, in the next chapter we consider the prospects for the emergence of sustained challenges to the deeply ingrained legitimating and distracting features of the pacification process and to the powerfully institutionalized and ever widening class inequalities of the late twentieth century.

NOTES

1. Robert Goodman, *The Last Entrepreneurs: America's Regional Wars for Jobs and Dollars* (New York: Simon and Schuster, 1979).

2. Joseph Weber and Blanca Riemer, "These Days Mack Trucks Isn't Built like Mack Trucks," *Business Week*, July 30, 1990, 40–41.

3. For details on incentive packages, see Peter Eisenger, *The Rise of the Entrepreneurial State* (Madison: University of Wisconsin Press, 1988); Milward H. Brinton and Heide H. Newman, "State Incentive Packages and the Industrial Location Decision," *Economic Development Quarterly* 3 (1989): 203–22; Robert Perrucci, *Japanese Auto Transplants in the Heartland* (New York: Aldine de Gruyter, 1994).

4. James Derk, "We Got It, Toyota!," *Indiana Business Magazine*, January 1996, 9–13.

5. "The New Transplants," *UAW Research Bulletin*, January–February 1995, 10–11.

6. Ibid.

7. Michelle Cottle, "The Real Class War," *Washington Monthly*, July–August 1997, 12–16.

8. "Unbalanced!: Bipartisan Budget Bill Boosts Billionaires," *Labor Party Press*, November 1997, 4–5.

9. Katherine Beckett, "Setting the Public Agenda: 'Street Crime' and Drug Use in American Politics," *Social Problems* 3 (1994), 425–47. Also see *Ageism on the Agenda*, special issue, *EXTRA!*, March–April 1997.

10. Earl Wysong and David Wright, "A Decade of DARE: Efficacy, Politics, and Drug Education," *Sociological Focus* 28 (1995): 283–311.

11. U.S. Department of Justice, Bureau of Justice Assistance. *Program Brief: An Introduction to DARE: Drug Abuse Resistance Education*, 2d ed. (Washington, D.C.: Bureau of Justice Assistance, 1991), 3–7.

12. Wysong and Wright, "A Decade of DARE," 285.

13. Tom Zoellner, "DARE Challenges Its Critics," *Salt Lake Tribune*, July 9, 1997.

14. For example, see Eric J. Jensen, Jurg Gerber, and Ginna M. Babcock, "The New War on Drugs: Grass Roots Movement or Political Construction?," *Journal of Drug Issues* 21

(1991): 651–67; James D. Orcutt and J. Blake Turner, "Shocking Numbers and Graphic Accounts: Quantified Images of Drug Problems in the Print Media," *Social Problems* 40 (1993): 190–206; and Mike Males, "Pot Boiler: Why Are Media Enlisting in the Government's Crusade against Marijuana?," *EXTRA!*, July–August 1997, 20–21.

15. Earl Wysong, Richard Aniskiewicz, and David Wright, "Truth *and* DARE: Tracking Drug Education to Graduation and as Symbolic Politics," *Social Problems* 41 (1994): 448–72.

16. For example, see Office of National Drug Control Policy, *The National Drug Control Strategy* (Washington, D.C.: National Criminal Justice Reference Service, 1992), 9.

17. Budget figures are from Office of National Drug Control Policy (ONDCP), *National Drug Control Strategy* (Washington, D.C.: National Criminal Justice Reference Service, 1992), 45, *National Drug Control Strategy* (1994), 79, and *National Drug Control Strategy* (1996), 61–62.

18. ONDCP, *National Drug Control Strategy* (Washington, D.C.: National Criminal Justice Reference Service, 1998), 59.

19. Wysong and Wright, "A Decade of DARE," 298.

20. *U.S. Code Annotated*, 20 U.S.C.A. sect. 3192, Amendment to Public Law 101-647, Cumulative Annual Pocket Part (St. Paul, Minn.: West Publishing, 1995), 337.

21. For examples see various issues of the *Congressional Record* that reference the DARE program from 1992 through 1996 listed in the bibliography.

22. See *U.S. Code Annotated*, Public Law 103-382, Title IV, Statutory Supplement 5A (St. Paul, Minn.: West Publishing, 1994). Also see Robert M. Wells, "House Education Bill," *Congressional Quarterly*, May 14, 1994, 1246-49; and Robert M. Wells, "Senate Panel Easily Approves $12.7 Billion Measure," *Congressional Quarterly*, June 18, 1994, 1632–33.

23. *Congressional Record, Title IV—Safe and Drug-Free Schools and Communities*, March 9, 1994, H1113–23.

24. U.S. Department of the Treasury, "Return of Organization Exempt from Income Tax—Form 990, DARE AMERICA," 95-4242541 (Washington, D.C., 1996).

25. U.S. Department of Justice, Program Brief, 11.

26. Dennis Cauchon, "Studies Find Drug Program Not Effective," *USA TODAY*, October 11, 1993, 1–2.

27. U.S. Department of the Treasury, "Form 990."

28. U.S. Senate Committee on Labor and Human Resources, *Drug Abuse, Prevention, and Treatment*, 100th Cong., 2d sess., 1988, 198.

29. See Everett M. Rogers, "Diffusion and Re-Invention of Project DARE," in *Organizational Aspects of Health Communication Campaigns: What Works?*, ed. Thomas E. Backer and Everett M. Rogers (Newbury Park, Calif.: Sage, 1993), 139–62. Also see U.S. House Committee on Education and Labor, Subcommittee on Elementary, Secondary, and Vocational Education, *Oversight Hearing on Drug Abuse Education Programs*, 101st Cong., 1st sess., 1990, serial 101-129.

30. Information from various sources, including DARE America's 1995 Form 990 Income Tax Return. Also see Cauchon, "Studies Find Drug Program Not Effective"; and U.S. House, *Oversight Hearing on Drug Abuse Education Programs*.

31. U.S. House, *Oversight Hearing on Drug Abuse Education Programs*, 57.

32. Ken Silverstein and Alexander Cockburn, "Why the Drug War Works: It's A Money/Class Thing, of Course," *CounterPunch*, June 15–30, 1998, 4–5.

33. "Spokane Just Says No to DARE Program," *Kokomo Tribune*, October 6, 1996.

34. Frances Fox Piven, "Poorhouse Politics," *Progressive*, February 1995, 22–24.

35. U.S. Department of Commerce, Bureau of the Census, *Statistical Abstract of the United States* (Washington, D.C.: U.S. Government Printing Office, 1997), 565–66, 779.

36. "Online Services: Top Ten Activities," *PC Magazine*, July 1997, 9. Also see Phil Lemmons, "Straight Talk about PC Costs," *PC World*, June 1997, 17.

37. U.S. Department of Commerce, Bureau of the Census, *Statistical Abstract of the United States* (Washington, D.C.: U.S. Government Printing Office, 1995), 572.

38. U.S. Department of Commerce, *Statistical Abstract of the United States* (1997), 565.

39. David Leonhardt, "Two-Tier Marketing," *Business Week*, March 17, 1997, 82–90.

40. Earl Wysong, "Class in the Movies," unpublished paper, 1996; Mick Martins and Mick Porter, *1995 Video Movie Guide* (New York: Ballantine Books, 1994).

41. Steven J. Ross, *Working-Class Hollywood: Silent Film and the Shaping of Class in America* (Princeton: Princeton University Press, 1998).

42. Robert W. McChesney, *Corporate Media and the Threat to Democracy* (New York: Seven Stories Press, 1997), 28.

43. Ross, *Working-Class Hollywood*, 255.

44. McChesney, *Corporate Media and the Threat to Democracy*, 28.

45. U.S. Department of Commerce, *Statistical Abstract of the United States* (1997), 578.

46. Richard Butsch, "Class and Gender in Four Decades of Television Situation Comedy: Plus ça Change . . . ," *Critical Studies in Mass Communications* 9 (1992): 387–99.

47. Lewis Freeman, "Social Mobility in Television Comedies," *Critical Studies in Mass Communication* 9 (1992): 400–406; quote, 405.

48. *TV Guide*, July 25–31, 1998.

49. *TV Guide*, July 26–August 1, 1997.

50. Sam Husseini, "Talking about Talk," *EXTRA!*, May–June 1996, 20.

51. Ronald Dahl, "Burned Out and Bored," *Newsweek*, December 15, 1997, 18.

52. Jeremy Smith, "Intellectual Snobs versus Political Slobs," *Dollars and Sense*, May–June 1998, 38–39.

53. Michael Golay and Carl Rollyson, *Where America Stands, 1996* (New York: Wiley, 1996), 137, 173.

54. *New York Times*, *The Downsizing of America* (New York: Random House, 1996), 318.

55. Miranda Spencer, "TV Nation: A Show for 'The Rest of Us,'" *EXTRA!*, November–December 1995, 24–25.

8

Class in the Twenty-first Century: Consolidation and Resistance

> Uninformed and misinformed; pauperized or over-worked; misled or betrayed
> by their leaders—financial, industrial, political and ecclesiastical, the people are
> suspicious, weary, and very, very busy, but they are, nonetheless, the first, last,
> and best appeal in all great human cases. . . . And, though each individual in the
> great crowd lacks some virtues, they all together have what no individual has, a
> combination of all the virtues.
>
> —Lincoln Steffens, *Upbuilders*, 1909

The stories of Forrest Gump and Jim Farley in chapter 1 of this volume focus attention on the intersection of social class and the American Dream. One shines as idealized fiction, the other illustrates the darkest side of reality, where privileged-class interests and power doom the dream to failure. There is no doubt which story is more popular. Grossing more than $329 million since its release in 1994,[1] *Forrest Gump* is the American Dream personified: its main character is the classic underdog achiever. But there's more. *Gump* also represents another important side of the American Dream: a commitment to the values of family, friends, community, and conscience.[2] The absence of those qualities in the hard-edged corporate boardrooms dominating the new class system of Jim Farley's world helped seal his fate. And Farley's economic free fall was not broken by a resilient social safety net. Despite popular enthusiasm for the sentimental Gump-like values of mutual compassion and shared sacrifices, these qualities are largely missing in action when it comes to providing meaningful assistance to the Jim Farleys of today's new working class. The chilling fact is that the downward mobility of Farley and millions like him actually serves the interests (at least in the short run) of those in the privileged class in the top diamond of the new class society.

Since chapter 1, we have tracked the contours and exposed the dark side of the new class society. From Jim Farley to the global economy and back to the culture industry, we have documented the corrosive effects of this system on the American Dream. And we have also tracked the processes by which privileged-class advantages have been ever more tightly institutionalized and legitimated. Our travels have taken us from Forrest Gump to the taboo land of class analysis, where the strange but vaguely familiar forms of icebergs, global sweatshops, invisible empires, stealth industries, classroom tracks, and pacification schemes cast dark shadows on the future.

So is it possible to transform the emerging new class society that doomed Jim Farley into a more open and equitable structure? Is an American class system possible that accommodates both sides of the dream: opportunities for Gump-like underdog achievement and a shared, institutionally based commitment to the values of mutual respect, support, and community? Is an American society possible where the needs of the many (the new working class) outweigh the power of the few (the privileged class)? Can we have a class structure with a human face? The current economic, political, and cultural landscape does not appear to favor any major transformations of the new class system toward a more equitable system. But lessons from the past as well as recent stirrings within the alternative power networks suggest some tantalizing possibilities.

In this final chapter we consider the prospects for continuity and change in the new class society through—with apologies to Charles Dickens—a kind of *Christmas Carol*-like set of Present, Past, and Future themes. The section titled "Reality Check of the Present" underscores the current imbalances in class power resources and reminds us that the structures of institutionalized capitalism and classism reinforce the new class society. In the "Past as Prologue?" section we revisit the class-based foundations of the American underdog tradition by recalling those historical moments when working-class Americans forged populist movements to contest the power of the privileged class.

Entering the twenty-first century, the "Future of Class" section is divided into three parts. It begins with a discussion of consolidation that considers how the struggles between the privileged class and the new working class on issues related to investment, consumption, and social and skill capital—resources at the heart of the new class society—are likely to unfold in the twenty-first century. Our assessment is based on the expectation that privileged-class leaders will pursue policies related to these forms of capital that will consolidate and reinforce privileged-class dominance.

The section subtitled "Resistance" presents an overview of selected examples from what we see as an emerging class-reform, activist coalition committed to reversing the increasing economic, political, and cultural inequalities of the new class society. Although many groups are part of the alternative power network coalition for change, our selections are limited to six cases. They were chosen because of their relatively recent emergence as reform agents and because of their shared concerns with structural reforms that unite economic, political, and cultural strands of change. Also, we see them as strikingly reminiscent of the American populist tradition in terms of their goals and the language and imagery they use in critiquing current class inequalities.

We conclude with a section called "Scrooge versus Structural Scenarios." In it, we contrast the "Scrooge scenario" for reform favored by privileged-class leaders with the populist "structural democracy scenario" favored by class-reform activists. As we will see, these scenarios represent very different approaches to reforming class inequities, with the former emphasizing the importance of individual conscience and the latter emphasizing the importance of democratic participation in developing structural changes in the economic, political, and cultural arenas of American society.

REALITY CHECK OF THE PRESENT

It is time to put economic class warfare aside.

—Congressman Bill Archer (R-Tex.), *Congressional Record*, June 26, 1997

"yada yada yada"

—Seinfeld, quoted by Rick Marin, *Newsweek*, January 12, 1998

On the cusp of the twenty-first century, it is clear that superclass "suits" (organizational elites typically sporting expensively tailored business suits) rule. But not in the old, easy-to-spot and deflate autocratic, robber-baron style. As we have seen, more and more, superclass "suits" affect a common touch—dressed-down, casual, and media savvy—with credentialed-class coaching and back-up as needed. We're all in this together, we are told. The message in the new class society is that social class (especially privileged-class origins) does not count in the competition for success. Class divisions are passé. High-tech skills, being a team player, and having a positive mental attitude, we are told, are the keys to success today. But are they?

The analysis of class relations in this book suggests that the balance of class power has shifted decidedly to the privileged class. For the past quarter century, starting in the mid-1970s, this class has been able to accumulate ever greater shares of income and wealth at the expense of the new working class. As we have seen, privileged-class dominance has been achieved by attacking workers' jobs and wages and by reducing spending on social programs, thereby requiring working-class members to pay more for their health care, education, housing, and retirement.

The consequences of thirty years of class warfare by the privileged against the new working class are revealed almost daily in the increasing polarization of social and economic conditions between the top 20 percent of society and the bottom 80 percent. Corporate profits in 1996 for the five hundred largest industrial and service companies were up sharply, reaching double-digit returns.[3] This growth in earnings and profits for multinational corporations occurred despite the fact that total revenue and employment was "flat" for the year, suggesting that increased profits are linked to lower costs of doing business. This phrase typically translates into fewer workers who are being paid less and forced to work harder, lower taxes on corporate revenues, and less government oversight of environment pollution and workplace health and safety. These seemingly obvious class inequalities become much less obvious after being filtered through the information industry and other powerful institutionalized forces. The filtering processes disguise privileged-class-biased corporate practices and government policies. And they legitimate the transfer of increasing shares of all capital forms—investment, consumption, skill and social—to those in the top tier of the new class system at the expense of those in the bottom tier.

This shift of wealth and power to the privileged class has been justified, in part, by the powerful new ideology of the global economy. This idea system focuses public attention on the need for American businesses and workers to accommodate new competitive forces in the global economy (e.g., workers who will work harder for less money and corporations that can invest more because governments tax and regulate them less). And it has been used over and over again to justify the economic changes that have led to the new class society. Superclass and credentialed-class corporate executives, politicians, media moguls, and policy experts have used the global economy mantra in the same way that the specter of international communism was used to justify repressive domestic political policies in the 1950s and 1960s. The geopolitical threat of communism has been transformed into the geoeconomic threat of global competition, which has been both created and managed by institutional capitalism.

Institutional Capitalism and Privileged-Class Dominance

The ability of the privileged class to devise, disguise, and legitimate corporate practices and government policies that serve its interests but are destructive to working-class interests is reinforced by several structures described earlier in this book. These class-biased structures and outcomes are typically both part of and also facilitated by the deeply embedded economic, political, and cultural power of institutional capitalism. This concept refers to the intercorporate-network model of business described in chapter 2—as opposed to earlier forms of family or managerial capitalism.[4] It involves large, often multinational, firms linked by numerous interlocks of directors who serve on several corporate boards at the same time. And it is driven by the impersonal principles of profit maximization, capital accumulation (especially through increases in corporate stock values), and the necessity of access to capital funds (to finance operations, mergers, and expansions). It is an institutionalized force of staggering size and power dominated by and serving privileged-class interests.

Under this system, investment, worker pay, promotion, security, and production policies of interlocked firms are dictated by how such policies can best serve the impersonal principles that drive the system—especially profit maximization. High profits maximize corporate access to capital pools controlled by investment firms and satisfy large individual and institutional shareholders' demands for the highest possible investment returns and for steady increases in the share values of the stock they hold. As the dominant form of business organization in the United States today, institutional capitalism drives the core sector of the economy and creates smaller firms in the periphery to service core needs. The result is a small number of core firms with superclass owners, major stockholders, and elite corporate managers, a relatively small number of high-paid credentialed-class positions, a shrinking number of middle-income blue-collar jobs, and expanding numbers of poorly paid positions in peripheral firms occupied by larger and larger numbers of new-working-class members.

Institutional capitalism was made possible in part by the legal standing accorded to corporations by shifts in laws governing the corporate chartering process and by the landmark 1886 U.S. Supreme Court case of *Santa Clara County v. Southern Pacific Railroad.* In that case, the Court invoked the fourteenth amendment and "defined corporations as 'persons' and ruled that California could not tax corporations differently than individuals."[5] The effect of this decision, which was made by the Court without hearing any formal arguments, conferred upon corporations the same legal rights and constitutional guarantees enjoyed by natural persons.[6] The extension of personlike legal rights and protections to corporations combined with their huge resources (even by 1886 standards) created an enormous power asymmetry between corporations and people in the American legal system and in the society generally. The social dangers posed by expanding corporate power and their potential to dominate all other social institutions were noted well before the 1886 case—by Abraham Lincoln. In an 1864 letter he warned that "as a result of the war, corporations have been enthroned and an era of corruption in high places will follow . . . until all wealth is aggregated in a few hands and the Republic is destroyed."[7]

One important result of institutional capitalism today is that the basic business practices guiding and the ideological premises underlying large U.S. corporations have spread to and infused the routine structures, policies, and practices of nearly all large-scale organizations in the society.[8] This includes government agencies, universities, schools, and even charities and churches. As massive corporations (and other types of large bureaucracies) have emerged (and merged) gradually over time, they have become an integral part of our collective experiences. Because they have such a pervasive physical presence and are often associated with the satisfaction of routine individual and social needs, it is hard to imagine how economic, political, and cultural activities—indeed, even society itself—could exist without large corporations—and similarly structured nonbusiness organizations. The huge organizations located in the economy and in the political and cultural arenas have become so much a part of the routine social landscape that they seem as natural as mountains, forests, rivers, and streams.

With multiple financial, personnel, and ideological links to other large organizations (e.g., government bureaucracies, universities, churches), large corporations populate and dominate the national economy, politics, popular culture, local communities, and how most people think about the new class society.[9] One example illustrating the penetration of American culture by ubiquitous corporations and the ideology and imagery associated with them is the increasing application of the business term *bottom line* to a variety of nonbusiness topics and activities. It has become a shorthand metaphor for the core or most critical feature of almost any activity or topic, such as personal health, family life, sex, movies, politics, or drug use—and many others.

Institutional capitalism is a powerful and pervasive organizational force field. It dominates the economic, political, and cultural arenas, shapes ideas and perceptions on a wide array of nonbusiness activities, and helps conceal the power of large corporations in creating, maintaining, and legitimating the new class system. But the hegemonic dominance of institutional capitalism in American society is rendered invisible by its saturation of the total social environment.

Institutional Classism and Privileged-Class Dominance

Institutional classism is another abstract label for a powerful but hidden force field that also helps reinforce and disguise privileged-class interests. At a general level, classism refers to the unspoken but widely accepted belief in American society that the values, social behavior, language patterns, and lifestyles of the privileged class are superior to those of the working class or the lower class.[10] Compared with racism, sexism, or even ageism, classism is largely a silent, hidden "ism"—partly because of the taboo nature of class in America. But classism is similar to racism and sexism in terms of its effects. It leads to prejudice toward, stereotyping of, and discrimination against members of the nonprivileged class—especially those in the lower segments of the working class. *White trash, redneck, trailer-park low-life, welfare bum*, and *slacker* are only a few of the many pejorative terms applied to groups clustered in the lower segments of the new class system.

Classism is based on and justified by a widely shared belief system sometimes called the ideology of meritocracy.[11] This idea system views class location as a reflection of talent and effort. It encourages the view that privileged-class positions are occupied by people who possess widely valued and admired traits such as high intelligence, achievement motivation, and altruism. It also encourages viewing members of the new working class (especially those at the lowest levels) as being justly placed in lower ranks because they obviously lack the valued qualities necessary to "succeed" in a merit-based economic system. The ideology of meritocracy helps justify and legitimate class inequalities by making class divisions seem naturally ordained and views those at the top as rare and gifted visionaries. This is obviously what billionaire John D. Rockefeller Sr. had in mind when he said, "I believe the power to make money is a gift of God. . . . Having been endowed with the gift I possess, I believe it is my duty to make money and still more money, and to use the money I make for the good of my fellow man according to the dictates of my conscience."[12]

Like racism and sexism, classism is embedded—or institutionalized—in the routine practices and policies of organizations dominated by privileged-class members such as corporations, government, the mass media, public schools, the criminal-justice system, and universities. As a result, the operations of nearly the entire organizational establishment of the society trend in directions that exclude, disadvantage, or otherwise marginalize people from the lower classes through everyday routine (but largely unrecognized) practices. Institutional classism refers to a form of hegemony whereby privileged-class-based ideas, values, norms, language styles, and social behaviors prevail in organizations dominated by this class. From schools to the workplace to government, the gatekeepers in privileged-class-controlled organizations actively screen out or marginalize working-class-based values, norms, language styles, and behaviors.

Such gatekeeping practices were evident in a recent study illustrating how Harvard law students "afflicted" with the stigma of working-class origins were subtly (but powerfully) encouraged to disguise this fact. In addition to their classroom work, they learned the importance of distancing themselves from the working-class stigma, as well as how to do it. This was necessary to increase their chances of being selected to join elite law firms and thereby maximize their own career opportunities. The acceptance of these students by privileged-class "organizational masters" in elite law firms required them to demonstrate an easy familiarity with elite cultural codes and conform to the cultural standards, social behaviors, style of dress, and patterns of speech of the privileged class.[13]

The hidden power of privileged-class communication styles illustrates yet another dimension of institutional classism. Teachers and professors in public schools and universities—especially those serving students where many already possess advanced levels of social capital—actively discourage working-class students from communicating in the language styles of their class and penalize their grades if they persist. The same pattern extends to hirings and promotions in the workplace—especially for positions above entry-level ranks—and to the conferring of legitimacy to political candidates by the mainstream media. The "elaborated code," encompassing more abstract conceptual references and complex sentences, routinely structures communication (written and spoken) among members of the privileged class.[14] As a kind of "gold standard," it is the only legitimate communication style or mode of expression accepted or rewarded in classrooms, boardrooms, and the formal political and policy-making arenas.

Hidden class-linked advantages or disadvantages associated with privileged-class gatekeeping practices and with the class-based hegemony of the elaborated code as a communication style are seldom noted or explored by social scientists, media commentators, or social pundits. In fact, the details of these phenomena are virtually unknown to the public. The placement of workers in advanced entry-level career positions as well as the pace of later career advancement are typically explained in mainstream academic research or in mass media profiles of "successful people" as functions of merit and talent and not as the result of class-biased gatekeeping practices. Similarly, the differential mastery by students of "proper" communication styles and forms (the elaborated code) is typically viewed as an indicator of merit and talent and not as the result of the advantages or disadvantages associated with privileged versus working-class origins and experiences.

Some features of privileged-class advantages are informally recognized among segments of the population, as in the commonly circulated aphorism (among the working class) concerning the basis of career success: "It's not what you know, but who you know." This statement reflects a kind of cynical realism among members of the working class, but it is obviously overly simplistic and misses the hidden institutional basis of privileged-class advantages.

As tips of the class inequalities iceberg, privileged-class gatekeeping practices and rewards for mastery of the elaborated code are but two examples of the myriad ways by which class-biased organizational routines, policies, and practices perpetuate privileged-class interests. They are only two of the many covert threads woven into the fabric of institutional classism. Their powerful presence as sifting and sorting instruments helps make the common economic, political, and cultural successes (and rare failures) of privileged-class offspring as well as the common failures and rare successes of working-class children within privileged-class-controlled organizations seem to be "fair" and "impartial" outcomes.

Our reality check of the present leads us to conclude that institutional capitalism and classism are powerful structures that reinforce the new class society in both obvious and subtle ways. Moreover, both structures are themselves embedded in the dominant power networks that span the economic, political, and cultural arenas of social life. As we have seen, the deeply entrenched force field of institutional capitalism generates an unequal hierarchy of class-based positions, rewards, and relationships. At the same time, the class-based inequalities produced by this system tend to be replicated as well as interpreted through institutional classism. The ideology of this system encourages viewing unequal class outcomes as legitimate, natural, and even inevitable or desirable by large numbers of people in all classes. Thus, classism as an institutionalized structure serves to perpetuate and reinforce—while also disguising—a variety of hidden privileged-class advantages and working-class disadvantages.

THE PAST AS PROLOGUE?

We meet in the midst of a nation brought to the verge of moral, political, and material ruin. Corruption dominates the ballot box, the legislatures, [and] the Congress. . . . The newspapers are subsidized or muzzled. . . . The fruits of the toil of millions are stolen to build up colossal fortunes. . . . From the same prolific womb of governmental injustice we breed two classes—paupers and millionaires.

—Preamble to the 1892 People's Party National Platform,
cited in Howard Zinn, *A People's History of the United States*, 1980

How long can the intensifying inequalities between the privileged class and the new working class continue? That's akin to asking, How long can the stock market keep going up? A typical buoyant headline from the late 1990s proclaimed, "Dow 12,000?" But some analysts expressed a more historically grounded sentiment: "You'd better enjoy the party while it's going on, because it's sure not going to last forever."[15] History, like the stock market, does not move in a straight line over time.

So what are the prospects that significant political or social movements will develop to alter the current imbalance of power that exists between the two great opposing classes in the double diamond? To avoid utopian visions or fantasies driven by hopes or dreams more than by reality, we look first to America's past. We focus on those times when the forces for change converged on a single project—to change the structure of society in order to reduce economic and social inequalities. Popular movements for change have gone by many labels, but "American populism" has endured as a common frame of reference describing many movements from the past aimed at reducing material inequalities. The next section considers lessons from the American populist tradition and provides a context for understanding contemporary reform projects aimed at reshaping the new class society.

Breaking the Taboo: The Recent Past

In the 1996 Republican Party primaries, Pat Buchanan was a long-shot outsider who desperately wanted to defeat front-runner Senator Bob Dole, long-time member and apologist of the privileged class. Buchanan knew that in order to have any chance to win his party's presidential nomination, he would have to appeal to working-class Americans who might not usually vote in a primary or even in the general election. Perhaps thinking like his old mentor, Richard Nixon, Buchanan must have thought, "How can I appeal to this 'silent majority'? How can I mobilize them to vote for me and not for Bob Dole?" The answer must have come to him as an epiphany: with a laserlike grasp of reality, he took the extraordinary step (for a politician) of telling the truth. His sound bites at times took on an almost Marxist tone of class analysis: "When AT&T lops off 40,000 jobs, the executioner that did it makes $5 million a year and AT&T stock soars"; "Mr. Dole put the interests of the big banks—Citibank, Chase Manhattan, Goldman Sachs—ahead of the American People"; "The voiceless men and women in this country have no one to represent them in Washington because the hierarchy of both parties really argues on behalf of these trade deals, which are often done for the benefit of corporations who shut their factories and move them overseas."[16]

In a New Hampshire primary stump speech Buchanan made a rambling allusion to earlier times when revolutionary fervor led the masses to attack elites and take what was rightfully theirs: "'You watch the establishment,' he urged supporters. . . . 'All the knights and barons will be riding into the castle and pulling up the drawbridge, because they're coming. All the peasants are coming with pitchforks after them.'"[17]

Buchanan's bombastic remarks sent shock waves through the privileged class and the presidential contenders from both parties. But consistent with the class taboo principle, in almost the blink of an eye the mainstream mass media rushed in to defuse the class content of Buchanan's campaign and to dissipate the emerging discussion of corporate profits and greed—without mentioning the superclass or its interests. As we noted earlier, the *New York Times*, in its role as premier dominator of the mainstream ideological process, took the extraordinary step of publishing the seven-part "Downsizing of America" series. Although it acknowledged some human costs associated with downsizing, the series' basic spin presented such practices as consistent with the long-term interests of all Americans. This effort—and others like it—effectively put the class genie back in the bottle and ensured that discussion of class remained verboten.

Breaking The Taboo: Lessons from History

What Pat Buchanan did in his surprising 1996 spring offensive against the superclass and corporate power was not new in American history. The wealthy and powerful, in the form of corporate executives, bankers, politicians, and bureaucrats, have often served as high-profile targets of criticism by individuals and groups attempting to mobilize discontented Americans for change. Historical movements condemning elite-class excesses and promoting working-class reforms have often juxtaposed obvious and easily understood class contrasts by using terms such as *the haves* versus the *have nots*, the *powerful* versus the *powerless*, and the *fat cats* versus the *common man*. Such references have often served as the images and language of American populism. This historical tradition of protest calling for reforms to reduce economic and social inequities has periodically emerged from the class-based grievances of the working-class majority.

Populist rhetoric has been used by numerous labor organizers, social movement leaders, and even, at times, mainstream politicians to shape and mobilize public discontent. In its classic form, populist messages seek to simultaneously elevate the masses and attack the privileged for their undeserved rewards. When the People's Party was formed in 1892, it pulled together debt-ridden small farmers, hundreds of discontented workers' groups, and several minor parties—all of whom were deeply dissatisfied with how the Democrats and Republicans had been running the country. More than a century ago, leaders of the People's Party praised the virtuous small farmers and laborers as the "producers" who created national prosperity that rightfully belonged to all Americans and heaped scorn on the "plutocrats," "parasites," and "moneyed aristocracy" who were said to wallow in idleness, extravagance, and waste. The use of sharply contrasting class-based images was a central feature of the populist message. As a noted historian of this tradition recently observed, "[Populism is] a language whose speakers conceive of ordinary people as a noble assemblage not bounded narrowly by class, view their elite opponents as self-serving, and seek to mobilize the former against the latter."[18]

The populist social movements of the nineteenth century were grounded in a rhetoric and ideology based on economic grievances and a defense of those who worked as small farmers, wage earners, and small-business people. But populist attacks on corporations, monopoly, and plutocrats were not aimed at the overthrow of capitalism. Rather, the populist reform message called for greater recognition of the importance of the common man in the economic, political, and social arenas and for a fair share of the fruits of workers' productive labor to be returned to these producers of wealth. The relatively modest scope of the populist reform agenda is underscored by author Michael Kazin's point that "through populism Americans have been able to protest social and economic inequalities without calling the entire system into question."[19] Kazin also argues that early populist critiques of American society attempted to build new bonds among people by returning to the core beliefs of the new American nation—rule by the people, reward for hard work and diligence, and faith in God.

The early moments of populism experienced through the People's Party at the end of the nineteenth century found expression in the twentieth century in different bases of discontent shared by widely varied groups. Throughout the twentieth century, populist rhetoric and movements have embraced an array of moral crusades. They began early in the century with the prohibitionists' war against alcohol and closed out the century with the religious right's attacks on the amoral elites who, it was claimed, were undermining the core values of the majority. Thus, American populism began the century as a left-liberal tradition aimed at attacking economic, political, and social privileges and inequalities but was later transformed and diverted into conservative forms of moral protest aimed primarily at defending the values of the "moral majority." The targets of populist attacks are superficially the same at both ends of the century: entrenched, irresponsible elites. But for early leftist populists, elite targets were symbolized by "fat cat" and "plutocrat" labels, whereas for contemporary rightist populists, evil is represented by "cultural elites" (as in Hollywood and the media) and by governmental elites who administer the growing bureaucratic state.[20]

As history illustrates, the American populist tradition has been both a powerful and ambivalent instrument for reform. Many real or aspiring leaders have picked up the populist instrument hoping to play a tune powerful enough to stir the sleeping masses into sweeping away corrupt elites. The power of that tradition rests with its roots in the early American experience stressing the dignity of the common man and a rejection of the "foreign" influences of aristocracy and elitism. This thread of populism can serve as a bond unifying people to act on behalf of the common good while eschewing privilege and unfair advantage. The ambivalence associated with the populist tradition stems from its majoritarian beliefs, reflected in the support for direct participatory democracy. The majoritarian emphasis does not sit well with members of religious or ethnic groups that are numerically small and therefore feel that their interests will be ignored by the usually white and Christian majority. The majoritarian emphasis also does not sit well with "privileged leftists" who support populist ideology but whose education and credentialed-class privileges make them wary of "marching with the people."

The ambivalence of the populist tradition is partly responsible for the liberal left's movement into identity movements and identity politics while seeking to give co-equal standing to the three major oppressions of class, race, and gender—which still excludes environmentalists, gays, the disabled, the aged, and numerous other groups with specific forms of grievances. The challenge facing the new-working-class majority in the United States involves finding ways to invoke the sentiment opposing privileged-class power of the populist tradition in ways that join the current disparate collection of disaffected groups, movements, and parties into a unified political movement. Only through unity can the new working class pool the modest organizational and personal resources its members possess into a substantial collective force for change—as in the aphorism of the hand and power: Each finger is only a modest force, but five fingers united transform the hand into a powerful fist.

THE FUTURE OF CLASS INEQUALITIES

Having recounted the past, what is the future of the new class society? We believe there is no single future. Rather, there are many possible futures. The future of class inequalities depends upon the extent to which the trends presented in the following three sections develop and unfold in the twenty-first century. It is likely that the consolidation trend will be powerful and difficult to change. We expect that privileged-class leaders will make every effort to pursue policies concerning investment, consumption, social, and skill capital that will consolidate and reinforce privileged-class dominance.

On the other hand, it is also likely that the current resistance trend to privileged-class policies that are increasing economic, political, and cultural inequities of the new class society will continue and grow. The growth of organized resistance to class inequalities may be one of the most encouraging stories (for the new working class) of the twenty-first century. Some of the groups involved in these struggles echo the American populist tradition in terms of their goals, language, and the images they use in critiquing unfair privileged-class advantages and class inequalities.

If the future does include reforms in the new class system, their substance will be critical to any meaningful changes in class inequities. Possibilities range from superficial and cosmetic to substantial and structural reforms. The final section, "The Scrooge Scenario versus the Structural Scenario," considers this issue.

The Future: Consolidation

> One class will have the autonomy to live how and where it wants; the other will be increasingly constrained and shut out. Pedigree and power, money and education will make the difference.
>
> —Jerry Adler, *Newsweek*, July 31, 1995

One future trend about which we are certain is that of continuity in the areas of class domination and class struggle. As we move into the twenty-first century, we expect the 20 million families making up the privileged class will continue to dominate virtually all of the elite decision-making positions as well as most of the professional and managerial information-generating and decision-executing positions in the major economic, political, and cultural institutions that make up the dominant power networks.

The domination by privileged-class members of the U.S. institutional infrastructure means that in their personal and public lives they will continue to make decisions that reflect institutional imperatives favoring an expansion of already concentrated wealth and power. These decisions can be expected to produce corporate and governmental practices and policies that disproportionately benefit privileged-class interests as against those of the working class. Thus, we expect the trend of the past thirty years, whereby ever larger shares of economic, political, and cultural resources have been shifted to the privileged class, to continue into the next century. By *continue* we mean that privileged-class leaders will pursue policies aimed at consolidating the gains made by this class over the past thirty years.

When we speak of consolidation, we refer to efforts to strengthen, deepen, and extend actions and policies that are already in place. We do not refer to totally new actions or policies, such as the ongoing attempt by the privileged class to convert the Social Security system into a private insurance scheme. As privileged-class consolidation efforts unfold, the quality of life among members of the new working class can be expected to deteriorate even further. This downward spiral will continue until and unless organized mass political and social resistance movements emerge—akin to those of the populist era—that will represent the interests and press the claims of the working class for a redress of its shared economic and political grievances.

The following five parts of this section consider how privileged-class-sponsored consolidation policies related to investment, consumption, social, and skill capital are likely to track into the next century. In focusing on the struggles surrounding these forms of capital, we expect that at least in the short term, privileged-class-controlled organizations in the economic, political, and cultural arenas will actively support policies that will strengthen and extend the advantages, interests, and power of this class at the expense of the new working class. We also expect that these same organizations will engage in activities aimed at concealing and legitimating corporate practices and governmental policies that shift increasing shares of all forms of capital to the privileged class at the expense of the new working class.

Investment Capital: Continued Export of U.S. Jobs

We have already discussed at length the loss of high-wage manufacturing jobs over the past thirty years. American corporations have moved production overseas or built new production facilities overseas in order to find lower-wage workers and governments that are indifferent to the security and safety of workers and protection of the environment. In chapters 3 and 4 we pointed out that the flight of U.S. capital has been greatly enhanced by the 1993 North American Free Trade Agreement (NAFTA), which political leaders claimed would stimulate trade between the United States, Mexico, and Canada. Although the Clinton administration has argued that it is good for the United States, there is no doubt that NAFTA has facilitated the shift of corporate production from the United States to Mexico.[21] Despite evidence that, by 1997, NAFTA had resulted in the loss of between 261,000 and 600,000 U.S. jobs, President Clinton requested that Congress grant him "fast-track" authority to negotiate an expansion of the treaty to other Latin American nations.[22] Any expansion of NAFTA would undoubtedly lead to more U.S. jobs being lost, as even more incentives would be created for shifting investment capital from U.S. plants to factories in low-wage nations.

As discussed in chapter 4, Clinton's request for fast-track authority to expand NAFTA was supported by major U.S. corporations and was also endorsed by virtually all major U.S. newspapers.[23] This request and the corporate support it evoked illustrate how U.S. trade policy is driven by superclass interests that in turn are grounded in and legitimated by the structures of institutional capitalism. But as we also noted in chapter 4, Clinton's proposal to extend NAFTA provoked unexpectedly stiff resistance from a labor-led coalition that included public interest, community, environmental, and religious groups as well as other organizations linked to the alternative power networks.

The opposition worked hard to expose NAFTA's anti-working-class record in the United States and Mexico in challenging Clinton's efforts to extend the treaty. Opponents cited evidence from several sources to make their case. For example, according to the Bronfenbrenner Report commissioned by the NAFTA Labor Secretariat (an organization created by "side agreements" to the NAFTA treaty), the passage of NAFTA increased U.S. plant closings in response to worker unionization drives: "Employers are [now] three times more likely to shut down the plant within two years of an organizing drive than they were in the late 1980s, before NAFTA."[24]

Various kinds of data were cited by opponents to illustrate that NAFTA had produced negative economic effects in both the United States and Mexico. For example, the 1993 pre-NAFTA U.S. trade record with Mexico included a $1.7 billion surplus, but in 1996 (post-NAFTA), the United States recorded a $16.8 billion trade deficit with Mexico. Also, the percentage of Mexicans considered "extremely poor" increased from 31 percent in 1993 to 50 percent in 1995.[25] Even the U.S. government provided the opposition with ammunition illustrating NAFTA's job loss effects in the United States in 1997: "The U.S. Department of Labor has certified that 154,180 [U.S.] workers have lost their jobs because production shifted to Mexico or Canada or because imports have increased from one of those countries."[26]

Despite widespread mainstream media accounts that portrayed fast-track opponents as irrational or delusional, the anti-fast-track coalition conveyed the evidence concerning NAFTA's antiworker effects to the public through alternative media sources and lobbied the sympathetic Democratic Caucus in the U.S. House of Representatives. Before the congressional vote, polls showed that 56 percent of Americans opposed granting fast-track authority to the president, and only 26 percent said they thought the United States benefited from NAFTA.[27]

The undeniably "high negatives" of the NAFTA record and the personal experiences of many U.S. workers with NAFTA's effects were major reasons that the labor-led coalition was able to effectively mobilize opposition and win the congressional vote against Clinton's fast-track request.[28] The defeat of fast track revealed that many working-class Americans believe more NAFTA-style policies will contribute to what Ross Perot called "the giant sucking sound" of more jobs leaving the United States—and that they are willing to actively oppose such policies. The battle illustrated that the continued export of U.S. jobs is not inevitable. It demonstrated that alternative-power-network organizations can successfully unite to resist privileged-class mobilization of dominant-power-network resources and policy preferences. However, despite the fast-track defeat, most privileged-class members continue to argue that more NAFTA-like policies are necessary to maintain U.S. competitiveness in the global economy.[29]

Privileged-class-supported, consolidation-style trade policies did not end with the vote against extending NAFTA. In 1998, the "free-trade" issue resurfaced in the form of the Multilateral Agreement on Investment (MAI). Because the MAI would promote a huge expansion of international corporate free-trade rights, it has been called the "big investors' Bill of Rights" and "'NAFTA on steroids.'"[30] The MAI negotiations began in 1995 with the idea of extending trade provisions found in both NAFTA and the GATT (the General Agreement on Tariffs and Trade). It would extend the free-trade provisions of GATT "by prohibiting signatory nations from impeding the flow of money and production facilities from one country to another." If passed, the MAI would explicitly subordinate "the right of elected governments to set national economic policy to the right of transnational corporations and investors to conduct business—investing and divesting—however they see fit."[31] Thus, its passage would undoubtedly facilitate the export of even more investment capital by the privileged class while further reducing job opportunities for the U.S. working class.

As the 1990s drew to a close, the MAI had a number of powerful supporters, including the Clinton administration, the United States Council for International Business (six hundred large U.S.-based multinationals), and transnational firms in the twenty-nine-member European Organization for Economic Cooperation and Development (OECD).[32] Despite this lineup of heavy-hitter support, by mid-1998 the proposed treaty had also begun to generate heated opposition from some of the same groups that helped defeat Clinton's request for fast-track trade authority.[33]

At the time of this writing, the combination of strong popular opposition and internal divisions within the business community makes U.S. and international agreement on and ratification of the MAI uncertain. In mid-December 1998, the OECD announced it was "no longer conducting negotiations for an MAI" and the treaty appeared to have stalled.[34] However, the MAI may turn out to be unnecessary for the superclass-dominated corporate community to achieve its international investment policy objectives. The investment policies mandated by the International Monetary Fund (IMF) in administering the 1998 Asian bail-out plan represent a kind of "regional MAI without the ratification process." The IMF plan requires the affected Asian nations' economies to be opened "to any private company to make any kind of investment" and to grant "'national treatment' for foreign investors." Now, "the IMF wants to rewrite its own Articles of Agreement to force all 180 of its affiliated nations to drop any remaining barriers to investment."[35] Thus, the IMF could, in effect, implement the key MAI features desired by superclass leaders of the international corporate community without resorting to the messy business of democratic national policy debates and votes. The MAI proposal and the possible IMF backdoor solution illustrate the determination of the superclass to extend consolidation-style trade policies into the next century.

Consumption Capital: Continued Inequality in Jobs, Wages, and Taxes

Privileged-class-based political and economic leaders argue that the U.S. economy and workers are doing fine. They point to the tremendous job growth that has occurred in the United States even while millions of jobs were being exported and while many large firms continue to report job cuts owing to corporate downsizing.

Although these leaders may be correct in terms of the net gain of new jobs created versus jobs lost to export and downsizing, most of the newly created jobs are at lower wages, with fewer benefits, and with more insecure job tenure than the jobs that were lost. The overall effect of these trends has been the imposition of intense pressures by employers on workers, resulting in the lowering of workers' real wages and a substantial weakening of workers' rights and bargaining power.[36]

Privileged-class leaders also point to the very low (5 percent range) unemployment rate of the late 1990s as evidence that overall the economy is strong and that everyone is benefiting as the Dow Jones average rises and inflation remains low. There are many problems with these interrelated claims. But the government's "official" unemployment rate is fatally flawed in two respects. First, it represents a serious underestimate of actual unemployment. The official estimate is based upon a monthly national sample survey of U.S. households, which asks people a series of questions about whether they are currently working or looking for work. Only those who are unemployed but claim to be actively looking for work are classified as unemployed. This approach excludes people who are unemployed but who have not looked for work in the past month. These "discouraged workers" have stopped looking for work because their experiences tell them the search is pointless. Also excluded are employed part-time workers who want full-time jobs but can't find them. The actual rate of unemployment and underemployment jumps to more than 12 percent when discouraged workers and part-time workers seeking full-time work are included.[37]

The emphasis by privileged-class leaders on expanding job opportunities and low unemployment serves to both mask and legitimate class inequalities linked directly to most workers' diminished access to consumption capital (income). The message sent to workers whose real wages have been declining since the 1970s and to the underemployed and unemployed by credentialed-class professionals who manage and spin economic news is essentially this: "The economy is booming. If you can't find a good job, it must be your fault!" In this way, privileged-class-scripted and mainstream-media-disseminated accounts of aggregate unemployment rates and other economic trends overreport the quantity of work available (creating the illusion of low unemployment) while also underreporting on the diminished quality of the jobs held by more and more members of the working class. Mainstream media reports ignore the reality that increasing numbers of jobs pay less than "living wages," provide few or no benefits, and offer little or no job security.[38]

The trends toward lower incomes and less economic security for most members of the working class are not accidental. They are the direct result of class-war consolidation practices and policies implemented by corporate and government actions throughout the 1970s, 1980s, and 1990s that have shifted consumption capital away from working-class wage earners to privileged-class groups. Examples of consolidation policies that would exacerbate current class-based income disparities and extend them into the next century are especially evident in recent governmental policy trends involving social programs and taxes.

Social Programs and the Declining Social Wage

The privileged class will continue to press for reductions in federal and state spending for programs that constitute the "social wage," which benefits all or some segments of the working class. In industrialized nations, the *social wage* refers to government policies ensuring minimum levels of citizens' material well-being through "social programs" such as health care, a mandated minimum wage, unemployment insurance, educational assistance, housing subsidies, income and food assistance to the poor, and old-age pensions.[39] Compared with that of other industrialized nations, the U.S. social wage is very modest and lacks health care guarantees. The major features were put in place in the 1930s; modest expansions occurred mainly in the 1960s with the passage of federal Medicare and Medicaid legislation.[40] However, in recent years the social wage has come under attack by privileged-class conservatives for allegedly breeding dependency on government and undercutting individual initiative.

Spending reductions have already occurred or are being planned in several areas including, for example, federal subsidies for education, housing, and welfare assistance. As a result, living costs for members of the working class are going up as real wages continue to fall (especially for the working poor), producing a free fall in the standard of living among the poorest segments of the new working class. This process is especially evident in the "welfare reform experiment." Organized and legitimated by credentialed-class elites acting on behalf of their own and superclass interests, the "reform" legislation capitalized on resentment among some segments of the working class toward entitlement programs serving the poor.

At the federal level, bipartisan congressional support led to the passage of the Personal Responsibility and Work Opportunity Reconciliation Act, which President Clinton signed into law in 1996. This measure not only sharply reduces benefits to the poor, it also imposes time restrictions on the number of years people are eligible for assistance and adds "training" requirements that move welfare recipients as quickly as possible into low-wage jobs. The net effects of this legislation include more downward pressures on wage levels (as thousands of new workers are added to the low-wage labor market), increases in the number of discouraged and underemployed workers, and rising levels of human misery as many of the poor lose minimal levels of support for food, housing, and health care.[41] Ironically, for the higher-wage members of the new working class who supported welfare "reform," as the poor are forced into the labor market, their presence helps drive down wage rates for all workers.[42]

Privileged-class leaders are also at work on two additional major policy efforts that would shift even more income from the working class to the privileged class. The first is the ongoing battle to extend the age at which retirees are enrolled in Medicare. Currently, retirees are eligible for Medicare at age sixty-five, but superclass-sponsored conservative "think tank" studies and policy papers are offered as justification for legislative proposals that would extend the age to sixty-seven.

Such an action would delay overall Medicare costs and also reduce government spending costs as those Americans who would have been covered at sixty-five and sixty-six die before reaching sixty-seven.[43]

The second effort, which has received cheers from the privileged class, is the initiative to recalculate the consumer price index (CPI), which is used by the federal government and many other governmental bodies and private firms to estimate the rate of inflation. The annual increase in the CPI is used as the basis for calculating (among other things) annual increases in Social Security checks paid to millions of older Americans. For example, if the CPI for 1999 is 3 percent, then a typical retiree receiving a monthly Social Security check of $800 would receive $824 in 2000. Political and economic elites know that they can reduce federal spending by billions of dollars if the CPI is "adjusted" downward by only 1 or 2 percent. Of course, if the CPI is adjusted downward, millions of low-income older Americans will lose benefits. At the same time, the privileged class can then make the case for further reductions in federal taxes, especially for high-income taxpayers.[44]

Continued Tax Inequalities: Wealth and Income

While the wages of the new working class are constrained, the income and wealth of the privileged class will continue to grow. Salaries of corporate executives, managers, and other members of the credentialed class are likely to continue to increase sharply into the twenty-first century, just as they have in the past three decades. Recent increases in stock prices have dramatically expanded the wealth of the privileged class, because this group owns most of the privately held stocks and mutual funds, bonds, and commercial properties in the United States. The trend of increasing concentration of wealth is also likely to continue well into the twenty-first century. And ironically, it is partly fueled by increasing economic insecurity among the new working class concerning retirement income. As benefit-defined pension plans (funded by corporate contributions) have been increasingly replaced by contribution-defined plans (funded by employee's contributions from wages; e.g., 401(k) plans), new-working-class members are forced into the stock market hoping for higher returns. Their stock purchases help drive up stock prices, which disproportionately benefit privileged-class stock owners.[45]

The expansion of privileged-class wealth and income received an additional boost from the Balanced Budget Reconciliation Act of 1997, brokered by President Clinton with the support of both Democratic and Republican members of Congress. As noted in chapter 4, this law will result in multibillion-dollar windfalls for the privileged class that will extend and expand income and wealth inequalities well into the twenty-first century. Two features of the law discussed in chapter 4 that are especially relevant in this regard are the reductions in the taxes on capital gains and reductions in inheritance taxes.

As we pointed out in chapter 4, wealth generated from increases in stock values is subject to capital gains taxes, but the 1997 law lowered the modest 28 percent rate of the early 1990s to 20 percent.[46] Because privileged-class members are the largest holders of capital (in the form of stocks and bonds), they will benefit the most, with the richest 1.4 percent of households enjoying an average annual "break of $21,850 apiece."[47] This change will increase both the wealth and income of privileged-class members well into the next century.

A second wealth- and income-extending benefit of the 1997 law involves the amount of personal wealth that can be transferred across generations free from federal taxation. In chapter 4 we pointed out that prior to the 1997 law, individuals could transfer estates valued at up to $600,000 to their children tax free (with husbands and wives permitted to transfer $1,200,000 tax free). After the 1997 law, these amounts increased to $1.2 million for an individual and $2.4 million for a couple.[48] Clearly this tax change affects only privileged-class members and will have the effect of reinforcing the intergenerational permanence of the new class system.

From these two 1997 tax law changes alone, apart from all other advantages associated with growing up in an affluent family, the sons and daughters of the privileged class will have their adult lives reinforced with enormous economic advantages. With policies such as these in place, to speak of equality of opportunity as the essence of the American Dream is more than a cruel joke. It approaches the Big Lie dimensions of the most distorted forms of propaganda.

Social and Skill Capital: Closing the Gates of Opportunity

Our distributional model views social and skill capital as critical factors influencing the processes through which varying levels of the other two capital forms are distributed (or redistributed) to individuals and groups. As we noted in chapter 1, social capital includes people's participation in various kinds of social networks, their acquisition of class-legitimating and class-enhancing formal credentials, and their possession of qualities valued and rewarded by various organizations (e.g., specialized talents and skills). Skill capital is closely related to social capital in that both are often linked to formal educational organizations that develop specialized talents, refine economically valued interests and skills, and help establish access to informal social and career networks of opportunities and practicing privileged-class professional mentors.

As the American economy is transformed by corporate strategies to maximize profit and per share value of stocks (downsizing, outsourcing, job transfers, globalization), the availability of "good jobs" has become increasingly problematic. The number of positions linked to high or even moderate levels of consumption capital (income) has always been finite, but in recent years those numbers have stagnated. Neither death or retirement of current workers nor economic expansion can be counted on to produce more "good job" openings as the economy is transformed. The situation is akin to a sports team in which only a limited number of player positions are available.

So how are the limited number of "good job" positions distributed among the large pool of aspirants? We believe social and skill capital play major roles in the distributional process in terms of providing access to these jobs and also in terms of explaining why it is fair and right for the holders of these jobs to occupy them. But as we have shown, the past three decades have witnessed an expansion of policies, programs, and trends that have restricted opportunities for members of the working class to cultivate social capital at individual or collective levels and to accumulate advanced levels of skill capital. For the younger cohorts of the working class, the result has been a dramatic decline in opportunities to access "good jobs" and to acquire the social and skill capital necessary for upward social mobility to professional careers in the privileged class.

Several kinds of corporate practices, government policies, and social trends are consolidating higher levels of social and skill capital in the hands of privileged-class members while decreasing access to these resources by working-class members. Although the list is long, it begins with the attack on public education by conservative privileged-class members and organizations. This group advocates decreased spending for all forms of public education, including college, while also supporting an expansion of school voucher systems and privatization schemes. These privileged-class-sponsored efforts are key examples of class consolidation policies related to social and skill capital. Already partially in place, these policies are reshaping how schools influence the distribution of social and skill capital resources to students in ways that will further disadvantage working-class children and reinforce the advantages of privileged-class children.

In state legislatures and the U.S. Congress, neoliberal privileged-class leaders are currently calling for cuts in funding for urban school programs because they claim more money will not solve problems of these schools. Their claim is based on social Darwinist assumptions that view the urban poor as an underclass so disorganized by antisocial values and hedonistic lifestyles that many of its children are beyond educational redemption—no matter how much money is spent on them.[49] Parallel to calls for deep cuts in publicly funded education are policies advocated by superclass-funded think tanks where marketplace competition for schools is viewed as a "solution" for those segments of the urban poor that might be redeemed by education. These "experts argue that education will only improve when poor children are given vouchers to attend private schools and private groups are allowed to start and run their own schools with unregulated public funds."[50]

Policies that defund public schools restrict working-class students' opportunities to participate in the kinds of social networks that would lead to the cultivation of an expanded circle of social ties and valued individual skills essential for acquiring a "good job" or a shot at upward social mobility. As high-quality educational experiences are made less accessible to working-class students and as their parents experience declining real incomes, the likelihood is reduced that such students will even aspire to (let alone acquire) the kinds of formal credentials and advanced skills necessary to access the declining pool of "good jobs" and professional careers.

Privileged-class efforts to defund public education also extend to the university level, as reflected in declining levels of state support for public universities combined with rapidly rising tuition costs. According to the Government Accounting Office, between 1980 and 1993 state governments reduced their contributions to public universities' operating revenues by 56 percent.[51] Also, during the 1987–96 period tuition rates at public universities increased by 132 percent.[52] The class-based social- and skill-capital implications of the combination of state defunding and increasing costs of college to students and parents are obvious. As state support drops and tuition costs escalate, fewer working-class students will be able to afford to attend college. Children from working-class families will face ever higher financial hurdles if they hope to attend college, as costs exceed the annual incomes (and maybe even the net worth) of their parents. Working-class children will find their choices increasingly limited to the cheapest forms of higher education. And these are likely to include more impersonal, technologically driven, narrowly focused, vocational-style programs that are connected to low-paid jobs with limited opportunities.

By contrast, children from the privileged class have few financial barriers to contend with when considering college attendance. Increasingly, only children from privileged-class families will have access to elite colleges and universities with programs taught by professional faculty and linked to job opportunity networks with higher starting salaries and long career ladders. Moreover, increasingly only children from privileged-class families will be able to realistically consider or afford professional degrees beyond the baccalaureate level. These factors (and others) will conspire to limit the chances of young men and women from the new working class to achieve significant, educationally linked opportunities for occupational and social mobility. Such circumstances will dramatically restrict their ability to access the formal credential dimension of both social and skill capital, but children from privileged-class backgrounds will be much less affected.

The decline of working-class access to social and skill capital resources produces less competition among privileged-class members for these resources. This means adult members of the privileged class will be able to reserve easier access to formal skills and a larger share of social capital resources for themselves and their children. These resources can then be used to legitimate a near monopoly by the privileged class on access to and legitimation of high levels of consumption and investment capital, which together almost permanently and exclusively cement membership in this class.

The Future: Resistance

> Once I saw the mountains angry, And ranged in battle-front. Against them stood a little man; I laughed and spoke to one near me, 'Will he prevail?' 'Surely,' replied this other; 'His grandfathers beat them many times.'
>
> —Stephen Crane, *The Red Badge of Courage and Other Writings*, 1960

The privileged-class-based consolidation policies and trends outlined in the preceding section are likely to produce increasing inequalities between the top 20 percent of privileged Americans and the remaining majority. Attempts by members of the new working class to increase their capital shares are likely to be kept in check by the continued mobilization of a variety of potent resources held by the privileged class and deployed along several fronts of the new class war. Any alteration in the distribution of capital resources will have to be initiated by reform-minded people, groups, and organizations grounded in the working class and perhaps linked to lessons from the populist tradition of the past.

Many of the themes, messages, and images that were part of the populist tradition reemerged in the 1990s and are being revised for a new century by a wide array of activist groups and organizations that are part of the alternative power networks. Many groups in these networks are working to reduce class inequalities (e.g., the Nader-founded Public Interest Group Complex, progressive and alternative media, Democratic Socialists of America, etc.), but our focus here is on six examples of organizational forces for economic, political, and cultural reform that emerged (or reemerged) in the 1990s. The revitalized AFL-CIO, United for a Fair Economy, the Program on Corporations, Law and Democracy, the Labor Party,

The Hand That Will Rule the World—One Big Union

Solidarity, June 30, 1917

the New Party, and Fairness and Accuracy in Media Reporting (FAIR) all reflect shared concerns with advancing working-class interests and democratic ideals. In many ways these groups are modern heirs to the populist tradition. They can be viewed as representing a kind of emerging "class warrior" activism committed to developing class consciousness among the new working class and to actively mobilizing a variety of economic, political, and cultural resources aimed at transforming the structural bases of the new class society and the many inequalities associated with it.

Organized Labor

In the late 1990s the AFL-CIO (American Federation of Labor and Congress of Industrial Organizations) reemerged as a major working-class force promoting economic and political changes that echo the populist tradition. The federation is the organizational foundation of the American labor movement, with 13 million members and annual revenues from union affiliates estimated at $6–8 billion.[53] The AFL-CIO shift to a more activist stance began after John Sweeney (former Service Employees' International Union officer) was elected president in 1995 over interim president Thomas Donahue in the first contested election for president of the organization in forty years.[54]

Although the AFL-CIO's most-high-profile programs initiated since the mid-1990s appear to be political in nature, their goals reflect both economic and political concerns. As we will see, recent federation programs are aimed at increasing workers' influence in the governmental and employer arenas in order to promote economic policies and business practices that will reduce class inequalities and increase workers' economic security. The federation's agenda for change reflects economic and political priorities, such as raising the minimum wage, supporting workers' strikes (as at United Parcel Service in 1997), protecting American workers' jobs (e.g., defeating fast-track authority to expand NAFTA), protecting Social Security, expanding public health care, increasing spending on education, and establishing closer links with trade unions on a global basis.[55]

The first major initiative under Sweeney to promote changes consistent with labor's interests was the federation's Labor '96 campaign. It involved a $35 million commitment by the AFL-CIO to mobilize union members for Democratic candidates and to pay for advertising in support of pro-union political candidates in the 1996 elections.[56] The relative success of that effort was evidenced in 1998 by the privileged-class-supported legislative backlash of proposals that would make it much more difficult for unions to do political fundraising among their own members.

As noted in chapter 4, this 1998 privileged-class-supported backlash involved the introduction in Congress by right-wing Republicans of the deceptively titled Worker Paycheck Protection Act and related ballot initiatives in California and other states. The proposed federal legislation would "require unions to obtain written permission from union members every year before spending money on politics."⁵⁷ The state initiatives asked voters to "decide whether unions should be barred from spending members' money on politics without every year getting their written permission."⁵⁸ Although both efforts failed, they illustrate that even modest union-sponsored programs challenging superclass interests will not go unchallenged by privileged-class leaders.

A second major AFL-CIO initiative for change unveiled in late 1996 was a long-term program titled "Organizing for Change," aimed at revitalizing the labor movement. The centerpiece of this effort was the federation's expansion of its organizing budget from $2.5 million in 1995 to $30 million in 1997.⁵⁹ It also included a Union Cities campaign aimed at using federation money to "transform central labor councils into organizing centers for their communities."⁶⁰

The organizing initiatives were reinforced by a new political strategy outlined by Sweeney in September 1997 at the federation's national convention in Pittsburgh. In contrast with past practices, Sweeney announced that in the 1998 and 2000 elections the federation would begin increasing its independence from the Democratic Party and winning Congress back for the Democrats would not be a primary goal of the organization. Instead, he said, "it is time for us to begin spending our money building real power by registering and mobilizing our own members."⁶¹ In general, this strategy meant the organization would begin to adopt an approach similar to that used by the Christian Coalition, endorsing "values and issues, not particular candidates and personalities."⁶² And it would produce a greater union presence in local and state politics. More specifically, this strategy committed the federation to registering 4 million new voters from union households and also to support union members running for offices at local, state, and national levels. The federation slogan, "2,000 by 2000," focused attention on its commitment to field two thousand union candidates for public offices by 2000—regardless of party labels or affiliations.⁶³

The outcomes of the AFL-CIO's revitalization and proactive strategies for change remain to be seen. Union efforts supporting economic and political changes that would advance working-class interests while challenging those of the privileged class are likely to face many stiff challenges. Union-sponsored reform efforts will be opposed by a wide array of privileged-class resources—including many organizations identified in earlier chapters. Also, some facets of union reforms are likely to be challenged by the little-known antiunion industry of fifteen hundred consultants who now "earn approximately $500 million each year advising corporations on how to keep unions out of their offices and factories."⁶⁴

Apart from privileged-class challenges, labor activists long critical of the AFL-CIO are yet to be convinced that its much publicized revitalization is more substance than sizzle. Shop-floor dissidents who favor what labor author Kim Moody calls "social movement unionism" (using democratic unions as a force to promote economic, political, and social justice) are skeptical that the sclerotic complacency of "business unionism" so typical of the AFL-CIO in the past is truly on the wane.[65] But despite criticisms from this group and from journalistic skeptics,[66] the AFL-CIO remains one of the most important organizational resources within the alternative power networks for promoting the economic, political, and cultural interests of the new working class.

United for a Fair Economy

Although unions remain the most resource-rich force pressing for economic and political reforms in the United States, new organizations emerged in the 1990s that highlighted growing class inequalities and helped call attention to the structural roots of these inequalities. One multidimensional activist organization working in these areas is United for a Fair Economy. This organization was created in 1996 out of the merger of the Share the Wealth Project and the Joint Project on Equality, both of which were founded in 1994. United for a Fair Economy is a "national organization that draws public attention to the growth of income and wealth inequality in the United States—and to the implications of this inequality for America's democracy, economy, and society."[67]

The organization disseminates information on wealth and income inequality via a number of publications, including a quarterly newsletter titled *Too Much*. In addition to serving as a kind of class-consciousness-raising organization, United for a Fair Economy is also involved in "advocacy and political action, community organizing and coalition building, research and media work, [and] arts and culture [projects]." In 1996 it presented "Growing Divide Workshops to over 15,000 participants in 450 training sessions for labor unions, business associations, schools, religious congregations, and community organizations across the United States."[68] Although most Americans have probably never heard of the organization, its publications and messages have been cited in various national publications such as the *Nation* and reported on broadcast media programs such as Jim Hightower's radio talk show (on independent stations).

Program on Corporations, Law, and Democracy

Another small, recently formed organization working to publicize class inequalities and to reform the organizational foundations of the corporate system that promotes privileged-class interests is the Program on Corporations, Law, and Democracy. Founded in 1993 by labor activist Richard Grossman and others, this organization is located in Provincetown, Massachusetts, and is best known as the leader of the "corporate charter movement." The purpose of the program is "to embolden citizens and lawmakers to toughen—or rather enforce—state corporate charter laws. These laws . . . give legislatures the power to limit corporations' activities and revoke their right to do business in their state."[69]

Although the program is unlikely to serve as more than a class-consciousness-raising force, perhaps in concert with other reform efforts that is a reasonable goal. The program is trying to introduce the topics of corporate origins, rights, and powers as public issues for democratic consideration and debate, but it also has a reform agenda in place. It recommends a number of possible actions that would place corporations back under the control of civil society:

- Recharter corporations to limit their powers and make them subordinate to the sovereign people.
- Establish worker and community control over production units of corporations in order to protect the property rights of workers and communities.
- Initiate referendum campaigns, or take action through legislative bodies—and in the courts—to strip from corporations constitutionally guaranteed rights intended for natural persons.[70]

A related reform suggested involves rewriting corporate law to require a reconfiguiring of corporate governance. For example, a typical twenty-person corporate board of directors could be required to include seven directors elected by shareholders, seven directors elected by employees, and six directors "elected by a number of other constituencies—such as consumers, suppliers, bondholders, and representatives of local communities."[71]

If implemented as policy, the actions listed above would significantly constrain corporate power and impact the current ability of corporations to serve primarily as agents of privileged-class interests. The program might be dismissed as unrealistic idealism, but it has succeeded in attracting growing public attention to an important structural dimension of class inequalities. By encouraging the growth of class consciousness and focusing public attention on a critical feature of the dominant economic power network, the program adds to the legitimacy of class analysis and helps break the silence of the class taboo.

Third-Party Challenges

Within the political arena, the Labor Party and the New Party are two new organizational forces, generally grounded in the populist tradition, that are dedicated to challenging or reforming privileged-class dominance of the current two-party system. "In 1991 delegates of the Oil, Chemical, and Atomic Workers union (OCAW) passed a resolution to launch Labor Party Advocates (LPA) and agitate within the ranks of labor for the founding of a labor party." Since 1991, LPA has not achieved its goal of recruiting 100,000 direct members. In fact, "membership leveled off well below even 10,000 direct members."[72] Even so, the LPA mobilized the resources necessary to create a new Labor Party. "In June [6–9] 1996, 1,400 elected delegates gathered in Cleveland, Ohio, to found the Labor Party."[73]

From 1991 through mid-1996, the LPA presented its views and activities in a newsletter titled *Labor Party Advocates*. Beginning in July 1996, the new Labor Party (formerly LPA) began publishing *Labor Party Press*, with a newspaper-like format, six times a year. The November 1996 issue of *Labor Party Press* introduced the party's campaign for a constitutional amendment (the twenty-eighth) to guarantee every American a job at a living wage. Since then, it has published updates on this campaign and publicized its 1998 Just Healthcare campaign (calling for universal health care and the elimination of health insurance companies). It also has reported on progress to solidify the party organization, and a variety of class-based stories on topics including Social Security, NAFTA, health care, the 1997 federal balanced-budget deal, and welfare reform. In each instance, the focus has been on reporting how the two major parties have crafted policies advancing privileged-class interests at the expense of the working class. The reports also often emphasize that the mainstream media have assisted in the formation of such policies while ignoring or concealing how these policies have eroded the living standards and quality of life for working-class Americans.

The Labor Party held its first Constitutional Convention in Pittsburgh, Pennsylvania, on November 13–15, 1998. A total of 1,414 elected delegates discussed the party's organizational structure, policies, and electoral strategies. The gathering was addressed by numerous labor leaders as well as by consumer advocate Ralph Nader and filmmaker Michael Moore "(who donated $10,000 in royalties from his new book to the Labor Party's educational arm)."[74] The future of the Labor Party is unclear, but the AFL-CIO's increasing interest in issue-oriented politics and campaigns could provide it with a boost in future elections. However, the AFL-CIO's extensive links to the Democratic Party makes it an uncertain partner. As one analyst observed, "Wary of upsetting the Democrats, the AFL-CIO and many of its major affiliates have kept their distance from the fledgling Labor Party."[75]

The New Party represents yet another recent political force organized to promote economic, political, and cultural changes that in many ways reflect the populist tradition. Growing out of Jesse Jackson's run for president in 1988, the New Party was founded in 1992, and by 1998 it included eleven thousand dues-paying members.[76] The basic goal of the New Party is to create a grassroots, mass political movement for change.[77] What kind of change? The party platform includes policies that, if enacted, would reverse many of the class-based inequalities that have produced the new class society over the past quarter century and would substantially alter the institutional structure that has contributed to the development of that system. The policies promoted include economic reforms (full employment, a shorter workweek, a guaranteed minimum income, a universal "social wage" covering—for example—health care and childcare), electoral reforms (public financing of elections, proportional representation), democratization of banking and financial systems, urban renewal, a more-progressive tax system, a ban on discrimination (by race, gender, age, ethnicity, or sexual orientation), reduced military spending, and new trade policies (to promote higher global living standards).[78]

The New Party began with a much more activist electoral stance than did the Labor Party (formerly LPA). In 1992 it backed a handful of candidates for local and state offices that grew to 25 in 1993, 70 in 1994–95, and 250 in 1996–97. The party's six-month budget to support its 1996–97 electoral activity—$696,598.81—

was tiny by major party standards.[79] Even so, by 1998 the New Party had won "150 electoral victories in races for city council, school board, county board, and state legislatures around the country."[80]

The New Party is continuing to expand through aggressive recruiting programs, and it has developed links to numerous progressive and labor organizations sympathetic to its goals and platforms. But as is the case for the Labor Party, the future of the New Party is uncertain. However, party leaders are optimistic, and they invoke memories from America's populist past as examples of what a "third force" can accomplish in American politics. As party organizer Dan Cantor observed, "I look at the Non-Partisan League model [of the 1915–21 era] and I think, that's what progressives need to be looking at today. . . . We need a party that breaks the barriers of conventional politics . . . so that progressive ideas and progressive candidates are no longer marginalized."[81]

The Labor Party and the New Party are only two of many political organizations that have emerged from the growing class inequalities spawned by the new class society. A detailed inventory of recent local and national progressive political challenges to the traditional two-party system was compiled by David Reynolds in his 1997 book, *Democracy Unbound*. However, as mentioned earlier, the success of these challenges remains to be seen, and the problems they confront are many. For example, the political-party identification of the U.S. adult population (at all degrees of attachment) was distributed in 1994 as follows: 47 percent Democrat, 43 percent Republican, 10 percent independent.[82] This distribution has remained relatively stable over the past twenty years and means that major shifts in party identification traditions would have to occur before any third party could accumulate a significant base of support. Of course, major shifts have occurred in the past (e.g., the rapid growth of the Republican Party in the 1850s and of several populist parties in the late 1800s and early 1900s) in the context of national economic and political crises. Thus, the recent growth of progressive third parties may well signal an emerging shift in the political landscape as groups organize to challenge the inequities in the new class society.

Media Reform: FAIR

Although Fairness and Accuracy in Media Reporting (FAIR) was organized in 1986, the 1990s witnessed its emergence as an increasingly important force in support of progressive economic, political, and cultural reforms within the mass media. The nature and goals of FAIR are printed inside the cover of each issue of *EXTRA!*, its bimonthly magazine with an annual paid or requested circulation of 18,500.[83] "FAIR is the national media watch group that offers well-documented criticism of media bias and censorship. . . . Ultimately, FAIR believes that structural reform is needed to break up the dominant media conglomerates, establish independent public broadcasting, and promote strong, non-profit alternative sources of information."[84]

In addition to publishing *EXTRA!*, FAIR also publishes *EXTRA!Update*, a four-page bimonthly newsletter, and it organizes and sponsors a number of activities in support of its goals of exposing media biases and censorship. These include maintaining a website (http://www.fair.org/fair/), producing and distributing FAIR's radio program, "CounterSpin," and selling products consistent with its goals, such as audiotapes from "CounterSpin" (and panel discussions), book-length compilations of selections from *EXTRA!*, and other books dealing with media issues. Compared with major media firms, FAIR is a small organization that relies mainly on *EXTRA!* subscriber revenues and donations to support a ten-person staff and an annual budget of less than $1 million.[85]

FAIR is one of many organizations that populate the alternative power networks, but it is especially significant because of its constant focus on the biases and power of the media. FAIR is not the only progressive organization that routinely critiques the economic, political, and cultural power of the mass media. But its consistent focus on mass media content makes it a valuable resource for understanding how privileged-class control of the media industry assists in maintaining and legitimating the new class society. FAIR's perspective and goals are consistent with many features of the populist tradition—especially its efforts to increase public class consciousness and critique the antidemocratic dangers and consequences of concentrated economic, political, and cultural power in the mass media.

The Superclass "Suits," The Dream, and the New Working Class

In contrast with the messages of class struggle outlined by the six reform groups aimed at reducing class inequalities, we find a constant win-win mainstream media spin on class-based issues such as labor-management conflicts over workers' concerns with wages and job security. "Refocus on the soaring stock market," workers are told. "Become an investor." In this way, concerns with class analysis and inequalities are transformed into the marginalized ravings of anachronistic cranks. Even so, class-reform-minded members of the alternative power networks confront the dominant-power-network players' script with an expose-and-challenge strategy, which seeks to unmask the reality of class interests and inequalities while stripping legitimacy away from the instruments of privileged-class power.

The mask-and-legitimate and expose-and-challenge approaches crash head-on today over a number of topics, but the prospects for and the means of achieving the American Dream strike especially bright sparks of conflict. The "suits" say, "The dream lives! It is alive and achievable for anyone with a positive mental attitude." How do they make the case? With the media awash in "bridge to the next century" and "information superhighway" metaphors, the new prosperity is claimed to be just around the corner. Success today, as pitched by credentialed-class hucksters, involves gleaming high-tech ventures where the road to the American Dream runs straight through multilevel marketing to a dot-com website.

By contrast, alternative-power-network-based class analysis says, "Welcome to the new American scheme!" Committed to exposing and challenging the mask-

and-legitimate myths disseminated by dominant-power-network representatives, class-reform analysts see a different reality. This view says, "Blinded by the fast-buck light, the success-cult members of the new working class either ignore or never see the class-biased cynical deception, distraction, and exploitation inherent in 'the dream lives' schemes." Today's hucksters play on the insecurities of life in the new working class and feed on the fading memory of a more open opportunity structure that, to some extent, accommodated and rewarded the aspirations and efforts of working-class members to achieve a "good job" or even some measure of upward social mobility.

Alternative-power-network-based critics who document the realities of the new class system are unlikely to be welcome guests at the rapidly metastasizing motivational and entrepreneurial seminars and computer workshops. These events, with their slavish odes to new opportunities for material enrichment and personal growth via "positive mental attitudes," multilevel-marketing schemes, web sites, chat rooms, and other cyberspace venues, typically not only charge admission up front but also close with a sales pitch at the end—often for motivational tapes or more computer hardware and software.

This bright and shiny view of new opportunities ushered in by computers today is attacked by the expose-and-challenge views of critics of the new class system. As they point out, a major function of computers is to speed-lash workers and consumers into a frenzy of tightly monitored, closely controlled, and cleverly manipulated production and consumption that perpetuates and reinforces the new class society. Moreover, the critics maintain that even as some machines are orchestrating the control processes, others are efficiently channeling most of the profits generated by computer-driven production and marketing to superclass owners and distributing generous rewards to credentialed-class "suits" in payment for their professional contributions to creating, maintaining, and justifying the new class system.

The alternative-power-network view that the privileged class oversees dominant power networks employing computer-based, worker-consumer control crashes head-on with the corporate ministry of information line that says classes do not count and computers are our pals. The "suits" say class inequalities are irrelevant, and computers are the way, the truth, and the light and the path to economic salvation and class mobility in the new American century. And woe unto those who fail to embrace the team-player mentality and the high-tech faith—for they shall be cast into the Lake of Economic Fire—meaning especially the marginalized contingent and excluded zones of the new working class. The "suits" say team play and the computer tide will raise all boats to new levels of prosperity, save our collective economic future, and ensure the American Dream as far as the eye can see over the horizon of the twenty-first century. It is a predictable mask-and-legitimate line. Alternative-power-network members disagree. Committed to an expose-and-challenge strategy but with severely limited resources, they are vulnerable to stigmatization through name-calling ("neo-Luddites") and institutional marginalization by the "suits." And they are vulnerable to the simplistic

Scrooge scenario for reform that deeply resonates within a working class that has been intensely socialized to the individualistic credo of American culture.

The Future: The Scrooge Scenario versus the Structural Scenario

In the world according to Dickens, reform is a function of conscience. In *A Christmas Carol*, the ghosts of Christmas Past, Present, and Future visit Ebenezer Scrooge. This gets results. Shown the consequences of his selfishness, Scrooge is appropriately appalled and transformed. He reforms his miserly ways, and the community becomes a better place. It is a powerful and comforting morality tale grounded in an unspoken assumption that the selfish pursuit by the rich of their narrow economic interests can be blunted and redirected by consciousness-raising experiences that awaken a latent social conscience.

The "Scrooge scenario" can be seen as a kind of pattern for reform favored and promoted by privileged-class leaders that focuses attention on individual renewal and personal commitment. Media accounts of political corruption involving PACs, influence peddlers, insiders, and fixers as well as economic warts such as sweatshops and child labor are portrayed as bad apples. The system is sound, we are told, we just need to replace rotten apples or force the bad apples to undergo a publicly reported transformation involving admissions of wrongdoing, acceptance of guilt, and repentance—along with promises to go forth and sin no more.

The "structural democracy scenario" places little faith in the Scrooge approach. Class reformers see undemocratic political, economic, and cultural structures controlled by the privileged class and unaccountable to the public as the problem. The populist-like "structural democracy scenario" is favored by many class-reform activists. The primary aim of this view is to revitalize the practice of democratic participation in politics and government and also extend the principles of democratic governance to the corporate structures that currently dominate the economic and cultural arenas of our society and undergird the many inequalities of the new class society.

Although the structural democracy project of resolving class inequalities is highly problematic and uncertain, we believe it can usefully serve as a point of departure for a national dialogue on the closeted, taboo subject of growing class inequalities. An increasingly class-conscious public can provide the economic, political, and human resources necessary to support existing and yet-to-be-established institutions committed to the interests of the new working class and to reforming the new class society.

As we have seen throughout this book, there is a real and pressing need for structural, not Scrooge-like, changes in our highly unequal new class system. The reforms proposed or initiated by organizations cited in this chapter provide some concrete examples of what real structural changes aimed at redressing class inequities might look like. Such reforms on a much wider scale are essential if we are to begin the process of melting the iceberg of inequality before it rips open the current version of the Titanic known as the new class society and sends our democratic experiment to a permanent resting spot at the bottom of history.

NOTES

1. Robert Famighetti, ed., *The World Almanac and Book of Facts, 1997* (Mahwah, N.J.: K-III Reference Corporation, 1996), 284. *Forrest Gump* is now (1999) the fourth U.S. film in gross receipts, after no. 1, *The Titanic* (1998; more than $500 million in the United States alone, more than $1 billion in worldwide receipts; David Ansen, "Our Titanic Love Affair," *Newsweek*, February 23, 1998, 60), and no. 2, *E.T.: The Extra-Terrestial* (1982; $400 million), and no. 3, *Jurassic Park* (1993; $357 million).

2. Charles Derber, *The Wilding of America* (New York: St. Martin's Press, 1996), 150.

3. Lixandra Urresta and Kenji Hosokawa, "The Fortune Global Five Hundred," *Fortune*, August 4, 1997, F1–12.

4. Michael Useem, *The Inner Circle* (New York: Oxford University Press, 1984), 172–200.

5. Joel Bleifuss, "Know Thine Enemy: A Brief History of Corporations," *In These Times*, February 8, 1998, 16–17.

6. Jim Hightower, "Chomp!," *Utne Reader*, March–April 1998, 60.

7. Quoted in Hightower, "Chomp!," 59.

8. Paul J. Dimaggio and Walter W. Powell, "The Iron Cage Revisited: Institutional Isomorphism and Collective Rationality in Organizational Fields," *American Sociological Review* 48 (1983): 147–60.

9. Charles Perrow, "A Society of Organizations," *Theory and Society* 20 (1991): 725–62.

10. Gregory Mantsios, "Class in America: Myths and Realities," in *Race, Class, and Gender in the United States*, ed. Paula S. Rothenberg (New York: St. Martin's Press, 1995), 131–43.

11. Robert Granfield, "Making It by Faking It," *Journal of Contemporary Ethnography* 20 (1991): 331–51.

12. Quoted in Matthew Josephson, *The Robber Barons* (New York: Harcourt, Brace and World, 1934), 325.

13. Robert Granfield and Thomas Koenig, "Pathways into Elite Law Firms: Professional Stratification and Social Networks," in *Research in Politics and Society*, vol. 4, *The Political Consequences of Social Networks*, ed. Gwen Moore and J. Allen Whitt (Greenwich, Conn.: JAI Press, 1992).

14. Basil Bernstein, *Class, Codes, and Control*, 3 vols. (London: Routledge and Kegan Paul, 1971–73).

15. Allan Sloan, "What Goes Up . . .," *Newsweek*, April 13, 1998, 42–43.

16. Francis X. Clines, "Fueled by Success, Buchanan Revels in Rapid-Fire Oratory," *New York Times*, February 15, 1996; Elizabeth Kolbert and Adam Clymer, "The Politics of Layoff: In Search of a Message," *New York Times*, March 8, 1996.

17. James Bennet, "Patrick J. Buchanan: Harsh Language for Party Leaders," *New York Times*, February 19, 1996.

18. Michael Kazin, *The Populist Persuasion* (New York: Basic Books, 1995), 1.

19. Ibid., 2.

20. Robert Parry, "The Right-Wing Media Machine," *EXTRA!*, March–April 1995, 6–10; also see Joseph L. Conn and Rob Boston, "Pat Robertson's Media Empire," *EXTRA!*, March–April 1995, 13–16.

21. Janine Jackson, "Broken Promises," *EXTRA!*, September–October 1997, 11–15.

22. David Elsila, "No More NAFTAs!," *UAW Solidarity*, April–May 1997, 10–12.

23. Janine Jackson, "Fast Track 1, Democracy 0," *EXTRA!*, November–December 1997, 9–10.

24. "NAFTA," *Labor Party Press*, July 1997, 8.

25. Ibid., 9.

26. "U.S. Trade Gap Sets Record," *UAW Solidarity*, May 1998, 7; also see: Jackson, "Broken Promises," 12.

27. "Fast-Track Media Misperceptions," *EXTRA!Update*, February 1998, 1.

28. William Grieder, "Saving the Global Economy," *Nation*, December 15, 1997, 11–16.

29. Joel Bleifuss, "Building the Global Economy," *In These Times*, January 11, 1998, 13.

30. Kim Moody, "NAFTA, WTO, MAI, IMF, FTAA, AGOA . . . Where Does It End?," *Labor Notes*, May 1998, 16.

31. Bleifuss, "Building the Global Economy," 13.

32. Ibid., 13–15.

33. "MAI Week of Action," and "Don't Let MAI Handcuff Democracy," *Public Citizen News*, March–April 1998, 15.

34. David Moberg, "Power Grab," *Progressive*, March 1998, 24–26. Quote from "MAI Roadshow Heads West," *Public Citizen News*, January–February 1999, 1.

35. Moody, "NAFTA, WTO, MAI, IMF, FTAA, AGOA," 16.

36. Stacie Garnett, "It's Tough to Be Young Today," *Dollars and Sense*, September–October 1997, 50.

37. Marc Breslow and Matthew Howard, "The Real Un(der)Employment Rate," *Dollars and Sense*, May–June 1995, 35.

38. Lawrence Mishel, Jared Bernstein, and John Schmitt, *The State of Working America, 1996–1997* (New York: M. E. Sharpe, 1997), 249–74.

39. Walter Korpi, *The Democratic Class Struggle* (London: Routledge, 1983).

40. Vicente Navarro, "Production and the Welfare State: The Political Context of Reforms," *International Journal of Health Services* 21 (1991): 585–614.

41. Neil deMause, "Out of Sight, Out of Mind," *EXTRA!*, November–December 1997, 25–27.

42. Teresa Amott, "Will the Economy Be Less Stable?," *Dollars and Sense*, November–December 1996, 22–23.

43. Robert Dreyfuss, "Neighbor to Neighbor Takes on Medicare Myths," *EXTRA!*, March–April 1997, 17–18.

44. Kim Moody, "America Gets a Virtual Raise," *Labor Notes*, February 1997, 15–16.

45. "Percent of Full-Time Employees Participating in Employer-Provided Benefit Plans, 1980–1991," *Monthly Labor Review*, February 1998, 103. Also see John Leland, "Blessed by the Bull," *Newsweek*, April 27, 1998, 51–53.

46. John Miller, "Tax Cuts: Clinton and Congress Feed the Wealthy," *Dollars and Sense*, November–December 1997, 43.

47. Michelle Cottle, "The Real Class War," *Washington Monthly*, July–August 1997, 13.

48. John Miller, "More Wealth for the Wealthy: The Estate Tax Giveaway and What to Do about It," *Dollars and Sense*, November–December 1997, 26–28, 33.

49. Mike Males, "Wild In Deceit: Why 'Teen Violence' Is Poverty Violence in Disguise," *EXTRA!*, March–April 1996, 7–9.

50. Noreen Connell, "Underfunded Schools: Why Money Matters," *Dollars and Sense*, March–April 1998, 14. Also see David Stratman, "School Reform and the Attack on Public Education," *Dollars and Sense*, March–April 1998, 7.

51. Stanley Aronowitz, "The New Corporate University: Higher Education Becomes Higher Training," *Dollars and Sense*, March–April 1998, 33.

52. Barbara McKenna, "Does College Cost Too Much?," *AFT on Campus*, March 1998, 8.

53. Ken Silverstein and Alexander Cockburn, "How's He Doing? Has Sweeney Changed Labor?," *CounterPunch*, July 16–31, 1997, 1.

54. Janine Jackson, "Moribund Militants: Corporate Media on (Re)Organized Labor," *EXTRA!*, January–February 1996, 6–7.

55. "The Steelworkers Contract with America," *Steelabor*, September–October 1996, 10–14.

56. Russ Davis, "AFL-CIO Unveils Program to Revitalize Labor Movement," *Labor Notes*, March 1997, 1, 14.

57. "Phony Paycheck Protection: It'll Cost You More than You Think," *UAW Solidarity*, March–April 1998, 10.

58. Suzanne Gordon, "Labor Needs More than PR to Beat New Curbs on Political Spending," *Labor Notes*, March 1998, 8.

59. Silverstein and Cockburn, "How's He Doing?," 1.

60. Davis, "AFL-CIO Unveils Program to Revitalize Labor Movement," 14.

61. David Glenn, "Adding Brains to Labor's New Political Muscle," *In These Times*, December 14, 1997, 22.

62. Glenn, "Adding Brains to Labor's New Political Muscle," 23.

63. Suzanne Wall, "Union Candidates Use a 'Bottom-Up' Approach to Winning Political Power," *Labor Notes*, April 1998, 3.

64. G. William Domhoff, *Who Rules America?: Power and Politics in the Year 2000* (Mountain View, Calif.: Mayfield, 1998), 304.

65. Kim Moody, *Workers in a Lean World: Unions in the International Economy* (New York: Verso, 1998).

66. Silverstein and Cockburn, "How's He Doing?," 1, 6–8.

67. "Programs and Achievements/Program Directions," brochure, ca. 1997, *United for a Fair Economy*, 37 Temple Place, fifth floor, Boston, MA 02111.

68. Ibid.

69. Craig Cox, "Taming the Corporate Beast," *Utne Reader*, March–April 1998, 60.

70. Joel Bleifuss, "The New Abolitionists," *In These Times*, April 1, 1996, 13.

71. Fred Block, "Toward Real Corporate Responsibility," *In These Times*, May 27, 1996, 27.

72. David Reynolds, *Democracy Unbound* (Boston: South End Press, 1997), 225, 228.

73. "Two Parties Give Us Six New Reasons for One Party for Us," *Labor Party Press*, March 1998, 1.

74. "Set to Organize," *Labor Party Press*, January 1999, 1, 4.

75. Glenn, "Adding Brains to Labor's New Political Muscle," 24.

76. John Nichols, "After Fusion: The New New Party," *In These Times*, March 22, 1998, 18.

77. Reynolds, *Democracy Unbound*, 186.

78. Nichols, "After Fusion: The New New Party," 18–19.

79. Daniel Cantor, *New Party* Membership Solicitation Letter, Pledge Form, and "It Adds Up," budget summary, September 1, 1996, 1–6 plus additional forms.

80. Nichols, "After Fusion: The New New Party," 18.

81. Quoted ibid., 20.

82. U.S. Department of Commerce, Bureau of the Census, *Statistical Abstract of the United States* (Washington, D.C.: U.S. Government Printing Office, 1997), 287.

83. "Statement of Ownership," *EXTRA!*, November–December 1997, 18.

84. "What's FAIR?," *EXTRA!*, March–April 1998, 2.

85. FAIR activities are summarized from various issues of *EXTRA!*, its bimonthly newsletter, *EXTRA!Update*, and contributor solicitation letters. Specific issues of *EXTRA!* used for the summary include January–February 1998 and November–December 1996. Information on FAIR's budget was computed on the basis of financial information included in an August 1996 solicitation letter listing FAIR's four-year total expenditures on all activities as slightly more than $2.8 million.

Bibliography

Adler, Jerry. "The Rise of the Overclass." *Newsweek* (July 31, 1995): 33–46.

AFL-CIO. "Executive PayWatch." 1997. <http://www.paywatch.com> (May 4, 1998): 1–4.

Ageism on the Agenda. Special issue. *EXTRA!* (March–April 1997).

Akre, Jane. "We Report, They Decide: Fox TV Censors Series on Milk Hazards." *National News Reporter* (June 1998): 12–13.

Alba, Richard D., and Gwen Moore. "Ethnicity in the American Elite." *American Sociological Review* 47 (June 1982): 373–83.

Albelda, Randy. "Farewell to Welfare but Not to Poverty." *Dollars and Sense* (November–December 1996): 16–19.

Alexander, Karl, Martha Cook, and Edward McDill. "Curriculum Tracking and Educational Stratification." *American Sociological Review* 43 (1982): 47–66.

Allen, Michael Patrick. "Elite Social Movement Organizations and the State: The Rise of the Conservative Policy-Planning Network." In *Research in Politics and Society*, vol. 4, *The Political Consequences of Social Networks*, ed. Gwen Moore and J. Allen Whitt. Greenwich, Conn.: JAI Press, 1992.

Alter, Jonathan, and Michael Isikoff. "The Beltway Populist." *Newsweek* (March 4, 1996): 24–27.

Amott, Teresa. "Will the Economy Be Less Stable?," *Dollars and Sense* (November–December 1996): 22–23.

Anderson, Charles H. *The Political Economy of Social Class.* Englewood Cliffs, N.J.: Prentice-Hall, 1974.

———. *Toward A New Sociology.* Homewood, Ill.: Dorsey Press, 1974.

Ansen, David. "Our Titanic Love Affair." *Newsweek* (February 23, 1998): 58–64.

Arenson, Karen W. "Cuts in Tuition Assistance Put College beyond Reach of Poorest Students." *New York Times*, January 27, 1997.

Aronowitz, Stanley. "The New Corporate University: Higher Education Becomes Higher Training." *Dollars and Sense* (March–April 1998): 32–35.

Aronowitz, Stanley, and William DiFazio. "High Technology and Work Tomorrow." *Annals of the American Academy of Political and Social Science* 544 (March 1996): 52–76.

Bagdikian, Ben H. *The Media Monopoly.* Boston: Beacon Press, 1997.

Baker, Dean. "Generation Excess." *EXTRA!* (March–April 1996): 12–13.

"Balance This." *In These Times* (May 13, 1996): 4–5.

Barlett, Donald L., and James B. Steele. *America: What Went Wrong?* Kansas City: Andrews and McMeel, 1992.

———. *America: Who Really Pays the Taxes?* New York: Touchstone, 1994.

———. "America: Who Stole the Dream?" *Indianapolis Star*, September 22–29, 1996; business section. Reprinted from the *Philadelphia Inquirer*.

Barnet, Richard J., and John Cavanagh. *Global Dreams: Imperial Corporations and the New World Order*. New York: Simon and Schuster, 1994.

Beckett, Katherine. "Setting the Public Agenda: 'Street Crime' and Drug Use in American Politics." *Social Problems* 3 (1994): 425–47.

Bendix, Reinhard, and Frank W. Howton. "Social Mobility and the American Business Elite—II." *British Journal of Sociology* 9 (1958): 1–14.

Bennet, James. "Patrick J. Buchanan: Harsh Language for Party Leaders." *New York Times*, February 19, 1996.

Bernstein, Aaron. "We Want You to Stay. Really." *Business Week* (June 22, 1998): 67–72.

Bernstein, Basil. *Class, Codes, and Control*. 3 vols. London: Routledge and Kegan Paul, 1971–73.

Blakely, Edward J., and Mary Gail Snyder. *Fortress America: Gated Communities in the United States*. Washington, D.C.: Brookings Institution Press, 1997.

Blau, Peter M., and Otis D. Duncan. *The American Occupational Structure*. New York: Wiley, 1967.

Bleifuss, Joel. "Building the Global Economy." *In These Times* (January 11, 1998): 13–15.

———. "Know Thine Enemy: A Brief History of Corporations." *In These Times* (February 8, 1998): 16–17.

———. "Money Talks, Democracy Walks." *In These Times* (May 16, 1994): 12–13.

———. "The New Abolitionists." *In These Times* (April 1, 1996): 12–13.

———. "The Terminators." *In These Times* (March 4, 1996): 12–13.

———. "Warfare or Welfare." *In These Times* (December 9, 1996): 12–14.

Block, Fred. "Toward Real Corporate Responsibility." *In These Times* (May 27, 1996): 25–27.

Bluestone, Barry, and Bennett Harrison. *The Deindustrialization of America*. New York: Basic Books, 1982.

Borosage, Robert L., and Ruy Teixeira. "The Politics of Money." *Nation* (October 21, 1996): 21–22.

Bowie, Nolan A. "On That Chart." *Nation* (June 3, 1996): 20.

Bowles, Samuel, and Herbert Gintis. *Schooling in Capitalist America: Educational Reform and the Contradictions of Economic Life*. New York: Basic Books, 1976.

Boyer, Gabriella. "Corporate America Stacks the NAFTA Debate." *Public Citizen* (July–August 1993): 26.

Breslow, Marc. "Congress for Sale." *Dollars and Sense* (July–August 1996): 43.

———. "Death by Devolution." *Dollars and Sense* (January–February 1996): 20–22, 38.

———. "Government of, by, and for the Wealthy." *Dollars and Sense* (July–August 1996): 23–24.

Breslow, Marc, and Matthew Howard. "The Real Un(der)Employment Rate." *Dollars and Sense* (May–June 1995): 35.

Brinton, Milward H., and Heide H. Newman. "State Incentive Packages and the Industrial Location Decision." *Economic Development Quarterly* 3 (1989): 203–22.

Buchanan, Patrick J. *The Great Betrayal: How American Sovereignty and Social Justice Are Being Sacrificed to the Gods of the Global Economy*. New York: Little, Brown, 1998.

Burris, Val. "Elite Policy-Planning Networks in the United States." In *Research in Politics and Society*, vol. 4, *The Political Consequences of Social Networks*, ed. Gwen Moore and J. Allen Whitt. Greenwich, Conn.: JAI Press, 1992.

Burstein, Rachel, and Larry Makinson, "The *Mother Jones* 400." *Mother Jones* (May–June 1997).

Butsch, Richard. "Class and Gender in Four Decades of Television Situation Comedy: Plus ça Change. . . ." *Critical Studies in Mass Communications* 9 (1992): 387–99.

Canham-Clyne, John. "When Elites Say 'Cut Medicare,' Press Debates 'How Much?'" *EXTRA!* (January–February 1996): 12–14.

Cauchon, Dennis. "Studies Find Drug Program Not Effective." *USA TODAY*, October 11, 1993.

"CEOs Play Reporter." *EXTRA!Update* (February 1996): 2.

"Chicken on Chechnya?" *Nation* (April 29, 1996): 3.

Church, George J. "Are We Better Off?" *Time* (January 29, 1996): 37–40.

Church, George J., and Richard Lacayo. "Social In-Security." *Time* (March 20, 1995): 24–32.

Cimini, Michael H., and Charles J. Muhl. "Twin Cities Nurses Reach Accord." *Monthly Labor Review* (August 1995): 74–75.

Clawson, Dan, Alan Neustadtl, and Denise Scott. *Money Talks*. New York: Basic Books, 1992.

Claybrook, Joan. "Why It's Their NAFTA, Not Ours, Not Yours." *Public Citizen* (November–December 1993): 2, 15.

Clines, Francis X. "Fueled by Success, Buchanan Revels in Rapid-Fire Oratory." *New York Times*, February 15, 1996.

Cohen, Jeff, and Norman Solomon. *Adventures in MediaLand*. Monroe, Maine: Common Courage Press, 1993.

Coleman, Richard D., and Lee Rainwater. *Social Standing in America*. New York: Basic Books, 1978.

Collins, Chuck. "Horatio Alger, Where Are You?" *Dollars and Sense* (January–February 1997): 9.

Collins, Randall. *The Credential Society*. New York: Academic Press, 1979.

———. "Functional and Conflict Theories of Educational Stratification." *American Sociological Review* 36 (1971): 1002–19.

Congressional Record. April 30, 1992, S5915–16.

———. July 21, 1992, H6333–34.

———. September 10, 1992, S13299.

———. June 8, 1993, S6963–64.

———. July 23, 1993, S9365.

———. September 8, 1993, E2099.

———. March 8, 1994, E373.

———. March 9, 1994, H1113–23.

———. April 21, 1994, S4598–99.

———. March 21, 1996, H2579.

———. May 8, 1997, S4236–38.

———. May 15, 1997, S4588–91.

———. June 26, 1997, H4668–H4813.

———. June 26, 1997, S6449–51.

———. June 27, 1997, S6678–79.

Conn, Joseph L., and Rob Boston. "Pat Robertson's Media Empire." *EXTRA!* (March–April 1995): 13–16.

Connell, Noreen. "Underfunded Schools: Why Money Matters." *Dollars and Sense* (March–April 1998): 14–17, 39.

Conniff, Ruth. "President Wellstone?" *Nation* (May 18, 1998): 11–16.

———. "Will Democrats Abandon Social Security?" *Progressive* (March 1999): 19–23.

Cooper, Marc. "Harley-Riding, Picket-Walking Socialism Haunts Decatur." *Nation* (April 8, 1996): 21–25.

———. "Labor-Latino Beat in CA." *Nation* (June 29, 1998): 5–6.

Cottle, Michelle. "The Real Class War." *Washington Monthly* (July–August 1997): 12–17.

Cox, Craig. "Taming the Corporate Beast." *Utne Reader* (March–April 1998): 60–61.

Crane, Stephen. *The Red Badge of Courage and Other Writings.* Ed. Richard Chase. Cambridge, Mass.: Riverside Press, 1960.

Crockett, Harry J., Jr. "The Achievement Motive and Differential Occupational Mobility in the United States." *American Sociological Review* 27 (1962): 191–204.

Croteau, David. "Challenging the 'Liberal Media' Claim." *EXTRA!* (July–August 1998): 4–9.

Cummings, Scott, and Del Taebel. "The Economic Socialization of Children: A Neo-Marxist Analysis." *Social Problems* 26 (December 1978): 198–210.

Dahl, Ronald. "Burned Out and Bored." *Newsweek* (December 15, 1997): 18.

Daniels, Arlene Kaplan. *Invisible Careers: Women Civic Leaders from the Volunteer World.* Chicago: University of Chicago Press, 1988.

Davies, Scott, and Neil Guppy. "Fields of Study, College Selectivity, and Student Inequalities in Higher Education." *Social Forces* 75 (June 1997): 1417–38.

Davis, James A., and Tom W. Smith. *General Social Surveys 1972–1989.* Chicago: National Opinion Research Center, 1989.

Davis, Russ. "AFL-CIO Unveils Program to Revitalize Labor Movement." *Labor Notes* (March 1997): 1, 14.

deMause, Neil. "Out of Sight, Out of Mind." *EXTRA!* (November–December 1997):25–27

Derber, Charles. *The Wilding of America.* New York: St. Martin's Press, 1996.

Derk, James. "We Got It, Toyota!" *Indiana Business Magazine* (January 1996): 9–13.

Dimaggio, Paul J., and Walter W. Powell. "The Iron Cage Revisited: Institutional Isomorphism and Collective Rationality in Organizational Fields." *American Sociological Review* 48 (1983): 147–60.

Dines, Gail. "Capitalism's Pitchmen." *Dollars and Sense* (May 1992): 18–20.

District of Columbia Bar. *1996–1997 Annual Report.* Washington, D.C.: D.C. Bar, 1997.

Dolan, Kerry A., ed. "The Global Power Elite." *Forbes* (July 28, 1997): 97–176.

———. "The World's Working Rich: United States." *Forbes* (July 6, 1998): 210–15.

Dolny, Michael. "What's in a Label?" *EXTRA!* (May–June 1998): 9–10.

Domhoff, G. William. *The Powers That Be.* New York: Vintage Books, 1978.

———. *Who Rules America Now?* Englewood Cliffs, N.J.: Prentice-Hall, 1983.

———. *State Autonomy or Class Dominance?* New York: Aldine de Gruyter, 1996.

———. *Who Rules America?: Power and Politics in the Year 2000.* Mountain View, Calif.: Mayfield Publishing, 1998.

Donnelly, David. "Maine Leads the Way." *Dollars and Sense* (July–August 1996): 34.

"Don't Let MAI Handcuff Democracy." *Public Citizen News* (March–April 1998): 15.

"Don't Let Them Fool You." *AFSCME Public Employee* (March–April 1998): 6–16.

Downs, Alan. *Corporate Executions.* New York: AMACOM, 1995.

Dreifus, Claudia. "Interview: Gore Vidal, The Writer as Citizen." *Progressive* (September 1986): 36–39.

Dreyfuss, Robert. "The End of Social Security as We Know It?" *Mother Jones* (November–December 1996): 50–58.

————. "Neighbor to Neighbor Takes on Medicare Myths." *EXTRA!* (March–April 1997): 17–18.

Drinkard, Jim. "Lobbying Costs Hit $100 Million a Month." *Indianapolis Star*, March 7, 1998.

DuBoff, Richard B. "Globalization and Wages: The Down Escalator." *Dollars and Sense* (September–October 1997): 36–40.

Duncan, Greg J., and Wei-Jun J. Yeung. "Extent and Consequences of Welfare Dependence among America's Children." *Children and Youth Services Review* 17 (1995): 157–82.

Dye, Thomas R. "Organizing Power for Policy-Planning: The View from the Brookings Institution." In *Power Elites and Organizations*, ed. G. William Domhoff and Thomas R. Dye. Newbury Park, Calif.: Sage, 1987.

Dye, Thomas. *Who's Running America?: The Clinton Years*. Englewood Cliffs, N.J.: Prentice-Hall, 1995.

Dylan, Bob. *Writings and Drawings by Bob Dylan*. New York: Knopf, 1973.

Ehrenreich, Barbara. "When Government Gets Mean: Confessions of a Recovering Statist." *Nation* (November 17, 1997): 11–16.

"The 89 Percent Liberal Media." *EXTRA!* (July–August 1998): 10.

Eisenger, Peter. *The Rise of the Entrepreneurial State*. Madison: University of Wisconsin Press, 1988.

Eitzen, D. Stanley, and Maxine Baca Zinn. *In Conflict and Order*. Boston: Allyn and Bacon, 1995.

Elsila, David. "No More NAFTAs!" *UAW Solidarity* (April–May 1997): 10–12.

Elsila, David, Michael Funke, and Sam Kirkland. "Blaming the Victim: The Propaganda War against Workers." *UAW Solidarity* (April 1992): 11–17.

Famighetti, Robert, ed. *The World Almanac and Book of Facts, 1997*. Mahwah, N.J.: K-III Reference Corporation, 1996.

Farley, John E. *Sociology*. Englewood Cliffs, N.J.: Prentice-Hall, 1990.

"Fast Track Falters in Major House Vote; UAW Steps Up Drive." *UAW Solidarity* (October 1997): 9.

"Fast Track Media Misperceptions." *EXTRA!Update* (February 1998): 1.

"Fast Track Sidetracked." *UAW Solidarity* (November 1997): 7.

Featherman, David L., and Robert M. Hauser. *Opportunity and Change*. New York: Academic Press, 1978.

Federal Election Commission. "Congressional Fundraising and Spending Up Again in 1996." Press release, April 14, 1997.

————. "Congressional Fundraising and Spending Up Again in 1996: Contributions from Individuals by Size of the Contribution." Press release, April 14, 1997.

————. "Congressional Fundraising and Spending Up Again in 1996: PAC Financial Activity, 1995–96." Press release, April 14, 1997.

————. "FEC Releases New PAC Count." Press release, July 28, 1989.

————. "1998 Congressional Candidates Raise $233 Million." Press release, March 6, 1998.

"Field Guide to TV's Lukewarm Liberals." *EXTRA!* (July–August 1998): 14–17.

Fineman, Howard. "Extreme Measures." *Newsweek* (March 4, 1996): 20–29.

Flanders, Laura. "Is It Real . . . Or Is It Astroturf?" *EXTRA!* (July–August 1996): 6.

Franklin, James C. "Industry Output and Employment Projections to 2006." *Monthly Labor Review* (November 1997): 39–57.

Frantz, Douglas. "Chiquita Scrutiny Continues despite Paper's Retraction." *Indianapolis Star*, July 19, 1998.

Freeman, Lewis. "Social Mobility in Television Comedies." *Critical Studies in Mass Communication* 9 (1992): 400–406.

"From the Left: More than a Figure of Speech?" *EXTRA!Update* (February 1996): 1.

Gallup, George, and S. F. Rae. *The Pulse of Democracy.* New York: Simon and Schuster, 1940.

Garnett, Stacie. "It's Tough to Be Young Today." *Dollars and Sense* (September–October 1997): 50.

Geoghagen, Thomas. "Overeducated and Underpaid." *New York Times,* June 3, 1997.

Gibbs, Nancy. "Cause Celeb." *Time* (June 17, 1996): 28–30.

Gilbert, Dennis, and Joseph A. Kahl. *The American Class Structure.* Chicago: Dorsey Press, 1987.

Ginsburg, Paul B., Jon R. Gabel, and Kelly A. Hunt, "Tracking Small-Firm Coverage, 1989–1996." *Health Affairs* 17 (January–February 1998): 167–71.

Gitlin, Todd. "Unum versus Pluribus." *Nation* (May 6, 1996): 28–34.

Glenn, David. "Adding Brains to Labor's New Political Muscle." *In These Times* (December 14, 1997): 22–25.

Glenn, Joshua, and Craig Cox. "Nader Wins!" *Utne Reader* (September–October 1996): 22.

Golay, Michael, and Carl Rollyson. *Where America Stands, 1996.* New York: John Wiley and Sons, 1996.

Gonnerman, Jennifer. "Media Watch." *In These Times* (December 25, 1995): 9.

Goodman, Robert. *The Last Entrepreneurs: America's Regional Wars for Jobs and Dollars.* New York: Simon and Schuster, 1979.

Gordon, David M. *Fat and Mean: The Corporate Squeeze of Working Americans and the Myth of Managerial "Downsizing."* New York: Free Press, 1996.

Gordon, Suzanne. "Labor Needs More than PR to Beat New Curbs on Political Spending." *Labor Notes* (March 1998): 8–9.

Granfield, Robert. "Making It by Faking It." *Journal of Contemporary Ethnography* 20 (1991): 331–51.

Granfield, Robert, and Thomas Koenig. "Pathways into Elite Law Firms: Professional Stratification and Social Networks." In *Research in Politics and Society,* vol. 4, *The Political Consequences of Social Networks,* ed. Gwen Moore and J. Allen Whitt. Greenwich, Conn.: JAI Press, 1992.

Granovetter, Mark. *Getting a Job: A Study of Contacts and Careers.* Cambridge: Harvard University Press, 1974.

Greenberg, Edward S. *Political Socialization.* New York: Atherton, 1970.

Greising, David. "It's the Best of Times—Or Is It?" *Business Week* (January 12, 1998): 36–38.

Grieder, William. "Saving the Global Economy." *Nation* (December 15, 1997): 11–16.

Gup, Ted. "Fakin' It." *Mother Jones* (May–June 1996): 53–54.

———. "The *Mother Jones* 400." *Mother Jones* (March–April 1996): 43.

Harrison, Bennett, and Barry Bluestone. "The Crisis of the American Dream." In *Great Divides,* ed. Thomas A. Shapiro. Mountain View, Calif.: Mayfield Publishing, 1998.

Hart, Peter, and Steve Rendall. "Meet the Myth Makers." *EXTRA!* (July–August 1998): 26–27.

Haveman, Ernest, and Patricia Salter West. *They Went to College.* New York: Harcourt, Brace, 1952.

Hearn, James. "Academic and Nonacademic Influences on the College Destinations of 1980 High School Graduates." *Sociology of Education* 64 (1991): 158–71.

Henriques, Diane B. "Ties that Bind: His Directors, Her Charity." *New York Times,* March 21, 1995.

Henson, Kevin D. *Just a Temp*. Philadelphia: Temple University Press, 1996.

Henwood, Doug. "American Dream: It's Not Working." *Christianity and Crisis* (June 8, 1992): 195–97.

———. "A Caste of Millions: 50 Million Americans Secede from the U.S. Leaving 200 Million in the Dust." *Utne Reader* (January–February 1992): 15.

Herman, Edward S. "The Media Mega-Mergers." *Dollars and Sense* (May–June 1996): 8–13

Herzenhorn, David. "The Story behind the Generous Gift to Harvard Law School." *New York Times*, April 7, 1995.

Hightower, Jim. "Chomp!" *Utne Reader* (March–April 1998): 57–61, 104.

———. "Homeless Electorate." *Dollars and Sense* (July–August 1996): 7.

Hipple, Steven, and Jay Stewart. "Earnings and Benefits of Contingent and Noncontingent Workers." *Monthly Labor Review* (October 1996): 22–30.

Hodge, Robert W., Paul M. Siegel, and Peter H. Rossi. "Occupational Prestige in the United States: 1925–1962." In *Class, Status, and Power*, ed. Reinhard Bendix and Seymour M. Lipset. New York: Free Press, 1966.

Hodge, Robert W., and Donald J. Treiman. "Class Identification in the United States." *American Journal of Sociology* 73 (March 1968): 535–47.

Hodge, Robert W., Donald J. Treiman, and Peter H. Rossi. "A Comparative Study of Occupational Prestige." In *Class, Status, and Power*, ed. Reinhard Bendix and Seymour M. Lipset. New York: Free Press, 1966.

Hodson, Randy, and Teresa A. Sullivan. *The Social Organization of Work*. Belmont, Calif.: Wadsworth, 1995.

Hoynes, William. "News for a Captive Audience: An Analysis of Channel One." *EXTRA!* (May–June 1997): 11–17.

Hurst, Charles E. *Social Inequality*. Boston,: Allyn and Bacon, 1995.

Husseini, Sam. "Talking about Talk." *EXTRA!* (May–June 1996): 20.

Husseini, Sam, and Normam Solomon. "The Right-Leaning Rolodex." *EXTRA!* (July–August 1998): 13.

"The Illusory Crisis." *In These Times* (January 6, 1997): 2.

"In Fact." *Nation* (August 26–September 2, 1996): 5.

Ireland, Doug. "Candidate Wellstone." *In These Times* (June 14, 1998): 12–15.

———. "Left Out in 2000." *In These Times* (February 21, 1999): 4.

Jackman, Mary R., and Robert W. Jackman. *Class Awareness in the United States*. Berkeley: University of California Press, 1982.

Jackson, Janine. "Broken Promises." *EXTRA!* (September–October 1997): 11–15.

———. "Economic Pack Journalism." *EXTRA!* (November–December 1996): 11–12.

———. "Fast Track 1, Democracy 0." *EXTRA!* (November–December 1997):9–10.

———. "Let Them Eat Baguettes." *EXTRA!* (March–April 1996): 14–15.

———. "Major Player or Big Bully?" *EXTRA!* (January–February 1997): 9–10.

———. "Moribund Militants: Corporate Media on (Re)Organized Labor." *EXTRA!* (January–February 1996): 6–7.

———. "We Feel Your Pain." *EXTRA!* (May–June 1996): 11–12.

Jaros, Dean. *Socialization to Politics*. New York: Praeger, 1973.

Jaszczak, Sandra, ed. *Encyclopedia of Associations*, 31st ed. Vol. 1. Detroit: Gale Research, 1996.

Jencks, Christopher, et al. *Inequality: Reassessment of the Effect of Family and Schooling in America*. New York: Harper and Row, 1972.

Jensen, Eric J., Jurg Gerber, and Ginna M. Babcock. "The New War on Drugs: Grass Roots Movement or Political Construction?" *Journal of Drug Issues* 21 (1991): 651–67.

Jezer, Marty. "Soft Money, Hard Choices." *Dollars and Sense* (July–August 1996): 30–34, 42.

Jones, Charisse. "Free from Want, but Just Getting By." *New York Times*, February 18, 1995.

Josephson, Matthew. *The Robber Barons*. New York: Harcourt, Brace and World, 1934.

Judis, John B. "The Most Powerful Lobby." *In These Times* (February 21, 1994): 22–23.

Kallick, David D. "Saving Social Security (From Its Saviors)." *In These Times* (March 7, 1999): 22–23.

Karen, David. "Toward a Political-Organizational Model of Gatekeeping: The Case of Elite Colleges." *Sociology of Education* 63 (1990): 227–40.

Katz, Michael B. *The Irony of Early School Reform*. Cambridge: Harvard University Press, 1968.

Katznelson, Ira, and Mark Kesselman. *The Politics of Power*. New York: Harcourt, Brace Janovich, 1975.

Kazin, Michael. *The Populist Persuasion*. New York: Basic Books, 1995.

Kerbo, Harold R. *Social Stratification and Inequality*. New York: McGraw-Hill, 1996.

Kerrey, Bob, and Alan K. Simpson. "How to Save Social Security." *New York Times*, May 23, 1995.

Kilgore, Sally. "The Organizational Context of Tracking in Schools." *American Sociological Review* 56 (1991): 189–203.

Knecht, G. Bruce. "Hard Copy: Magazine Advertisers Demand Prior Notice of 'Offensive' Articles." *Wall Street Journal*, April 30, 1997.

Knoke, David. *Organized for Action: Commitment in Voluntary Associations*. New Brunswick: Rutgers University Press, 1981.

Kolbert, Elizabeth, and Adam Clymer. "The Politics of Layoff: In Search of a Message." *New York Times*, March 8, 1996.

Kominski, Robert, and Rebecca Sutterlin. *What's It Worth?: Educational Background and Economic Status*. U.S. Bureau of the Census, Household Economic Studies P70-32. Washington, D.C.: U.S. Government Printing Office, 1992.

Koretz, Gene. "Downsizing's Painful Effects." *Business Week* (April 13, 1998): 23.

Korpi, Walter. *The Democratic Class Struggle*. London: Routledge, 1983.

Kozol, Jonathan. *Savage Inequalities: Children in America's Schools*. New York: Harper, 1991.

Krugman, Paul. "The Spiral of Inequality." *Mother Jones* (November–December 1996): 44–49.

Lee, Martin A., and Norman Solomon. "Does the News Media Have a Liberal Bias?" In *Taking Sides*, ed. Kurt Finsterbusch and George McKenna. Guilford, Conn.: Duskin Publishing Group, 1996.

Lehmann, Chris. "Michael and Me." *In These Times* (October 14, 1996): 39–40.

Leland, John. "Blessed by the Bull." *Newsweek* (April 27, 1998): 51–53.

Lemmons, Phil. "Straight Talk about PC Costs." *PC World* (June 1997): 17.

Leonhardt, David. "Two-Tier Marketing." *Business Week* (March 17, 1997): 82–90.

Levy, Clifford J. "New York Attorney General Remakes Staff by Patronage." *New York Times*, November 10, 1995.

Lewis, Charles. "The Buying of the President." *Dollars and Sense* (July–August 1996): 28, 41.

Lieberman, Trudy. "Social Insecurity: The Campaign to Take the System Private." *Nation* (January 27, 1997): 11–18.

"Lifestyles of the Rich and Fatuous." *EXTRA!Update* (April 1994): 2.

Lipset, Seymour M., and Reinhard Bendix. *Social Mobility in Industrial Society*. Berkeley: University of California Press, 1959.

Litt, Edgar. "Civic Education, Community Norms, and Political Indoctrination." *American Sociological Review* 28 (February 1963): 69–75.

Longworth, R. C., and Sharman Stein. "Middle-Class Muddle." *Indianapolis Star*, September 24, 1995.

Lustig, Jeffrey. R. "The Politics of Shutdown." *Journal of Economic Issues* 19 (1985): 123–59.

MacEwan, Arthur. "Ask Dr. Dollar." *Dollars and Sense* (May–June 1998): 42.

"MAI Roadshow Heads West." *Public Citizen News* (January–February 1999): 1.

"MAI Week of Action." *Public Citizen News* (March–April 1998): 15.

Makinson, Larry. *The Big Picture: Money Follows Power Shift on Capitol Hill.* Washington, D.C.: Center for Responsive Politics, 1997.

Males, Mike. "Pot Boiler: Why Are Media Enlisting in the Government's Crusade against Marijuana?" *EXTRA!* (July–August 1997): 20–21.

———. "Wild in Deceit: Why 'Teen Violence' Is Poverty Violence in Disguise." *EXTRA!* (March–April 1996): 7–9.

Manilov, Marianne. "Channel One, Joe Camel, Potato Chips, and ABC." *EXTRA!* (July–August, 1996): 18–19.

Mantsios, Gregory. "Class in America: Myths and Realities." In *Race, Class, and Gender in the United States*, ed. Paula S. Rothenberg. New York: St. Martin's Press, 1995.

———. "Media Magic: Making Class Disappear." In *Race, Class, and Gender in the United States*, ed. Paula S. Rothenberg. New York: St. Martin's Press, 1995.

Marin, Rick. "Jerry Seins Off." *Newsweek* (January 12, 1998): 54–57.

Marin, Rick, and Yahlin Chang. "The Katie Factor." *Newsweek* (July 6, 1998): 53–58.

Martin, Mick, and Mick Porter. *1995 Video Movie Guide*. New York: Ballantine, 1994.

Masci, David. "Senate Foes Likely to Derail Striker Replacement Bill." *Congressional Quarterly* (July 9, 1994): 1873.

———. "Senate Rejects Striker Bill; More Action Unlikely." *Congressional Quarterly* (July 16, 1994): 1936.

McChesney, Robert W. *Corporate Media and the Threat to Democracy*. New York: Seven Stories Press, 1997.

———. "The Global Media Giants." *EXTRA!* (November–December 1997): 11–18.

McKenna, Barbara. "Does College Cost Too Much?" *AFT on Campus* (March 1998): 8.

McKenzie, Evan. *Privatopia*. New Haven: Yale University Press, 1994.

McNamee, Mike. "Social Security Reform: Ready for Prime Time?" *Business Week* (January 19, 1998): 33.

"Media Myths and Facts." *UAW Solidarity* (April 1992): 17.

Meyers, Mike. "No Doom and Gloom, Americans Better Off." *Kokomo Tribune*, September 12, 1996.

Miller, Ellen, and Randy Kehler. "Mischievous Myths about Money in Politics." *Dollars and Sense* (July–August 1996): 22–23.

Miller, John. "More Wealth for the Wealthy: The Estate Tax Giveaway and What to Do about It." *Dollars and Sense* (November–December 1997): 26–28, 33.

———. "Tax Cuts: Clinton and Congress Feed the Wealthy." *Dollars and Sense* (November–December 1997): 43.

Miller, John, and Ramon Castellblanch. "Does Manufacturing Matter?" *Dollars and Sense* (October 1988): 6–8.

Miller, Mark C. "Free the Media." *Nation* (June 3, 1996): 9–15.

———. "The National Entertainment State." *Nation* (June 3, 1996).

Miller, S. M. "Born on Third Base: The Sources of Wealth of the 1996 *Forbes* 400." *United for a Fair Economy* (February 1997).

Mines, Luke. "Globalization in the Classroom." *Nation* (June 1, 1998): 22–24.

Mishel, Lawrence, and Jared Bernstein. *The State of Working America, 1992–1993.* Washington, D.C.: Economic Policy Institute, 1993.

Mishel, Lawrence, Jared Bernstein, and John Schmitt. *The State of Working America, 1996–1997.* Armonk, N.Y.: M. E. Sharpe, 1997.

Moberg, David. "Power Grab." *Progressive* (March 1998): 24–26.

Monroe, Ann. "Getting Rid of the Gray." *Mother Jones* (July–August 1996): 29.

Moody, Kim. "America Gets a Virtual Raise." *Labor Notes* (February 1997): 15–16.

———. "NAFTA, WTO, MAI, FTAA, AGOA. . . . Where Does It End?" *Labor Notes* (May 1998): 16, 10.

———. *Workers in a Lean World: Unions in the International Economy.* New York: Verso, 1998.

Moore, Michael. "Banned by Borders." *Nation* (December 2, 1996): 10.

———. *Downsize This!* New York: Crown Publishers, 1996.

———. "Is the Left Nuts? (Or Is It Me?)." *Nation* (November 17, 1997): 16–18.

Moore, Stephen. "How to Slash Corporate Welfare." *New York Times,* April 5, 1995.

Morin, Richard, and John M. Berry. "Reality Check: The Economic Perception Gap." *Washington Post,* October 13–15, 1996.

Murray, Charles. "The Shape of Things to Come." *National Review* (July 8, 1991): 29–30.

Nader, Ralph. "Product Libel." *Public Citizen News* (May–June 1998): 4.

"NAFTA." *Labor Party Press* (July 1997): 8–9.

Naureckas, Jim. "Corporate Censorship: The Case of NBC." *EXTRA!* (November–December 1995): 13.

———. "Editor's Note: The Media-Republican Complex." *EXTRA!* (November–December 1995): 2.

———. "From the Top: What Are the Politics of Network Bosses?" *EXTRA!* (July–August 1998): 21–22.

Navarro, Vicente. "Medical History as Justification Rather than Explanation: A Critique of Starr's *The Social Transformation of American Medicine.*" *International Journal of Health Services* 14 (1984): 511–28.

———. "The Politics of Health Care Reform in the United States, 1992–1994: A Historical Review." *International Journal of Health Services* 25 (1995): 185–201.

———. "Production and the Welfare State: The Political Context of Reforms." *International Journal of Health Services* 21 (1991): 585–614.

Neather, Andy. "The Temp-ing of America." *UAW Solidarity* (January–February 1995): 10–14.

Neustadtl, Alan, and Dan Clawson. "Corporate Political Groupings: Does Ideology Unify Business Political Behavior?" *American Sociological Review* 53 (1988): 172–90.

"The New Transplants." *UAW Research Bulletin* (January–February 1995): 10–11.

New York Times. The Downsizing of America. New York: Random House, 1996.

Newman, Katherine S. *Falling from Grace: The Experience of Downward Mobility in the American Middle Class.* New York: Free Press, 1988.

Nichols, John. "After Fusion: The New New Party." *In These Times* (March 22, 1998): 18–20.

"No Sweat?" *UAW Solidarity* (June–July 1997): 9.

"No Sweat over Sweatshops." *EXTRA!Update* (June 1998): 3.

Noble, David F. *Forces of Production: A Social History of Industrial Automation.* New York: Knopf, 1984.

Noble, Douglas D. "Schools as 'Instructional Delivery Systems.'" *In These Times* (November 30, 1992): 28–29.

Nye, Peter. "Lobbying and Gift Reform Shines Sunlight on Influence Peddling." *Public Citizen* (January–February 1996): 1, 3.

Office of Congressman Dick Armey. "Washington's Lobbying Industry: A Case for Tax Reform—Executive Summary" (June 19, 1996).

Office of Management and Budget. *Budget of the United States Government: Fiscal Year 1999.* Washington, D.C.: U.S. Government Printing Office, 1998.

Office of National Drug Control Policy. *The National Drug Control Strategy.* Washington, D.C.: National Criminal Justice Reference Service, 1992, 1994, 1996, 1998.

Office of Technology Assessment. *Technology and Structural Unemployment.* Washington, D.C.: Congress of the United States, 1986.

Oliver, Melvin, Thomas M. Shapiro, and Julie E. Press. "'Them That's Got Shall Get': Inheritance and Achievement in Wealth Accumulation." In *Research in Politics and Society,* vol. 15, ed. Richard E. Ratliffe, Melvin Oliver, and Thomas M. Shapiro. Greenwich, Conn.: JAI Press, 1995.

"The 100 Largest U.S. Multinationals." *Forbes* (July 17, 1995): 274–76.

"Online Services: Top Ten Activities." *PC Magazine* (July 1997): 9.

Orcutt, James D., and J. Blake Turner. "Shocking Numbers and Graphic Accounts: Quantified Images of Drug Problems in the Print Media." *Social Problems* 40 (1993): 190–206.

Orum, Anthony M., and Roberta S. Cohen. "The Development of Political Orientations among Black and White Children." *American Sociological Review* 38 (1973): 62–74.

Pace, Eric. "B. Gerald Cantor, Philanthropist and Owner of Rodin Collection, Is Dead at 79." *New York Times,* July 6, 1996.

Parenti, Michael. *Power and the Powerless.* New York: St. Martin's Press, 1978.

———. "The Super Rich Are Out of Sight." *Dollars and Sense* (May–June 1998): 36–37.

Parry, Robert. "The Right-Wing Media Machine." *Extra!* (March–April 1995): 6–10.

———. "Who Buys the Right?" *Nation* (November 18, 1996): 5–6.

Paulin, Geoffrey, and Brian Riordon. "Making It on Their Own: The Baby Boom Meets Generation X." *Monthly Labor Review* (February 1998): 10–21.

"Paycheck Deception Act: Don't Let Them Fool You." *AFSCME Public Employee* (March–April 1998): 7–19.

"Percent of Full-Time Employees Participating in Employer-Provided Benefit Plans, 1980–1991" *Monthly Labor Review* (February 1998): 103.

Perkins, Joseph. "Caught in the News Media's Liberal Bias." *Indianapolis Star,* July 18, 1998.

Perrow, Charles. "A Society of Organizations." *Theory and Society* 20 (1991): 725–62.

Perrucci, Carolyn Cummings, and Robert Perrucci. "Social Origins, Educational Contexts, and Career Mobility." *American Sociological Review* 35 (1970): 451–63.

Perrucci, Robert. *Japanese Auto Transplants in the Heartland.* New York: Aldine de Gruyter, 1994.

———. "The Significance of Intra-Occupational Mobility." *American Sociological Review* 26 (1961): 874–83.

Perrucci, Robert, and Bonnie L. Lewis. "Interorganizational Relations and Community Influence Structure." *Sociological Quarterly* 30 (1989): 205–23.

Perrucci, Robert, and Marc Pilisuk. "Leaders and Ruling Elites: The Interorganizational Basis of Community Power." *American Sociological Review* 35 (1970): 1040–57.

Phillips, Kevin. "Fat City." *Time* (September 26, 1994): 49–56.

"Phony Paycheck Protection: It'll Cost You More than You Think." *UAW Solidarity* (March–April 1998): 10–11.

Piven, Frances Fox. "Poorhouse Politics." *Progressive* (February 1995): 22–24.

Polivka, Anne E. "Contingent and Alternative Work Arrangements, Defined." *Monthly Labor Review* (October 1996): 3–9.

Pomery, John. "Running Deficits with the Rest of the World—Part I." *Focus on Economic Issues.* West Lafayette, Ind.: Purdue Center for Economic Education, Fall 1987.

Postman, Neil. "Virtual Students, Digital Classroom."*Nation* (October 9, 1995): 377–82.

Press, Eyal. "Spin Cities." *Nation* (November 18, 1996): 30–33.

Public Citizen Health Research Group. "Health Care Costs: Executive Compensation." *Health Letter* (April 1996): 12.

Purdue Research Foundation. *Home for High-Tech Business.* West Lafayette, Ind.: Purdue Research Park, 1998.

Quinn, Jane Bryant. "Savings at Risk." *Newsweek* (December 11, 1995): 54–55.

Rampton, Sheldon, and John Stauber. "Oprah's Free—Are We?" *EXTRA!* (May–June 1998): 11–12.

———. "This Report Brought to You by Monsanto." *Progressive* (July 1998): 22–25.

Reich, Robert B. "Broken Faith: Why We Need to Renew the Social Contract." *Nation* (February 16, 1998): 11–17.

———.*The Next American Frontier.* New York: Times Books, 1983.

———. "Secession of the Successful." *New York Times Magazine,* January 20, 1991, 16–17, 42–45.

———. *The Work of Nations: Preparing Ourselves for the Twenty-first Century.* New York: Knopf, 1991.

———. "Your Country Needs You." *UAW Solidarity* (December 1995): 24.

Reingold, Jennifer, Richard A. Melcher, and Gary McWilliams. "Special Report: Executive Pay." *Business Week* (April 20, 1998): 64–70.

Reynolds, David. *Democracy Unbound.* Boston: South End Press, 1997.

Rich, Elizabeth H., ed. *The Foundation Directory, 1998 Edition.* New York: Foundation Center, 1998.

"The Rich Get a Good Return on Their Campaign Investments." *Sanders Scoop* (Winter 1998): 1.

Roberts, Johnnie L. "Mergers' Main Men." *Newsweek* (July 29, 1996): 42–48.

Rogers, Everett M. "Diffusion and Re-Invention of Project DARE." In *Organizational Aspects of Health Communication Campaigns: What Works?,* ed. Thomas E. Backer and Everett M. Rogers. Newbury Park, Calif.: Sage, 1993.

Rosenthal, Robert, and Lenore Jacobson. *Pygmalion in the Classroom.* New York: Holt, Rinehart and Winston, 1968.

Ross, Steven J. *Working-Class Hollywood: Silent Film and the Shaping of Class in America.* Princeton: Princeton University Press, 1998.

Rubin, Beth A. *Shifts in the Social Contract.* Thousand Oaks, Calif.: Pine Forge Press, 1996.

Ryscavage, Paul. "A Surge in Growing Income Inequality?" *Monthly Labor Review* (August 1995): 51–61.

Salant, Jonathan D. "Financial Reports Show Members Still Take Lobbies' Free Rides." *Congressional Quarterly Weekly Report* (June 17, 1995): 1709.

———. "'97 Lobbying Topped $1 Billion Mark." *Indianapolis Star,* July 8, 1998.

Samuelson, Robert J. "Can Clinton Do a Nixon?" *Newsweek* (December 9, 1996): 32.

———. "Confederacy of Dunces." *Newsweek* (September 23, 1996): 65.

———. "Down with the Media Elite!?" *Newsweek* (July 13 1998): 47.

———. "Great Expectations." *Newsweek* (January 8, 1996): 24–33.

Schaefer, Richard T., and Robert P. Lamm. *Sociology*. New York: McGraw-Hill, 1998.

Schellhardt, Timothy D. "Are Layoffs Moral? One Firm's Answer: You Ask, We'll Sue." *Wall Street Journal*, August 1, 1996.

Schiff, Bob. "Bogus Comparisons." *Public Citizen* (Spring 1996): 15.

Schiller, Herbert I. "On That Chart." *Nation* (June 3, 1996): 16–17.

Schlozman, Kay L., and John T. Tierney. *Organized Interests and American Democracy*. New York: Harper and Row, 1986.

Schor, Juliet B. "Keeping Up with the Trumps: How the Middle Class Identifies with the Rich." *Washington Monthly* (July–August 1998): 34–37.

Schrammel, Kurt. "Comparing the Labor Market Success of Young Adults from Two Generations." *Monthly Labor Review* (February 1998): 3–9.

Seider, Maynard S. "American Big Business Ideology: A Content Analysis of Executive Speeches." *American Sociological Review* 39 (1974): 802–15.

Seldes, George. "Is the Entire Press Corrupt?" *EXTRA!* (November–December 1994): 26–27.

"Set to Organize." *Labor Party Press* (January 1999): 1, 4.

Sewell, William A., A. O. Haller, and G. W. Ohlandorf. "The Educational and Early Occupational Status Attainment Process." *American Sociological Review* 35 (1970): 1014–27.

Sewell, William A., and Vimal Shah. "Parents' Education and Children's Educational Aspirations and Achievements." *American Sociological Review* 33 (1968): 191–209.

Shaiken, Harley. *Work Transformed: Automation and Labor in the Computer Age*. New York: Holt, Rinehart and Winston, 1985.

Sherman, Scott. "An Appeal to Reason." *Nation* (March 10, 1997): 15–19.

Shuldiner, Allan, and Tony Raymond. *Who's in the Lobby?: A Profile of Washington's Influence Industry*. Washington, D.C.: Center for Responsive Politics, 1998.

Silverstein, Ken. "Manufactured News." *EXTRA!* (January–February 1997): 23–24.

Silverstein, Ken, and Alexander Cockburn. "How's He Doing? Has Sweeney Changed Labor?" *CounterPunch* (July 16–31, 1997): 1, 6–8.

———. "Our Little Secret: Life on the Fast Track." *CounterPunch* (September 1–15, 1997): 2–3.

———. "Why the Drug War Works: It's A Money/Class Thing, of Course." *CounterPunch* (June 15–30, 1998): 4–5.

Silvestri, George T. "Occupational Employment to 2005." *Monthly Labor Review* (November 1995): 60–84.

Simmons, Robert G., and Morris Rosenberg. "Functions of Children's Perceptions of the Stratification System." *American Sociological Review* 36 (1971): 235–49.

Sirico, Robert A. "The Capitalist Ethic: True Morality." *Forbes* (December 2, 1996): 85.

Sloan, Allan. "The Hit Men." *Newsweek* (February 26, 1996): 44–48.

———. "What Goes Up . . . ." *Newsweek* (April 13, 1998): 42–43.

Smith, Jeremy. "Intellectual Snobs versus Political Slobs." *Dollars and Sense* (May–June 1998): 38–39.

Smith, Wesley J. "Nobody's Nader." *Mother Jones* (July–August 1996): 61–63.

"Social (In-)Security." *Nation* (June 1, 1998): 3–5.

Soley, Lawrence C. *Leasing the Ivory Tower: The Corporate Takeover of Academia*. Boston: South End Press, 1996.

———. "The Power of the Press Has a Price." *EXTRA!* (July–August 1997): 11–13.

Solomon, Norman. "The Media's Favorite Think Tank." *EXTRA!* (July–August 1996): 9–12.

———. "Media Moguls on Board." *EXTRA!* (January–February 1998): 19–22.

Solowey, Fred J. "Selling Social Insecurity." *EXTRA!* (March–April 1998): 22–23.

"Soundbites." *EXTRA!* (May–June 1996): 5.

"Soundbites." *EXTRA!* (September–October 1996): 5.

Spencer, Miranda. "TV Nation: A Show For 'The Rest of Us.'" *EXTRA!* (November–December 1995): 24–25.

"Spokane Just Says No to DARE Program." *Kokomo Tribune*, October 6, 1996.

"Statement of Ownership." *EXTRA!* (November–December 1997): 18.

Stauber, John, and Sheldon Rampton. *Toxic Sludge Is Good for You: Lies, Damn Lies, and the Public Relations Industry*. Monroe, Maine: Common Courage Press, 1996.

———. "Watching the Watchdogs: How Corporate PR Keeps Tabs on Reporters." *EXTRA!* (May–June 1996): 22.

"The Steelworkers Contract with America." *Steelabor* (September–October 1996): 10–14.

Steffens, Lincoln. *Upbuilders*. 1909. Seattle: University of Washington Press, 1968.

Stendler, Cecelia Burns. *Children of Brasstown: Their Awareness of the Symbols of Social Class*. Urbana: University of Illinois Press, 1949.

Stevenson, Richard W. "Trade Deficits for 1997 Hit Nine-Year High." *New York Times*, February 20, 1998.

———. "U.S. to Report to Congress NAFTA Benefits Are Modest." *New York Times*, July 11, 1997.

Stillman, Don. "The Devastating Impact of Plant Relocations." *Working Papers* (July–August 1978): 42–53.

Stohl, Michael, and Harry R. Targ. *Global Political Economy in the 1980s*. Cambridge, Mass.: Schenkman, 1982.

Stone, Oliver. "On That Chart." *Nation* (June 3, 1996): 18.

Stone, Peter H. "The Nicotine Network." *Mother Jones* (May–June 1996): 50–52.

Stratman, David. "School Reform and the Attack on Public Education." *Dollars and Sense* (March–April 1998): 7.

Tasini, Jonathan. "Lost in the Margins: Labor and the Media." *EXTRA!* (Summer 1990): 2–6.

———. "Media Stereotypes about Unions." *EXTRA!* (Summer 1990): 4.

Thomas, Evan, and Gregory L. Vistica. "Fallout from a Media Fiasco." *Newsweek* (July 20, 1998): 24–26.

Thompson, Hunter S. *Generation of Swine*. New York: Vintage Books, 1988.

Tilly, Charles. *Half a Job: Bad and Good Part-Time Jobs in a Changing Labor Market*. Philadelphia: Temple University Press, 1996.

Tobiasen, Linda G., ed. *The Foundation Grants Index, 1996*. New York: Foundation Center, 1995.

"The Top Paid CEOs." *Forbes* (May 18, 1998): 224–99.

Tudor, Jeannette F. "The Development of Class Awareness in Children." *Social Forces* 49 (1971): 470–76.

Turner, Richard, and Peter Annin. "Leaving Messages, Sending Messages." *Newsweek* (July 13, 1998): 64–65.

Turque, Bill. "Picking a Fight about the Future." *Newsweek* (December 9, 1996): 30–31.

Turque, Bill, and Bob Cohen. "Why Clinton Won't Play Class War." *Newsweek* (April 25, 1995): 31–32.

"Two Parties Give Us Six New Reasons for One Party for Us." *Labor Party Press* (March 1998): 1.

Uchitelle, Louis. "U.S. Corporations Expanding Abroad at a Quicker Pace." *New York Times*, July 25, 1998.

Uchitelle, Louis, and N. R. Kleinfield. "On Battlefield of Business, Millions of Casualties." *New York Times*, March 3, 1996.

"Unbalanced!: Bipartisan Budget Bill Boosts Billionaires." *Labor Party Press* (November 1997): 4–5.

Urresta, Lixandra, and Kenji Hosokawa. "The Fortune Global Five Hundred." *Fortune* (August 4, 1997): F1–12.

U.S. Congress. House Committee on Education and Labor, Subcommittee on Elementary, Secondary, and Vocational Education. *Oversight Hearing on Drug Abuse Education Programs.* 101st Cong., 1st sess. Serial 101-129. Washington, D.C.: U.S. Government Printing Office, 1990.

———. House Committee on Ways and Means. *Comprehensive Tax Reform.* 99th Cong., 1st sess. Serial 99-41. Washington, D.C.: U.S. Government Printing Office, 1985.

———. *Impact, Effectiveness, and Fairness of the Tax Reform Act of 1986.* 101st Cong., 2d sess. Serial 101-92. Washington, D.C.: U.S. Government Printing Office, 1990.

———. Senate Committee on Labor and Human Resources. *Drug Abuse, Prevention, and Treatment.* 100th Cong., 2d sess. Washington, D.C.: U.S. Government Printing Office, 1988.

U.S. Department of Commerce. Bureau of the Census. *Statistical Abstract of the United States.* Washington, D.C.: U.S. Government Printing Office, 1995.

———. *Statistical Abstract of the United States.* Washington, D.C.: U.S. Government Printing Office, 1997.

U.S. Department of Education. National Center for Educational Statistics. *The Condition of Education, 1996.* NCES 96-304. Ed. Thomas Smith. Washington, D.C.: U.S. Government Printing Office, 1996.

———. *Digest of Educational Statistics, 1997.* NCES 98-015. Ed. Thomas D. Snyder, Charlene M. Hoffman, and Clair M. Geddes. Washington, D.C.: U.S. Government Printing Office, 1997.

U.S. Department of Justice. Bureau of Justice Assistance. *Program Brief: An Introduction to DARE: Drug Abuse Resistance Education.* 2nd ed. Washington, D.C.: Bureau of Justice Assistance, 1991.

U.S. Department of the Treasury, Internal Revenue Service. "Return of Organization Exempt from Income Tax: Form 990: DARE America." 95-4242541. Washington, D.C., 1995, 1996.

———. *Statistics of Income, 1995: Individual Income Tax Returns.* Publication 1304. Washington, D.C.: U.S. Government Printing Office, 1997.

———. *The Statistics of Income. SOI Bulletin.* Washington, D.C.: U.S. Government Printing Office, Winter 1997–98.

"U.S. Trade Gap Sets Record." *UAW Solidarity* (May 1998): 7.

Useem, Michael. *The Inner Circle.* New York: Oxford University Press, 1984.

Vanderpool, Tim. "Secession of the Successful." *Utne Reader* (November–December, 1995): 32–34.

Vanneman, Reeve, and Lynn Weber Cannon. *The American Perception of Class.* Philadelphia: Temple University Press, 1987.

Vidal, Gore. "The End of History." *Nation* (September 30, 1996): 11–18.

Wall, Suzanne. "Union Candidates Use a 'Bottom-Up' Approach to Winning Political Power." *Labor Notes* (April 1998): 3.

"Washington Wire." *Wall Street Journal*, January 31, 1997.

Weber, Joseph, and Blanca Riemer. "These Days Mack Trucks Isn't Built like Mack Trucks." *Business Week* (July 30, 1990): 40–41.

Weinstein, James. "Social Security versus Securities." *In These Times* (June 28, 1998): 1.

Wells, Robert M. "House Education Bill." *Congressional Quarterly* (May 14, 1994): 1246–49.

———. "Senate Panel Easily Approves $12.7 Billion Measure." *Congressional Quarterly* (June 18, 1994): 1632–33.

Wellstone, Paul. "The People's Trust Fund." *Nation* (July 27–August 3, 1998): 4–5.

Wenglinsky, Harold. "How Money Matters: The Effect of School District Spending on Academic Achievement." *Sociology of Education* 70 (July 1997): 221–37.

Wessel, David. "Again, the Rich Get Richer, but This Time They Pay More Taxes." *Wall Street Journal*, April 2, 1998.

"What Is the 'Paycheck Deception Act'?" *AFSCME Public Employee* (March–April 1998): 10–11.

"What's FAIR?" *EXTRA!* (March–April 1998): 2.

"Where's the Power: Newsroom or Boardroom?" *EXTRA!* (July–August 1998): 23.

"Who's Behind It?" *AFSCME Public Employee* (March–April 1998): 8–9.

Wiedenbaum, Murray L. *Business, Government, and the Public.* Englewood Cliffs, N.J.: Prentice-Hall, 1977.

Wohl, R. Richard. "The 'Rags to Riches Story': An Episode of Secular Idealism." In *Class, Status, and Power*, ed. Reinhard Bendix and Seymour M. Lipset. New York: Free Press, 1966.

Wolfe, Alan. *The Seamy Side of Democracy.* New York: David McKay, 1973.

Wolff, Edward N. *Top Heavy.* New York: Twentieth Century Fund, 1996.

Wright, Erik O. *Classes.* London: Verso, 1985.

———. *Interrogating Inequality.* London: Verso, 1994.

WuDunn, Sheryl. "When Lifetime Jobs Die Prematurely: Downsizing Comes to Japan, Fraying Old Workplace Ties." *New York Times*, June 12, 1996.

Wysong, Earl. "Class in the Movies." Unpublished paper, 1996.

———. *High Risk and High Stakes: Health Professionals, Politics, and Policy.* Westport, Conn.: Greenwood Press, 1992.

Wysong, Earl, Richard Aniskiewicz, and David Wright. "Truth *and* DARE: Tracking Drug Education to Graduation and as Symbolic Politics." *Social Problems* 41 (1994): 448–72.

Wysong, Earl, and David Wright. "A Decade of DARE: Efficacy, Politics, and Drug Education." *Sociological Focus* 28 (1995): 283–311.

Zachary, G. Pascal, and Bob Ortega. "Age of Angst: Workplace Revolution Boosts Productivity at Cost of Job Security." *Wall Street Journal*, March 10, 1993.

Zinn, Howard. *A People's History of the United States.* New York: Harper Colophon Books, 1980.

Zoellner, Tom. "DARE Challenges Its Critics." *Salt Lake Tribune*, July 9, 1997.

Zuckman, Jill. "Senate Foes Ready to Block Striker Replacement Bill." *Congressional Quarterly* (June 19, 1993): 1579.

Zweigenhaft, Richard L., and G. William Domhoff. *Diversity in the Power Elite: Have Women and Minorities Reached the Top?* New Haven: Yale University Press, 1998.

Index

293

Index

About the Authors

Robert Perrucci is professor of sociology at Purdue University. He is the author of numerous articles and books, including *Japanese Auto Transplants in the Heartland: Corporatism and Community*, and *Plant Closings: International Context and Social Costs*.

Earl Wysong is associate professor of sociology at Indiana University Kokomo. His research focuses on the intersection of class, power, and organizations. He is the author of *High Risk and High Stakes: Health Professionals, Politics and Policy* and has published articles on organizations, class power, and public policies.